W9-BHZ-347

Authors

L. Carey Bolster
Supervisor of Mathematics
Baltimore County Public Schools
Towson, Maryland

H. Douglas Woodburn
Chairman of the Mathematics Department
Perry Hall Junior High School
Baltimore County, Maryland

Joella H. Gipson
Associate Professor of Education
Wayne State University
Detroit, Michigan

Reader/Consultants

Robert Y. Hamada
Supervisor, Mathematics
Los Angeles City Unified School District
Los Angeles, California

Sidney Sharron
Supervisor, Educational Communications and Media Branch
Los Angeles City Unified School District
Los Angeles, California

ISBN: 0-673-13182-3

345678910-KPK-90898887868584838281

Acknowledgments

For permission to reproduce photographs, forms, and other visual material on the pages indicated, acknowledgment is made to the following:

Photo of city on cover courtesy of Orban/Free Lance Photographers Guild.

Photo on 4-5 courtesy of Elizabeth Hamlin/Stock, Boston.

7UP liter bottle on 46 courtesy of The Seven-Up Company.

Deposit slip on 88 and check on 90 courtesy of Gary-Wheaton Bank. Names, William J. Engelmeyer and Marjorie Lynn Engelmeyer, used by permission.

Puzzle on 99 from *Puzzle Quiz and Stunt Fun*, by Jerome S. Meyer. Reprinted by permission of Dover Publications, Inc.

Promissory note on 108 courtesy of Sparks State Bank, Sparks, Maryland.

CTA transfer on 169 reprinted by permission of Chicago Transit Authority.

Table on 234 adapted from "Averages for Selected Metropolitan Areas for All Major Lenders," from Federal Home Loan Bank Board *News*. Courtesy of Federal Home Loan Bank Board.

Floor plans of "Arlington I" and "The Cambridge" and illustrations of "Arlington Colonial" and "Cambridge Tudor" on 243-244 courtesy of Levitt Homes, a Subsidiary of Levitt Corporation, and the architects, Salvatore Balsamo & Associates, Inc.

Form on 249 and 251 adapted from "Cooling-Load Estimate Form for Room Air-Conditioners." Reprinted by permission of Association of Home Appliance Manufacturers.

Form W-2 on 260 courtesy of Internal Revenue Service.

Illinois State Capitol Building on 274-275 courtesy of Illinois State Historical Library.

Certificate of deposit on 304 courtesy of Glenview State Bank, Glenview, Illinois.

1925 Studebaker on 345 courtesy of Studebaker Worthington, Inc.

Simplicity pattern #5113 on 346 courtesy of Simplicity Pattern Co., Inc. Copyright © 1972 Simplicity Pattern Co., Inc., 200 Madison Avenue, New York, New York 10016.

Rugs on 350-351 courtesy of Columbia-Minerva Company.

Mosaic table on 351 reprinted by permission of *American Home* Crafts. Copyright © 1977 American Home Publishing Company.

Tables for wage-bracket method of withholding on 402-405 courtesy of Internal Revenue Service.

1976 Tax Tables on 407-409 courtesy of Internal Revenue Service.

Consumer and Career Mathematics

L. Carey Bolster

H. Douglas Woodburn

Joella H. Gipson

Scott, Foresman and Company
Editorial Offices: Glenview, Illinois

Regional Sales Offices: Palo Alto, California •
Tucker, Georgia • Glenview, Illinois •
Oakland, New Jersey • Dallas, Texas

unit 1 Mathematics Skills

Chapter 1

Whole Numbers, Decimals, and Fractions

Chapter 2

Equations, Proportions, and Percent

Chapter 3

Measurement and Statistics

Income, Banking, and Credit

Chapter 4
Income

Chapter 5
Personal Banking

Chapter 6
Consumer Credit

unit 3 Transportation

Chapter 7
Buying a Car

Chapter 8
Automobile Operating Expenses

Chapter 9
Travel

Housing

Chapter 10

Renting and Decorating a Home

Chapter 11

Buying a Home

Chapter 12

Building a Home

 Taxes, Insurance, and Investments

Chapter 13

Income Tax

Chapter 14

Health, Life, and Retirement Insurance

Chapter 15

Investments

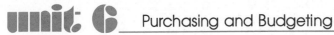

 Purchasing and Budgeting

unit one

Mathematics Skills

Chapter 1

Whole Numbers, Decimals, and Fractions

Chapter 2

Equations, Proportions, and Percent

Chapter 3

Measurement and Statistics

Chapter 1

Whole Numbers, Decimals, and Fractions

The need to understand and compute with numbers is essential to functioning in our society. Computation is involved in many jobs, in consumer purchases, and even in driving a car.

POLAKOW MANUFACTURING COMPANY

TEST FOR EMPLOYMENT

Show all your work and your answers on this paper.

1. Add.

$$\begin{array}{r} 358 \\ +\ 297 \\ \hline \end{array}$$

5. Add.

15.2 + 3 + 4.

2. Subtract.

$$\begin{array}{r} 6062 \\ -\ 329 \\ \hline \end{array}$$

6. Subtract.

54 − 38.25

3. Multiply.

7. Multiply.

Rounding Whole Numbers and Decimals

If there is no need to be exact, numbers are often rounded to make them easier to read at a glance. Thus, "22,357 people attended the game" might appear in the newspaper as "more than 22,000 people attended the game."

This table shows the place value of each digit in 22,357.

billions	hundred millions	ten millions	millions	hundred thousands	ten thousands	thousands	hundreds	tens	ones	tenths	hundredths	thousandths	ten-thousandths	hundred-thousandths	millionths
					2	2,	3	5	7						

problem A

Round 34,695 to the nearest hundred.

solution

Look at the digit to the *right* of the hundreds place. If it is 5 or greater, round up to 700. If it is 4 or less, round down to 600.

34,695
↑ 5 or greater. Round up.

34,700 Rounded to the nearest hundred

problem B

Round 469.2043 to the nearest hundredth.

solution

Look at the digit to the *right* of the hundredths place. It it is 5 or greater, round up to .21. If it is 4 or less, round down to .20.

469.2043
↑ 4 or less. Round down.

469.20 Rounded to the nearest hundredth

exercises

set A Round each number to the nearest thousand, the nearest hundred, and the nearest ten.

1. 1536
2. 2321
3. 4872
4. 824
5. 927
6. 5013
7. 6007
8. 80,089
9. 7002.5
10. 16,010.3

set B Round each number to the nearest whole number, the nearest tenth, and the nearest hundredth.

11. 12.684
12. 5.271
13. 13.882
14. 17.5039
15. 47.973
16. 126.1293
17. 320.709
18. 97.005
19. 100.084
20. 10.002

set C Round to the nearest dollar and to the nearest cent.

21. \$6.035
22. \$15.183
23. \$26.852
24. \$98.789
25. \$124.374
26. \$175.896
27. \$70.049
28. \$62.0034
29. \$50.499
30. \$16.2708

31. The official attendance at the game was 16,485. The announcer said, "We have a crowd of well over ______ thousand."

32. Bob calculates that he owes the city treasury \$27.3287 in tax. Round this to the nearest cent to find the amount that Bob must pay.

Adding and Subtracting Whole Numbers and Decimals

John plans to buy 1 carton of milk for \$1.57, a roast for \$3.27, and a package of cheese for \$1.19. To be sure he will have enough money at the check-out counter, he estimates the prices at \$2, \$3, and \$1, for a total of \$6.

In many situations, it is practical to estimate a sum or difference. An estimate can also be used to decide if a computed answer is reasonable.

problem A

28 + 34 + 76 + 98

solution

Estimate. Round each number to the nearest ten and add.		Find the sum.
28 ⟶	30	28
34 ⟶	30	34
76 ⟶	80	76
98 ⟶	+ 100	+ 98
	240	236

■ *When adding or subtracting decimals, write the problem vertically so that the decimal points line up.*

problem B

.341 + 1.98 + 3.01 + .05

solution

Estimate. Round each number to the nearest whole number and add.		Find the sum.
.341 ⟶	0	.341
1.98 ⟶	2	1.98
3.01 ⟶	3	3.01
.05 ⟶	+ 0	+ .05
	5	5.381

problem C

44.3 − 15.791

solution

Estimate. Round each number to the nearest whole number and subtract.

$$\begin{array}{lr} 44.3 \longrightarrow & 44 \\ 15.791 \longrightarrow & -\ 16 \\ \hline & 28 \end{array}$$

Find the difference.

$$\begin{array}{r} 44.300 \\ -\ 15.791 \\ \hline 28.509 \end{array}$$

exercises

For each exercise, estimate the sum or difference. Then compute each answer.

set A

1. 42 + 28 + 39
2. 23 + 46 + 67
3. 74 + 12 + 18
4. 78 + 43 + 37
5. 86 + 51 + 17
6. 62 + 29 + 43
7. 88 + 56 + 25 + 34
8. 97 + 8 + 17 + 18
9. 21 + 94 + 32 + 13
10. 19 + 99 + 62 + 53
11. 356 + 217 + 592
12. 101 + 463 + 786

set B

13. 4.7 + 1.28
14. 6.4 + 2.08
15. 18.75 + 9.23
16. 63.91 + 40.15
17. 1.82 + 3.47 + 1.3
18. 1.31 + .35 + 2.5
19. 1.33 + 6.57 + 2.91
20. 7.62 + 5.07 + 3.94
21. 2.34 + 6.19 + 5.28 + 4.05
22. 1.84 + 3.71 + 8.65 + 7.54
23. .57 + .93 + .15 + .08
24. .094 + .89 + 1.04 + .36

set C

25. 34 − 19
26. 82 − 38
27. 67 − 42
28. 91 − 7
29. 47.3 − 21.2
30. 95.65 − 8.16
31. 24.7 − 15.9
32. 80.6 − 48.9
33. 73.21 − 41.6
34. 40.933 − 36.2
35. 67.14 − 25.8
36. 91.702 − 36.13
37. 72.6 − 5.81
38. 83.73 − 17.008
39. 45.6 − 14.986
40. 9.84 − .779
41. 18 − 5.6
42. 27 − 12.45
43. 53 − 37.9
44. 61 − 42.16
45. 53.8 − 9
46. 27.31 − 18

set D

47. Estimate the total cost of these items: notebook, $2.79; paper, $.89; pen, $1.29; and paper clips, $.65.
48. Find the actual cost of the items in exercise 47. How much change would you receive if you paid for them with a $20 bill?

Multiplying Whole Numbers

A farmer has planted 265 acres of corn. Based on past experience, he expects a yield of 115 bushels per acre. From this, he estimates that his total production will be 100 × 300, or 30,000 bushels of corn.

■ *When multiplying whole numbers that end in zeros, multiply the nonzero digits. Then count the zeros in both factors and write that many in your answer.*

problem A

700 × 5000

solution

	Factor		Factor		Product
	700	×	5000	=	▒
Think	7	×	5	=	35
so	700	×	5000	=	3,500,000
	2 zeros		3 zeros		5 zeros

problem B

437 × 68

solution

Estimate. Round each factor so that only the first digit is not zero.

$$\begin{array}{ccc} 437 & \times & 68 \\ \downarrow & & \downarrow \\ 400 & \times & 70 = 28{,}000 \end{array}$$

Find the product.

$$\begin{array}{r} 437 \\ \times\ \ 68 \\ \hline 3496 \longleftarrow 8 \times 437 \\ 26220 \longleftarrow 60 \times 437 \\ \hline 29716 \end{array}$$

exercises

set A Find the product.

1. 50 × 90
2. 700 × 60
3. 40 × 400
4. 7 × 2000
5. 9000 × 8
6. 4000 × 3000
7. 600 × 800
8. 9 × 700
9. 9000 × 600
10. 60 × 500
11. 800 × 50
12. 60 × 300
13. 90 × 20
14. 5000 × 4
15. 90 × 900
16. 50 × 200
17. 300 × 8
18. 40 × 9000
19. 320 × 1000
20. 100 × 1400
21. 2200 × 30
22. 110 × 600
23. 210 × 40
24. 410 × 600
25. 5100 × 300
26. 8100 × 6000
27. 930 × 500
28. 520 × 700

set B Estimate. Then find the product.

29. 53 × 26
30. 93 × 81
31. 57 × 18
32. 88 × 27
33. 25 × 38
34. 48 × 65
35. 34 × 97
36. 67 × 79
37. 184 × 75
38. 610 × 64
39. 467 × 13
40. 319 × 59
41. 304 × 58
42. 903 × 96
43. 802 × 43
44. 704 × 91
45. 237 × 456
46. 381 × 952
47. 228 × 307
48. 502 × 805
49. 512 × 691
50. 698 × 724
51. 1203 × 45
52. 4216 × 37
53. 8253 × 94
54. 6271 × 83
55. 8002 × 173
56. 4099 × 496
57. 4204 × 506
58. 9307 × 705

set C

59. Soybeans planted on 373 acres of land are expected to yield 33 bushels per acre. Estimate the total production of soybeans on this land.
60. Les can type 52 words per minute. If he types for 28 minutes, can he finish a 1275-word manuscript?
61. Chairs must be set up in the school cafeteria. There are to be 62 rows of chairs with 20 chairs in each row. How many chairs are needed?
62. Jeanette makes $19 a day assisting the owner of a day-care center. She worked 14 days last month. How much did she earn?

Multiplying Decimals

Members of the school band are having a series of car washes to raise money for new uniforms. They expect to clean 275 cars for $1.25 each. The treasurer estimates that they will raise about $1.00 × 300, or $300.

■ *When multiplying decimals, multiply as with whole numbers. Then add the number of decimal places in each factor to find the number of decimal places in the product.*

problem A

.8 × .06

solution

Think	8	×	6	=	48
so	.8	×	.06	=	.048
	1 decimal place		2 decimal places		3 decimal places

problem B

800 × .007

solution

Think	8	×	7	=	56
so	800	×	7	=	5600
then	800	×	.007	=	5.600, or 5.6
	0 decimal places		3 decimal places		3 decimal places

problem C

914.37 × .069

solution

Estimate. Round each factor so that only one digit is not zero.

$$\begin{array}{l} 914.37 \times .069 \\ \downarrow \qquad\quad \downarrow \\ 900 \quad \times .07 = 63.00 \end{array}$$

Find the product.

$$\begin{array}{r} 914.37 \leftarrow \text{2 decimal places} \\ \times \quad .069 \leftarrow \text{3 decimal places} \\ \hline 8\,22933 \\ 54\,86220 \\ \hline 63.09153 \leftarrow \text{5 decimal places} \end{array}$$

exercises

set A Find the product.

1. .4 × .2
2. .3 × .1
3. .08 × .8
4. .7 × .03
5. .04 × .8
6. .09 × .04
7. .6 × .06
8. .008 × .7
9. 6 × .03
10. .005 × 5
11. .5 × .07
12. .09 × .08
13. .4 × .05
14. 9 × .009
15. 2 × .005
16. .006 × .008
17. .12 × .02
18. 11 × .003
19. .001 × .01
20. .21 × .2

set B Find the product.

21. 700 × .06
22. 80 × .2
23. .9 × 300
24. 70 × .04
25. .03 × 5000
26. .03 × 30
27. 600 × .05
28. .007 × 20
29. 5000 × .8
30. 900 × .006
31. .07 × 7000
32. .09 × 700
33. .06 × 400
34. 11 × .008
35. 120 × .03
36. 1300 × .002
37. .007 × 1100
38. 2000 × .0012
39. .005 × 500
40. .007 × 700

set C Estimate. Then find the product.

41. 38.7 × .62
42. 11.9 × 4.7
43. 9.58 × .014
44. 9.3 × 45.7
45. 2.59 × 35
46. .413 × 5.5
47. 4.51 × .094
48. 8.808 × 1.5
49. .3304 × 78
50. .601 × .807
51. .0227 × .609
52. 4.001 × 87.7
53. 57.35 × .00436
54. 5.603 × 3.41
55. .946 × .0167
56. .0293 × .38
57. .058 × .0442
58. 61.91 × .873
59. 5.319 × .0176
60. 90.42 × .0943

set D

61. Band uniforms cost $95.85 each. Estimate the cost of 75 uniforms.
62. Maria multiplied 2.16 by .075 on her calculator. The answer displayed was 16.2. Is this answer reasonable?
63. Pat makes $3.79 per hour. How much does he make in 5.5 hours?
64. An automobile dealer sold 114 small cars last year for an average price of $3685.73. Find his total sales.

Dividing Whole Numbers and Decimals

Judy has $11.25. She wants to buy several scarves that are on sale for $3.49 each. She divides $11.25 by $3.49 to find that she can buy 3 scarves.

problem A

$3329 \div 52$

solution

Dividend		Divisor		Quotient
3329	÷	52	=	▦

```
      64←——Quotient
52)3329
  − 312 ←——52 × 6
    209
  − 208←——52 × 4
      1←——Remainder
```

Use estimation to decide if the answer is reasonable. Round the quotient and the divisor and multiply.

$60 \times 50 = 3000$

Since 3000 is close to 3329, the estimation indicates that the answer, 64 R1, is reasonable.

■ *When dividing decimals, write the divisor as a whole number by moving the decimal point. Then move the decimal point in the dividend the same direction and the same number of places. Add zeros if necessary.*

problem B

Find the quotient to the nearest thousandth.

$34.564 \div .12$

solution

```
     2 88.0333 ≈ 288.033
.12)34.56 4000
    24
    10 5
     9 6
       96
       96
         4
         0
         40
         36
          40
          36
           40
           36
            4
```

Continue the division to the fourth decimal place. Then round to thousandths.

Use estimation to decide if the answer is reasonable. Round the quotient and the divisor and multiply.

$300 \times .1 = 30.0$

Since 30 is close to 34.564, the estimation indicates that the answer is reasonable.

exercises

set A Find the quotient. Estimate to decide if the answer is reasonable.

1. $2848 \div 8$

2. $1729 \div 7$

3. $1137 \div 9$

4. $1834 \div 6$

5. $4765 \div 7$

6. $7344 \div 17$

7. $13{,}608 \div 63$

8. $862 \div 23$

9. $3875 \div 78$

10. $7998 \div 39$

11. $11{,}682 \div 56$

12. $36{,}565 \div 85$

13. $204{,}136 \div 34$

14. $147{,}613 \div 29$

15. $95{,}140 \div 19$

16. $919{,}078 \div 913$

set B Find the quotient to the nearest thousandth. Estimate to decide if the answer is reasonable.

17. $27.6 \div 14$

18. $.156 \div 3$

19. $1.168 \div 27$

20. $42.89 \div 32$

21. $70.52 \div 125$

22. $.0589 \div 8.2$

23. $11.53 \div 2.6$

24. $4.4 \div 1.82$

25. $1.9 \div 3.56$

26. $8 \div .4$

27. $93 \div .31$

28. $6.04 \div 9.71$

29. $.641 \div .07$

30. $.0091 \div .23$

31. $.801 \div .578$

32. $.2161 \div .036$

set C

33. Chiang has $2.85. He wants to buy some cans of oil that cost $.53 each. How many cans will he be able to buy?

34. Robert is organizing teams for the park district field day. There are 156 children to be put on 12 teams. How many children will be on each team?

Renaming Fractions and Mixed Numbers

A recipe called for $2\frac{1}{2}$ cups of flour. Margaret's large measuring cup was filled, so she used a half-cup measure. Since $2\frac{1}{2}$ is the same as $\frac{5}{2}$, she used 5 half-cup measures of flour.

■ *The value of a fraction does not change if the numerator and the denominator are multiplied (or divided) by the same number.*

problem A

Which is greater, $\frac{1}{6}$ or $\frac{3}{8}$?

solution

$\frac{1}{6}$ 1 ⟵ numerator, 6 ⟵ denominator

Write the fractions with a common denominator. Then compare.

To find a common denominator, list the multiples of 8 until you find a multiple of 6.

8 16 **24** — 24 is a common multiple of 6 and 8.

Write each fraction with a denominator of 24.

$$\frac{1}{6} = \frac{1 \times 4}{6 \times 4} = \frac{4}{24}$$

$$\frac{3}{8} = \frac{3 \times 3}{8 \times 3} = \frac{9}{24}$$

The common denominator is 24.

Since $\frac{9}{24} > \frac{4}{24}$

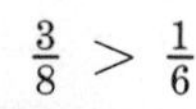

$\frac{3}{8} > \frac{1}{6}$

problem B

Rename $\frac{36}{48}$ in lowest terms.

solution

$\frac{36}{48} = \frac{36 \div 6}{48 \div 6} = \frac{6}{8}$

$\frac{6}{8} = \frac{6 \div 2}{8 \div 2} = \frac{3}{4}$

$\frac{36}{48} = \frac{3}{4}$

$\frac{3}{4}$ is in lowest terms because no number greater than 1 will divide both 3 and 4 evenly.

problem C

Write $\frac{27}{11}$ as a mixed number.

solution

$\frac{27}{11} = 27 \div 11$

$$\begin{array}{r} 2\frac{5}{11} \\ 11\overline{)27} \\ -22 \\ \hline 5 \end{array}$$

Divide the numerator by the denominator. Write the remainder as a fraction.

$\frac{27}{11} = 2\frac{5}{11}$

problem D

Write $3\frac{2}{5}$ as a fraction.

solution

$3\frac{2}{5} = \frac{5 \times 3 + 2}{5} = \frac{17}{5}$

$3\frac{2}{5} = \frac{17}{5}$

Multiply 3 by 5 to find the number of fifths in 3. Then add 2.

exercises

set A Tell which is greater.

1. $\frac{2}{3}$ $\frac{5}{6}$ **5.** $\frac{5}{6}$ $\frac{8}{9}$ **9.** $\frac{1}{2}$ $\frac{5}{8}$

2. $\frac{3}{4}$ $\frac{7}{12}$ **6.** $\frac{5}{8}$ $\frac{7}{12}$ **10.** $\frac{4}{9}$ $\frac{1}{2}$

3. $\frac{1}{3}$ $\frac{2}{5}$ **7.** $\frac{1}{2}$ $\frac{3}{5}$ **11.** $\frac{5}{16}$ $\frac{1}{2}$

4. $\frac{4}{7}$ $\frac{1}{2}$ **8.** $\frac{4}{9}$ $\frac{5}{12}$ **12.** $\frac{7}{11}$ $\frac{1}{2}$

set B Rename in lowest terms.

13. $\frac{4}{16}$ **16.** $\frac{24}{40}$ **19.** $\frac{63}{81}$

14. $\frac{8}{10}$ **17.** $\frac{16}{80}$ **20.** $\frac{24}{72}$

15. $\frac{18}{24}$ **18.** $\frac{22}{66}$ **21.** $\frac{42}{56}$

set C Write as a mixed number.

22. $\frac{28}{5}$ **25.** $\frac{36}{27}$ **28.** $\frac{42}{12}$

23. $\frac{14}{3}$ **26.** $\frac{24}{7}$ **29.** $\frac{23}{16}$

24. $\frac{12}{8}$ **27.** $\frac{36}{11}$ **30.** $\frac{71}{8}$

set D Write as a fraction.

31. $1\frac{3}{4}$ **34.** $9\frac{4}{5}$ **37.** $3\frac{7}{10}$

32. $2\frac{5}{16}$ **35.** 4 **38.** $4\frac{5}{12}$

33. $8\frac{2}{3}$ **36.** 3 **39.** $5\frac{1}{16}$

set E

40. How many quarter-cup measures should you use to measure $2\frac{3}{4}$ cups of rice?

41. If you need tacks longer than $\frac{3}{8}''$, should you use $\frac{3}{4}''$ or $\frac{5}{16}''$ tacks?

Multiplying and Dividing Fractions and Mixed Numbers

Luis has a 30-gallon water tank in his camping trailer. He knows that one gallon of water weighs about $8\frac{1}{4}$ pounds. If he fills the tank before leaving for his vacation, he estimates that he will be pulling about 30×8, or 240 pounds of extra weight.

problem A

$1\frac{5}{6} \times 2\frac{2}{7}$

solution

Estimate the product by rounding each mixed number to the nearest whole number. If the fraction is $\frac{1}{2}$ or greater, round up. If the fraction is less than $\frac{1}{2}$, round down.

$$1\frac{5}{6} \times 2\frac{2}{7}$$
$$\downarrow \quad\quad \downarrow$$
$$2 \times 2 = 4$$

Find the product.

$1\frac{5}{6} \times 2\frac{2}{7} = \frac{11}{6} \times \frac{16}{7}$ — Write the mixed numbers as fractions.

$= \frac{11}{\cancel{6}_{3}} \times \frac{\cancel{16}^{8}}{7}$ — Simplify by dividing a numerator and a denominator by the same number.

$= \frac{88}{21}$ — Multiply the numerators and the denominators.

$= 4\frac{4}{21}$ — Simplify the answer.

■ *The product of a number and its reciprocal is 1. To divide fractions, multiply the dividend by the reciprocal of the divisor.*

problem B

$5\frac{3}{8} \div 3\frac{1}{2}$

solution

Estimate the quotient by rounding each mixed number to the nearest whole number.

$$5\frac{3}{8} \div 3\frac{1}{2}$$
$$\downarrow \qquad \downarrow$$
$$5 \div 4 \approx 1$$

Find the quotient.

$5\frac{3}{8} \div 3\frac{1}{2} = \frac{43}{8} \div \frac{7}{2}$	Write the mixed numbers as fractions.
$= \frac{43}{8} \times \frac{2}{7}$	The reciprocal of $\frac{7}{2}$ is $\frac{2}{7}$.
$= \frac{43}{\cancel{8}_4} \times \frac{\cancel{2}^1}{7}$	Simplify.
$= \frac{43}{28}$	Multiply.
$= 1\frac{15}{28}$	Simplify the answer.

exercises

set A Find the product.

1. $\frac{1}{2} \times \frac{5}{6}$
2. $\frac{1}{4} \times \frac{2}{3}$
3. $\frac{3}{5} \times \frac{5}{6}$
4. $\frac{7}{10} \times \frac{15}{28}$
5. $\frac{1}{5} \times 4$
6. $\frac{7}{8} \times 6$

Estimate. Then find the product.

7. $5\frac{1}{3} \times \frac{1}{2}$
8. $2\frac{5}{8} \times \frac{5}{6}$
9. $3\frac{3}{4} \times 1\frac{1}{5}$
10. $4\frac{1}{6} \times 5\frac{1}{10}$
11. $2\frac{3}{16} \times 1\frac{2}{5}$
12. $1\frac{3}{4} \times 6\frac{2}{3}$
13. $2\frac{11}{12} \times 6$
14. $4 \times 8\frac{3}{8}$
15. $\frac{1}{2} \times \frac{2}{3} \times \frac{5}{8}$
16. $\frac{1}{2} \times 4\frac{1}{2} \times 3\frac{1}{3}$

set B Find the quotient.

17. $\frac{1}{2} \div \frac{2}{3}$
18. $\frac{3}{4} \div \frac{2}{3}$
19. $\frac{5}{6} \div \frac{7}{9}$
20. $\frac{5}{8} \div \frac{15}{16}$
21. $4 \div \frac{1}{2}$
22. $\frac{2}{3} \div 6$

Estimate. Then find the quotient.

23. $1\frac{2}{3} \div \frac{7}{9}$
24. $3\frac{1}{3} \div \frac{5}{6}$
25. $2\frac{1}{2} \div 3\frac{3}{8}$
26. $5\frac{1}{4} \div 4$
27. $3 \div 1\frac{1}{3}$
28. $6\frac{1}{8} \div 1\frac{3}{4}$
29. $10\frac{5}{6} \div 4\frac{1}{3}$
30. $12\frac{3}{8} \div 8\frac{1}{4}$

set C

31. Helen is mailing 4 copies of a book that weighs $2\frac{1}{2}$ pounds. What is the weight of all of the books?

32. Henry wants to make 5 columns on a sheet of paper that is $8\frac{1}{2}$ inches wide. How wide should each column be?

Adding and Subtracting Fractions and Mixed Numbers

Lucille wants to make 6 quarts of punch for a party. She estimates that this recipe will make only 3 + 1 + 1, or 5 quarts of punch.

here's what's cookin'

Party Punch

Mix together:

$2\frac{1}{2}$ qt. cranberry juice cocktail
$\frac{3}{4}$ qt. pineapple juice
$1\frac{1}{4}$ qt. ginger ale

■ ***To add or subtract fractions, first write the fractions with a common denominator.***

problem A

$21\frac{3}{5} + 3\frac{2}{3}$

solution

Estimate the sum by rounding each mixed number to the nearest whole number.

$$\begin{array}{rcr} 21\frac{3}{5} & \longrightarrow & 22 \\ 3\frac{2}{3} & \longrightarrow & +\ 4 \\ \hline & & 26 \end{array}$$

Find the sum. First write the fractions with a common denominator.

$$\begin{array}{rcr} 21\frac{3}{5} & = & 21\frac{9}{15} \\ +\ 3\frac{2}{3} & = & 3\frac{10}{15} \\ \hline & & 24\frac{19}{15} \end{array}$$

Add the numerators. Use the common denominator.

Add the whole numbers.

$24 + 1\frac{4}{15} = 25\frac{4}{15}$ Simplify the answer.

problem B

$31\frac{3}{8} - 4\frac{7}{8}$

solution

Estimate the difference by rounding each mixed number to the nearest whole number.

$$\begin{array}{rcr} 31\frac{3}{8} & \longrightarrow & 31 \\ 4\frac{7}{8} & \longrightarrow & -\ 5 \\ \hline & & 26 \end{array}$$

Find the difference.
Since $\frac{7}{8}$ cannot be subtracted from $\frac{3}{8}$, rename $31\frac{3}{8}$.

$$\begin{array}{rcr} 31\frac{3}{8} & = & 30\frac{11}{8} \\ -\ 4\frac{7}{8} & = & 4\frac{7}{8} \\ \hline & & 26\frac{4}{8} = 26\frac{1}{2} \end{array}$$

$31\frac{3}{8} = 30 + 1\frac{3}{8} = 30 + \frac{11}{8}$

Subtract the numerators. Use the common denominator. Subtract the whole numbers and simplify.

15. $1\frac{3}{4} + 1\frac{1}{10}$

16. $2\frac{5}{7} + 3\frac{2}{3}$

17. $6\frac{1}{3} + 4\frac{1}{4}$

18. $4\frac{7}{8} + 1\frac{4}{5}$

19. $8\frac{1}{16} + 2\frac{7}{8}$

20. $4\frac{3}{5} + 5\frac{2}{3}$

21. $2\frac{1}{4} + 1\frac{1}{5} + 4\frac{1}{2}$

22. $10\frac{2}{3} + 3\frac{5}{8} + 4\frac{1}{6}$

set B Find the difference.

23. $\frac{5}{8} - \frac{1}{2}$

24. $\frac{3}{5} - \frac{1}{2}$

25. $\frac{11}{12} - \frac{2}{3}$

26. $\frac{3}{4} - \frac{2}{5}$

27. $\frac{7}{8} - \frac{5}{6}$

28. $\frac{1}{3} - \frac{1}{4}$

29. $\frac{3}{8} - \frac{1}{3}$

30. $\frac{1}{2} - \frac{2}{7}$

31. $4 - \frac{3}{5}$

32. $10 - \frac{5}{16}$

Estimate. Then find the difference.

33. $6\frac{1}{8} - 2\frac{7}{8}$

34. $27\frac{1}{3} - 18\frac{2}{3}$

35. $16 - 4\frac{3}{8}$

36. $11 - 2\frac{5}{12}$

37. $12\frac{1}{3} - 7\frac{1}{9}$

38. $14\frac{5}{8} - 5\frac{1}{4}$

39. $15\frac{1}{2} - 1\frac{11}{16}$

40. $17\frac{1}{6} - 9\frac{2}{3}$

41. $12\frac{3}{5} - 4\frac{3}{4}$

42. $16\frac{2}{9} - 2\frac{5}{6}$

43. $10\frac{1}{3} - 4\frac{7}{8}$

44. $11\frac{1}{4} - 3\frac{5}{6}$

exercises

set A Find the sum.

1. $\frac{1}{8} + \frac{1}{3}$

2. $\frac{5}{6} + \frac{1}{4}$

3. $\frac{3}{7} + \frac{1}{2}$

4. $\frac{3}{4} + \frac{4}{5}$

5. $\frac{9}{16} + \frac{5}{8}$

6. $\frac{1}{12} + \frac{2}{3}$

7. $\frac{1}{4} + \frac{5}{9}$

8. $\frac{3}{7} + \frac{1}{3}$

9. $\frac{1}{2} + \frac{5}{8} + \frac{5}{6}$

10. $\frac{2}{3} + \frac{1}{2} + \frac{3}{5}$

Estimate. Then find the sum.

11. $2\frac{1}{3} + 4\frac{5}{6}$

12. $7\frac{3}{5} + 9\frac{1}{10}$

13. $12\frac{3}{8} + \frac{2}{3}$

14. $3\frac{5}{7} + \frac{1}{2}$

set C

45. How much punch does the recipe on page 18 actually make? How much more liquid would Lucille have to add in order to have 6 quarts?

46. Laurie needs the following lengths of molding: $8\frac{3}{4}''$, $9\frac{1}{8}''$, and $7\frac{3}{16}''$. Can she cut these 3 pieces from one 25″ strip of molding?

CALCULATOR EXERCISES

Write $14\frac{5}{12}$ as a decimal. Round to the nearest thousandth.

First write $\frac{5}{12}$ as a decimal.

$\frac{5}{12} = 5 \div 12 \approx 0.4166666$ From the calculator

$\frac{5}{12} \approx 0.417$ Rounded to the nearest thousandth

Since $14\frac{5}{12} = 14 + \frac{5}{12}$

$14\frac{5}{12} \approx 14 + 0.417$

$14\frac{5}{12} \approx 14.417$

Write each number as a decimal. Round to the nearest thousandth.

1. $\frac{5}{6}$

2. $\frac{7}{9}$

3. $\frac{11}{13}$

4. $\frac{20}{21}$

5. $\frac{5}{8}$

6. $\frac{23}{40}$

7. $\frac{7}{18}$

8. $\frac{37}{60}$

9. $\frac{15}{52}$

10. $\frac{13}{16}$

11. $\frac{75}{70}$

12. $\frac{36}{17}$

13. $\frac{97}{37}$

14. $\frac{111}{24}$

15. $\frac{114}{15}$

16. $2\frac{4}{5}$

17. $10\frac{7}{8}$

18. $14\frac{5}{12}$

19. $27\frac{11}{16}$

20. $31\frac{1}{15}$

21. $40\frac{1}{18}$

22. $2\frac{2}{11}$

23. $3\frac{5}{9}$

24. $17\frac{3}{11}$

25. $20\frac{33}{111}$

26. $53\frac{4}{9}$

27. $12\frac{4}{99}$

28. $15\frac{13}{99}$

29. $8\frac{17}{99}$

30. $6\frac{35}{99}$

change of pace

In the game of chess, queens can capture opposing queens by moving any number of spaces horizontally, vertically, or diagonally.

Use a 5 by 5 grid as a chessboard. Place 3 white queens and 4 black queens on the chessboard so that the queens cannot capture each other.

On another 5 by 5 grid, place 3 white queens and 5 black queens so that the queens cannot capture each other.

Chapter 1

review

Rounding whole numbers and decimals, pages 4-5

1. Round 7481 to the nearest thousand, the nearest hundred, and the nearest ten.

2. Round 23.716 to the nearest whole number, the nearest tenth, and the nearest hundredth.

Adding and subtracting whole numbers and decimals, pages 6-7

3. $26 + 52 + 63$

4. $2.1 + .36 + 5.82$

5. $91 - 57$

6. $65.2 - 23.74$

Multiplying whole numbers, pages 8-9

7. 30×700

8. 576×42

Multiplying decimals, pages 10-11

9. $50 \times .07$

10. 5.23×6.7

Dividing whole numbers and decimals, pages 12-13

11. $2883 \div 7$

12. $9312 \div 16$

Find the quotient to the nearest hundredth.

13. $43.6 \div 7$

14. $84.1 \div .24$

Renaming fractions and mixed numbers, pages 14-15

Tell which is greater.

15. $\frac{1}{3}$ $\frac{5}{12}$

16. $\frac{2}{3}$ $\frac{3}{5}$

Rename in lowest terms.

17. $\frac{8}{24}$

18. $\frac{12}{20}$

Write as a mixed number.

19. $\frac{28}{3}$

20. $\frac{35}{6}$

Write as a fraction.

21. $1\frac{2}{3}$

22. $4\frac{3}{5}$

Multiplying and dividing fractions and mixed numbers, pages 16-17

23. $\frac{1}{3} \times \frac{5}{7}$

24. $1\frac{1}{6} \times 2\frac{2}{3}$

25. $\frac{3}{4} \div \frac{1}{5}$

26. $3\frac{1}{2} \div 1\frac{1}{4}$

Adding and subtracting fractions and mixed numbers, pages 18-19

27. $\frac{3}{4} + \frac{1}{5}$

28. $2\frac{1}{3} + 3\frac{7}{8}$

29. $\frac{7}{8} - \frac{2}{9}$

30. $5\frac{2}{3} - 2\frac{1}{9}$

Chapter 1

test

1. Round 3172 to the nearest thousand, the nearest hundred, and the nearest ten.

2. Round 58.326 to the nearest whole number, the nearest tenth, and the nearest hundredth.

3. $32 + 74 + 25$

4. $8.12 + 3.27 + 5.64$

5. $83 - 26$

6. $57.36 - 24.71$

7. 20×800

8. 324×67

9. $.7 \times .04$

10. 4.62×3.8

11. $3728 \div 6$

12. $9776 \div 13$

Find the quotient to the nearest hundredth.

13. $56.2 \div 9$

14. $15.55 \div 3.2$

Tell which is greater.

15. $\frac{3}{4}$ $\frac{11}{12}$

16. $\frac{5}{8}$ $\frac{2}{3}$

Rename in lowest terms.

17. $\frac{5}{20}$

18. $\frac{16}{28}$

Write as a mixed number.

19. $\frac{27}{5}$

20. $\frac{35}{4}$

Write as a fraction.

21. $1\frac{1}{4}$

22. $4\frac{2}{3}$

Compute.

23. $\frac{1}{2} \times \frac{3}{8}$

24. $1\frac{3}{4} \times 3\frac{1}{3}$

25. $\frac{5}{6} \div \frac{4}{5}$

26. $2\frac{2}{3} \div 1\frac{1}{2}$

27. $\frac{2}{3} + \frac{1}{4}$

28. $2\frac{2}{5} + 1\frac{1}{3}$

29. $\frac{11}{12} - \frac{2}{3}$

30. $4\frac{7}{12} - 1\frac{1}{2}$

Chapter 2

Equations, Proportions, and Percent

Many everyday problems at home and on the job involve using equations, proportions, or percent.

DIRECTIONS: TO MAKE FROM ONE GLASS TO 8 QUARTS, USE THE FOLLOWING DIRECTIONS:
SCOOP
HOUSEHOLD MEASURE
QUANTITY
ICE WATER
½ SCOOP
1½ TABLESPOONS
TO MAKE 8
2 SCOOPS
6 TABLESPOONS
TO MAKE
8 SCOOPS
1⅔ CUPS
TO MAKE
(4 QUARTS
—
ENTIRE CONTENTS OF CAN
TO MAKE 8
NUTRITION INFORMATION PER SERVING
SERVING SIZE: 8 FL. OZ. SERVINGS PER
CALORIES 90
PROTEIN 0
CARBOHYDRATE 22
FAT 0
PERCENTAGE OF U.S. RECOMMENDED DAILY ALLOWANCES (U.S. RDA)* VITAMIN C 15%

Addition and Subtraction Equations

Sale-Saturday Only
Save $17.33
You Pay Only
$49.98

Larry cannot go shopping until Monday. He could solve the equation $r - \$17.33 = \$49.98$ to find that he will have to pay \$67.31 for the jacket on Monday.

■ *To solve an equation, add, subtract, multiply, or divide each side by the same number.*

problem A

Solve this equation. $a + 2 = 3.2$

solution

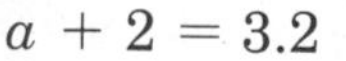

$a + 2 = 3.2$	2 is added to a.
$a + 2 - 2 = 3.2 - 2$	To undo the addition, subtract 2 from each side of the equation.
$a = 1.2$	

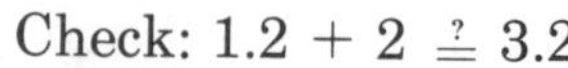

Check: $1.2 + 2 \stackrel{?}{=} 3.2$	Substitute 1.2 for a in the original equation.
$3.2 = 3.2$	

problem B

Solve this equation. $n - 8 = 9.4$

solution

$n - 8 = 9.4$	8 is subtracted from n.
$n - 8 + 8 = 9.4 + 8$	To undo the subtraction, add 8 to each side of the equation.
$n = 17.4$	
Check: $17.4 - 8 \stackrel{?}{=} 9.4$	Substitute 17.4 for n in the original equation.
$9.4 = 9.4$	

exercises

Solve and check.

set A

1. $a + 2.1 = 6$
2. $b + 3.01 = 4$
3. $9.2 = c + 2.9$
4. $28 + d = 37$
5. $f + 1.87 = 3.4$
6. $4 = 3.3 + x$

set B

7. $g - 13 = 10$
8. $h - .25 = 1.13$
9. $.09 = k - .7$
10. $m - 2 = 4$
11. $7 = n - 17$
12. $a - .03 = 1.8$

set C

13. $14 + m = 26$
14. $30 = a + 4.3$
15. $t - .329 = .601$
16. $r + 2.08 = 3$
17. $4.6 = s - 1$
18. $22 = v + 18$
19. $w - 45.19 = 6$
20. $7.5 = 4.11 + x$
21. $6 = y - 47$
22. $z + 100 = 499$
23. $p - 83 = 8$
24. $4.9 = a - 33.7$
25. $3.3 + b = 6.06$
26. $s + 10.6 = 30$
27. $3.9 = z - 5.15$
28. $d - 2.7 = 7.4$
29. $98.6 + g = 132$

Write an equation for each exercise. Then solve and check.

30. A baseball glove is on sale for $13.40. This is a savings of $2.10. What is the regular price of the glove?
31. After receiving a 27¢ per hour raise, Libby now makes $6.35 per hour. What was she earning before her raise?
32. Jenny currently pays $64.63 per month for health insurance. If she insures her son with this policy, she will pay a total of $76.52 per month. What is the cost of insuring Jenny's son?

Multiplication and Division Equations

The cashier collected \$885 from dance tickets which sold for \$2.50 each. She solved the equation $\$2.50n = \$885$ to find that 354 tickets had been sold.

problem A

Solve this equation. $.3n = 36$

solution

$.3n = 36$ — $.3n$ means $.3 \times n$.

$\frac{.3n}{.3} = \frac{36}{.3}$ — To undo the multiplication, divide each side by .3.

$n = 120$

Check: $.3(120) \stackrel{?}{=} 36$

$36 = 36$

Substitute 120 for n in the original equation.

problem B

Solve this equation. $\frac{x}{4} = 3.7$

solution

$\frac{x}{4} = 3.7$ — $\frac{x}{4}$ means x is divided by 4.

$\frac{x}{4}(4) = 3.7(4)$ — To undo the division, multiply each side by 4.

$x = 14.8$

Check: $\frac{14.8}{4} \stackrel{?}{=} 3.7$

$3.7 = 3.7$

Substitute 14.8 for x in the original equation.

problem C

Solve this equation. $3m + 4m = 35$

solution

$3m + 4m = 35$ — $3m$ and $4m$ are like terms because 3 and 4 are each multiplied by m.

$7m = 35$ — Combine the like terms. $3m + 4m = (3 + 4)m = 7m$

$\frac{7m}{7} = \frac{35}{7}$ — To undo the multiplication, divide each side by 7.

$m = 5$

Check: $3(5) + 4(5) \stackrel{?}{=} 35$ — Substitute 5 for m in the original equation.

$15 + 20 \stackrel{?}{=} 35$

$35 = 35$

exercises

Solve and check.

set A

1. $3a = 141$
2. $1.2b = 8.4$
3. $153 = 9c$
4. $.8x = 72$
5. $3.15 = 3.5z$

set B

6. $\frac{d}{5} = .08$
7. $\frac{f}{.2} = 3$
8. $.45 = \frac{g}{.7}$
9. $\frac{r}{.8} = 19$
10. $.04 = \frac{h}{25}$

set C

11. $7a + 8a = 45$
12. $10c - 2c = 32$
13. $99 = 5t + 6t$
14. $.2d + 2.2d = 48$
15. $84 = 15x - 8x$

set D

16. $.5r = 17.5$
17. $3.5 = .07x$
18. $17c + 28c = 45$
19. $47y = 0$
20. $2b + 2b + 3b = 56$
21. $.09z = 8.1$
22. $105 = 16q - q$
23. $1.08 = .27s$
24. $12a + a = 26$
25. $318x - 167x = 0$
26. $\frac{d}{.5} = .8$
27. $\frac{f}{.16} = .6$
28. $\frac{x}{5.07} = 1.1$
29. $\frac{k}{4.018} = 0$
30. $.22 = \frac{m}{1.7}$

Write an equation for each exercise. Then solve and check.

31. Hot chocolate sells for \$.35 a cup at the football games. The booster club collected \$61.25 from hot chocolate sales. How many cups were sold?
32. Tim and Alex earned \$25 one Saturday for preparing a garden for planting. Since Alex worked 4 times as long as Tim, he will receive 4 times as much money as Tim. How much will each boy receive?

Two-Step Equations

Adam wants to make \$30 this week from his part-time job making deliveries. He is paid \$2.50 per hour and has already made \$7.50 this week. Adam can use the equation $\$2.50h + \$7.50 = \$30$ to find that he must work 9 hours more to reach his goal.

problem A

Solve this equation. $3x + 2 = 11$

solution

$$3x + 2 = 11$$

2 is added to $3x$.

$$3x + 2 - 2 = 11 - 2$$

$$3x = 9$$

To undo the addition, subtract 2 from each side.

$$\frac{3x}{3} = \frac{9}{3}$$

$$x = 3$$

To undo the multiplication, divide each side by 3.

$$\text{Check: } 3(3) + 2 \stackrel{?}{=} 11$$

$$9 + 2 \stackrel{?}{=} 11$$

$$11 = 11$$

Substitute 3 for x in the original equation.

problem B

Solve this equation. $\frac{x}{4} - 7 = 1.7$

solution

$$\frac{x}{4} - 7 = 1.7$$

7 is subtracted from $\frac{x}{4}$.

$$\frac{x}{4} - 7 + 7 = 1.7 + 7$$

To undo the subtraction, add 7 to each side.

$$\frac{x}{4} = 8.7$$

$$\frac{x}{4}(4) = 8.7(4)$$

To undo the division, multiply each side by 4.

$$x = 34.8$$

Check: $\frac{34.8}{4} - 7 \stackrel{?}{=} 1.7$

$8.7 - 7 \stackrel{?}{=} 1.7$

$1.7 = 1.7$

Substitute 34.8 for x in the original equation.

exercises

Solve and check.

set A

1. $5a + 3 = 8$
2. $3s - 14 = 16$
3. $7n + 2 = 65$
4. $11 = 6 + 2r$
5. $0 = 2b - 7$

set B

6. $\frac{m}{2} + 3 = 6$
7. $\frac{a}{3} - 7 = 5$
8. $\frac{t}{7} + 9 = 10$
9. $24 = 11 + \frac{c}{4}$
10. $4 = \frac{x}{6} + 4$

set C

11. $20 = 5z - 20$
12. $12 + 2c = 12$
13. $.5y + 4 = 8$
14. $43 = 7 + 3w$
15. $9x - 98 = .01$
16. $.2y - .2 = 20$
17. $1.3 = .4b - 2.7$
18. $2.8 = .7 + 3x$
19. $1.2 + 6m = 2.4$
20. $.9n - 4.7 = 1.6$
21. $.1x - .1 = .1$
22. $41 = 32 + \frac{y}{9}$
23. $\frac{x}{.2} + .6 = 1.5$
24. $2.9 + \frac{d}{5} = 3.5$
25. $\frac{g}{.01} - 11 = 3$
26. $1 = \frac{b}{.1} - 39$
27. $5.3 + \frac{w}{1.9} = 15.3$
28. $\frac{a}{.9} + .9 = .9$

Write an equation for each exercise. Then solve and check.

29. Martha is paid $2.75 per hour and has earned $24.75 this week. To earn a total of $55, how many more hours must she work?
30. Ollie is sawing pieces of wood from a 90″ plank. He wants one piece to be 15″ long. The remainder of the plank is to be cut into 4 pieces of equal length. How long will each of these pieces be?

Ratio and Proportion

Leroy wanted to make 10 cups of lemonade. It takes 3 tablespoons of mix to make 2 cups of lemonade. He wrote this proportion.

$$\frac{3}{2} = \frac{x}{10} \begin{array}{l} \leftarrow \text{Tablespoons of mix} \\ \leftarrow \text{Cups of lemonade} \end{array}$$

He solved the proportion and found that he would need 15 tablespoons of mix.

■ *Equal ratios form a proportion. Two ratios are equal if their cross-products are equal. If the cross-products are not equal, the ratios are not equal.*

problem A

Find the cross-products of these ratios. Tell whether the ratios are equal.

$\frac{.16}{36}$ $\frac{.04}{9}$

solution

$$\frac{.16}{36} \times \frac{.04}{9}$$

$.16 \times 9 \stackrel{?}{=} 36 \times .04$ Write the cross-products.

$1.44 = 1.44$

$\frac{.16}{36} = \frac{.04}{9}$ The cross-products are equal, so the ratios are equal.

problem B

Solve the proportion. $\frac{3}{10} = \frac{n}{8}$

solution

$$\frac{3}{10} = \frac{n}{8}$$

$3 \times 8 = 10 \times n$ — Write the cross-products.

$24 = 10n$

$\frac{24}{10} = \frac{10n}{10}$ — To undo the multiplication, divide each side by 10.

$2.4 = n$

Check:

$\frac{3}{10} \stackrel{?}{=} \frac{2.4}{8}$ — Substitute 2.4 for n in the original equation.

$3 \times 8 \stackrel{?}{=} 10 \times 2.4$ — Write the cross-products.

$24 = 24$ — The cross-products are equal, so the ratios are equal and $n = 2.4$.

exercises

set A Find the cross-products. Tell whether the ratios are equal.

1. $\frac{7}{28}$ $\frac{3}{12}$
2. $\frac{20}{100}$ $\frac{7}{35}$
3. $\frac{5}{6}$ $\frac{37}{42}$
4. $\frac{30}{8}$ $\frac{70}{21}$
5. $\frac{24}{64}$ $\frac{3}{8}$
6. $\frac{20}{35}$ $\frac{12}{21}$
7. $\frac{11}{12}$ $\frac{44}{48}$
8. $\frac{32}{63}$ $\frac{4}{9}$
9. $\frac{8}{1.2}$ $\frac{2}{.3}$
10. $\frac{3.5}{4.2}$ $\frac{10}{14}$
11. $\frac{10.8}{6}$ $\frac{3.6}{2}$
12. $\frac{.6}{9}$ $\frac{.4}{6}$
13. $\frac{.5}{.25}$ $\frac{.4}{.2}$
14. $\frac{.3}{.5}$ $\frac{3}{4.5}$
15. $\frac{50.4}{100}$ $\frac{4.2}{9}$
16. $\frac{75}{81}$ $\frac{2.5}{2.7}$

set B Solve and check.

17. $\frac{a}{20} = \frac{6}{8}$
18. $\frac{11}{33} = \frac{c}{15}$
19. $\frac{12}{d} = \frac{4}{3}$
20. $\frac{24}{9} = \frac{8}{f}$
21. $\frac{x}{5} = \frac{3}{4}$
22. $\frac{16}{g} = \frac{10}{2}$
23. $\frac{3}{5} = \frac{h}{7}$
24. $\frac{24}{25} = \frac{6}{w}$
25. $\frac{.75}{1} = \frac{30}{x}$
26. $\frac{r}{14} = \frac{.7}{10}$
27. $\frac{.5}{.9} = \frac{s}{36}$
28. $\frac{x}{1.4} = \frac{2.4}{2.8}$
29. $\frac{.03}{.5} = \frac{t}{.1}$
30. $\frac{.06}{v} = \frac{.3}{4}$
31. $\frac{y}{1.6} = \frac{1.5}{4.8}$
32. $\frac{.25}{.3} = \frac{100}{x}$

set C

33. Three teaspoons of mix make 24 ounces of iced tea. How much mix is needed to make 40 ounces of iced tea?
34. One bag of fertilizer treats 10,000 square feet of lawn. How many bags are required for 25,000 square feet?

CALCULATOR EXERCISES

Solve the proportions.

1. $\frac{n}{875} = \frac{48}{125}$

2. $\frac{n}{215} = \frac{456}{2580}$

3. $\frac{628}{54} = \frac{2198}{n}$

4. $\frac{87}{522} = \frac{n}{1578}$

5. $\frac{1029}{n} = \frac{392}{104}$

6. $\frac{376}{1504} = \frac{385}{n}$

7. $\frac{n}{2619} = \frac{969}{5529}$

8. $\frac{225}{750} = \frac{n}{2500}$

9. $\frac{16.5}{28} = \frac{74.25}{n}$

10. $\frac{27.6}{46} = \frac{n}{299}$

11. $\frac{27}{8.532} = \frac{75}{n}$

12. $\frac{n}{520} = \frac{46.8}{156}$

13. $\frac{53}{3.71} = \frac{n}{.2597}$

14. $\frac{n}{3.32} = \frac{33.2}{13.28}$

15. $\frac{133.2}{n} = \frac{2.22}{.037}$

16. $\frac{12.87}{14.3} = \frac{n}{12.87}$

17. $\frac{237.6}{39.6} = \frac{n}{6.6}$

18. $\frac{49.71}{149.13} = \frac{16.57}{n}$

19. $\frac{16.83}{n} = \frac{.561}{.3892}$

20. $\frac{n}{986.3} = \frac{18.88}{394.52}$

21. $\frac{.984}{13.71} = \frac{n}{53.469}$

22. $\frac{n}{.2667} = \frac{4.04}{.0762}$

23. $\frac{.796}{3.4} = \frac{4.776}{n}$

24. $\frac{2.552}{11.6704} = \frac{n}{2.9176}$

25. Chris plans to travel 75 miles each day on a long distance bike trip. At that rate, how long will it take her to travel 458 miles? (Round the answer to the nearest day.)

26. Shirts are sale priced at 3 for \$11.79. At that rate, how much will 2 shirts cost?

27. If 7 packs of gum sell for \$.99, how many packs of gum can be bought for \$2.57? (Round the answer to the nearest whole number.)

28. One inch on a scale drawing represents an actual distance of 36 feet. How many feet are represented by $7\frac{1}{8}$ inches on the scale drawing? (Hint: You could write $7\frac{1}{8}$ as a decimal.)

change of pace

How observant are you? Make a drawing of the buttons on a telephone and see if you can place the correct numerals and letters on the buttons.

Writing Percents, Decimals, and Fractions

Mrs. Lupe is completing her state tax forms. She changes $2\frac{1}{2}\%$ to .025 so that she can multiply on a calculator.

■ *Percent means hundredths.*

$1\% = .01 = \frac{1}{100}$

problem A

Write $5\frac{1}{4}\%$ as a decimal.

solution

$5\frac{1}{4}\% = 5.25\%$	Write $\frac{1}{4}$ as .25.
$5.25\% = .0525$	Drop the percent sign and move the decimal point two places to the left.

problem B

Write .163 as a percent.

solution

$.163 = 16.3\%$	Move the decimal point two places to the right and attach the percent sign.

problem C

Write 20% as a fraction.

solution

$20\% = \frac{20}{100}$	Drop the percent sign and write the number over 100.
$20\% = \frac{1}{5}$	Rename $\frac{20}{100}$ in lowest terms.

problem D

Write $\frac{7}{8}$ as a percent.

solution

First write $\frac{7}{8}$ as a decimal.

$$\begin{array}{r} .875 \\ 8\overline{)7.000} \\ \underline{6\,4} \\ 60 \\ \underline{56} \\ 40 \\ \underline{40} \end{array}$$

Divide the numerator by the denominator.

Then write the decimal as a percent.

$\frac{7}{8} = .875 = 87.5\%$

exercises

set A Write as a decimal.

1. 23%
2. 7%
3. 2%
4. 14%
5. 13.5%
6. 9.25%
7. 8.75%
8. 24.8%
9. $3\frac{1}{2}\%$
10. $4\frac{3}{4}\%$
11. $32\frac{1}{4}\%$
12. $12\frac{1}{8}\%$
13. 135%
14. 216%
15. 107%

set B Write as a percent.

16. .43
17. .71
18. .09
19. .1
20. .027
21. .314
22. .225
23. .468
24. .1975
25. .2325
26. .0745
27. .0375
28. 1.25
29. 3.74
30. 2.465

set C Write as a fraction in lowest terms.

31. 10%
32. 70%
33. 25%
34. 50%
35. 40%
36. 75%
37. 60%
38. 35%
39. 21%
40. 47%
41. 18%
42. 61%
43. 93%
44. 109%
45. 107%

set D Write as a percent.

46. $\frac{3}{4}$
47. $\frac{1}{2}$
48. $\frac{1}{4}$
49. $\frac{4}{5}$
50. $\frac{8}{20}$
51. $\frac{17}{25}$
52. $\frac{27}{50}$
53. $\frac{1}{20}$
54. $\frac{2}{25}$
55. $\frac{5}{8}$
56. $\frac{9}{16}$
57. $\frac{12}{32}$
58. $\frac{1}{8}$
59. $\frac{11}{5}$
60. $\frac{27}{4}$

set E

61. Michiko's answer to a problem was 0.1325 on her calculator display. Write this as a percent.

62. A record shop advertises all records at a 15% discount. Write the discount as a fraction.

Save 25%
Palm Tree
Regularly $15,
Now reduced $3

Percent Problems

A consumer could check the accuracy of this ad by finding that \$3 is 20% of \$15. The ad is incorrect!

■ *Percent problems can be solved by writing and solving an equation. First write the information in this form:*

_______% of _______ is _______

problem A

In one class, 16% of the students have red hair. There are 50 students in the class. How many of them have red hair?

solution

__*% of* _________ *is* _________

16*% of* all students *are* red-haired

16*% of* 50 *are* ▒

Write and solve the equation.

16*% of* 50 *are* ▒

$.16 \times 50 = n$

$8.00 = n$

There are 8 students with red hair.

problem B

There are 38 women and 57 men employed in one office building. What percent of the employees are women?

solution

__% *of* __________ *is* ________

__% *of* employees *are* women

▒ *of* 95 *are* 38

Write and solve the equation.

▒ *of* 95 *are* 38

$m \times 95 = 38$

$\frac{m \times 95}{95} = \frac{38}{95}$

$m = .4 = 40\%$

40% of the employees are women.

problem C

An ad says, "20% off our regular price! Save \$39!" What is the regular price?

solution

__% *of* __________ *is* __________

20% *of* regular price *is* amount saved

20% *of* ▒ *is* \$39.00

Write and solve the equation.

20% *of* ▒ *is* \$39.00

$.20 \times n = \$39.00$

$\frac{.20n}{.20} = \frac{\$39.00}{.20}$

$n = \$195.00$

The regular price is \$195.00.

exercises

set A

1. 3% of 75 is ▒.
2. 12.5% of 20 is ▒.
3. 6.3% of 37 is ▒.
4. Find 14% of 231.
5. Find $2\frac{1}{2}$% of \$300.
6. Find 85% of 25.
7. What number is 16% of 28?
8. What number is 4.75% of 15?
9. What number is $5\frac{1}{4}$% of 80?

set B

10. ▒% of 48 is 7.2.
11. ▒% of 60 is 2.1.
12. ▒% of 88 is 77.44.
13. What percent of 20 is 15?
14. What percent of 64 is 40?
15. What percent of 25 is 2?
16. 12 is what percent of 80?
17. 21 is what percent of 350?
18. 675 is what percent of 1000?

set C

19. 11% of ▒ is 22.
20. 86% of ▒ is 77.4.
21. $6\frac{1}{4}$% of ▒ is 7.5.
22. 8% of what number is 36?
23. 52% of what number is 5.72?

24. 20.2% of what number is 13.13?

25. 21 is 70% of what number?

26. 36 is 25% of what number?

27. 2.5 is 40% of what number?

set D

28. Sharon bought a sofa for $375. Her state has a sales tax of 5% of the selling price. How much tax did Sharon pay?

29. Information on a milk carton indicates that 9 grams of protein is about 14% of the U.S. Recommended Daily Allowance of protein. Find the Recommended Daily Allowance of protein to the nearest gram.

30. Tina had a new ignition system installed in her car. The total bill was $73, which included a labor charge of $12. What percent of the total charge was the charge for labor? (Round the answer to the nearest whole percent.)

31. A research study indicates that 9% of peanut butter is saturated fat. How many grams of fat are in 500 grams of peanut butter?

32. The Federal Reserve Bank estimates that for each group of 200 checks sent to be processed, 1 is returned because it is incorrectly written. What percent of the checks are returned?

33. There are 8346 registered voters in a certain school district. It is expected that 35% of these people will vote in the next school board election. How many people are expected to vote? (Round the answer to the nearest whole number.)

34. Conrad works for his grandfather's landscaping service. He is paid 7.5% of the firm's profits. What will the firm's profits have to be in order for Conrad to make $1200 this year?

35. Radial tires usually cost $54 each. One store is offering to sell the tires at a savings of $14.04. What percent of the original cost will be saved by buying a tire on sale?

36. A state supervisor indicated that his staff of 24 bank examiners was only 44% of the number of examiners needed to do the work assigned. How many examiners did the supervisor claim that the job required? (Round the answer to the nearest whole number.)

37. Store A is offering a color TV set at a sale price of $399.95. Store B is advertising the same set for "20% off the regular price of $479.95." Which store is offering a lower price?

38. A commuter ticket costs $42.40. A 10.5% fare increase has been proposed by the railroad. What will the new ticket cost? (Round the answer to the nearest cent.)

Chapter 2

review

Addition and subtraction equations, pages 24-25

Solve.

1. $d + 3.5 = 8$

2. $15.8 = m + 7.3$

3. $f - .74 = 7.25$

4. $5.8 = g - 2.15$

Multiplication and division equations, pages 26-27

Solve.

5. $8x = 424$

6. $17.5 = 2.5t$

7. $\frac{b}{9} = .24$

8. $3a + 9a = 48$

Two-step equations, pages 28-29

Solve.

9. $7c + 2 = 37$

10. $5y - 17 = 23$

11. $53 = 3w + 8$

12. $\frac{x}{2} + 2 = 5$

Ratio and proportion, pages 30-31

Find the cross-products. Tell whether the ratios are equal.

13. $\frac{50}{65}$ $\frac{4}{5}$

14. $\frac{9}{24}$ $\frac{1.2}{3.2}$

Solve the proportions.

15. $\frac{c}{56} = \frac{3}{7}$

16. $\frac{.25}{2} = \frac{11}{t}$

Writing percents, decimals, and fractions, pages 34-35

Write as a decimal.

17. 57%

18. $5\frac{3}{4}\%$

Write as a percent.

19. .06

20. .465

Write as a fraction in lowest terms.

21. 41%

22. 38%

Write as a percent.

23. $\frac{19}{25}$

24. $\frac{9}{16}$

Percent problems, pages 36-38

25. Find 6% of 527.

26. $37\frac{1}{2}\%$ of 64 is what number?

27. 9 is what percent of 60?

28. What percent of 56 is 49?

29. 24% of what number is 10.8?

30. 12% of what number is 18?

Chapter 2

test

Solve.

1. $a + 7 = 11$
2. $14.7 = x + 4$
3. $p - 6 = 5.2$
4. $9 = h - 12$
5. $6t = 162$
6. $4.2 = 3a$
7. $\frac{d}{7} = .14$
8. $4t + 5t = 36$
9. $6x + 4 = 22$
10. $9b - 14 = 31$
11. $40 = 4r + 8$
12. $\frac{s}{3} + 2 = 6$

Find the cross-products. Tell whether the ratios are equal.

13. $\frac{3}{8} \quad \frac{12}{32}$
14. $\frac{5.6}{8.1} \quad \frac{8}{9}$

Solve the proportions.

15. $\frac{2}{3} = \frac{n}{39}$
16. $\frac{3.2}{d} = \frac{16}{7}$

Write as a decimal.

17. 49%
18. $21\frac{1}{2}\%$

Write as a percent.

19. .24
20. .327

Write as a fraction in lowest terms.

21. 39%
22. 24%

Write as a percent.

23. $\frac{7}{20}$
24. $\frac{3}{8}$

Compute.

25. Find 8% of 43.
26. $12\frac{1}{2}\%$ of 88 is what number?
27. 7 is what percent of 25?
28. What percent of 125 is 15?
29. 18% of what number is 4.5?
30. 15% of what number is 18?

Chapter 3

Measurement and Statistics

Understanding the metric system and interpreting statistics are necessary skills for many workers and consumers.

Estimated Budget for Pollution Control, 1983
Type
Percent of budget
Air pollution 43%
Water pollution 46%
Solid waste 11%
1kg×5g
METRIC-AIDS

Metric Units of Length

To determine the size of rug to buy, Heidi measured her bedroom with a meter stick. The room is 3.1 meters by 3.9 meters.

■ *Commonly used metric units of length are the* ***millimeter*** *(mm), the* ***centimeter*** *(cm), the* ***meter*** *(m), and the* ***kilometer*** *(km).*

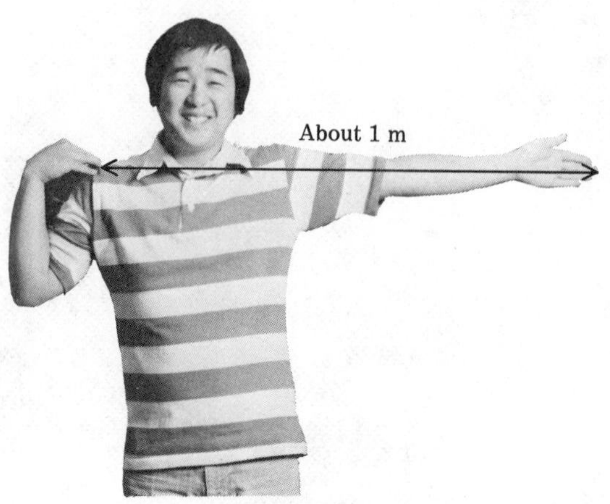

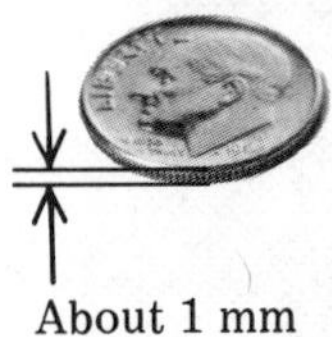

The thickness of a dime is about 1 millimeter.

For some adults, the distance from one shoulder to the opposite fingertip is about 1 meter.

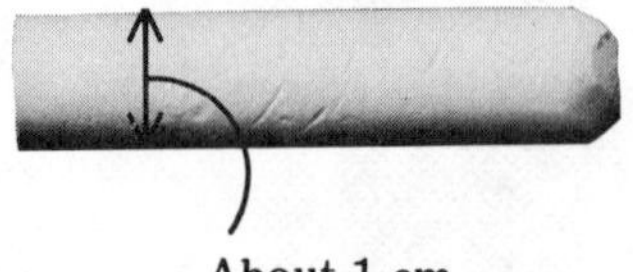

The width of a piece of chalk is about 1 centimeter.

The length of this airport runway is about 1 kilometer.

There are 100 centimeters in 1 meter.
There are 1000 millimeters in 1 meter.
There are 1000 meters in 1 kilometer.

problem A

Choose the most sensible measure for the length of a pen.

15 mm   15 cm   15 m

solution

Use the references on page 42 to make a sensible selection.

A pen is about 15 cm long.

problem B

Choose the most sensible measure for the height of a room.

0.5 m   1.1 m   2.5 m

solution

Use the reference to a meter on page 42 to make a sensible selection.

A room is about 2.5 m high.

exercises

set A Choose the most sensible measure.

1. Average depth of the Atlantic Ocean
   3.87 cm   3.87 m   3.87 km
2. Length of a nail
   78 mm   78 cm   78 m
3. Wheelbase of a mid-sized car
   300 mm   300 cm   300 m
4. Height of a giant redwood tree
   110 cm   110 m   110 km
5. Length of a peanut
   14 mm   14 cm   14 m
6. Height of a toaster
   18 mm   18 cm   18 m
7. Distance from Denver to New Orleans
   2130 cm   2130 m   2130 km

set B Choose the most sensible measure.

8. Height of an adult
   165 cm   250 cm   315 cm
9. Distance from New York to Los Angeles
   62 km   342 km   4590 km
10. Man's neck size
    17 cm   38 cm   52 cm
11. Length of a hockey rink
    60 m   180 m   275 m
12. Diameter of a long-playing record album
    0.8 cm   12 cm   30 cm
13. Width of a telephone cord
    4 mm   14 mm   28 mm
14. Width of a lane on an expressway
    0.5 m   3 m   10 m

set C

15. Estimate the length of your classroom in meters.
16. Estimate the height of the blackboard in centimeters.
17. Estimate the length of the blackboard.
18. Estimate the height of your teacher.
19. Estimate the length of a paper clip.
20. Estimate the distance from Boston to Washington, D.C.

Area and Volume

The custodian at the high school needs to find the area of the basketball court so that he can order varnish to refinish it. The court is 28 meters by 15 meters, or 420 square meters, in area.

■ *Some metric units of area are the* ***square millimeter*** *(mm^2), the* ***square centimeter*** *(cm^2), the* ***square meter*** *(m^2), and the* ***square kilometer*** *(km^2).*

problem A

Find the area of this card.

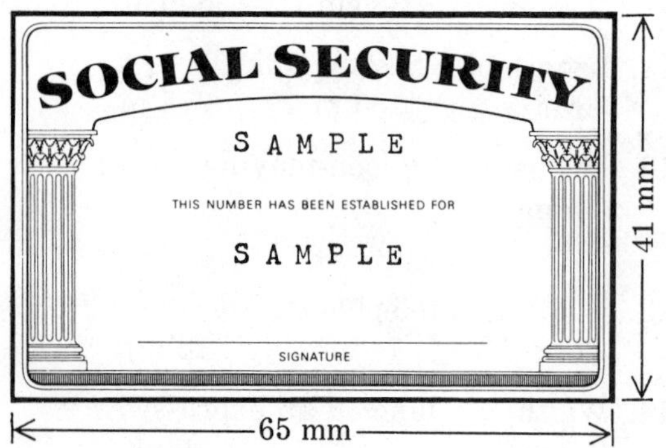

solution

The area is the length times the width.

$A = l \times w$

$A = 65 \text{ mm} \times 41 \text{ mm}$

$A = 2665 \text{ mm}^2$

■ *Some metric units of volume are the* ***cubic millimeter*** *(mm^3), the* ***cubic centimeter*** *(cm^3), and the* ***cubic meter*** *(m^3).*

problem B

Find the volume of this box of cereal. Round the answer to the nearest tenth of a cubic centimeter.

solution

The volume is the length times the width times the height.

$V = l \times w \times h$

$V = 17.2 \text{ cm} \times 5.9 \text{ cm} \times 24.4 \text{ cm}$

$V = 2476.112 \text{ cm}^3$

$V \approx 2476.1 \text{ cm}^3$

exercises

set A Use the given dimensions to find the area of each rectangle. Round each answer to the nearest tenth of a square unit.

	Length	Width
1.	28 mm	14 mm
2.	6.2 m	3.5 m
3.	4.1 km	2.3 km
4.	17.3 cm	25.9 cm
5.	11.6 m	27.8 m

set B Use the given dimensions to find the volume of each box. Round each answer to the nearest tenth of a cubic unit.

	Length	Width	Height
6.	37 mm	13 mm	17 mm
7.	8.0 m	4.0 m	2.3 m
8.	9.0 cm	2.7 cm	4.3 cm
9.	8.1 m	6.2 m	3.7 m
10.	27.7 cm	21.5 cm	1.9 cm

set C

11. Find the area of a soccer field that measures 105 meters by 70 meters.

12. Kenji wants to carpet 3 rooms. The dimensions of the rooms are 5.3 m by 4.8 m, 3.7 m by 4.3 m, and 3.1 m by 3.4 m. He saw an ad that said "3 rooms of carpeting—only $200 (maximum 35 m^2)." Find the area Kenji has to carpet. Round the area of each room to the nearest tenth of a square meter. Is the carpeting in the ad enough for Kenji's 3 rooms?

13. Find the volume of a package of gum. The package is 74 mm long, 20 mm wide, and 12 mm high.

14. How many cubic meters of sand are needed to fill a sandbox 1.7 m long, 1.5 m wide, and 0.3 m deep? Round the volume to the nearest tenth of a cubic meter.

15. Find the area of the triangular section of this house. The formula for the area of a triangle is $A = \frac{1}{2} \times b \times h$. Round the area to the nearest tenth of a square meter.

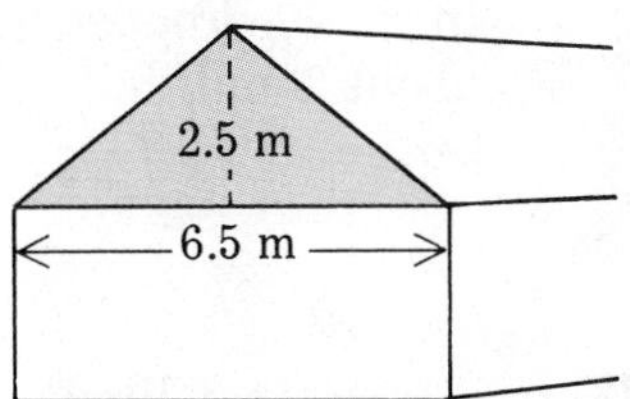

Metric Units of Capacity and Mass

Mary Elizabeth is mixing a solution of plant food. Using a ratio of 1 to 12, she mixes 50 milliliters of plant food with 600 milliliters of water.

■ *Commonly used metric units of capacity are the* ***liter*** *(L) and the* ***milliliter*** *(mL).*

The amount of liquid in this bottle is 1 liter.

The amount of liquid in an eyedropper is about 1 milliliter.

There are 1000 milliliters in 1 liter.

■ *Commonly used metric units of mass are the* ***kilogram*** *(kg), the* ***gram*** *(g), and the* ***milligram*** *(mg).*

The mass of your math book is about 1 kilogram.

The mass of a dollar bill is about 1 gram.

The mass of an aspirin is about 325 milligrams.

There are 1000 grams in 1 kilogram.

There are 1000 milligrams in 1 gram.

problem A

Choose the more sensible measure for a full tank of gasoline in a car.

60 mL   60 L

solution

Use the references on page 46 to make a sensible selection.

A full tank of gasoline is about 60 liters.

problem B

Choose the most sensible measure for the mass of a sports car.

5 kg   43 kg   980 kg

solution

Use the reference to a kilogram on page 46 to make a sensible selection.

The mass of a sports car is about 980 kilograms.

exercises

set A Choose the more sensible measure of capacity.

1. Glass of milk
   250 mL   250 L
2. Bottle of antifreeze
   2 mL   2 L
3. Washing machine
   40 mL   40 L

Choose the most sensible measure for the mass of each object.

4. Woman
   59 mg   59 g   59 kg
5. Vitamin pill
   350 mg   350 g   350 kg
6. Box of potato chips
   240 mg   240 g   240 kg

set B Choose the most sensible measure for the mass of each object.

7. New baby
   3.5 kg   10.4 kg   126.1 kg
8. Box of cereal
   8 g   57 g   312 g
9. Bag of sugar
   2 kg   17 kg   175 kg

Choose the more sensible measure of capacity.

10. Bottle of nail polish
    25 mL   200 mL
11. Can of paint
    4 L   25 L
12. Tube of toothpaste
    15 mL   150 mL

set C

13. Estimate the capacity of a pail of water in liters.
14. Estimate the capacity of a coffee cup in milliliters.
15. Estimate the mass of a loaf of bread in grams.
16. Estimate the mass of a portable television set in kilograms.

Renaming Metric Units of Measure

Manuel has a 946-milliliter bottle of fruit drink and a 1-liter pitcher. He knows that 946 mL is .946 L, so the pitcher will hold all of the fruit drink.

Metric prefixes	
kilo-	thousand
hecto-	hundred
deka-	ten
deci-	tenth
centi-	hundredth
milli-	thousandth

■ *To rename a larger metric unit of measure as a smaller unit, multiply by the correct power of 10.*

kilo-	hecto-	deka-	meter liter gram	deci-	centi-	milli-

Spaces to the right:	3	2	1
Multiply by:	1000	100	10

problem A

6.5 g = ▒ mg

solution

You are moving 3 spaces to the right on the chart. Multiply by 1000.

6.5 × 1000 = 6500

6.5 g = 6500 mg

■ *To rename a smaller metric unit of measure as a larger unit, divide by the correct power of 10.*

Look again at the chart on page 48.
If you move:

1 space to the left, divide by 10.
2 spaces to the left, divide by 100.
3 spaces to the left, divide by 1000.

problem B

2 cm = ▒ m

solution

You are moving 2 spaces to the left on the chart. Divide by 100.

$2 \div 100 = 0.02$

2 cm = 0.02 m

exercises

set A

1. 5 m = ▒ cm

2. 0.8 km = ▒ m

3. 9.3 cm = ▒ mm

4. 2.1 m = ▒ mm

5. 12.75 m = ▒ cm

6. 3 L = ▒ mL

7. 0.5 L = ▒ mL

8. 45 kg = ▒ g

9. 2.1 g = ▒ mg

10. 0.84 kg = ▒ g

set B

11. 935 m = ▒ km

12. 160.4 cm = ▒ m

13. 429 mm = ▒ m

14. 1250 m = ▒ km

15. 67 mm = ▒ cm

16. 1578 mL = ▒ L

17. 84 mL = ▒ L

18. 716 g = ▒ kg

19. 1375 mg = ▒ g

20. 42.6 g = ▒ kg

set C

21. 23 km = ▒ m

22. 971 m = ▒ km

23. 18 cm = ▒ mm

24. 3.5 m = ▒ mm

25. 6 cm = ▒ m

26. 14 L = ▒ mL

27. 250 mL = ▒ L

28. 837 g = ▒ kg

29. 1296 mg = ▒ g

30. 8.3 kg = ▒ g

31. Will 300 centimeters of model train track fit along the edge of a board that is 2.5 meters long?

32. To find the amount of paint needed for the baseboards of a room, find the area to be covered. The baseboards are 31.6 meters long and 9 centimeters high. Find the area in square meters.

Temperature

Perry heard on the radio that the temperature was -25 degrees Celsius (-25°C) and that the wind speed was 15 kilometers per hour (15 km/h). In a wind-chill table, he found that these conditions make it feel like -38°C without the wind. The combined effect of temperature and wind is often called the **wind-chill factor.**

Wind-Chill Table

Wind speed (km/h)	Thermometer reading (°C)								
	0	-5	-10	-15	-20	-25	-30	-35	-40
	Equivalent temperature (°C)								
Calm	0	-5	-10	-15	-20	-25	-30	-35	-40
10	-4	-10	-15	-21	-27	-32	-38	-43	-49
15	-8	-14	-20	-26	-32	-38	-45	-51	-57
20	-10	-17	-23	-30	-37	-43	-50	-56	-63
25	-12	-19	-26	-33	-40	-47	-54	-61	-68
30	-14	-21	-28	-36	-43	-50	-57	-64	-71
35	-16	-23	-30	-38	-45	-52	-60	-67	-74
40	-17	-24	-32	-39	-47	-54	-62	-69	-77
45	-18	-25	-33	-41	-48	-56	-64	-71	-79
50	-19	-26	-34	-42	-50	-57	-65	-73	-81
55	-19	-27	-35	-43	-51	-59	-67	-74	-82
60	-20	-28	-36	-44	-52	-60	-68	-76	-83

Little danger   Increasing danger   Great danger

Danger from freezing of exposed flesh
(For properly clothed persons)

■ *Temperature can be measured with several different scales. The Celsius scale is commonly used in countries that use the metric system.*

problem A

Choose the more sensible temperature for a winter day in Gary, Indiana.

-10°C   20°C

solution

Consult the thermometer shown here.

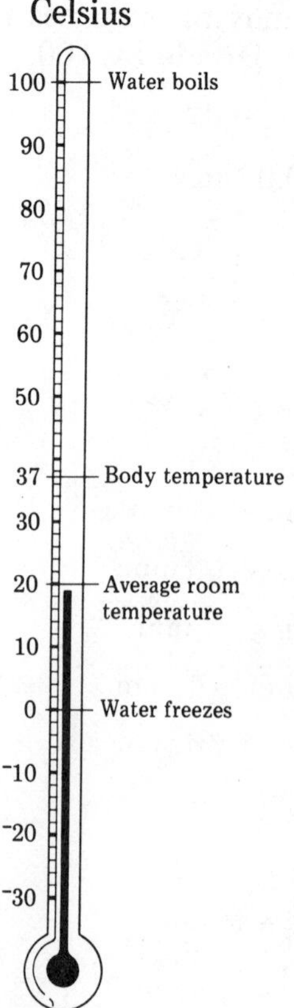

The more sensible temperature is -10°C, or 10° *below* zero.

problem B

Choose the more sensible oven setting for cooking meat loaf.

125°C   175°C

solution

Consult the oven dial shown here.

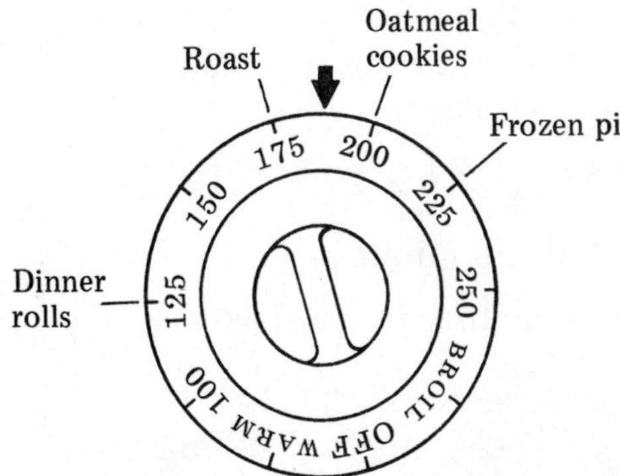

The more sensible oven setting is 175°C.

exercises

set A Choose the more sensible temperature.

1. Normal January day in Miami, Florida
   19°C   60°C
2. Normal January day in Philadelphia, Pennsylvania
   $^-34$°C   1°C
3. Normal July day in Milwaukee, Wisconsin
   10°C   21°C
4. Normal July day in San Antonio, Texas
   28°C   85°C
5. Sick person
   39.8°C   100.4°C
6. Setting on a home thermostat
   20°C   50°C

set B Choose the more sensible oven setting.

7. Cook frozen dinner.
   150°C   225°C
8. Bake chocolate-chip cookies.
   125°C   200°C
9. Keep pancakes warm.
   125°C   225°C
10. Cook pot roast.
    175°C   225°C
11. Cook frozen pizza.
    100°C   225°C
12. Bake a cake.
    175°C   250°C

set C For exercises 13–15, use the wind-chill table on page 50.

13. The temperature is $^-10$°C and the wind is 30 km/h. Find the wind-chill factor.
14. The temperature is $^-10$°C and the wind is 45 km/h. Find the wind-chill factor.
15. Between what two wind-chill factors does the danger from freezing of exposed flesh change from "little danger" to "increasing danger"?
16. The temperature is 2°C. Would you go to a football game with or without a jacket?
17. The temperature is 25°C. Would you go water skiing or ice skating?

Time

Fran's plane departs at 4:10 P.M. and travels for 3 hours 25 minutes. By adding, she knows the plane will arrive at 7:35 P.M.

■ *The abbreviation* A.M. *means before noon.* P.M. *means after noon. Midnight is 12:00* P.M.

problem A

A trip to Crystal Lake takes 4 hours 45 minutes on the train. This is followed by a bus ride of 2 hours 30 minutes. What is the total time of the trip?

solution

First add the hours.

4 hr. + 2 hr. = 6 hr.

Then add the minutes.

45 min. + 30 min. = 75 min.

75 min. is more than 1 hr.
75 min. = 60 min. + 15 min.
75 min. = 1 hr. 15 min.

Then add the hours and the minutes.

6 hr. + 1 hr. 15 min. → 7 hr. 15 min.

The total time of the trip is 7 hours 15 minutes.

problem B

A movie starts at 11:20 A.M. and runs for 2 hours 15 minutes. At what time does the movie end?

solution

First add the hours to the starting time. Recall that the first hour after noon is 1:00 P.M.

11:20 A.M. + 2 hr. → 1:20 P.M.

Then add the minutes.

1:20 P.M. + 15 min. → 1:35 P.M.

The movie ends at 1:35 P.M.

problem C

Mr. Bedoni went to sleep at 10:30 P.M. and woke up at 6:15 A.M. How long did he sleep?

solution

First find the number of hours. Recall that the first hour after midnight is 1:00 A.M.

10:30 P.M. to 5:30 A.M. → 7 hr.

Then find the number of minutes remaining.

5:30 A.M. to 6:15 A.M. → 45 min.

Mr. Bedoni slept for 7 hours 45 minutes.

exercises

set A

1. Add 3 hours 15 minutes to 5 hours 20 minutes.
2. Add 2 hours 35 minutes to 7 hours 50 minutes.
3. Add 4 hours 25 minutes to 3 hours 55 minutes.

set B

4. Add 3 hours 20 minutes to 8:15 A.M.
5. Add 6 hours 5 minutes to 9:25 A.M.
6. Add 8 hours 15 minutes to 10:10 P.M.

set C

7. How much time is there from 4:30 P.M. to 7:40 P.M.?
8. How much time is there from 7:15 A.M. to 3:35 P.M.?
9. How much time is there from 11:45 P.M. to 6:20 A.M?

set D

10. A plane departs at 10:10 A.M. and travels for 3 hours 15 minutes. What time does the plane arrive?
11. A concert started at 8:30 P.M. and was over at 11:50 P.M. How long did the concert last?
12. Chuck put his dinner of beef stew in the oven at 4:30 P.M. The stew takes 1 hour 45 minutes to cook. When will it be ready?
13. Audrey spent two days removing the finish on a set of shelves. She worked 3 hours 20 minutes on Tuesday and 4 hours 45 minutes on Saturday. Find the total time Audrey spent on the shelves.
14. Karen starts school at 8:25 A.M. and leaves at 3:10 P.M. How long is she in school?
15. Peggy left home at 11:35 A.M. She spent 2 hours 15 minutes shopping. What time did she finish shopping?
16. A car was parked in a parking lot from 8:50 A.M. until 9:20 P.M. How long was the car parked?
17. Sally and Nick are going to a movie that ends at 10:35 P.M. It will take about 1 hour 20 minutes to drive home. Will they be home by midnight?

Bar Graphs and Line Graphs

Government statistics are often published in the form of a graph.

problem A

Make a **bar graph** using these statistics for predicted energy sources for the United States in 1985.

Hydro	5 quadrillion BTU's
Nuclear	7 quadrillion BTU's
Coal	23 quadrillion BTU's
Oil	29 quadrillion BTU's
Gas	22 quadrillion BTU's

solution

List the five energy sources on the vertical scale.

Units on the horizontal scale can be in quadrillion BTU's. Because the largest number is 29, the scale can stop at 30. Draw bars to show the predicted number of BTU's for each energy source.

Write a title for the graph.

Predicted Energy Sources for the United States in 1985

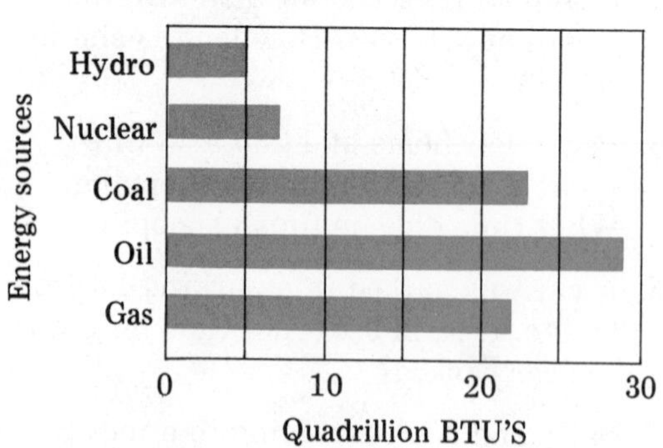

problem B

Make a **line graph** to show the amount spent on recreation by Americans between 1950 and 1975.

1950	$11,147,000,000
1955	$14,078,000,000
1960	$18,295,000,000
1965	$26,298,000,000
1970	$40,653,000,000
1975	$65,999,000,000

solution

Draw and label the vertical and the horizontal scales. The broken vertical scale means that numbers are missing.

Find the line for 1950. Mark a point just above $11 billion. Locate the points for the other years. Connect the points with lines.

Write a title for the graph.

Amount Spent on Recreation by Americans

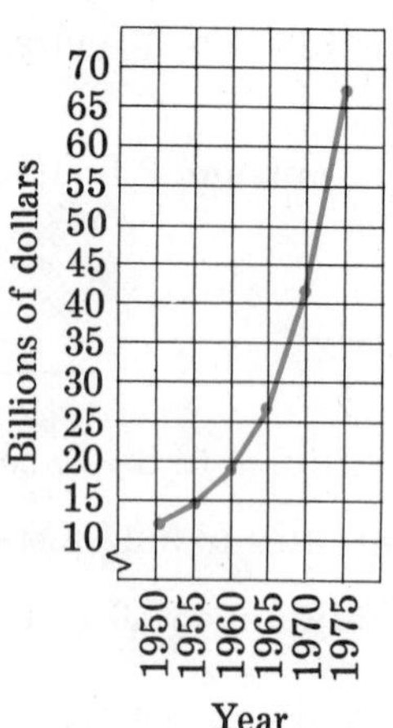

exercises

set A Make a bar graph for each set of data.

1. 1975 world wheat production by region

Far East	74 million metric tons
Near East	29 million metric tons
Africa	6 million metric tons
Latin America	15 million metric tons
North America	75 million metric tons
Western Europe	53 million metric tons
Eastern Europe	25 million metric tons
USSR	66 million metric tons

2. Retail store sales in 1975 by department

Automotive	$102 billion
Furniture and appliances	$26 billion
Lumber, building, hardware	$24 billion
Apparel	$27 billion
Food	$132 billion
Eating and drinking places	$48 billion
Gasoline service stations	$44 billion

3. Employees in non-agricultural occupations in 1975 by job category

Mining	745,000
Contract construction	3,457,000
Manufacturing	18,347,000
Transportation and public utilities	4,498,000
Wholesale, retail trade	16,947,000
Finance, insurance, real estate	4,223,000
Service	13,995,000
Government	14,773,000

(*Hint:* One scale could be "Millions of people.")

set B Make a line graph for each set of data.

4. Number of work stoppages (strikes) in the U.S.

1950	4,800	1965	4,000
1955	4,300	1970	5,700
1960	3,300	1975	5,000

5. Percent of profit for U.S. aircraft industries

1960	7.4%	1970	6.8%
1965	15.1%	1975	11.0%

6. Average hourly earnings in U.S. manufacturing industries

1950	$1.44	1965	$2.61
1955	$1.86	1970	$3.36
1960	$2.26	1975	$4.81

7. People unemployed in the U.S.

1970	4,088,000
1971	4,993,000
1972	4,840,000
1973	4,304,000
1974	5,076,000
1975	7,830,000

8. Number of U.S. banks

1925	26,479	1955	14,309
1935	16,047	1965	14,295
1945	14,542	1975	15,108

9. Total deposits in U.S. banks

1925	$51,641,000,000
1935	$51,149,000,000
1945	$151,033,000,000
1955	$208,850,000,000
1965	$362,611,000,000
1975	$897,101,000,000

Circle Graphs

Some statistics have more meaning if they are displayed in a **circle graph.**

problem A

The circle graph below shows the breakdown of passenger car production in U.S. plants by the "big four" automakers for the 1976 model year. If 7,999,304 cars were produced, about how many cars were produced by the American Motors Corporation? Round your answer to the nearest whole number.

Passenger Car Production, 1976 Model Year

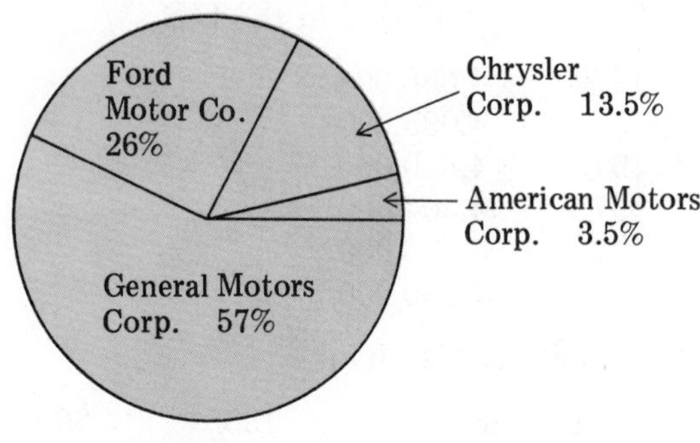

solution

3.5% of 7,999,304 is ▒

$.035 \times 7{,}999{,}304 = n$

$279{,}976 \approx n$

American Motors Corporation produced about 279,976 cars for the 1976 model year.

■ *A central angle is an angle whose vertex is the center of a circle.*

problem B

Make a circle graph to show what percent of a school's newspaper subscriptions were purchased by each group.

Female students	53%
Male students	37%
Teachers	7.2%
Others	2.8%

solution

Write each percent as a decimal. Then multiply by 360° to find the size of each central angle. Round the answers to the nearest degree.

Female students	$.53 \times 360° \approx 191°$
Male students	$.37 \times 360° \approx 133°$
Teachers	$.072 \times 360° \approx 26°$
Others	$.028 \times 360° \approx 10°$

Use a protractor to draw a circle and each central angle. Label each section. Write a title for the graph.

Newspaper Subscriptions

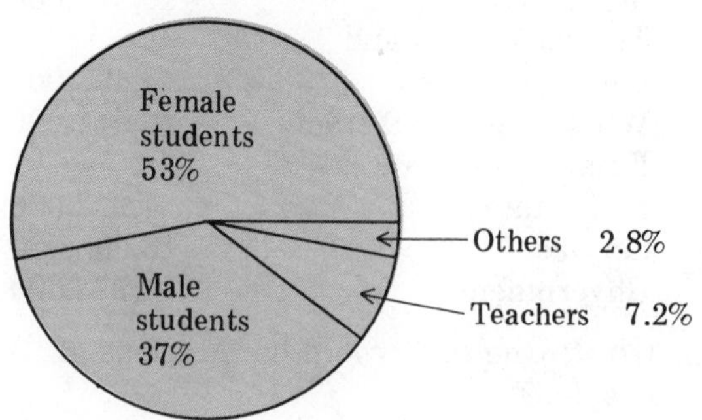

exercises

set A Use the circle graph in problem A on page 56 for exercises 1-3. About how many cars were produced by each corporation? Round each answer to the nearest whole number.

1. Chrysler Corporation

2. Ford Motor Company

3. General Motors Corporation

Use the circle graph in problem B on page 56 for exercises 4-7. If the school had 857 subscriptions, about how many subscriptions were sold to each group? Round each answer to the nearest whole number.

4. Female students

5. Male students

6. Teachers

7. Others

set B Make a circle graph for each set of data.

8. Estimated budget for pollution control in 1983

Type	Percent of budget
Air pollution	43%
Water pollution	46%
Solid waste	11%

9. U.S. states: minimum driving ages

Age	Percent of states
15 yr.	10%
16 yr.	76%
17 yr.	8%
18 yr.	4%
21 yr.	2%

10. Amounts outstanding on non-installment credit (1975)

Type	Percent of credit
Single-payment loans	37.3%
Charge accounts	28.4%
Service credit	34.3%

11. U.S. dollars spent on food and live animal imports (1975)

Commodity	Percent spent
Meat	15.7%
Cheese	2.2%
Fish	18.7%
Grains	2.5%
Fruit and nuts	8.8%
Vegetables	4.9%
Sugar	25.7%
Coffee, green	21.5%

set C For exercises 12 and 13, make a circle graph for each set of data.

12. Females employed (1975)

Category	Percent of employed
White-collar workers	63%
Blue-collar workers	14%
Service workers	21.6%
Farm workers	1.4%

13. Males employed (1975)

Category	Percent of employed
White-collar workers	41%
Blue-collar workers	45.4%
Service workers	8.6%
Farm workers	5%

14. If 33,553,000 women were employed in 1975, about how many women were employed in each category in exercise 12?

15. If 51,230,000 men were employed in 1975, about how many men were employed in each category in exercise 13?

Mean, Median, and Mode

Leah is a forward for the Prairie City High School basketball team. In the last 3 games she scored 9, 9, and 15 points, for a total of 33 points. Her average for the 3 games is 33 ÷ 3, or 11 points.

■ *In a set of numbers, the number that appears most often is the* ***mode.*** *The sum of a set of numbers divided by the number of addends is the average, or the* ***mean.*** *When a set of numbers is arranged in order, the middle number is the* ***median.***

problem A

Find the mode of this set of numbers.

4, 13, 1, 6, 11, 8, 10, 11, 12, 11

solution

Arrange the numbers in order.

1, 4, 6, 8, 10, $\underbrace{11, 11, 11,}$ 12, 13

The mode is 11, the number that appears most often.

Some sets of numbers have no mode. Some sets of numbers have more than one mode.

problem B

Find the mean of this set of numbers.

7, 6, 3, 10, 7, 2, 2

solution

Add the numbers.

$$\begin{array}{r} 7 \\ 6 \\ 3 \\ 10 \\ 7 \\ 2 \\ +\ 2 \\ \hline 37 \end{array}$$

Divide the sum by the number of addends.

$$7\overline{)37.000} = 5.285$$

The mean, rounded to the nearest hundredth, is 5.29.

problem C

Find the median of this set of numbers.

7, 9, 11, 10, 8, 10, 7

solution

Arrange the numbers in order.

$\underbrace{11, 10, 10,}$ 9, $\underbrace{8, 7, 7}$

The median is 9. There are as many numbers before 9 as after it.

problem D

Find the median of this set of numbers.

10, 3, 12, 1

solution

Arrange the numbers in order.

$\underbrace{1, 3,}$ $\underbrace{10, 12}$

There is no middle number in the set. The median is halfway between 3 and 10.

$$\frac{3 + 10}{2} = \frac{13}{2} = 6\tfrac{1}{2}$$

The median is $6\frac{1}{2}$.

exercises

set A Find the mode for each set of numbers.

1. 8, 9, 7, 2, 3, 7, 6
2. 309, 305, 309, 301, 301
3. 47, 21, 89, 8, 21
4. 29, 23, 21, 25, 27, 31, 29
5. 10.3, 10.1, 10.01, 10.25, 10.01

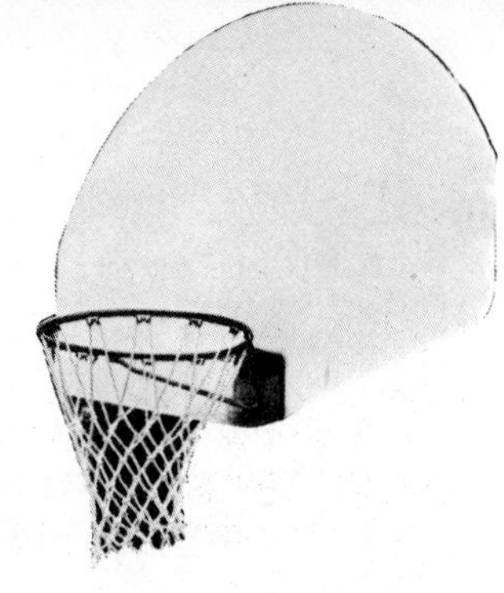

6. 116, 132, 116, 104, 132, 127
7. 9, 7, 13, 5, 3, 11
8. 20, 18, 13, 15, 15, 18, 20, 15
9. 2.1, 2.25, 2.5, 2.04, 2.35, 2.5
10. 73, 87, 78, 69, 73, 58

set B

Exercises 11–20. Find the mean for each set of numbers in exercises 1–10. Round the answers to the nearest hundredth.

set C

Exercises 21–25. Find the median for each set of numbers in exercises 1–5.

set D

Exercises 26–30. Find the median for each set of numbers in exercises 6–10.

set E

31. Find the mean, median, and mode for this set of test scores. Round the mean to the nearest hundredth. 88, 72, 83, 47, 93, 77, 75, 80, 37, 84, 56, 86, 93, 73, 82, 85, 42
32. Find the mean, median, and mode for these heights in centimeters. 189, 175, 154, 167, 190, 175

CALCULATOR EXERCISES

Find the mean for each set of numbers. Round the answers to the nearest hundredth.

1. 282, 919, 464, 737
2. 1537, 2491, 1764, 3248, 2073
3. 1234, 5678, 6789
4. 1122, 3344, 5566, 7788, 9900
5. 27,634 47,092 90,185 53,264 36,243
6. 364,257 423,765 170,843 857,091 963,251
7. 84,076.3 65,308.7 58,732.1 42,435.4 93,457.8
8. 525.371 976.32 624.57 425.09 139.84 840.16
9. 532.96 4.308 3.54 647.91 17.852
10. 17.562 3.354 23.98 22.731 104.16 .634

Find the mean for each set of data. Round the answers to the nearest whole number.

11. Number of students attending school during a 1-week period

Monday	1,842
Tuesday	1,730
Wednesday	1,753
Thursday	1813
Friday	1,647

12. Salaries in one department

Baker	$6,790
Carson	$13,500
Mason	$8,470
Omachi	$20,620
Pena	$18,575
Roberts	$7,250
Thomas	$10,825

13. Attendance at football games

Sept. 22	62,153
Sept. 29	48,139
Oct. 6	57,204
Oct. 13	64,379
Oct. 20	35,702
Oct. 27	71,428

14. U.S. Automobile production

1973	9,667,152
1974	7,324,504
1975	6,717,043
1976	7,999,304

15. Newspaper subscriptions

1974	1,112,653
1975	1,273,468
1976	947,305
1977	985,651
1978	1,104,289

Chapter 3

review

Metric units of length, pages 42-43

Choose the most sensible measure.

1. Length of a paper clip
   3 mm 3 cm 3 m
2. Length of a tennis court
   4 m 24 m 125 m

Area and volume, pages 44-45

3. Find the area of a rectangle that measures 7 meters by 4.8 meters.
4. Find the volume of a box that measures 14.3 cm by 7.2 cm by 5.6 cm.

Metric units of capacity and mass, pages 46-47

Choose the more sensible measure.

5. Gas tank of a motorcycle
   13 mL 13 L
6. Portable typewriter
   5 g 5 kg
7. Can of soup
   45 mL 200 mL
8. Can of peaches
   25 g 600 g

Renaming metric units of measure, pages 48-49

9. 34 cm = ▒ m
10. 7.63 kg = ▒ g

Temperature, pages 50-51

Choose the more sensible temperature.

11. Ice-skating weather
    −10°C 10°C

Time, pages 52-53

12. How much time is there from 10:35 A.M. to 2:20 P.M.?

Bar graphs and line graphs, pages 54-55

13. Make a bar graph for the data given.

1974 gold production by country

Canada	52 thousand kilograms
United States	35 thousand kilograms
Japan	32 thousand kilograms
Ghana	19 thousand kilograms
Philippines	17 thousand kilograms
Australia	16 thousand kilograms
West Germany	10 thousand kilograms

Circle graphs, pages 56-57

14. Make a circle graph for the data given.

Advertising expenditures (1975)

Source	Percent of total
Newspapers	30%
Television	19%
Direct mail	15%
Radio	7%
Other	29%

Mean, median, and mode, pages 58-59

For exercises 15-16, use the set of numbers below.

23, 16, 24, 10, 14, 28, 21, 12, 28, 24

15. Find the mean.
16. Find the median.

Chapter 3

test

Choose the most sensible measure.

1. Width of a pencil
   8 mm 8 cm 8 m

2. Height of a 4-year-old
   80 cm 250 cm 410 cm

3. Find the area of a rectangle that measures 3 meters by 7.2 meters.

4. Find the volume of a box that measures 12 cm by 9 cm by 6.5 cm.

Choose the more sensible measure.

5. Carton of orange juice
   900 mL 900 L

6. Package of bacon
   450 g 450 kg

7. Bottle of apple juice
   35 mL 600 mL

8. Whole chicken
   1.2 kg 24.5 kg

9. 3.7 m = ▒ cm

10. 482 g = ▒ kg

Choose the more sensible temperature.

11. Warm shower
    26°C 80°C

12. How much time is there from 1:10 P.M. to 5:45 P.M.?

13. Make a line graph for the data given.

    Marriages in the United States

1935	1,300,000
1945	1,600,000
1955	1,500,000
1965	1,800,000
1975	2,100,000

14. The circle graph below shows annual housing expenses in the United States. Find the amount of money spent on property taxes by a family that spends $5000 per year on housing.

Annual Housing Expenses (1975)

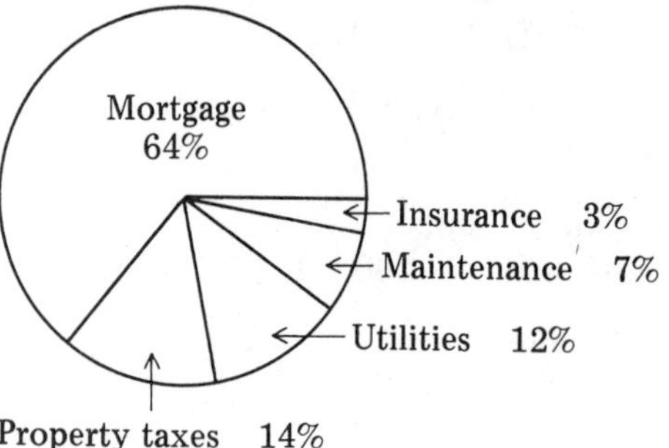

For exercises 15-16, use the set of numbers below.

3, 10, 13, 6, 12, 1, 6, 13, 8, 14, 13

15. Find the mean.

16. Find the median.

Unit 1

Choose the best answer.

1. Round 4753 to the nearest hundred.

A 5000 **C** 4700

B 4800 **D** 4750

2. 96.27 − 64.83

A 161.10 **C** 31.44

B 32.64 **D** 32.34

3. 783 × 94

A 73,602 **C** 66,502

B 68,592 **D** 72,602

4. 8.32 × 4.7

A 3.8104 **C** 39.104

B 381.04 **D** 38.104

5. 28.236 ÷ 3.9

A .724 **C** 7.31

B .731 **D** 7.24

6. Rename $\frac{12}{20}$ in lowest terms.

A $\frac{6}{10}$ **C** $\frac{4}{5}$

B $\frac{3}{4}$ **D** $\frac{3}{5}$

7. $\frac{9}{11} \div \frac{3}{5}$

A $\frac{33}{45}$ **C** $1\frac{7}{11}$

B $1\frac{4}{11}$ **D** $\frac{27}{55}$

8. $3\frac{3}{4} + 1\frac{1}{6}$

A $4\frac{11}{12}$ **C** $4\frac{4}{10}$

B $3\frac{4}{10}$ **D** $3\frac{1}{8}$

9. Solve. $d - 251 = 347$

A $d = 598$ **C** $d = 116$

B $d = 96$ **D** $d = 104$

10. Solve. $384 = 16y$

A $y = 6144$ **C** $y = 24$

B $y = 368$ **D** $y = 400$

11. Solve. $8b + 42 = 138$

A $b = 12$ **C** $b = 14.5$

B $b = 22.5$ **D** $b = 16$

12. Solve. $\frac{6}{c} = \frac{21}{28}$

A $c = 4.5$ **C** $c = 9$

B $c = 8$ **D** $c = 98$

13. Write 8% as a decimal.

A .8 **C** 8

B .008 **D** .08

14. 15% of what number is 90?

A 6 **C** .16

B 600 **D** 60

15. Choose the most sensible measure for the length of an adult's hand.

A 19 mm **C** 19 m

B 19 cm **D** 19 km

16. Find the area of a rectangle that measures 6 meters by 9.7 meters.

A 582 m^2 **C** 474 m^2

B 47.4 m^2 **D** 58.2 m^2

17. Choose the most sensible measure for a container of liquid bleach.

A 4 mL **C** 4 L

B 23 mL **D** 68 L

18. Choose the most sensible measure for a package of cheese.

A 475 g **C** 475 kg

B 47 mg **D** 47 kg

19. 9.8 m = ▒ cm

A 9800 **C** 98

B .0098 **D** 980

20. 3476 g = ▒ kg

A .3476 **C** 3.476

B 347.6 **D** 34.76

21. Choose the most sensible water temperature for outdoor swimming.

A 23°C **C** 79°C

B 4°C **D** 101°C

22. Add 3 hours 25 minutes to 4:15 P.M.

A 7:30 P.M. **C** 7:40 P.M.

B 1:10 P.M. **D** 8:40 P.M.

23. The circle graph below shows the major cost items in building a home. Find the amount of money spent for labor on a house that cost $58,000 to build.

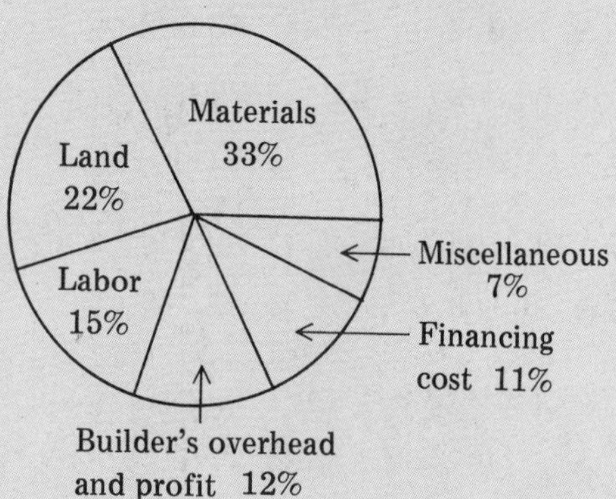

A $12,760 **C** $12,750

B $8700 **D** $6960

24. Find the mode of the following set of numbers.

13, 18, 4, 15, 9, 18, 21

A 15 **C** 17

B 14 **D** 18

unit two

Income, Banking, and Credit

Chapter 4

Income

Chapter 5

Personal Banking

Chapter 6

Consumer Credit

Chapter 4

Income

Most people have jobs to earn money for their living expenses. Employers use a variety of methods to compute gross pay for employees.

Hourly Rate and Overtime Rate

Jose Betances works as a mailer for a stereo manufacturer. He was hired to work 8 hours a day, 5 days a week.

If he works more than 8 hours in one day, Jose is paid at an **overtime rate** for the extra hours. The overtime rate is usually 1.5 times the regular hourly rate. This is often called **time and a half.**

Jose's **gross pay** is the sum of his regular pay and his overtime pay.

problem

This week Jose worked his regular 40 hours and an additional 4.7 hours of overtime. If his regular hourly rate is \$5.00 per hour, what is his gross pay this week?

solution

Find Jose's regular pay.

$\$5.00 \times 40 = \$200.00$

Find his overtime rate.

$\$5.00 \times 1.5 = \$7.50$

Find his overtime pay.

$\$7.50 \times 4.7 = \$35.25$

Find Jose's gross pay.

\$200.00	Regular pay
+ 35.25	Overtime pay
\$235.25	Gross pay

exercises

Complete the table to find the gross pay for employees with these jobs. Round the answers to the nearest cent.

	Job	Regular hours	Regular hourly rate	Regular pay	Overtime hours	Overtime rate (time and a half)	Overtime pay	Gross pay
	Mailer	40	$5.00	$200.00	4.7	$7.50	$35.25	$235.25
1.	Steamfitter	40	$6.28	**a.**	0	**b.**	**c.**	**d.**
2.	Sheet-metal worker	38	$6.38	**a.**	0	**b.**	**c.**	**d.**
3.	Pipefitter	40	$4.28	**a.**	5	**b.**	**c.**	**d.**
4.	Operating engineer	40	$5.06	**a.**	6	**b.**	**c.**	**d.**
5.	Mold maker	40	$4.18	**a.**	8	**b.**	**c.**	**d.**
6.	Millwright	40	$4.52	**a.**	12	**b.**	**c.**	**d.**
7.	Machinist	40	$5.56	**a.**	2.4	**b.**	**c.**	**d.**
8.	Ironworker	40	$6.80	**a.**	15	**b.**	**c.**	**d.**
9.	Die maker	40	$4.80	**a.**	3.5	**b.**	**c.**	**d.**
10.	Draftsperson	40	$4.50	**a.**	6.8	**b.**	**c.**	**d.**
11.	Instrument technician	40	$4.58	**a.**	5.2	**b.**	**c.**	**d.**

12. Ann Altaha works in a physical testing department. Her regular hourly rate is $5.26 for a 40-hour week. She is paid double time (two times the hourly rate) for each hour she works on a holiday. She is paid time and a half for all other overtime. One week Ann worked 53.6 hours, including 8 hours on Labor Day. Find her gross pay for that week. Round the answers to the nearest cent.

Hourly Rate Plus Tips

Earl Jackson is a waiter in a large restaurant in Chicago. His weekly pay is determined by both his hourly rate and the tips he earns. Earl gives part of his tips to other employees who give service to his customers.

problem

Earl's hourly rate is \$3.15 for a 40-hour week. In one week, he worked 40 hours and earned \$215 in tips. Earl gave 25% of his tips to other employees. What was Earl's gross pay for the week?

solution

Find Earl's regular pay.

$\$3.15 \times 40 = \$126.00$

Find Earl's earnings in tips.

$100\% - 25\% = 75\%$ Earl's share of the tips

75% of \$215

$.75 \times \$215 = \$161.25$ Earl's earnings in tips

Find his gross pay.

\$126.00	Regular pay
+ 161.25	Earnings in tips
\$287.25	Gross pay

exercises

Find each person's gross pay for the week.

	Name	Hourly rate	Hours worked	Tips	
				Amount	Gives to others
1.	Linda Taylor	$2.75	40	$250	———
2.	Phillip Witt	$2.55	25	$115	———
3.	David Glenn	$2.70	40	$164	20%
4.	Vicki Feustle	$3.00	35	$183	25%
5.	Dick Grove	$2.20	40	$212	15%
6.	Irene Luciano	$3.10	36.4	$148	15%
7.	Clyde Beagle	$3.25	34.7	$143	10%

8. Roger Marks is a porter. He earns $3.25 per hour plus tips. If he worked 35 hours and made $175 in tips, what is his gross pay?

9. Sue Bowersoc is a barber. She charges $4.75 for each haircut. Find her gross pay if she gave 65 haircuts and earned $32.50 in tips.

10. Ray Inada is a musician earning $5.20 per hour for a 40-hour week. He makes time and a half for overtime. One week, Ray worked 45 hours and made $185 in tips. Find his gross pay.

Move 3 matches in the figure below to make 3 squares that are the same size.

Remove 4 matches from the figure below so that exactly 3 squares remain.

Straight Commission

Pat Bowen works part-time selling products for Home Cosmetics, Inc. She is paid a **commission** on all of the sales she makes. This means that she keeps a certain portion of the money from the sales as her pay.

Since this is the only pay that Pat earns for her work, this type of wage system is called straight commission.

problem

One of Pat's customers ordered two bottles of perfume which cost \$6.90 each. Pat's commission on the perfume is 40%. How much did Pat earn on this sale?

solution

Find the amount of the sale.

$\$6.90 \times 2 = \$13.80$

Find Pat's earnings.

40% of \$13.80

$.40 \times \$13.80 = \$5.52$

Pat earned \$5.52 on this sale.

exercises

Every two weeks, Home Cosmetics offers a different sales campaign. Since the items are on sale, the commissions vary.

Find the amount Pat would make by selling each of these items for the given commission. Round to the nearest cent.

	Item	Sale price	Commission
1.	Night cream	$2.49	45%
2.	Cleansing cream	$1.99	45%
3.	Eyeshadow	$2.29	43%
4.	Mascara	$3.99	43%
5.	Rouge compact	$3.19	37%
6.	Moisturizer	$1.99	35%
7.	Lipstick	$1.69	41%
8.	After-shave lotion	$5.99	33%
9.	Pre-shave lotion	$.99	20%
10.	Air freshener	$1.29	25%

The commission on each item listed below is 40%. Complete the table.

	Item	Quantity	Price each	Total price	Commission earned
11.	Bath crystals	2	$5.20	**a.**	**b.**
12.	Suntan lotion	3	$1.40	**a.**	**b.**
13.	Eyeliner	1	$4.50	**a.**	**b.**
14.	Hand lotion	2	$3.50	**a.**	**b.**
15.	Perfumed soap	3	$3.00	**a.**	**b.**
16.	Hair spray	2	$2.25	**a.**	**b.**
17.	Bath powder	1	$4.50	**a.**	**b.**

18. Find the total amount of the sale and the total commission earned.

career

Bookkeeper

Career Cluster: Business Detail

Carolyn Tarahata owns Business Services, Inc. Her firm prepares payroll information for Becker's Home Center. Carolyn must compute the gross pay for each employee.

problem

Greg Ritter is paid $75 a week and a commission of 1.5% on all sales delivered. Last week, he sold $7400 worth of furniture. Orders totaling $475 were canceled. How did Carolyn compute Greg's gross pay for the week?

solution

Find the total sales delivered.

$\$7400 - \$475 = \$6925$

Find Greg's commission earnings.

1.5% of $6925

$.015 \times \$6925 = \$103.875$

Greg's commission earnings are $103.88, rounded to the nearest cent.

Find his gross pay.

$ 75.00	Weekly salary
+ 103.88	Commission earnings
$178.88	Gross pay

exercises

Use the information below to compute the gross pay for each of the Becker employees.

	Name	Total sales	Cancellations	Commission	Weekly salary
1.	Mary Andrulewicz	$8500	$900	1.5%	$75
2.	Ed Armacost	$7860	$295	1.5%	$80
3.	Brian Prescott	$10,432	$357	2%	$80
4.	Judy Funk	$9136	$425	2%	$80
5.	Lorraine Hill	$11,089	$718	1.5%	$90
6.	Louise Hiura	$9976	$387	1.5%	$90
7.	Edna Kane	$7659	$195	3%	$75
8.	Roy Tom	$8564	$87	2%	$80

9. Jerry Cohen sells springs and mattresses. He receives a salary of $95 a week and a commission of 2% on all sales over $800. Last week he sold $1500 worth of bedding. Find his gross pay.

10. Neil McCall receives a salary of $90 a week, plus a commission of 1.5% on all sales over $1800. Last week he sold $3700 worth of carpeting. Find Neil's gross pay.

11. Shannon Michaels sells major appliances. Her salary is $480 per month, plus a commission of 3.5% on all sales over $8000. Find her gross pay for the month if her sales were $12,400.

12. Dick Nair sells tires for a monthly salary of $340 and a 2% commission on all sales over $4800. If he sold $4658 worth of tires last month, what was his gross pay?

Graduated Commission

Scott Palmer sells pipe and steel products for large construction projects. He is paid a monthly salary and **graduated commissions.** His commission rate depends on his total sales.

problem

Scott's monthly salary is \$350. In addition, he receives 5% commission on the first \$9000 of his sales, and 6% commission on all sales over \$9000.

Last month, Scott sold \$17,000 worth of products. What was his gross pay?

solution

Find Scott's commission earnings.

.05 × \$9000 = \$450.00	5% of \$9000
\$17,000 − \$9000 = \$8000	Sales over \$9000
.06 × \$8000 = \$480.00	6% of sales over \$9000
\$450 + \$480 = \$930	Total commission earnings

Find Scott's gross pay.

\$350	Monthly salary
+ 930	Commission earnings
\$1280	Gross pay

exercises

Find the gross pay from the total sales and the commissions given below.

	Salary	Commission	Total sales
1.	\$400	5% of first \$5000; 6% of sales over \$5000	\$9500
2.	\$535	3.5% of first \$2000; 5% of sales over \$2000	\$8200
3.	\$375	8% of first \$5000; 10% of sales over \$5000	\$7000
4.	\$475	5.5% of first \$8500; 7% of sales over \$8500	\$8450
5.	\$0	10% of all sales, plus 5% of sales over \$4300	\$8865
6.	\$0	4% of first \$1500; 5% of sales over \$1500 and less than \$3000; 7% of sales over \$3000	\$19,800

CALCULATOR EXERCISES

Employers may use selling cost percentage as one means of comparing the work of their salespersons. The lower the selling cost percentage, the more efficient the salesperson.

Selling cost percentage is the ratio, expressed as a percent, of the person's total earnings to his or her total sales.

Connie sold $87,000 worth of goods last year. Her total salary was $12,300 plus a commission of 2% of all of her sales.

To find her selling cost percentage, first find Connie's total earnings.

$.02 \times \$87{,}000 = \$1740$ Commission earnings

$\$12{,}300 + \$1740 = \$14{,}040$ Total earnings

Divide her total earnings by her total sales. Round to five decimal places.

$\$14{,}040 \div \$87{,}000 \approx .16138$

The selling cost percentage is 16.138%.

exercises

Find each selling cost percentage.

	Salary	Commission	Sales
1.	$5823	5% of all sales	$65,000
2.	$7123	7.25% of all sales	$88,500
3.	$6100	6.135% of all sales	$74,865
4.	$5036	3.35% of first $1800; 4.7% of sales over $1800	$89,547
5.	$4538	5.5% of first $20,000; 8.5% of sales over $20,000	$133,457
6.	$0	10.23% straight commission	$158,889
7.	$0	11.85% straight commission	$126,453
8.	$3500	11.21% straight commission	$117,582
9.	$0	3.47% of first $25,000; 6.23% of sales over $25,000 and less than $50,000; 7.35% of sales over $50,000	$298,468
10.	$6000	3.73% of first $45,000; 6.85% of sales over $45,000 and less than $90,000; 7.35% of sales over $90,000	$215,386

Net Pay

Each pay period, employers subtract a specified amount from employees' gross pay to send to the federal government for income taxes.

The amount deducted is determined by the employee's gross pay, marital status, and number of **exemptions.** An exemption is a family member legally dependent on the taxpayer for support. If they wish, taxpayers may claim fewer exemptions than they are entitled to claim.

The Internal Revenue Service of the United States Treasury Department provides tables which employers may use to determine the amount to withhold for federal income taxes. The tables are on pages 402–405.

problem

Marge Schaffer is single and earns $155 a week as a keypunch operator. She claims exemptions for herself and her father. How much is withheld from her paycheck each week for federal income taxes?

solution

Use the table for single persons.

SINGLE PERSONS - Weekly Pay Period

And the wages are-		Exemptions claimed		
At least	But less than	0	1	2
$120	$125	$18.00	$14.90	$12.00
125	130	19.20	15.90	13.00
130	135	20.30	17.00	14.00
135	140	21.50	18.20	15.00
140	145	22.60	19.30	16.00
145	150	23.80	20.50	17.10
150	160	25.50	22.20	18.90
160	170	27.80	24.50	21.20
170	180	30.10	26.80	23.50
180	190	32.40	29.10	25.80

$155 is "at least $150 but less than $160." Marge claims 2 exemptions.

The amount of tax withheld is $18.90.

EARNINGS STATEMENT | DETACH BEFORE CASHING

RATE	HOURS	EARNINGS	TYPE	CLOCK NO./IDENT.	NAME	DEPARTMENT		PERIOD ENDING
5 00	31 00	155 00	R	132	SCHAFFER, MARGE	08		1 7 77

DEDUCTIONS THIS PAY

FED. WITH. TAX	F.I.C.A.	S.U.I./DIS.	STATE WITH. TAX	CITY WITH. TAX
18 90	9 07	13 75	3 88	

GROSS PAY	NET PAY	GROSS PAY	FED. WITH. TAX	F.I.C.A.	S.U.I./DIS.	STATE WITH. TAX	CITY WITH. TAX
155 00	109 40	155 00	18 90	9 07	13 75	3 88	

EARNINGS THIS PAY | YEAR-TO-DATE TOTALS

exercises

Use the appropriate table from pages 402–405 to find the amount withheld each week for federal income taxes.

	Gross pay	Marital status	Exemptions claimed
1.	$100	Single	1
2.	$58	Single	1
3.	$175	Single	2
4.	$437	Single	3
5.	$437	Single	0
6.	$437	Married	0
7.	$437	Married	3
8.	$323	Married	2
9.	$418	Married	6
10.	$287	Married	5
11.	$247	Single	1
12.	$415	Married	4
13.	$112	Married	3
14.	$343	Single	1
15.	$542	Married	5

Each pay period, part of every employee's paycheck is withheld under the Federal Insurance Contributions Act (FICA). The federal government uses this money to provide retirement income, survivors' benefits, and medical costs benefits to qualified persons.

All employed persons pay *5.85% of the first $16,500 of their gross income* to the federal government for **social security** (FICA deductions).

The employer must also pay the government an amount equal to the employee's deduction. Both amounts are credited to the employee's social security account.

exercises

Find the amount withheld from these paychecks for social security.

	Gross pay to date	Gross pay this paycheck
16.	$6358.07	$138.81
17.	$2009.18	$94.65
18.	$197.67	$46.73
19.	$7885.60	$226.80
20.	$5421.45	$500.00
21.	$4960.48	$181.53
22.	$10,965.00	$674.26
23.	$12,376.14	$1547.02
24.	$25,980.90	$885.46
25.	$31,664.00	$938.17

problem

Elena's paycheck shows that her gross pay so far this year totals $10,483.12. This pay period, her gross pay is $375.56. How much is withheld this pay period for social security?

solution

Elena has not yet earned $16,500 this year. Her employer is still required to withhold 5.85% of her gross pay for this pay period.

5.85% of $375.56

$.0585 \times \$375.56 \approx \$21.97$

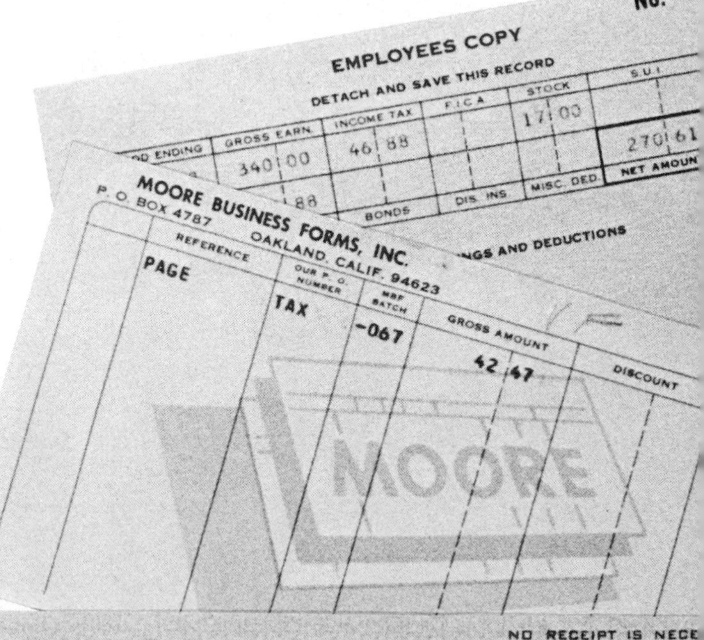

Net pay, sometimes called **take-home pay,** is the amount left after all deductions have been subtracted from gross pay.

Some states require deductions for state or local income taxes. Sometimes union dues, insurance payments, and other deductions are also made.

problem

John Santini is married and claims 3 exemptions. He earned \$227.85 this week. So far this year, his gross pay totals \$8202.60. His weekly union dues and insurance payments are \$4.23. Find John's net pay.

solution

Find the total of all deductions.

From the table on page 404, the federal income tax withheld is \$25.00.

Since John has not earned \$16,500, 5.85% is withheld for social security.

$.0585 \times \$227.85 \approx \$13.33$ Social security

\$25.00	Federal income tax
13.33	Social security
+ 4.23	Union dues and insurance
\$42.56	Total deductions

Find John's net pay.

\$227.85	Gross pay
− 42.56	Total deductions
\$185.29	Net pay

exercises

Find the amounts withheld from each paycheck for federal income tax and social security. Then find the net pay.

				This Week's Paycheck				
	Marital status	Exemptions claimed	Gross pay to date	Gross pay	Federal tax	Social security	Other deductions	Net pay
	Married	3	\$8202.60	\$227.85	\$25.00	\$13.33	\$4.23	\$185.29
26.	Single	1	\$8695.00	\$202.21	**a.**	**b.**	——	**c.**
27.	Single	2	\$12,425.37	\$375.52	**a.**	**b.**	——	**c.**
28.	Married	2	\$11,560.09	\$235.92	**a.**	**b.**	\$5.75	**c.**
29.	Married	4	\$7543.81	\$179.60	**a.**	**b.**	\$2.19	**c.**
30.	Single	1	\$14,000.00	\$311.11	**a.**	**b.**	\$9.16	**c.**
31.	Married	5	\$22,820.00	\$447.45	**a.**	\$0	\$13.87	**b.**
32.	Single	1	\$19,865.32	\$389.51	**a.**	**b.**	\$15.43	**c.**
33.	Married	4	\$13,860.50	\$294.90	**a.**	**b.**	\$9.75	**c.**
34.	Married	3	\$24,347.90	\$518.02	**a.**	**b.**	——	**c.**
35.	Single	0	\$6218.69	\$565.27	**a.**	**b.**	——	**c.**

Jobs in Classified Ads

Most newspapers have a "help wanted" section in their classified ads. People looking for a job use this section to determine the jobs available in the area.

problem

Olivia is looking for a job as a typist. She finds the two ads shown in her local newspaper. Which job pays more? How much more per year does it pay?

A.
STAFF TYPIST
$9300 yr. Exp. and refs. req. 60 wpm

B.
TYPIST
$175 WK
Gen. ofc. typist position with C.P.A. firm. Type reports, ans. phones, other gen. ofc. duties. 50 wpm skills.

solution

Find the amount job B pays in a year.

$\$175 \times 52 = \$9100$

Find how much more job A pays in a year.

$\$9300 - \$9100 = \$200$

Job A pays $200 more per year than job B.

exercises

Use these advertisements and the methods of the previous lessons in this chapter to answer the questions.

C.
KEYPUNCH OPERATOR
$8500 yr. Exper. Good work background. 2nd, 3rd shifts.

D.
KEYPUNCH OPERATOR
Openings for exp. keypunchers. 4-12 midnight. 37.5 hr. wk. $6.50/hr. Good benefits.

E.
FACTORY BRANCH SALES
Consumer protection products. Openings in installation and marketing. No. exp. nec. Complete train. $5.57/hr.

F.
JEWELRY REPAIR
Exp. person to do bench work. All co. benefits: life ins., medical ins., pd. vac. and sick leave. $6.75/hr. for 40 hr. Overtime at time and a half.

G.
SALES
Containers
$13-$14,500 or more
Container mfr. seeks college grad with a couple years sales exp. to sell to distributors, institutions and end users. Exp. only. 20% comm.

H.
SECRETARY
BILINGUAL/SPANISH
Shorthand and good typing skills required for bilingual position. Excellent benefits. $10,200

I.
SALES
PACKAGING MATERIALS
$20,000-$25,000
Packaging mfr. offers solid position. Above fig. reps. 1st yr. salary plus established comms. Co. auto, expense acct., complete fringe package. Send resume.

J.

> STUDENTS—Full or part-time for summer. Pick up and del. Must have car. Up to $3 per hr. in commissions.

K.

> SALES
> JEWELRY STORE
> Exc. salary and comm. No jewelry exp. nec. We're looking for bright, ambitious people. Bring school records and references.

L.

> WAITRESSES
> Only exp. need apply. Full time. Great hrs., many benefits. Guar. salary.

1. Charles is looking for a job as a keypunch operator. Which of the two jobs advertised (C and D) pays more per year? How much more does it pay? (Do not include any calculations for overtime.)

2. Harry Klein was hired as a jewelry repairman (F). The first four weeks, he worked 37.5, 40, 45, and 39.5 hours. What was his gross pay for this four-week period?

3. Barbara accepted the job (G) selling containers for a straight commission of 20%. Her first three sales were for $3456, $6598, and $5653. How much did she earn from these sales?

4. Randy is a student working part-time making deliveries (J). His commission is 30% of the price of the goods. He worked 50 hours and delivered goods worth $369. What did Randy earn from these deliveries? Did he make $3 per hour as advertised?

5. Frank Leong was hired to sell jewelry (K). His salary is $200 per month plus 3% commission on his first $2000 in sales, and 4% commission on all sales over $2000. What was his gross pay for the month if he sold $7500 worth of jewelry?

6. Sandra took the job in packaging materials sales (I) for $600 per month. The first year, she sold $10,500 worth of goods each month for a straight commission of 12%. Did she make $20,000 to $25,000 that year as advertised?

7. Ramon wants to change jobs. His present job pays $5.75 per hour, but he spends $15.60 per week to commute to work. The factory branch sales position (E) is within walking distance of his home. How much money would he gain or lose each week if he took the advertised job? (Do not include any calculations for deductions from gross pay.)

8. Eileen interviewed for the job as a waitress (L). She was told that she could choose the method for computing her pay—$2.40 per hour plus tips, or $200 per week with no tips. The other waitresses told her that the tips usually averaged about $18 per day. Assume that the job is for 5 days, and a total of 40 hours a week. Which pay arrangement would be better?

9. Consuela is considering accepting the job of bilingual secretary (H). She is single and claims 1 exemption. She would have deductions from her gross pay for federal income tax and social security. What will her net pay be each week if she takes the job?

skills tune-up

Rounding whole numbers and decimals, pages 4–5

Round each number to the nearest thousand, the nearest hundred, and the nearest ten.

1. 667
2. 924
3. 1245
4. 7959
5. 5043
6. 1998
7. 65,186
8. 71,541
9. 882.5
10. 28,033.8

Round each number to the nearest whole number, the nearest tenth, and the nearest hundredth.

11. 3.279
12. 11.754
13. 74.518
14. 20.203
15. 152.795
16. 647.026
17. 391.482
18. 18.907
19. 84.671
20. 100.346

Subtracting whole numbers and decimals, pages 6–7

1. 88 − 57
2. 72 − 15
3. 93 − 27
4. 83 − 6
5. 34 − 25
6. 66 − 62
7. 56.1 − 43.6
8. 91.5 − 32.9
9. 42.16 − 29.45
10. 98.23 − 71.63
11. 40.18 − 24.37
12. 26.63 − 17.3
13. 16.322 − 12.84
14. 83.974 − 36.38
15. 55.729 − 38.384
16. 81.043 − 18.477
17. .95 − .597
18. 72.38 − 36.41
19. 9.41 − 8.81
20. 3.16 − 2.53
21. 8.603 − 3.5
22. 41.002 − 25
23. 89 − 17.6
24. 33 − 9.8
25. 8 − 3.61
26. 49 − 16.05

Multiplying whole numbers, pages 8–9

1. 150 × 10
2. 60 × 60
3. 70 × 600
4. 400 × 400
5. 300 × 1800
6. 4000 × 120
7. 30 × 6000
8. 200 × 15,000
9. 1000 × 3400
10. 200 × 230
11. 400 × 860
12. 1700 × 2100
13. 900 × 160
14. 7 × 43
15. 26 × 17
16. 35 × 130
17. 27 × 291
18. 85 × 25
19. 2109 × 15
20. 822 × 45
21. 281 × 346
22. 329 × 1485
23. 34 × 10,126
24. 9478 × 23
25. 2453 × 2608
26. 1815 × 4470

Chapter 4

review

Hourly rate and overtime rate, pages 68–69

1. Don Marcy makes $4.86 per hour for a 40-hour work week. Find his gross pay if he works 40 hours in one week.

2. Kay Soto earns $4.50 per hour for a 40-hour work week, and time and a half for overtime. One week she worked 56 hours. Find her gross pay.

Hourly rate plus tips, pages 70–71

3. Mary Harvey makes $3.50 per hour plus tips. One week she worked 35 hours and earned $39.20 in tips. She gives 15% of her tips to other employees. Find Mary's gross pay for the week.

Straight commission, pages 72–73

4. Dwayne Johnson, a route salesman, makes 15% straight commission. One week, he had sales of $1560. What was his gross pay for the week?

Bookkeeper, pages 74–75

5. Dotty Koontz receives a salary of $100 per week and a commission of 5% of all sales delivered. Last week, she had sales of $3000 and cancellations of $1200. Find Dotty's gross pay.

Graduated commission, page 76

6. Dale Keller is paid $350 per month and a commission of 3% of the first $2000 of his sales, and 4.5% of all his sales over $2000. He sold $3500 worth of lumber last month. What was his gross pay?

Net pay, pages 78–81

7. Max Steiner is married and claims four exemptions. He makes $289.46 per week. Use the table on page 404 to find the amount withheld from his weekly paycheck for federal income taxes.

8. Max makes less than $16,500 per year. Find the amount withheld from his paycheck each week for social security.

9. In addition to federal income tax and social security, Max has other deductions totaling $2.35 each week. What is Max's net pay each week?

Jobs in classified ads, pages 82–83

10. Use the ads shown. Which receptionist job pays more per week? How much more does it pay each week?

A.
RECEPTIONIST
SMALL OFFICE
$165 WEEK

Wonderful all public contact job. You'll be the one to greet and direct everyone, be on phones, and give info. Must type, be personable, enjoy people. Will train.

B.
RECEPTIONIST

Professional organization is seeking an individual to become the front office receptionist. Duties are to greet clients, keep daily records of staff, make airline reservations, and various other duties. $3.85/hr. 40 hr. wk.

Chapter 4

test

1. Sheila makes $4.95 per hour for a 40-hour week. Find her gross pay if she works 40 hours in one week.
2. Eric earns $6.00 per hour for a 40-hour week and time and a half for overtime. One week he worked 54 hours. What was his gross pay?
3. Rick is a porter. He is paid $2.85 per hour plus all of his tips. Last week he worked 30 hours and made $120 in tips. What was his gross pay?
4. Elaine sells books for a straight commission of 30%. Last week she sold $800 worth of books. How much did she earn?
5. Kristen receives a salary of $90 per week, plus a commission of 10% on all of her sales that are delivered. She sold $2000 worth of furniture last week and had only $200 worth of cancellations. What was her gross pay?
6. Marjorie sells appliances. She is paid $100 per week plus commissions of 3% of the first $2000 of sales, and 4% of all sales over $2000. Last week, she sold $4000 worth of appliances. What was her gross pay?
7. Julio makes $200 per week. He is single and claims only one exemption. Use the table on page 403 to find the amount withheld from his paycheck each week for federal income taxes.
8. How much is withheld from Julio's weekly paycheck for social security?
9. Julio also has $3.15 deducted each week for insurance. What is his net pay?
10. Use the ads shown. Which job pays more for a 40-hour work week? How much more does it pay?

A. AUTO BODY—$300/wk. guar. Must have 5 yrs. exp. Gd. Ref.

B. AUTO BODY—$8.50/hr. 40 hr. wk. Must have 8 yrs. exp. Gd. Ref.

Chapter 5

Personal Banking

Banks provide many services for business, industry, and individuals. Savings and checking accounts are two of the most commonly used services.

Deposit Slips

Bill and Lynn Engelmeyer want to open a checking account. They know that paying bills regularly by check is safer and more convenient than carrying around large sums of money.

The manager of the bank explains that they must put money in the bank to establish their account. This is called a **deposit.**

problem

Bill and Lynn decide to deposit their paychecks. They want to keep $25 for spending money. The amounts of their paychecks are $237.31 and $176.25. How do the Engelmeyers fill out the deposit slip?

solution

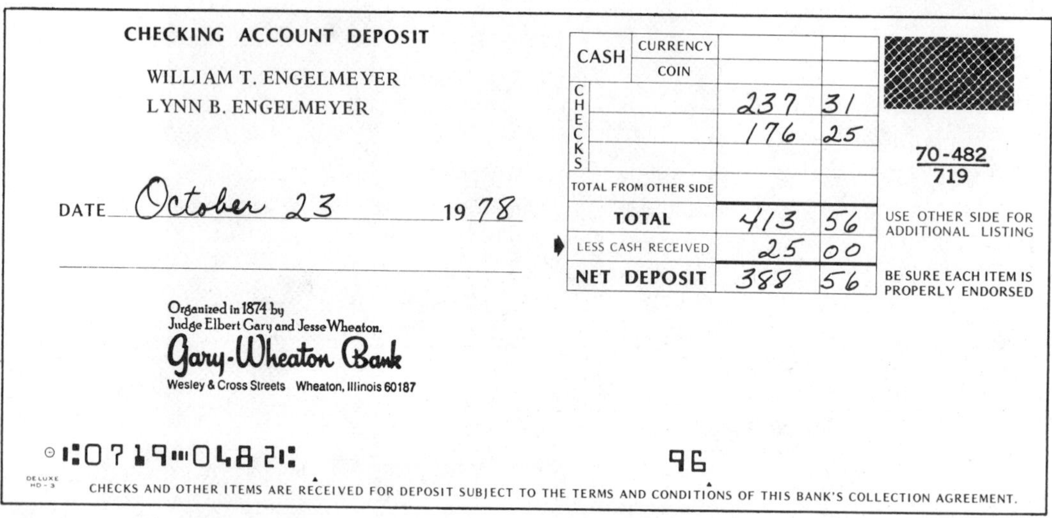

CHECKING ACCOUNT DEPOSIT

WILLIAM T. ENGELMEYER
LYNN B. ENGELMEYER

DATE October 23 19 78

CASH	CURRENCY		
	COIN		
CHECKS		237	31
		176	25
TOTAL FROM OTHER SIDE			
TOTAL		413	56
LESS CASH RECEIVED		25	00
NET DEPOSIT		388	56

70-482
719

USE OTHER SIDE FOR ADDITIONAL LISTING

BE SURE EACH ITEM IS PROPERLY ENDORSED

Organized in 1874 by
Judge Elbert Gary and Jesse Wheaton.
Gary-Wheaton Bank
Wesley & Cross Streets Wheaton, Illinois 60187

⑆0719⑉0482⑆ 96

DELUXE HD-3

CHECKS AND OTHER ITEMS ARE RECEIVED FOR DEPOSIT SUBJECT TO THE TERMS AND CONDITIONS OF THIS BANK'S COLLECTION AGREEMENT.

List each check separately and add.

$$\begin{array}{r l} \$237.31 & \\ +\ 176.25 & \\ \hline \$413.56 & \text{Total} \\ -\ 25.00 & \text{Less cash received} \\ \hline \$388.56 & \text{Net deposit} \end{array}$$

They want to keep $25 in cash. Subtract to find the **net deposit.**

The Engelmeyers are depositing $388.56. They will also receive $25 of their money in cash.

exercises

In exercises 1–4, complete the deposit slips.

1.

CASH	CURRENCY		
	COIN	7	86
CHECKS		18	84
		27	36
		16	25
TOTAL FROM OTHER SIDE			
TOTAL		a.	
LESS CASH RECEIVED			
NET DEPOSIT		b.	

2.

CASH	CURRENCY		
	COIN	18	56
CHECKS		205	16
		19	43
		8	62
TOTAL FROM OTHER SIDE			
TOTAL		a.	
LESS CASH RECEIVED		32	00
NET DEPOSIT		b.	

3.

CASH	CURRENCY		
	COIN	54	75
CHECKS		218	97
		108	29
		37	17
TOTAL FROM OTHER SIDE			
TOTAL		a.	
LESS CASH RECEIVED		75	00
NET DEPOSIT		b.	

4.

CASH	CURRENCY		
	COIN	37	17
CHECKS		49	26
		123	47
		35	91
TOTAL FROM OTHER SIDE			
TOTAL		a.	
LESS CASH RECEIVED		65	00
NET DEPOSIT		b.	

5. Roy had these checks to deposit: \$23.78, \$116.29, \$108.25, and \$8.75. If he wanted \$75 in cash, how much did he deposit in his account?

6. Linda had these checks to deposit: \$208.36, \$97.18, \$29.16, and \$8.64. If she wanted \$35 in cash, how much did she deposit in her account?

The Engelmeyers must **endorse** their checks before depositing them. When they do this, they give the bank the legal right to cash the checks.

problem

How should Bill Engelmeyer endorse his paycheck to deposit it in the Gary-Wheaton Bank?

solution

Bill writes on the back of his paycheck:

Pay to the order of
Gary-Wheaton Bank
for deposit only.
William T Englemeyer

exercises

7. How should James B. Jones endorse his paycheck to deposit it in the Valley National Bank?

8. How should Charlene M. Green endorse her paycheck to deposit it in the Citizens' National Bank?

9. If Cindy Wallace's full name is Cynthia Ann Wallace, how should she endorse a check to deposit it in the State Bank of Georgetown?

10. Arthur Gordon's nickname is Sonny. How should Sonny endorse a check to deposit it in the City National Bank?

Checks and Check Stubs

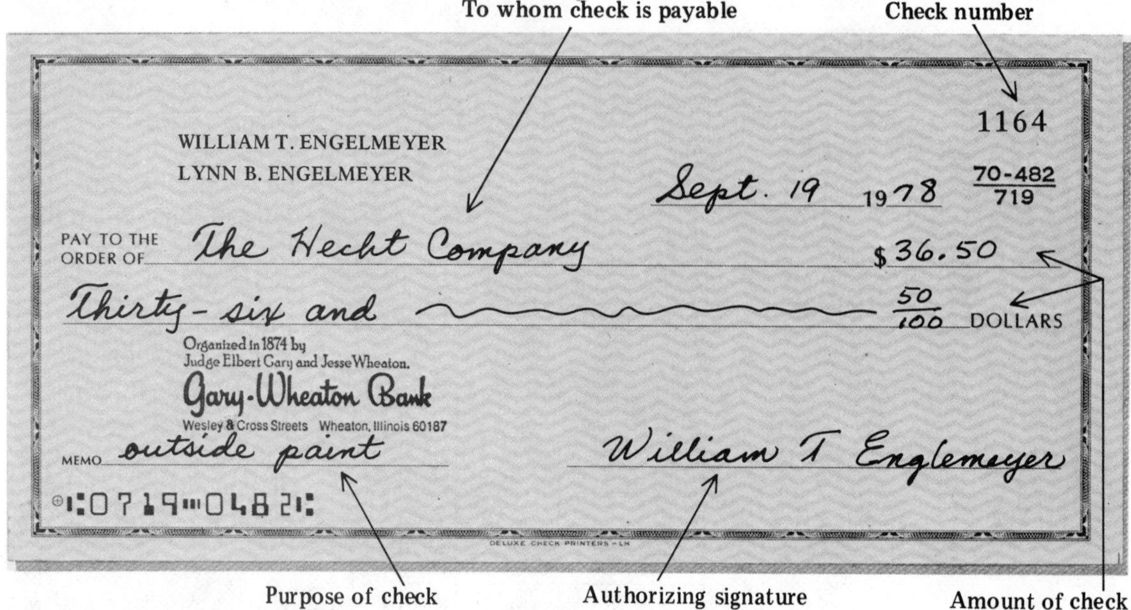

On the completed **check** above, the amount of the check is written in both words and numbers. If there is a difference between these amounts, the bank accepts the amount written in words.

problem

How should $457.17 be written in words on a check?

solution

Always use the entire space provided so that no one can change the amount that is written.

Four hundred fifty-seven and ~ 17/100 Dollars

exercises

Write these amounts in words as they would appear on a check.

1. $27.81
2. $45.63
3. $60.00
4. $72.54
5. $15.00
6. $18.08
7. $395.13
8. $639.00
9. $1002.30

When a check is written, the **stub** should be filled in completely. The stub is a record of the check that stays in the checkbook.

problem

If the balance brought forward was $347.50 and a deposit of $63.20 was made, how should Bill complete the stub for the check shown on page 90?

solution

No. 1164 $ 36.50
Sept. 19 19 78
To The Hecht Co. (paint)

Bal. For'd.	347	50
Deposits	63	20
"		
"		
Total	410	70
This Check	36	50
Bal. For'd.	374	20

Fill in the top of the stub by using the information from the check.

List the balance brought forward from the last stub.
List all deposits since the last stub was completed.

Add to find the total.
List the amount of this check.
Subtract to find the balance that should be carried forward to the next stub.

exercises

Find the balance carried forward.

10.

Bal. For'd.	65	29
Deposits		
"		
"		
Total	a.	
This Check	18	40
Bal. For'd.	b.	

11.

Bal. For'd.	86	20
Deposits	37	50
"	23	16
"		
Total	a.	
This Check	48	95
Bal. For'd.	b.	

12.

Bal. For'd.	17	86
Deposits	39	42
"	8	63
"	13	87
Total	a.	
This Check	15	29
Bal. For'd.	b.	

13. The balance brought forward was $475.80. Deposits of $163.20 and $87.25 were made. The amount of this check is $287.45. Find the balance carried forward to the next stub.

14. The balance carried forward was $189.53. Checks for $17.86 and $9.32 were deposited. If the amount of this check is $57.15, find the balance carried forward to the next stub.

Check Registers

Some people use a **check register** rather than check stubs to record their checks. The same information is written on both.

problem

David Halstead had a balance of $231.18 in his account. On September 29, he wrote check number 342 for $189.00. This check was made out to Realty Associates to pay his rent. How should David record this check in his check register?

solution

CHECK NO.	DATE	DESCRIPTION	AMOUNT OF CHECK		√	AMOUNT OF DEPOSIT		BALANCE	
								231	18
342	9/29	Realty Associates (rent)	189	00				42	18

Subtract to find the new balance.

$231.18 − $189.00 = $42.18

problem

David deposited his paycheck of $203.14 on October 2. What entry should he make in his check register?

solution

CHECK NO.	DATE	DESCRIPTION	AMOUNT OF CHECK		√	AMOUNT OF DEPOSIT		BALANCE	
								231	18
342	9/29	Realty Associates (rent)	189	00				42	18
	10/2	paycheck				203	14	245	32

Add to find the new balance.

$42.18 + $203.14 = $245.32

exercises

Copy the check register form shown above. Make additional entries to show these checks and deposits in David's account.

1. Oct. 4, check #343 to H-1 Insurance Agency for car insurance payment, $63.10
2. Oct. 7, check #344 to Marloff's Hardware Store for paint, $12.38
3. Oct. 9, check #345 to BankAmericard for September charges, $33.56
4. Oct. 12, check #346 to Dr. William Edelhart for dental exam, $25
5. Oct. 16, deposit paycheck of $203.14
6. Oct. 18, deposit refund check from J. C. Penney for $8.89
7. Oct. 18, check #347 to Central Utilities Services for the electric bill, **$15.34**
8. Oct. 23, check #348 to General Telephone Company for the phone bill, $18.93
9. Oct. 28, check #349 to Lou's Auto Repair for engine tune-up, $57.66
10. Oct. 30, deposit paycheck of $203.14
11. Oct. 30, check #350 to Realty Associates for rent, $189.00
12. Oct. 30, check #351 to Jenness Furniture Store for a chair, $109.20

Reconciling a Bank Statement

Each month Dianne Starr receives a **bank statement** for her checking account. With the statement are all of Dianne's **canceled checks,** the checks that the bank has paid from her account during the month.

Dianne **reconciles** the bank statement with her check register. This means that she makes the balances from her check register and the bank statement agree.

Sometimes Dianne has recorded deposits and checks in her check register that are not listed on the bank statement. These are called **outstanding deposits** and **outstanding checks.**

The **service charge** listed on the bank statement is the amount the bank charges for handling the account.

problem

Information from Dianne's bank statement for one month is shown. Her check register balance is $510.79. How does Dianne reconcile her statement?

First National Bank		
CHECKING ACCOUNT INFORMATION		
STATEMENT DATE		07-24-78
NO. OF CHECKS		9
BALANCE FORWARD		$166.10
DEPOSIT TOTAL		954.57
CHECK TOTAL		727.90
SERVICE CHARGE		1.75
ENDING BALANCE		$391.02
CHECK #	DATE	AMOUNT
323	07-02	$ 60.00
324	07-03	49.25
325	07-07	60.00
326	07-18	10.20
327	07-18	19.95
328	07-18	50.00
330	07-19	120.50
331	07-24	350.25
333	07-23	7.75
	DEPOSITS	
	07-06	$100.00
	07-18	703.97
	07-20	150.60

solution

Dianne compares the amount of each check and each deposit in her check register with the canceled checks and the amounts listed on her bank statement.

She notices that there is an outstanding deposit of $150. There are three outstanding checks: #329 for $8.75, #332 for $15.50, and #334 for $7.75.

She then completes the forms on the back of her bank statement.

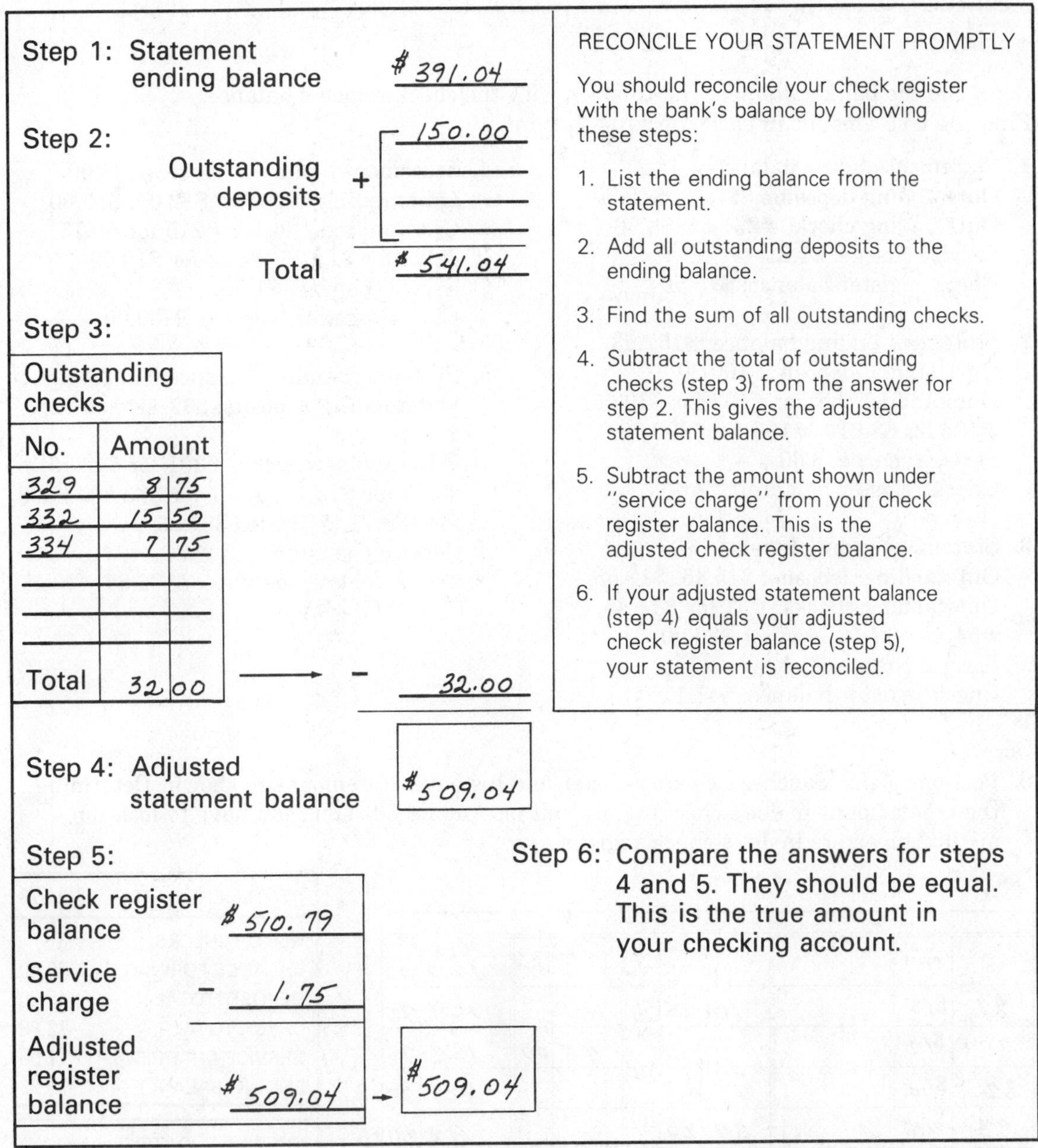

Step 1: Statement ending balance $391.04

Step 2: Outstanding deposits + 150.00

Total $541.04

Step 3:

Outstanding checks	
No.	Amount
329	8 75
332	15 50
334	7 75
Total	32 00

→ − 32.00

Step 4: Adjusted statement balance $509.04

Step 5:

Check register balance $510.79

Service charge − 1.75

Adjusted register balance $509.04 → $509.04

RECONCILE YOUR STATEMENT PROMPTLY

You should reconcile your check register with the bank's balance by following these steps:

1. List the ending balance from the statement.
2. Add all outstanding deposits to the ending balance.
3. Find the sum of all outstanding checks.
4. Subtract the total of outstanding checks (step 3) from the answer for step 2. This gives the adjusted statement balance.
5. Subtract the amount shown under "service charge" from your check register balance. This is the adjusted check register balance.
6. If your adjusted statement balance (step 4) equals your adjusted check register balance (step 5), your statement is reconciled.

Step 6: Compare the answers for steps 4 and 5. They should be equal. This is the true amount in your checking account.

Since her adjusted statement balance is the same as her adjusted check register balance, Dianne's statement is reconciled.

She records the $1.75 service charge in her check register. Now her register balance shows $509.04, the true amount in her account.

exercises

Reconcile the bank statement information with the check register balance. Find the true amount in each checking account.

1. Statement ending balance: $44.27
   Outstanding deposits: $27.70, $12.30
   Outstanding check: #221 for $9.98
   Service charge: $1.21
   Check register balance: $75.50

2. Statement ending balance: $157.93
   Outstanding deposit: $100.00
   Outstanding checks: #103 for $10.00, #104 for $24.13, #106 for $200.00
   Service charge: $.60
   Check register balance: $24.40

3. Statement ending balance: $67.38
   Outstanding deposits: $15.45, $12.55
   Outstanding checks: #51 for $18.45, #54 for $17.12, #55 for $20.20
   Service charge: $1.50
   Check register balance: $41.11

4. Statement ending balance: $235.00
   Outstanding deposits: $12.00, $13.00
   Outstanding checks: #215 for $9.75, #221 for $11.25, #222 for $10.00
   Service charge: $1.00
   Check register balance: $230.00

5. Statement ending balance: $392.41
   Outstanding deposits: $32.41, $50.12, $49.46
   Outstanding checks: #301 for $42.75, #303 for $73.12, #307 for $63.30, #308 for $88.71, #311 for $81.80
   Service charge: $2.15
   Check register balance: $176.87

6. Portions of Joe Sanchez's check register and his bank statement are shown. Determine the true amount in Joe's checking account on August 30. You may have to look for arithmetic errors in Joe's check register.

CHECK NO.	DATE		AMOUNT OF CHECK		√	AMOUNT OF DEPOSIT		BALANCE	
								120	00
81	8/5		10	25				109	75
	8/9					45	00	154	75
82	8/10		25	35				129	40
83	8/15		37	20				92	20
84	8/15		13	23				79	97
	8/27					47	00	126	97
	8/30					5	60	132	57
85	8/30		32	52				100	05

STATEMENT DATE		08-21-78
NO. OF CHECKS		3
BALANCE FORWARD		$120.00
DEPOSIT TOTAL		45.00
CHECK TOTAL		72.80
SERVICE CHARGE		1.50
ENDING BALANCE		$ 90.70
CHECK #	DATE	AMOUNT
81	08-09	$10.25
82	08-14	25.35
83	08-21	37.20
	DEPOSITS	
	08-11	$45.00

CALCULATOR EXERCISES

1. Complete the check register below by filling in the balances on each line.

CHECK NO.	DATE		AMOUNT OF CHECK		✓	AMOUNT OF DEPOSIT		BALANCE	
								1005	07
101	3/1		103	82					
102	3/4		111	26					
103	3/7		72	25					
104	3/8		201	44					
	3/9					173	53		
105	3/10		386	89					
106	3/11		75	53					
107	3/11		195	40					
	3/11					713	98		
108	3/18		521	57					
109	3/19		92	75					
110	3/21		118	65					
	3/21					428	60		
111	3/23		219	74					
112	3/23		123	90					
113	3/24		78	65					
	3/24					628	35		
114	3/25		77	78					
115	3/25		35	40					
116	3/29		187	65					
117	3/30		213	14					
118	3/30		97	80					

2. Reconcile the check register in exercise 1 with the bank statement below.

STATEMENT DATE		03-26-78
NO. OF CHECKS		10
BALANCE FORWARD		$1005.07
DEPOSIT TOTAL		1316.11
CHECK TOTAL		1891.08
SERVICE CHARGE		1.40
ENDING BALANCE		$ 428.70
CHECK #	DATE	AMOUNT
101	03-03	$103.82
102	03-07	111.26
104	03-09	201.44
105	03-14	386.89
107	03-13	195.40
108	03-20	521.57
109	03-21	92.75
110	03-24	118.65
112	03-25	123.90
115	03-26	35.40
	DEPOSITS	
	03-09	$173.53
	03-13	713.98
	03-21	428.60

career

Personal Banking Representative

Career Cluster: Business Contact

Debbie Haverl is a personal banking representative for the Edgar State Bank. Her job is to help the bank's customers understand the services offered by the bank.

John and Andrea Warren want to open a savings account. The amount the Warrens deposit is called the **principal.** The amount that the bank will pay the Warrens for leaving their money in a savings account is called the **interest.**

Debbie explains that the bank uses the **simple interest formula** to compute the interest on many types of accounts.

$I = p \times r \times t$

I is the amount of interest paid.

p is the principal.

r is the interest rate, expressed as a decimal or as a fraction.

t is the length of time in years.

problem

Andrea deposited \$300 in a savings account that pays $4\frac{1}{4}\%$ simple interest per year. If she leaves her money in the account for 3 months, how much interest will she earn?

solution

$4\frac{1}{4}\% = .0425 = \frac{425}{10{,}000}$

3 months is $\frac{3}{12}$ or $\frac{1}{4}$ year.

$I = p \times r \times t$

$I = \$300 \times \frac{425}{10{,}000} \times \frac{1}{4}$

$I = \$3.1875$

Andrea's account will earn \$3.19, rounded to the nearest cent.

exercises

Compute the simple interest paid on each of these savings accounts.

	Principal	Interest rate	Time
1.	\$50	4%	2 mo.
2.	\$200	$5\frac{1}{2}\%$	1 yr.
3.	\$350	6.5%	18 mo.
4.	\$175	5.25%	8 mo.
5.	\$348	$6\frac{1}{2}\%$	15 mo.
6.	\$225	6.75%	30 mo.
7.	\$285	4.25%	27 mo.
8.	\$615	7%	10 mo.
9.	\$425	$6\frac{1}{4}\%$	38 mo.
10.	\$3210	7.75%	1 yr. 9 mo.
11.	\$3750	$7\frac{1}{4}\%$	4 mo.
12.	\$2940	5%	2 yr. 4 mo.
13.	\$5000	$6\frac{1}{4}\%$	3 yr. 3 mo.
14.	\$1290	4.75%	2 yr. 6 mo.
15.	\$720	$5\frac{1}{2}\%$	3 yr. 5 mo.

change of pace

This is a diagram of something of vast importance to our world. Among other things, it provides food, employment, recreation, and adventure for thousands of people. What is it?

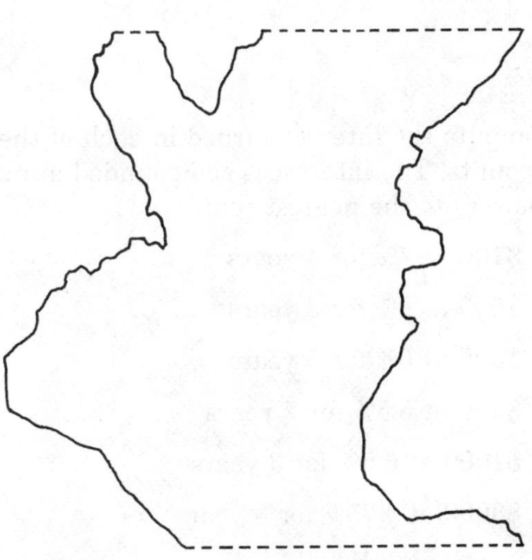

Compound Interest

Greater Returns!
1st Federal of Wilmette offers you higher i
bank in a variety of higher-paying account
The Savings Professionals who can help
Portfolio for a proper "mix" of short and
and passbook accounts. Wise planning
highest earnings along with accessibility
the time to save more—at the 1st!
Earn 5.39% annual yield
Earn 6.00% annual yield
Earn 6.81% annual
Earn 7.08% annual
Earn 7.90% annual
Earn 8.17% annual
save for a rainy day

Tom Yazzie placed his money in a savings account that pays **compound interest.** This means that the interest is computed on the principal *and* on the interest previously earned.

problem

Tom deposits $1000 in a savings account that pays 7% interest compounded annually. How much interest will this account earn in two years?

solution

Interest compounded annually is computed once each year. Find the interest for each year by using the simple interest formula.

Year	Principal plus previous interest	Interest for the year $p \times r \times t = I$
1	$1000	$1000 × .07 × 1 = $70.00
2	$1070	$1070 × .07 × 1 = $74.90
		Total interest $144.90

Tom's account will earn $144.90 in interest in two years.

exercises

Compute the interest earned in each of these savings accounts. The interest is compounded annually. Round answers to the nearest cent.

1. $100 at 7% for 4 years

2. $500 at 8% for 3 years

3. $300 at 6% for 5 years

4. $250 at 5.5% for 2 years

5. $1000 at 6.5% for 3 years

6. $3000 at 4.75% for 3 years

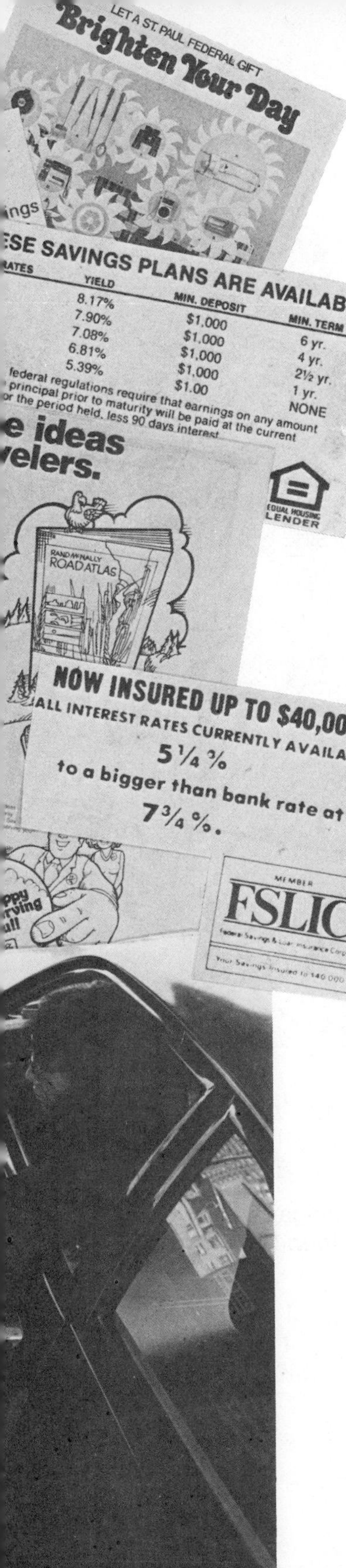

Interest compounded quarterly is computed every three months. Interest compounded semiannually is computed every six months.

problem

Alicia Melendez deposited $1500 in a savings account that pays 8% interest compounded quarterly. How much interest will her account earn in one year?

solution

Compute the interest for each three-month period by using the simple interest formula. Round to the nearest cent.

Qtr.	Principal plus previous interest	Interest this quarter $p \times r \times t = I$
1	$1500.00	$1500.00 × .08 × .25 = $30.00
2	$1530.00	$1530.00 × .08 × .25 = $30.60
3	$1560.60	$1560.60 × .08 × .25 ≈ $31.21
4	$1591.81	$1591.81 × .08 × .25 ≈ $31.84
		Total interest $123.65

Alicia's account will earn $123.65 in interest.

exercises

Find the interest earned in these savings accounts.

7. $400 at 5% compounded quarterly for 1 year
8. $300 at 6% compounded semiannually for 2 years
9. $560 at 8% compounded semiannually for 3 years
10. $220 at 7% compounded quarterly for 1 year
11. $1000 at 5.5% compounded semiannually for 2 years
12. $500 at 6% compounded quarterly for 1 year
13. $500 at 6% compounded semiannually for 1 year
14. $500 at 6% compounded annually for 1 year

Compound Interest Tables

COMPOUND INTEREST TABLE

No. of Periods	1.5%	2%	2.5%	3%	3.5%	4%	5%	6%	7%	8%
1	1.0150	1.0200	1.0250	1.0300	1.0350	1.0400	1.0500	1.0600	1.0700	1.0800
2	1.0302	1.0404	1.0506	1.0609	1.0712	1.0816	1.1025	1.1236	1.1449	1.1664
3	1.0457	1.0612	1.0769	1.0927	1.1087	1.1248	1.1576	1.1910	1.2250	1.2597
4	1.0614	1.0824	1.1038	1.1255	1.1475	1.1699	1.2155	1.2625	1.3108	1.3605
5	1.0773	1.1041	1.1314	1.1593	1.1877	1.2167	1.2763	1.3382	1.4026	1.4693
6	1.0934	1.1262	1.1597	1.1941	1.2293	1.2653	1.3401	1.4186	1.5007	1.5869
7	1.1098	1.1487	1.1887	1.2299	1.2723	1.3159	1.4071	1.5036	1.6058	1.7138
8	1.1265	1.1717	1.2184	1.2668	1.3168	1.3686	1.4775	1.5938	1.7182	1.8059
9	1.1434	1.1951	1.2489	1.3048	1.3629	1.4233	1.5513	1.6895	1.8385	1.9990
10	1.1605	1.2190	1.2801	1.3439	1.4106	1.4802	1.6289	1.7908	1.9672	2.1589
11	1.1779	1.2434	1.3121	1.3842	1.4600	1.5395	1.7103	1.8983	2.1049	2.3316
12	1.1956	1.2682	1.3449	1.4258	1.5111	1.6010	1.7959	2.0122	2.2522	2.5182
13	1.2136	1.2936	1.3785	1.4685	1.5640	1.6651	1.8856	2.1329	2.4098	2.7196
14	1.2318	1.3195	1.4130	1.5126	1.6187	1.7317	1.9799	2.2609	2.5785	2.9372
15	1.2502	1.3459	1.4483	1.5580	1.6753	1.8009	2.0789	2.3966	2.7590	3.1722
16	1.2690	1.3728	1.4845	1.6047	1.7340	1.8730	2.1829	2.5404	2.9522	3.4259
17	1.2880	1.4002	1.5216	1.6528	1.7947	1.9479	2.2920	2.6928	3.1588	3.7000
18	1.3073	1.4282	1.5597	1.7024	1.8575	2.0258	2.4066	2.8543	3.3799	3.9960
19	1.3270	1.4568	1.5987	1.7535	1.9225	2.1068	2.5270	3.0256	3.6165	4.3157
20	1.3469	1.4859	1.6386	1.8061	1.9898	2.1911	2.6533	3.2071	3.8697	4.6610
21	1.3671	1.5157	1.6796	1.8603	2.0594	2.2788	2.7860	3.3996	4.1406	5.0338
22	1.3876	1.5460	1.7216	1.9161	2.1315	2.3699	2.9253	3.6035	4.4304	5.4365
23	1.4084	1.5769	1.7646	1.9736	2.2061	2.4647	3.0715	3.8198	4.7405	5.8715
24	1.4295	1.6084	1.8087	2.0328	2.2833	2.5633	3.2251	4.0489	5.0724	6.3412
25	1.4509	1.6407	1.8539	2.0938	2.3673	2.6658	3.3864	4.2919	5.4274	6.8485

Compound interest tables are designed to allow people to compute compound interest without as much calculating.

To use the table, follow these steps:

1. Divide the annual interest rate by the number of times the interest is compounded each year.
2. Multiply the number of years by the number of times the interest is compounded each year to find the total number of periods.
3. Read the entry from the table by using the row and column determined by steps 1 and 2.
4. Multiply the principal by the entry from the table. Round to the nearest cent, if necessary.
5. Subtract the original principal from the answer for step 4 to find the total amount of interest earned.

problem

Ginnie Leatherman has $500 in a savings account that pays 7% interest compounded semiannually. How much interest will her account earn in 3 years?

solution

Step 1	$7\% \div 2 = 3.5\%$
Step 2	$3 \times 2 = 6$
Step 3	1.2293 from the table
Step 4	$\$500 \times 1.2293 = \$614.65$
Step 5	$\$614.65 - \$500.00 = \$114.65$

Ginnie's account will earn $114.65 in interest in three years.

exercises

Use the compound interest table to find the interest earned by each account.

	Principal	Annual interest rate	Time	Compounded
1.	$100	5%	4 years	Annually
2.	$370	7%	5 years	Annually
3.	$750	8%	15 years	Annually
4.	$435	6%	8 years	Annually
5.	$400	10%	3 years	Semiannually
6.	$850	7%	8 years	Semiannually
7.	$575	8%	11 years	Semiannually
8.	$1000	6%	12 years	Semiannually
9.	$2000	8%	5 years	Quarterly
10.	$1500	6%	6 years	Quarterly
11.	$1800	10%	4 years	Quarterly
12.	$2500	12%	3 years	Quarterly

skills tune-up

Multiplying decimals, pages 10-11

1. $.5 \times .7$
2. $.8 \times .3$
3. $.04 \times .4$
4. $.01 \times .6$
5. $.02 \times .09$
6. $.4 \times .08$
7. $.004 \times .02$
8. $.03 \times .011$
9. $200 \times .7$
10. $.9 \times 600$
11. $400 \times .08$
12. $.05 \times 110$
13. $.007 \times 300$
14. $800 \times .006$
15. $.005 \times .004$
16. $.002 \times .007$
17. $4000 \times .0011$
18. 8.3×1.7
19. 6.24×5.6
20. 9.1×3.46
21. $16.2 \times .015$
22. 5.814×6.29
23. 36.01×4.263
24. $7.49 \times .6008$
25. $28.124 \times .056$
26. $4.627 \times .0037$

Ratio and proportion, pages 30-31

Find the cross-products. Tell whether the ratios are equal.

1. $\frac{6}{30}$ $\frac{4}{20}$
2. $\frac{3}{13}$ $\frac{5}{15}$
3. $\frac{10}{12}$ $\frac{12}{14}$
4. $\frac{2.1}{.7}$ $\frac{6}{2}$
5. $\frac{.16}{.06}$ $\frac{.55}{.40}$
6. $\frac{25.5}{15.3}$ $\frac{.5}{.3}$

Solve and check.

7. $\frac{4}{3} = \frac{n}{27}$
8. $\frac{25}{a} = \frac{5}{20}$
9. $\frac{x}{42} = \frac{5}{14}$
10. $\frac{16}{3} = \frac{8}{c}$
11. $\frac{18}{d} = \frac{2.4}{2.8}$
12. $\frac{1.5}{.6} = \frac{a}{.36}$
13. $\frac{.03}{.27} = \frac{9}{y}$
14. $\frac{28}{x} = \frac{24}{.18}$

Writing percents, decimals, and fractions, pages 34-35

Write as a decimal.

1. 17%
2. 8%
3. 1%
4. 25%
5. 96%
6. 3%
7. 99%
8. $6\frac{1}{4}$%
9. 7.75%
10. 15.6%
11. $12\frac{1}{2}$%
12. 1.5%
13. 6.75%
14. $1\frac{1}{2}$%
15. 32.8%
16. 8.5%
17. $5\frac{3}{4}$%
18. 924%
19. $37\frac{1}{2}$%
20. 103%
21. 856%
22. $16\frac{1}{8}$%
23. 160%
24. 305%

Write as a fraction in lowest terms.

25. 50%
26. 90%
27. 35%
28. 75%
29. 60%
30. 37%
31. 24%
32. 83%
33. 20%
34. 15%
35. 9%
36. 56%
37. 33%
38. 5%
39. 45%
40. 87%
41. 95%
42. 67%
43. 110%
44. 675%
45. 350%
46. 140%

Chapter 5

review

Deposit slips, pages 88-89

1. Complete the deposit slip.

CASH	CURRENCY		
	COIN	8	75
CHECKS		29	80
		37	40
		5	23
TOTAL FROM OTHER SIDE			
TOTAL		a.	
LESS CASH RECEIVED		25	00
NET DEPOSIT		b.	

Checks and check stubs, pages 90-91

2. Find the balance carried forward for this stub.

Bal. For'd.	93	57
Deposits	95	76
"	17	29
"		
Total	a.	
This Check	75	20
Bal. For'd.	b.	

Check registers, pages 92-93

For exercises 3 and 4, copy the check register shown after exercise 4. Make the correct entries and compute the balances.

3. Oct. 8, check #127 to ABC Hardware Store for tools, $34.70

4. Oct. 9, deposit paycheck of $136.18

Reconciling a bank statement, pages 94-96

5. The ending balance on a bank statement is $196.50. There are outstanding checks for $19.70 and $125.25, and an outstanding deposit of $57.56. Find the adjusted statement balance.

6. The bank statement in exercise 5 shows a service charge of $.60. The check register has a balance of $109.86. Do the balances reconcile?

Personal banking representative, pages 98-99

7. A savings account pays 4.5% simple interest. Find the amount of interest that $1500 will earn in eight months.

Compound interest, pages 100-101

8. Find the amount of interest earned in 2 years by an account of $1300 that pays 8% interest compounded annually.

9. A savings account of $1000 earns 6% interest compounded quarterly. Find the amount of interest earned in 1 year.

Compound interest tables, pages 102-103

10. Use the table on page 102 to find the amount of interest earned on $400 at 7% interest compounded semiannually for 5 years.

CHECK NO.	DATE	DESCRIPTION	AMOUNT OF CHECK		✓	AMOUNT OF DEPOSIT		BALANCE	
								283	26

Chapter 5

test

1. Complete the deposit slip.

CASH	CURRENCY		
	COIN		
CHECKS		18	50
		43	82
		459	27
TOTAL FROM OTHER SIDE			
TOTAL		a.	
LESS CASH RECEIVED		35	00
NET DEPOSIT		b.	

2. Find the balance carried forward for this stub.

Bal. For'd.	100	69
Deposits	47	29
"	126	35
"		
Total	a.	
This Check	225	80
Bal. For'd.	b.	

For exercises 3 and 4, copy the check register shown after exercise 4. Make the correct entries and compute the new balances.

3. Nov. 16, check #311 to Uptown Auto Shop for repairs, $78.16

4. Nov. 20, deposit paycheck of $126.74

5. The ending balance on Ann Umeki's bank statement is $147.80. She has an outstanding deposit of $57.26. There are outstanding checks for $37.86, $29.40, and $75.84. What is Ann's adjusted statement balance?

6. Ann's check register balance is $63.21. If the bank statement contains a service charge of $1.25, do the balances reconcile?

7. A savings account of $700 earns 6.5% simple interest. Find the amount of interest the account will earn in 6 months.

8. A savings account pays 7% interest compounded annually. Compute the amount of interest on an account of $500 after 2 years.

9. A savings account of $2000 earns 8% interest compounded semiannually. Find the amount of interest earned in 1 year.

10. Use the table on page 102 to find the amount of interest on $5000 at 8% compounded quarterly for 4 years.

CHECK NO.	DATE	DESCRIPTION	AMOUNT OF CHECK		✓	AMOUNT OF DEPOSIT		BALANCE	
								114	53

Consumer Credit

More than 70 million credit cards are in circulation today. The uses and abuses of credit must be understood by each consumer.

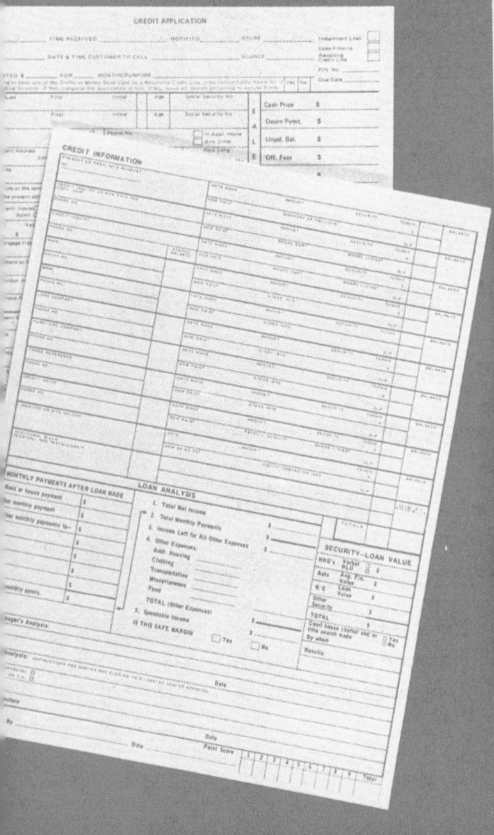

Promissory Notes

$____________

SPARKS, MD., ____________ 19___

____________ AFTER DATE, I, WE, OR EITHER OF US, PROMISE TO PAY TO THE ORDER OF ____________

____________ $\frac{}{100}$ DOLLARS

AT THE SPARKS STATE BANK, SPARKS, MARYLAND WITH INTEREST FOR VALUE RECEIVED

And to secure the payment of said amount the makers and endorsers of this note hereby authorize any attorney of any Court to appear for them or any of them in such Court in term time or vacation, or before any Justice of the Peace at any time before or after the maturity of this note, and confess judgment without process in favor of the holder of this note for such amount as may appear to be unpaid thereon, together with all costs and 15 per cent. for attorney's fees for collection, and hereby waive all right to stay of execution and exemption under the laws of the United States, State of Maryland or any other State, and also waive right to supersede such judgment. The maker or makers and all other parties hereto, whether endorsers, sureties or guarantors, severally waive presentment, demand, protest and notice, and consent to any extension of the time of the payment hereof made after maturity by agreement with the maker, or makers, with or without notice.

WITNESS ____________

ADDRESS ____________ ____________ (SEAL)

DUE ____________ NO. ____________ ____________ (SEAL)

Dennis Nelson is opening a coin-operated laundry. He wants to borrow money from his bank to pay for the dryers.

The bank requires that he sign a **promissory note.** He agrees to repay the **principal**, the amount borrowed, along with **interest,** by a certain date. The interest is the amount the bank charges Dennis for the use of the money.

The bank uses the simple-interest formula to compute the amount of interest.

$I = p \times r \times t$

Banks commonly express the time of a promissory note by using the **ordinary method.** Under this method, a year has 12 months of 30 days each, for a total of 360 days.

problem

Dennis signs a promissory note for \$2400 due in 120 days. The interest rate is 9.5% per year. Find the amount of interest and the total amount due in 120 days.

solution

$120 \text{ days} = \frac{120}{360} \text{ year} = \frac{1}{3} \text{ year}$

$9.5\% = .095 = \frac{95}{1000}$

$I = p \times r \times t$

$I = \$2400 \times \frac{95}{1000} \times \frac{1}{3}$

$I = \$76.00$ Amount of interest

Find the total amount due in 120 days.

\$2400	Principal
+ 76	Amount of interest
\$2476	Total amount due

exercises

Find the amount of interest. Use the ordinary method to express days or months as years. Round the answer to the nearest cent.

1. $850 at 8% for 90 days
2. $1100 at 9% for 30 days
3. $730 at 7.5% for 60 days
4. $1500 at 8.5% for 120 days
5. $2000 at 9% for 1 day
6. $600 at 7.5% for 15 days
7. $2300 at 9% for 4 months
8. $1350 at 8.5% for 8 months
9. $500 at 7% for 15 months
10. $4850 at 8% for 18 months

Find the amount of interest and the total amount due on these promissory notes.

11. 120 days AFTER DATE I, WE, OR EITHER OF US, PROMISE TO PAY TO THE ORDER OF First National Bank
One thousand eight hundred and 00/100 DOLLARS
WITH INTEREST FOR VALUE RECEIVED AT 8 % PER YEAR.

12. 1 yr. 3 mo. AFTER DATE I, WE, OR EITHER OF US, PROMISE TO PAY TO THE ORDER OF Prairie State Bank
Nine hundred twenty-five and 00/100 DOLLARS
WITH INTEREST FOR VALUE RECEIVED AT 8.5 % PER YEAR.

13. 2 yr. 6 mo. AFTER DATE, I, WE, OR EITHER OF US, PROMISE TO PAY TO THE ORDER OF Lincoln Bank
Two thousand four hundred and 00/100 DOLLARS
WITH INTEREST FOR VALUE RECEIVED AT 9 % PER YEAR.

14. 50 days AFTER DATE I, WE, OR EITHER OF US, PROMISE TO PAY TO THE ORDER OF Northeast National Bank
Nine hundred seventy-five and 00/100 DOLLARS
WITH INTEREST FOR VALUE RECEIVED AT 7.5 % PER YEAR.

Credit Card Finance Charges

Marilyn Bishop has a department store credit card that allows her to charge all of her purchases at that store. Once a month, she is sent a statement of the balance due on her account.

When she pays less than the full amount owed, she has to pay a **finance charge** the next month. The finance charge is the amount that the store charges for the privilege of delaying payment.

The finance charge on Marilyn's account is computed on the amount that remains after the store subtracts her payments from her unpaid balance. There is no finance charge on new purchases.

Marilyn checks her statement by computing the balance in her account according to the store's methods.

problem

Marilyn's unpaid balance from last month is \$87.50. This month, she has made a payment of \$20.00 and purchases totaling \$23.18. The finance charge is 1.5% per month. What is the amount of the finance charge? What is the new balance in her account?

solution

Find the amount of the finance charge.

\$87.50	Unpaid balance
− 20.00	Payment
\$67.50	Balance after payment

\$67.50	Balance after payment
× .015	1.5% = .015
\$1.0125 ≈ \$1.01	Amount of finance charge, rounded to the nearest cent

Find the new balance.

\$67.50	Balance after payment
1.01	Amount of finance charge
+ 23.18	Purchases
\$91.69	New balance

exercises

Complete the table. The finance charge is 1.5% per month of the balance after payments.

	Unpaid balance	Payments	Balance after payments	Amount of finance charge	Purchases	New balance
1.	\$47.16	\$0	a.	b.	\$0	c.
2.	\$79.62	\$0	a.	b.	\$46.13	c.
3.	\$126.38	\$20.00	a.	b.	\$0	c.
4.	\$48.18	\$25.00	a.	b.	\$30.57	c.
5.	\$72.33	\$50.00	a.	b.	\$9.98 \$14.68	c.
6.	\$42.75	\$10.00	a.	b.	\$6.23 \$10.39	c.
7.	\$83.77	\$10.00	a.	b.	\$17.43 \$12.21	c.
8.	\$234.90	\$36.00	a.	b.	\$18.95 \$19.34	c.
9.	\$83.21	\$83.21	a.	b.	\$20.94	c.
10.	\$23.14	\$10.00 \$13.14	a.	b.	\$0	c.
11.	\$8.19	\$8.19	a.	b.	\$35.60	c.
12.	\$0	\$0	a.	b.	\$12.00 \$16.49 \$49.40	c.

career

Credit Counselor

Career Cluster: Social Service

Ted Kitcheyan is a counselor for a consumer protection agency. He helps people understand the costs of buying on credit.

Lee Gilbert has a credit card for a company that uses the **average daily balance** to compute finance charges. Ted explained that the company computes the unpaid balance in the account each day of the month. The finance charge is based on the average of these daily unpaid amounts.

problem

Lee's unpaid balance on November 1 was \$132.40. He charged \$13.14 worth of gasoline on November 15. On November 21, he made a payment of \$20.

The finance charge is 1.5% per month of the average daily unpaid balance. There is no finance charge on new purchases. What is the amount of the finance charge for Lee's account on November 30? What is his new balance?

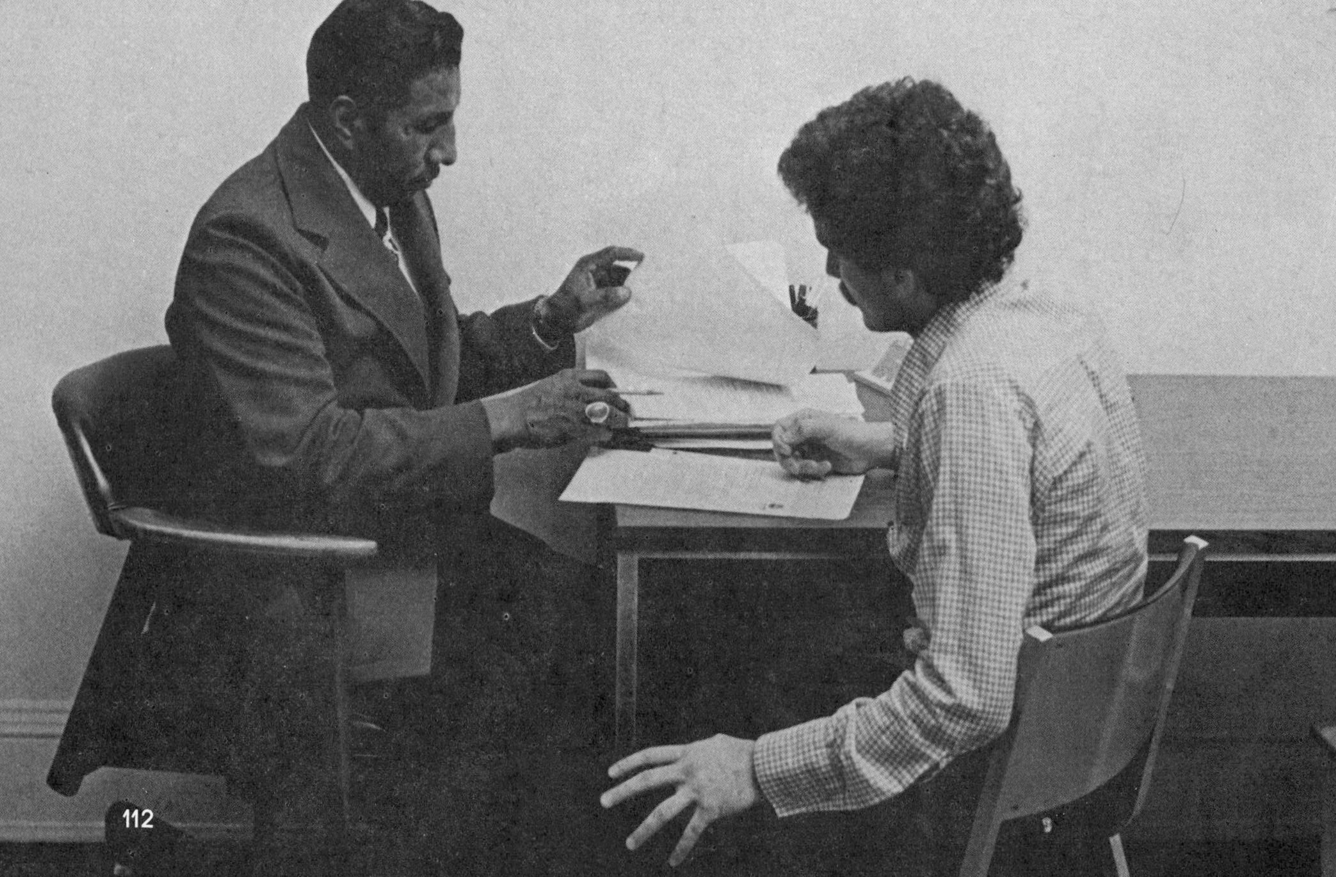

solution

New purchases are not used to compute the average daily balance. The chart below shows the computation.

Dates	Payment	Unpaid balance	Days	Weighted balance (Unpaid balance × Days)
Nov. 1–20	———	\$132.40	20	\$2648.00
Nov. 21	\$20.00	\$112.40	1	\$112.40
Nov. 22–30	———	\$112.40	9	\$1011.60
		Total	30	\$3772.00

The total days should equal the number of days in the month being used. November has 30 days.

Find the average daily balance.

Total weighted balance		Total days		Average daily balance	
\$3772.00	÷	30	≈	\$125.73	Rounded to the nearest cent

Find the amount of the finance charge.

Average daily balance		Monthly rate		Amount of finance charge	
\$125.73	×	.015	≈	\$1.89	Rounded to the nearest cent

Find the new balance.

\$132.40	Unpaid balance
− 20.00	Payment
\$112.40	Balance after payment

\$112.40	Balance after payment
1.89	Amount of finance charge
+ 13.14	Purchases
\$127.43	New balance

exercises

Each exercise gives all of the activity in one account for one month.

For exercises 1–5, the finance charge is 1% per month of the average daily unpaid balance. There is no finance charge on new purchases. Find the amount of the finance charge and the new balance in the account at the end of the month.

1. April 1: Unpaid balance is $145.00.
   April 11: Payment of $15.00
   No new purchases
2. January 1: Unpaid balance is $34.00.
   January 7: Payment of $10.00
   New purchases of $18.66
3. May 1: Unpaid balance is $235.89.
   No payment during the month
   New purchases of $76.54 and $33.65
4. March 1: Unpaid balance is $18.00.
   No payments or purchases
5. February 1: No unpaid balance
   No payment during the month
   New purchases of $8.67

For exercises 6–10, the finance charge is 1.5% per month of the average daily unpaid balance. There is no finance charge on new purchases. Find the amount of the finance charge and the new balance in the account at the end of the month.

6. July 1: Unpaid balance is $45.63.
   No payment during the month
   New purchases of $57.27
7. September 1: Unpaid balance is $88.14.
   September 22: Payment of $25.00
   No new purchases during the month
8. October 1: Unpaid balance is $133.84.
   October 15: Payment of $30.00
   New purchases of $4.78
9. August 1: Unpaid balance is $108.75.
   August 21: Payment of $60.00
   New purchases of $32.98 and $45.60
10. November 1: No unpaid balance
    No payment during the month
    New purchases of $55.73, $64.92, and $55.78

CALCULATOR EXERCISES

Some companies *do* include new purchases when they determine a customer's average daily unpaid balance. They do this only when the customer has an unpaid balance from the previous month.

Marla Tate has a credit card from a company that uses this method. The finance charge is 1.5% per month. Use the chart below to find the amount of the finance charge and the new balance in Marla's account on December 31.

	Dates	Payments	Purchases	Unpaid balance	Days	Weighted balance (Unpaid balance × Days)
	Dec. 1–8	——	——	$435.78	8	$3486.24
1.	Dec. 9	——	$23.97	$459.75	1	**a.**
2.	Dec. 10	$50.00	——	$409.75	**a.**	**b.**
3.	Dec. 11–14	——	——	**a.**	**b.**	**c.**
4.	Dec. 15	——	$12.31	**a.**	**b.**	**c.**
5.	Dec. 16–23	——	——	**a.**	**b.**	**c.**
6.	Dec. 24	——	$18.99	**a.**	**b.**	**c.**
7.	Dec. 25–28	——	——	**a.**	**b.**	**c.**
8.	Dec. 29	——	$15.79	**a.**	**b.**	**c.**
9.	Dec. 30–31	——	——	**a.**	**b.**	**c.**
10.	Total	**a.**	**b.**	——	31	**c.**

11. Find the average daily unpaid balance.

Total weighted balance		Total days		Average daily balance
	÷	31	=	

12. Find the amount of the finance charge.

Average daily balance		Monthly rate		Finance charge
	×	.015	=	

13. Find the new balance in the account.

Unpaid balance	$435.78
Total of payments	−
Balance after payments	
Balance after payments	
Total of purchases	
Finance charge	+
New balance	

Minimum Payments on Charge Accounts

Most companies that issue credit cards require the customer to make a **minimum payment.** The amount of the payment depends on the balance in the account.

A minimum-payment schedule may look like this:

New balance	Minimum payment
$0 to $10	Amount of balance
$10.01 to $100	$10
$100.01 to $200	$20
$200.01 to $400	15% of balance
Over $400	20% of balance

problem

Donald Reade had an unpaid balance in his account of $198.42. During the month, he made a payment of $20. Then he charged the purchase of kitchen cabinets that cost $227.68. His statement shows a finance charge of $2.68.

What is the new balance in Donald's account at the end of the month? What is the minimum payment required by the payment schedule?

solution

$198.42	Unpaid balance
− 20.00	Payment
$178.42	Balance after payment

$178.42	Balance after payment
2.68	Finance charge
+ 227.68	Purchases
$408.78	New balance

The minimum payment is 20% of $408.78.

$.20 \times \$408.78 \approx \$81.76$ Minimum payment, rounded to the nearest cent

exercises

Find the new balance in each account. Then use the schedule on page 116 to find the minimum payment.

	Unpaid balance	Payment	Balance after payment	Finance charge	Purchases	New balance	Minimum payment
	$198.42	$20.00	$178.42	$2.68	$227.68	$408.78	$81.76
1.	$52.16	$10.00	**a.**	$.78	$11.76	**b.**	**c.**
2.	$85.49	$10.00	**a.**	$1.13	$76.35	**b.**	**c.**
3.	$127.36	$20.00	**a.**	$1.61	$85.50	**b.**	**c.**
4.	$178.28	$20.00	**a.**	$2.37	$107.00	**b.**	**c.**
5.	$225.93	$35.00	**a.**	$2.86	$0	**b.**	**c.**
6.	$418.73	$125.00	**a.**	$4.41	$0	**b.**	**c.**
7.	$129.68	$120.00	**a.**	$.15	$0	**b.**	**c.**
8.	$629.58	$629.58	**a.**	$0	$9.55	**b.**	**c.**
9.	$386.27	$60.00	**a.**	$4.89	$134.77	**b.**	**c.**
10.	$455.39	$95.00	**a.**	$5.41	$60.67	**b.**	**c.**

The first person to sail alone around the world was Captain Joshua Slocum. He returned to Newport, Rhode Island, on June 27, 1898, to end his 74,000 kilometer voyage. His trip took 3 years, 2 months, and 2 days.

Use the diagram to discover an unusual fact about Captain Slocum. The key to unraveling the diagram is the number 11.

C	M	T	L	O	O	I	N	M
C								T
S								O
I								A
T				11				W
H								N
I								A
D								O
W	K	P	W	S	D	N	O	U

Level-Payment Loans

For many people, the best credit arrangement is a **level-payment loan.** This type of loan is repaid in equal monthly **installments.**

The calculations needed to determine the amount of the payment are very complicated, so lenders use a table like the one on page 406.

problem

Donna Delfonso wants to borrow $300 to pay dental bills. She plans to repay the loan in 6 equal monthly installments. The interest on the loan will be 9% per year of the unpaid balance. What will Donna's monthly payment be?

solution

Use the portion of the table shown.

Annual rate	Monthly Payment per $1 Borrowed 6 mo.	12 mo.
7%	.17008	.08653
8%	.17058	.08699
8.5%	.17082	.08722
9%	.17107	.08745
9.5%	.17131	.08768
10%	.17156	.08792

Find the row for an annual rate of 9% and the column for 6 monthly payments. The entry from the table is .17107.

Multiply this number by the amount borrowed.

$\$300 \times .17107 \approx \$51.32$ Rounded to the nearest cent

The monthly payment will be $51.32.

exercises

Use the table on page 406 to find the amount of the monthly payment for each of these level-payment loans. Round the answers to the nearest cent.

1. $500 at 8.5% for 6 months
2. $350 at 10% for 12 months
3. $700 at 9.5% for 6 months
4. $875 at 12% for 36 months
5. $300 at 22% for 30 months
6. $1100 at 14% for 24 months
7. $950 at 16% for 24 months
8. $950 at 16% for 36 months
9. $2500 at 18% for 18 months
10. $2500 at 12% for 18 months

Each month, part of the payment is used to pay one month's interest. The rest of the payment reduces the amount owed.

problem

How much will Donna still owe on her \$300 loan after she has made the first payment?

solution

Find the amount of interest for one month. Use the formula for simple interest.

$9\% = \frac{9}{100}$

$1 \text{ mo.} = \frac{1}{12} \text{ year}$

$I = p \times r \times t$

$I = \$300 \times \frac{9}{100} \times \frac{1}{12}$

$I = \$2.25$

Find the amount still owed after the first payment.

\$300.00	Amount owed
+ 2.25	Interest for 1 month
\$302.25	Total owed

\$302.25	Total owed
− 51.32	Payment
\$250.93	Amount still owed

exercises

Complete the table to find Donna's schedule for repaying the loan.

	End of month	Amount owed	Interest for 1 month	Total owed	Payment	Amount still owed
	1	\$300.00	\$2.25	\$302.25	\$51.32	\$250.93
11.	2	\$250.93	a.	b.	\$51.32	c.
12.	3	a.	b.	c.	\$51.32	d.
13.	4	a.	b.	c.	\$51.32	d.
14.	5	a.	b.	c.	\$51.32	d.
15.	6	a.	b.	c.	\$51.32	d.
16.	Total	——	a.	——	b.	——

Installment Buying

Instead of paying the full price at the time of purchase, people often pay only part of the price, the **down payment.** The remainder is **financed,** paid in monthly installments. Buying on an installment plan is similar to borrowing money with a level-payment loan.

Like all credit arrangements, buying on an installment plan costs more than paying in cash. The additional cost is the finance charge.

problem

Mr. and Mrs. Jamison are buying a color television set. The price, including tax, is $522.85. They sign an installment contract, agreeing to pay 10% of the price as a down payment. The remainder, plus a finance charge, will be paid in 18 monthly installments of $30.47 each. What is the amount of the finance charge on the Jamisons' purchase?

solution

Find the amount of the down payment.

$522.85	Cash price
× .10	10% = .10
$52.285 ≈ $52.29	Down payment

Find the amount financed.

$522.85	Cash price
− 52.29	Down payment
$470.56	Amount financed

Find the total paid in installments.

$30.47	Installment payment
× 18	Number of payments
$548.46	Total paid in installments

Find the amount of the finance charge.

$548.46	Total paid in installments
− 470.56	Amount financed
$77.90	Finance charge

exercises

Complete the table to find the amount of the finance charge on each item.

	Item	Cash price	Down payment	Amount financed	Installments			Finance charge
					Number of months	Monthly amount	Total paid in installments	
	TV set	$522.85	10%	$470.56	18	$30.47	$548.46	$77.90
1.	Tool set	$225.75	———	$225.75	12	$20.91	a.	b.
2.	Lawn mower	$234.15	———	$234.15	18	$15.16	a.	b.
3.	Refrigerator	$529.95	$60.00	a.	24	$23.92	b.	c.
4.	Rug	$162.75	$25.00	a.	12	$12.76	b.	c.
5.	Water heater	$149.20	$15.00	a.	30	$5.72	b.	c.
6.	Typewriter	$270.89	$30.00	a.	24	$12.26	b.	c.
7.	Furniture	$358.60	10%	a.	36	$11.99	b.	c.
8.	Air conditioner	$397.95	20%	a.	24	$16.20	b.	c.
9.	Oven	$367.45	30%	a.	36	$9.56	b.	c.
10.	Sewing machine	$280.35	10%	a.	30	$10.76	b.	c.

Use the table on page 406 and the method shown on page 118 to find the amount of the monthly payment for these installment plans. Also find the total paid in installments and the amount of the finance charge.

	Amount financed	Annual rate	Installments			Finance charge
			No. of months	Monthly amount	Total paid	
11.	$500	16%	12	a.	b.	c.
12.	$500	16%	24	a.	b.	c.
13.	$500	16%	36	a.	b.	c.
14.	$500	18%	12	a.	b.	c.
15.	$500	18%	24	a.	b.	c.
16.	$500	18%	36	a.	b.	c.
17.	$600	16%	24	a.	b.	c.
18.	$600	16%	36	a.	b.	c.

Comparing Credit Plans

People can often find more than one credit plan to finance a major purchase. They should compare the plans before deciding which one to use.

problem

Phyllis needs to buy a new \$1850 furnace. She can borrow \$1850 from her credit union at an annual rate of 12%. She would repay the credit union \$87.08 per month for 2 years.

She could also finance the \$1850 through the dealer at an annual rate of 16%. She would pay the dealer \$65.05 per month for 36 months. What is the cost of credit for each plan? Which plan costs less?

solution

Find the cost of borrowing the money from the credit union.

$\$87.08 \times 24 = \$2089.92$ Total repaid

\$2089.92	Total repaid
− 1850.00	Amount borrowed
\$239.92	Cost of borrowing from the credit union

Find the cost of financing through the dealer.

$\$65.05 \times 36 = \$2341.80$ Total repaid

\$2341.80	Total repaid
− 1850.00	Amount financed
\$491.80	Cost of financing through the dealer

Borrowing from the credit union would cost Phyllis less.

exercises

Two appliance dealers are offering the same model of home freezer for $379.95.

1. Dealer A will finance the purchase for 18 months with monthly payments of $24.81. What is the cost of credit for this plan?
2. Dealer B offers a 24-month payment plan with monthly payments of $18.97. What is the cost of credit for this plan?
3. Which plan costs less?

Al needs to borrow $500 to install new equipment in his machine shop.

4. He can borrow the money on a level-payment loan and repay it in 6 monthly installments of $85.66 each. What is the cost of credit for this plan?
5. He can borrow the money on a promissory note at 9.5% interest for 6 months. What is the cost of credit for this plan?
6. Which plan costs less?

Gladys needs to borrow $2100 to pay medical expenses.

7. She can borrow the money at 10% for 30 months on a level-payment loan. Find the amount of the monthly payment for this loan. (See page 118.)
8. She can borrow the money at 12% for 36 months on a level-payment loan. Find the amount of the monthly payment for this loan.
9. Gladys knows that the most she can repay is $70 per month. Which credit plan will fit into her budget?

George is buying a motorbike for $485.79.

10. He can use his credit card to make the purchase. Use the schedule on page 116 to find the amount of his minimum monthly payment for the first month.
11. George could buy the bike on an installment plan. The contract calls for 18 monthly payments and an annual rate of 20%. What would be the amount of his monthly payment? (See page 118.)
12. Which monthly payment is less?

Emily owes $400 on one of her credit-card accounts. She is trying to decide how to pay it.

13. She could borrow $400 from her savings and loan association at 11%. She would repay the loan in 4 payments of $102.30 each. Find the cost of credit for this plan.
14. She could pay $100 per month on her charge account and pay finance charges of 1.5% per month on the unpaid balance. Complete the table to find the cost of credit for this plan.

Unpaid balance	Payment	Balance after payment	Finance charge (1.5%)	New balance
$400	$100	$300	$4.50	$304.50
$304.50	$100			
	$100			
	$100			
		$0	$0	$0
Total	——	——		——

15. Which plan costs less?

skills tune-up

Dividing whole numbers, pages 12-13

Find the quotient.

1. 5208 ÷ 2
2. 2777 ÷ 8
3. 1281 ÷ 7
4. 4836 ÷ 6
5. 4961 ÷ 3
6. 2496 ÷ 5
7. 4413 ÷ 99
8. 1843 ÷ 17
9. 6179 ÷ 59
10. 8471 ÷ 43
11. 2265 ÷ 55
12. 3192 ÷ 36
13. 5954 ÷ 13
14. 4432 ÷ 78
15. 9848 ÷ 47
16. 9639 ÷ 81
17. 2861 ÷ 63
18. 74,525 ÷ 23
19. 38,024 ÷ 56
20. 53,585 ÷ 69
21. 410,785 ÷ 71
22. 306,949 ÷ 84
23. 595,882 ÷ 72
24. 496,318 ÷ 706
25. 72,741 ÷ 835

Dividing decimals, pages 12-13

Find the quotient to the nearest thousandth.

1. 16.54 ÷ 9
2. 40.4 ÷ 6
3. 13.78 ÷ 21
4. 43.92 ÷ 53
5. 4.079 ÷ 45
6. 1.968 ÷ 76
7. .0065 ÷ .34
8. .0172 ÷ .62
9. .8 ÷ 7.4
10. 1.2 ÷ 3.3
11. 47.94 ÷ 7.5
12. 10.46 ÷ 4.9
13. .685 ÷ .15
14. 2.632 ÷ .46
15. 84 ÷ .3
16. 45 ÷ .9
17. 8.7 ÷ 1.54
18. 2.55 ÷ 8.65
19. 5.64 ÷ 7.19
20. 5.78 ÷ 3.75
21. .1565 ÷ 2.91
22. .618 ÷ .316
23. .992 ÷ .714
24. .3922 ÷ .081
25. .5927 ÷ .082

Multiplying fractions and mixed numbers, pages 16-17

1. $\frac{2}{5} \times \frac{1}{3}$
2. $\frac{3}{4} \times \frac{1}{4}$
3. $\frac{3}{5} \times \frac{1}{3}$
4. $\frac{1}{3} \times \frac{1}{2}$
5. $\frac{5}{6} \times \frac{3}{5}$
6. $\frac{7}{16} \times \frac{4}{7}$
7. $\frac{5}{9} \times 12$
8. $30 \times \frac{3}{10}$
9. $\frac{2}{5} \times 4\frac{1}{2}$
10. $5\frac{1}{4} \times \frac{2}{7}$
11. $5\frac{5}{8} \times \frac{8}{9}$
12. $3\frac{3}{4} \times 1\frac{1}{2}$
13. $\frac{1}{2} \times 6\frac{1}{4}$
14. $4 \times 1\frac{6}{7}$
15. $2\frac{4}{5} \times 2\frac{1}{7}$
16. $1\frac{1}{2} \times 8\frac{1}{2}$
17. $6 \times 2\frac{5}{8}$
18. $9\frac{3}{4} \times 2\frac{2}{3}$
19. $\frac{5}{6} \times \frac{9}{14} \times \frac{2}{3}$
20. $4 \times 6\frac{3}{4} \times \frac{2}{5}$

Chapter 6

review

Promissory notes, pages 108–109

A promissory note for $1800 is due in 60 days. The interest rate is 8.5%.

1. Find the amount of interest due in 60 days.
2. Find the total amount due in 60 days.

Credit card finance charges, pages 110–111

Unpaid balance: $127.30 Payment: $20.00 Finance charge: 1.5% per month of the balance after payments

3. Find the amount of the finance charge on this account.

Credit counselor, pages 112–114

September 1: Unpaid balance is $90.60. September 11: Payment of $30.00 No purchases during the month.

4. Find the average daily balance in this account during the month of September.

Minimum payments on charge accounts, pages 116–117

Unpaid balance: $75.00 Payment: $20.00 Purchases: $55.00 Finance charge: $.83

5. What is the new balance in this account?
6. Find the minimum payment required on this account. (Use the minimum-payment schedule on page 116.)

Level-payment loans, pages 118–119

7. Find the amount of the monthly payment on a level-payment loan of $600 at 12% for 18 months. (Use the table on page 406.)

Installment buying, pages 120–121

Cash price: $375.16 Down payment: 10% Payment plan: 24 monthly payments of $16.85 each

8. What is the amount financed by this installment plan?
9. What is the total paid in installments?

Comparing credit plans, pages 122–123

10. What is the cost of credit for the installment plan of exercises 8–9?

Chapter 6

test

1. A promissory note for $2000 is due in 90 days. The interest rate is 9%. Find the amount of interest due in 90 days.

2. Find the total amount due in 90 days on the promissory note of exercise 1.

Unpaid balance: $150.00 Payment: $30.00 Finance charge: 1% per month of the balance after payments

3. Find the amount of the finance charge on the account above.

April 1: Unpaid balance is $75.00. April 21: Payment of $15.00 No purchases during the month

4. Find the average daily balance in the account above during April.

Unpaid balance: $45.00 Payment: $10.00 Purchases: $25.00 Finance charge: $.53

5. What is the new balance in the account above?

6. What is the minimum payment required on the new balance of exercise 5? (Use the minimum-payment schedule on page 116.)

7. Find the amount of the monthly payment on a level-payment loan of $1000 at 14% for 24 months. (Use the table on page 406.)

Cash price: $450.00 Down payment: $90.00 Payment plan: 24 monthly payments of $18.00 each

8. What is the amount financed by the installment plan above?

9. What is the total paid in installments for the plan of exercise 8?

10. What is the cost of credit for the installment plan of exercises 8–9?

Unit 2

Choose the best answer.

1. Carol earns $4.50 per hour as a typist. What is her gross pay for working a 38-hour week?

   A $167.00 C $171.38

   B $161.00 D $171.00

2. Ralph made $178 in tips during one week. He gives 20% of his tips to other employees. What was Ralph's share of the tips for this week?

   A $160.20 C $35.60

   B $142.40 D $124.60

3. Ted sells cleaning supplies to factories for a straight commission of 40%. How much did he earn on a sale of $982?

   A $589.20 C $396.80

   B $362.80 D $392.80

4. Maria sells sewing machines. She is paid $105 per week plus a commission of 6% of all sales over $1000. Last week she sold $1800 worth of sewing machines. What was her gross pay?

   A $48 C $213

   B $153 D $108

5. The weekly gross pay earned by Dion Davis is $180. His deductions are $25.80 for federal income taxes and $10.53 for social security. What is Dion's net pay?

   A $154.20 C $143.67

   B $36.33 D $169.47

6. Su Lin had these checks to deposit: $135.48, $97.20, and $9.34. If she wanted $80 in cash, how much did she deposit in her account?

   A $162.02 C $106.54

   B $242.02 D $322.02

7. Laura Whitebird had a balance of $1479.28 in her checking account. She wrote a check for $387.09. Find the new balance.

   A $1866.37 C $1092.19

   B $1112.21 D $1092.21

8. The ending balance on a bank statement is $427.32. There is one outstanding deposit of $150.50 and one outstanding check of $39.84. What is the adjusted statement balance?

   A $316.66 C $236.98

   B $617.66 D $537.98

9. A savings account of $1600 earns 5% simple interest. Find the amount of interest the account will earn in 9 months.

A $60 **C** $720

B $80 **D** $50

10. Use the table on page 102 to find the amount of interest on $300 at 6% compounded annually for 3 years.

A $357.30 **C** $358.23

B $57.30 **D** $58.23

11. A promissory note for $1500 is due in 30 days. The interest rate is 8%. Find the amount of interest due in 30 days. (Use the ordinary method of 360 days in a year.)

A $120 **C** $10

B $360 **D** $240

12. Unpaid balance: $95.50
Payment: $50.00
Finance charge: 1.5% per month of the balance after payments

Find the amount of the finance charge on this account. Round the answer to the nearest cent.

A $1.43 **C** $.68

B $.75 **D** $.71

13. Find the minimum payment required on a charge account with a new balance of $230.20. (Use the table on page 116.)

A $20.00 **C** $34.58

B $46.04 **D** $34.53

14. Find the amount of the monthly payment on a level-payment loan of $500 at 10% for 18 months. (Use the table on page 406.)

A $30.03 **C** $30.26

B $30.08 **D** $30.96

15. The Wilsons need to finance $495 for the purchase of a sofa. There will be 12 monthly installments of $45.84 each. Find the total paid in installments.

A $594.00 **C** $560.08

B $549.08 **D** $550.08

16. What is the amount of the finance charge for the installment plan in exercise 15?

A $54.08 **C** $99.00

B $55.08 **D** $65.08

unit three

Transportation

Chapter 7

Buying a Car

Chapter 8

Automobile Operating Expenses

Chapter 9

Travel

Chapter 7

Buying a Car

We are a mobile society. Almost 140 million cars and trucks are on the road today. Buying an automobile is a major expense for most consumers.

Buying a Used Car

Teri Bright wants to buy a used car. She must consider the **total cost** of the car. Besides price, the total cost includes **sales tax,** a **title fee,** a **license plate fee,** and any repairs needed on the car.

problem

Teri wants to buy a used car from a friend. The price of the car is $985. The state sales tax is 4% of the price of the car. There is a title fee of $3.00. The license plate fee is $18.00. Teri took the car to a mechanic and found that the car needed a tune-up that would cost $62.45. What is the total cost of the car?

solution

Find the state sales tax.

4% of $985

.04 × $985 = $39.40

Find the total cost of the car.

$985.00	Price
39.40	Sales tax
3.00	Title fee
18.00	License plate fee
+ 62.45	Repairs
$1107.85	Total cost

The total cost of the car is $1107.85.

exercises

Complete the table for each used car.

	Price	Sales tax	Amount of sales tax	Title fee	License plate fee	Repairs	Total cost
	$985	4%	$39.40	$3.00	$18.00	$62.45	$1107.85
1.	$725	5%	a.	$8.00	$20.00	$42.50	b.
2.	$1200	4%	a.	$4.00	$30.00	$81.45	b.
3.	$2000	3%	a.	$5.50	$22.00	—	b.
4.	$1395	—	—	$10.00	$54.00	$160.00	a.
5.	$1860	7%	a.	$6.00	$18.00	—	b.
6.	$2995	6%	a.	$9.50	$75.00	—	b.
7.	$3575	—	—	$7.00	$100.00	$57.95	a.
8.	$4350	4.5%	a.	$12.50	$48.00	—	b.
9.	$2765	2.5%	a.	$3.50	$35.00	$64.15	b.

Floyd Gates wants to buy a used car. The state sales tax is 4%. There is a city sales tax of 1.5%. The title fee in his state is $4.50. Floyd can buy a 6-month license plate for $15.00.

10. The price of a subcompact car is $870.

a. Find the state sales tax.

b. Find the city sales tax.

c. The car needs new spark plugs. Floyd can do the work himself for a cost of $11.80. Find the total cost of the car.

11. The price of a compact car is $920.

a. Find the state sales tax.

b. Find the city sales tax.

c. This car is from a dealer and does not need any repairs. Find the total cost of the car.

12. Find the difference in the total costs for the subcompact and the compact cars.

Martha O'Brien wants to buy a used car. The state sales tax is 5%. The title fee is $6.00.

13. The price of a full-sized car is $1595. The license plate fee is $34.00. The car needs a new muffler that would cost $125. What is the total cost of the car?

14. The price of a mid-sized car is $1625. The license plate fee is $22.00. The car needs new brakes that will cost $75.35. What is the total cost of the car?

15. Find the difference in the total costs for the full-sized and the mid-sized cars.

Buying a New Car

The **standard equipment** and some of the **optional equipment** (options) for a mid-sized car are listed below. The **sticker price** of a car is the **base price** plus the cost of the optional equipment.

Mid-Sized Car (2-door model) Standard Equipment Base Price: $4725	
V-6 engine	Coil spring suspension, front and rear
3-speed manual transmission	Front and rear energy-absorbing bumpers
Fiberglass-belted, blackwall tires	Bumper protective strips, front and rear

Mid-Sized Car (2-door model) Optional Equipment			
Engine		**Tires**	
V-8 engine with 2-barrel carburetor	$167	Fiberglass-belted, whitewall tires (with V-6 engine only)	$41
V-8 engine with 4-barrel carburetor	$222	Steel-belted, blackwall tires	
Chassis		with V-6 engine	$67
Power steering	$147	with V-8 engine	N.E.C.*
Power front disc brakes (required with V-8 engine)	$61	Steel-belted, whitewall tires	
Automatic transmission	$282	with V-6 engine	$110
Entertainment		with V-8 engine	$43
AM radio	$79	Steel-belted, wide-oval, billboard-lettered tires	
AM-FM radio	$142	with V-6 engine	$136
AM-FM stereo radio with front and rear dual speakers	$233	with V-8 engine	$69
AM-FM stereo radio and tape player with front and rear dual speakers	$337	**Appearance and protection**	
Rear-seat speaker (single)	$21	Styled wheel covers	$57
Front and rear dual speakers	$44	Deluxe wire wheel covers	$99
Under-dash citizens band transceiver	$195	Hatch roof	$587
Comfort and convenience		Landau top	$120
Air conditioner	$499	Vinyl top	$111
Speed control	$80	Protective body-side moldings	$27
Tinted glass	$54	Door-edge guards	$9
Power windows	$108	Bumper guards, front and rear	$38
Electric rear-window defogger	$82	Special order paint	$134
		Body-side accent stripe	$45

*no extra charge

problem

The options Fred Gonzales wants on his new mid-sized car are automatic transmission, AM-FM radio, air conditioning, and steel-belted whitewall tires. Find the sticker price of Fred's car.

solution

Add to find the sticker price.

$4725	Base price
282	Automatic transmission
142	AM-FM radio
499	Air conditioner
+ 110	Steel-belted, whitewall tires
$5758	Sticker price

exercises

Find the sticker price of a mid-sized car with the options given. Use the base price and the list of options on page 134.

1. AM-FM stereo radio with front and rear dual speakers
   Air conditioner
   Tinted glass
   Fiberglass-belted, whitewall tires
   Landau top
2. V-8 engine with 4-barrel carburetor
   Power steering
   Power front disc brakes
   Automatic transmission
   AM-FM stereo radio and tape player with front and rear dual speakers
   Power windows
   Steel-belted, blackwall tires
   Bumper guards, front and rear
3. AM radio
   Rear-seat speaker
   Under-dash citizens band transceiver
   Air conditioner
   Speed control
   Styled wheel covers
   Vinyl top
   Special order paint

Nancy Fox wants to buy a new mid-sized car. She does not want to spend more than $5700. In exercises 4 and 5, find the sticker price of a car with the options listed. Tell whether Nancy could buy the car.

4. AM-FM radio
   Air conditioner
   Electric rear-window defogger
   Steel-belted, whitewall tires
   Deluxe wire wheel covers
   Protective body-side moldings
5. Power steering
   AM-FM radio
   Front and rear dual speakers
   Steel-belted, wide-oval, billboard-lettered tires
   Hatch roof
   Door-edge guards
   Body-side accent stripe

Jay Eigel wants to buy a new mid-sized car. The options that he wants are a V-8 engine with 2-barrel carburetor, power steering, power front disc brakes, and automatic transmission.

6. Find the sticker price of Jay's car.

Jay would also like an AM-FM radio, at least one extra speaker, and tires that are not standard.

7. List the least expensive additional equipment for Jay's car.
8. What is the sticker price of the car in exercise 7?
9. List the most expensive additional equipment for Jay's car.
10. What is the sticker price of the car in exercise 9?

Making an Offer for a New Car

Bud Ritter wants to buy a new car. He knows that people often negotiate the price of a car. To determine a reasonable price to offer to pay, some people follow this guideline:

> 90% of the sticker price is a reasonable offer for a new car.

The **selling price** of a car is the price finally agreed upon by the customer and the salesperson.

problem

Bud has selected a new subcompact car. The sticker price is $4480. Bud decides to follow the guideline. What will be Bud's first offer for the car?

solution

Find 90% of $4480.

$.90 \times \$4480 = \$4032$

Bud offers to buy the car for $4032.

After further discussion, the salesperson and Bud agree on a selling price of $4275.

exercises

Use the guideline on page 136 to find a reasonable offer for each car listed.

	Model	Sticker price
1.	Mid-sized	$6250
2.	Subcompact	$3740
3.	Full-sized	$7685
4.	Sports car	$5325
5.	Compact	$4910
6.	Station wagon	$6435
7.	Mid-sized	$5870
8.	Full-sized	$8265
9.	Subcompact	$4190
10.	Compact	$5345

A selling price of $5980 was agreed upon for the car in exercise 1.

11. Find the amount of the state sales tax if the tax is 6% of the selling price of the car.

12. The title fee is $4.50 and the license plate fee is $54.00. Find the total cost of the car.

A selling price of $3565 was agreed upon for the car in exercise 2.

13. Find the amount of the state sales tax if the tax is 5% of the selling price of the car.

14. The title fee is $8.50. The license plate fee is $35.00. Find the total cost of the car.

Shopping for a New Car

Dudley and Amy Davis want to buy a compact station wagon. They know the model they want and the options. They plan to **trade-in** the car they own now. The dealer offers them a **trade-in allowance** on their present car. The selling price less the trade-in allowance is the **net price,** the price the customer pays for the new car.

problem

Amy and Dudley have shopped at three car dealers and found these prices for the same car.

Dealer	Selling price	Trade-in allowance
Penn Sales Inc.	$4560	$825
Richard Motors	$4500	$830
Walker Motors Ltd.	$4455	$775

Which car dealer offers the lowest net price?

solution

For each dealer, subtract the trade-in allowance from the selling price of the new car. The difference is the net price of the car.

Penn Sales Inc. $\$4560 - \$825 = \$3735$

Richard Motors $\$4500 - \$830 = \$3670$

Walker Motors Ltd. $\$4455 - \$775 = \$3680$

Richard Motors offers the lowest net price of $3670.

exercises

For each exercise, find the net price at each dealer. Which car dealer offers the lowest net price?

1. Subcompact model

Dealer	Selling price	Trade-in allowance
a. Suburban Ltd.	$3885	$1260
b. Oak St. Motors	$3930	$1200
c. Field Sales	$4070	$1330

2. Compact model

Dealer	Selling price	Trade-in allowance
a. Pollard Motors	$4560	$585
b. Colonial Motors	$4590	$575
c. Central Sales	$4470	$500

3. Mid-sized model

Dealer	Selling price	Trade-in allowance
a. Lutz Motor Co.	$5650	$2480
b. Oak Park Sales	$5845	$2570
c. Heritage Ltd.	$5725	$2610

4. Full-sized model

Dealer	Selling price	Trade-in allowance
a. Cass St. Motors	$7340	$3580
b. Harris Inc.	$7265	$3425
c. North Motors	$7485	$3610

5. Station wagon

Dealer	Selling price	Trade-in allowance
a. Serota Motors	$6795	$1165
b. Prospect Sales	$6875	$1350
c. Viking Motors	$6680	$1030

6. Sports car

Dealer	Selling price	Trade-in allowance
a. Village Imports	$8360	$2435
b. Congress Motors	$8425	$2675
c. Nortown Imports	$8595	$2760

For each model in exercises 1–6, tell which price was used to determine the lowest net price. Was the lowest, middle, or highest selling price used? Was the lowest, middle, or highest trade-in allowance used? For Dudley and Amy Davis, the middle selling price and the highest trade-in allowance gave them the best deal.

	Model	Selling price	Trade-in allowance
	Compact station wagon	middle	highest
7.	Subcompact	a.	b.
8.	Compact	a.	b.
9.	Mid-sized	a.	b.
10.	Full-sized	a.	b.
11.	Station wagon	a.	b.
12.	Sports car	a.	b.

Financing a Car

Walter Choi is buying a new compact car. He must **finance** the car because he cannot pay the total cost of the car. Financing a car is very similar to installment buying. The down payment when you finance a car could include a **deposit** made at the time you order the car and a trade-in allowance on a used car. It could also include an amount paid when you pick up the car, called **cash on delivery.** The sum of the down payment and the total paid in monthly installments is the **deferred-payment price.**

problem

The total cost of the car Walter wants is $5460. His down payment is $1300. Walter can finance the rest of the cost for 36 months. His monthly payment will be $138.15. Find the finance charge for Walter's loan.

solution

Find the deferred-payment price.

Down payment		Total paid in monthly installments		Deferred-payment price
$1300	+	($138.15 × 36)		
$1300	+	$4973.40	=	$6273.40

Find the finance charge.

Deferred-payment price		Total cost		Finance charge
$6273.40	−	$5460	=	$813.40

The finance charge for Walter's loan is $813.40.

exercises

For each car financed, find the deferred-payment price and the finance charge.

	Model	Total cost	Down payment	Installments: Monthly payment	Installments: Number of months	Deferred-payment price	Finance charge
	Compact	$5460	$1300	$138.15	36	$6273.40	$813.40
1.	Compact	$4540	$1550	$139.36	24	a.	b.
2.	Full-sized	$5885	$1450	$155.93	36	a.	b.
3.	Station wagon	$6340	$2475	$230.35	18	a.	b.
4.	Subcompact	$3452	$1075	$89.87	30	a.	b.
5.	Mid-sized	$5735	$3575	$191.92	12	a.	b.
6.	Sports car	$6155	$3420	$98.87	36	a.	b.
7.	Full-sized	$7215	$3300	$107.00	48	a.	b.
8.	Compact	$4860	$750	$246.85	18	a.	b.
9.	Mid-sized	$5625	$3350	$106.04	24	a.	b.
10.	Subcompact	$3795	$1060	$250.74	12	a.	b.

career

Automobile Salesperson

Career Cluster: Social Service

Dorothy Gant is a car salesperson. For each car she sells, her commission is 25% of the dealer's **profit.** The profit is the selling price of the car less the amount the dealer paid for the car.

The dealer Dorothy works for also has a bonus plan. This plan is based on the number of cars sold by each salesperson.

Number of cars sold	Bonus
10–12	\$10 per car
13–15	\$13 per car
16 or more	\$15 per car

problem

During January, Dorothy sold 14 cars. The dealer's profit on the cars was \$4250. What was Dorothy's gross pay for January?

solution

Find her commission earnings.

25% of \$4250

$.25 \times \$4250 = \$1062.50$ Commission earnings

Find her bonus earnings.

Number of cars		Amount per car		Bonus earnings
14	×	\$13.00	=	\$182.00

Find Dorothy's gross pay.

	\$1062.50	Commission earnings
+	182.00	Bonus earnings
	\$1244.50	Gross pay

Dorothy's gross pay for January was \$1244.50.

exercises

Complete the table below showing Dorothy Gant's earnings for the year.

	Month	Number of cars sold	Dealer's profit	Commission earnings	Bonus earnings	Gross pay
	January	14	$4250	$1062.50	$182.00	$1244.50
1.	February	12	$3550	**a.**	**b.**	**c.**
2.	March	15	$4485	**a.**	**b.**	**c.**
3.	April	16	$4825	**a.**	**b.**	**c.**
4.	May	18	$5300	**a.**	**b.**	**c.**
5.	June	20	$5875	**a.**	**b.**	**c.**
6.	July	17	$5150	**a.**	**b.**	**c.**
7.	August	15	$4535	**a.**	**b.**	**c.**
8.	September	8	$2360	**a.**	**b.**	**c.**
9.	October	17	$5065	**a.**	**b.**	**c.**
10.	November	13	$3945	**a.**	**b.**	**c.**
11.	December	11	$3325	**a.**	**b.**	**c.**
12.	Total	**a.**	———	**b.**	**c.**	**d.**

Assume Dorothy sold one more car in February for $275 profit.

13. What would her commission earnings be for February?

14. What would her bonus earnings be for February?

15. What would her gross pay be for February?

CALCULATOR EXERCISES

In the fall, customers can buy the new model cars. At this time, the car manufacturer and the dealer usually offer customers a discount to sell last year's models.

The sticker price of a compact car is \$4795.26. The dealer is offering a discount of 5%. Find the selling price of the car.

Find 5% of \$4795.26.

$.05 \times \$4795.26 \approx \$239.76$ Rounded to the nearest cent

Subtract the discount.

$\$4795.26 - \$239.76 = \$4555.50$

The selling price of the car is \$4555.50.

Find the amount of the discount and the selling price of each car. Round the answers to the nearest cent.

	Model	Sticker price	Discount	Amount of discount	Selling price
	Compact	\$4795.26	5%	\$239.76	\$4555.50
1.	Full-sized	\$7356.28	5%	**a.**	**b.**
2.	Compact	\$4395.12	10%	**a.**	**b.**
3.	Mid-sized	\$5784.36	15%	**a.**	**b.**
4.	Station wagon	\$6883.84	10%	**a.**	**b.**
5.	Subcompact	\$3692.73	5%	**a.**	**b.**
6.	Sports car	\$6718.46	15%	**a.**	**b.**
7.	Compact	\$4637.21	20%	**a.**	**b.**
8.	Full-sized	\$8423.95	10%	**a.**	**b.**
9.	Subcompact	\$3745.39	5%	**a.**	**b.**
10.	Mid-sized	\$6371.47	15%	**a.**	**b.**

change of pace

Many Americans take for granted the water available in their homes. They can get a glass of water just by turning on the faucet. However, water conservation is becoming a major concern in many areas.

The U.S. receives 700 billion gallons of water from the environment each day. We use about 400 billion gallons daily. People who have compared population growth and other factors concerned with our water supplies, claim that we will soon exceed our share of water if our methods of use do not change. It is predicted that by the year 2000, Americans will use between one and two trillion gallons of water daily.

The average American uses 60 gallons of water per day in the home.

1. How many gallons of water does the average American use in one week?
2. How many gallons of water does the average American use in one year?
3. How many gallons of water does a family of four use in one week?
4. How many gallons of water does a family of four use in one year?
5. The average American uses 22 gallons of water to bathe each day. If you had a reduced-flow shower head installed, you could save 12% of the water used. How much water would be saved in one day? in one week? in one year?
6. A pinhole leak from a faucet wastes 170 gallons of water a day. How many gallons would be wasted in one week? in one year?
7. There are about 10 million people in the New York City area. About how much water is used in New York City in one day? in one week? in one year?
8. There are about 3,100,000 people in the San Francisco area. About how much water is used in San Francisco in one day?
9. In order to conserve water, the people of San Francisco could use only 50 gallons of water per day. If they did, how much water could be saved per day in San Francisco?
10. An open fire hydrant will release 30 gallons of water per second. How much water would be lost in one day?

skills tune-up

Subtracting whole numbers and decimals, pages 6-7

1. 87 − 53
2. 65 − 36
3. 33 − 9
4. 60 − 7
5. 92 − 25
6. 59 − 50
7. 84.3 − 63.2
8. 72.6 − 3.7
9. 45.34 − 27.14
10. 81.94 − 27.46
11. 42.27 − 21.3
12. 70.23 − 24.5
13. 7.051 − 3.27
14. 56.239 − 23.67
15. 89.104 − 67.832
16. 46.019 − 43.347
17. .37 − .007
18. 38.57 − 7.539
19. 62.7 − 61.8
20. 19.2 − 18.6
21. 21.789 − 16
22. 7.006 − 5
23. 68 − 41.4
24. 72 − 29.3
25. 3 − 1.04
26. 46 − 29.32

Writing percents, decimals, and fractions, pages 34-35

Write as a decimal.

1. 29%
2. 5%
3. 9%
4. 16%
5. 82%
6. 2%
7. 73%
8. $3\frac{3}{4}\%$
9. 18.42%
10. 6.3%
11. $67\frac{1}{2}\%$
12. 4.5%
13. 8.25%
14. $10\frac{1}{2}\%$
15. 18.4%
16. 7.5%
17. $8\frac{1}{4}\%$
18. 525%
19. $20\frac{1}{2}\%$
20. 115%
21. 405%
22. $5\frac{3}{8}\%$
23. 250%
24. 400%

Write as a percent.

25. .56
26. .83
27. .03
28. .08
29. .5
30. .17
31. .49
32. .9
33. .053
34. .528
35. .339
36. .075
37. .906
38. .159
39. .0125
40. .8237
41. .3225
42. .0875
43. .9054
44. 3.87
45. 5.06
46. 2.48
47. 1.121
48. 8.675

Percent problems, pages 36-38

1. 35% of 14 is ▒.
2. $3\frac{1}{4}\%$ of 600 is ▒.
3. Find 75% of 52.
4. Find 85% of 435.
5. What number is 9.2% of 2250?
6. What number is 5% of 340?
7. What number is 25% of 950?
8. 44% of ▒ is 11.
9. 65% of ▒ is 517.4.
10. 12% of ▒ is 40.8.
11. $3\frac{1}{2}\%$ of ▒ is 42.
12. 95% of ▒ is 57.
13. 82% of what number is 2.46?
14. 5.1 is 60% of what number?
15. ▒% of 1500 is 315.
16. ▒% of 190 is 5.7.
17. ▒% of 60 is 9.
18. ▒% of 48 is 6.
19. ▒% of 225 is 27.
20. What percent of 50 is 16?
21. What percent of 175 is 168?
22. 66 is what percent of 150?

Chapter 7

review

Buying a used car, pages 132-133

The price of a used car is \$1475.

1. The state sales tax is 5% of the price of the car. Find the amount of the state sales tax.
2. The title fee is \$6.50 and the license plate fee is \$32. The car needs repairs that will cost \$47.25. Find the total cost of the car.

Buying a new car, pages 134-135

3. The base price of a mid-sized car is \$4725. Find the sticker price of the car with these options. (Use the table on page 134.)

   Power steering
   AM-FM radio
   Air conditioner
   Bumper guards, front and rear

Making an offer for a new car, pages 136-137

4. A subcompact car has a sticker price of \$4290. Find a reasonable offer for the car. (Use the guideline that 90% of sticker price is a reasonable offer.)

Shopping for a new car, pages 138-139

5. The selling price of a new car is \$4360. The trade-in allowance on a used car is \$685. Find the net price.

Financing a car, pages 140-141

The total cost of Sam's new car is \$5725. He made a down payment of \$1700. Sam can finance the car for 24 months. His monthly payment is \$193.24.

6. Find the deferred-payment price.
7. Find the finance charge.

Automobile salesperson, pages 142-143

Tom Willis is an automobile salesperson. During November he sold 15 cars with a dealer's profit of \$4515.

8. Find Tom's commission earnings if he is paid 20% of the dealer's profit.
9. The dealer Tom works for follows the bonus plan shown on page 142. Find Tom's bonus earnings for November.
10. Find Tom's gross pay for November.

Chapter 7

test

The price of a used car is $2425.

1. Find the state sales tax if the tax is 3% of the price of the car.
2. The title fee is $7.00. The license plate fee is $45.00. Find the total cost of the car.
3. The base price of a mid-sized car is $4725. Find the sticker price of the car with the options listed. (Use the table on page 134.)

   Automatic transmission
   AM radio
   Tinted glass
   Fiberglass-belted, whitewall tires
   Landau top

4. A mid-sized car has a sticker price of $6140. Find a reasonable offer for the car. (Use the guideline that 90% of sticker price is a reasonable offer.)
5. The selling price of a new car is $6850. The trade-in allowance on a used car is $2475. Find the net price.

The total cost of Kate's new car is $4875. She made a down payment of $1300. Kate is financing the car for 36 months. Her monthly payment is $118.73.

6. Find the deferred-payment price.
7. Find the finance charge.

Janice Whitecrow is a car salesperson. During September she sold 12 cars with a dealer's profit of $3560.

8. Find Janice's commission earnings if she is paid 25% of the dealer's profit.
9. The dealer Janice works for uses the bonus plan shown on page 142. Find Janice's bonus earnings for September.
10. Find Janice's gross pay for September.

Chapter 8

Automobile Operating Expenses

How much does it cost to own and maintain your car? The typical automobile costs about $2000 per year to operate.

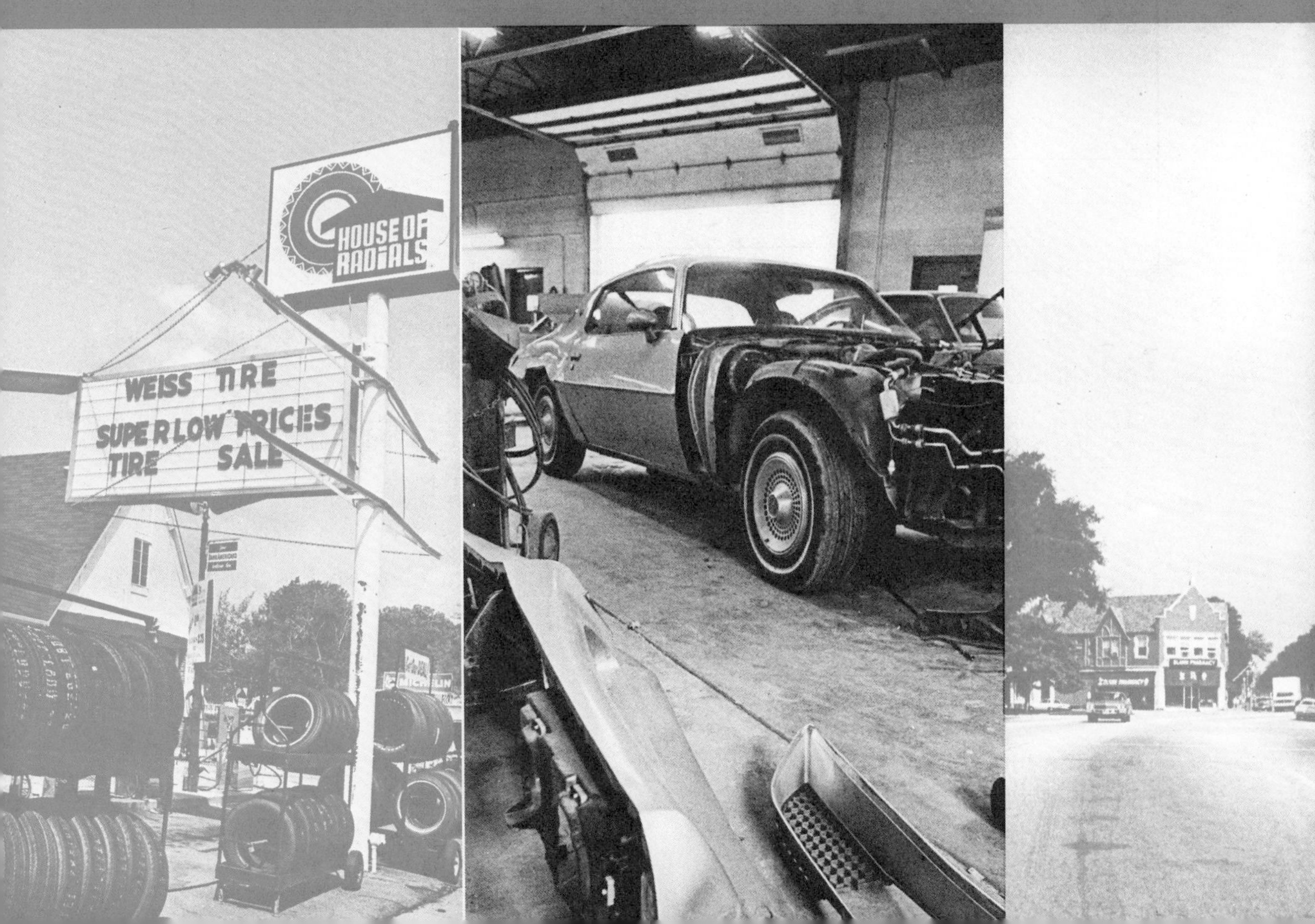

Finding Gasoline Costs

Your car's **fuel consumption,** the distance it travels on one liter of gasoline, can affect your gasoline costs.

Monica Shang and her brother Vincent kept records of how much gasoline they bought during October. Each of them started with a full tank of gasoline and filled the tank each time they needed more gas. Most of their driving is in the city.

problem

Monica drives a 6-cylinder mid-sized car. Find her car's fuel consumption. Then find the cost of the gasoline for each kilometer she traveled.

Oct.	Reading	Gasoline	Cost
1	15,302.5 km	full	---
16		45.7 L	\$ 8.22
31	15,975.2 km	56.3 L	\$10.13
		102.0 L	\$18.35

solution

Find the distance traveled.

15,975.2 km	Oct. 31 reading
−15,302.5 km	Oct. 1 reading
672.7 km	Distance traveled

Find the fuel consumption.

$$\frac{\text{Distance traveled}}{\text{Amount of gasoline}} = \text{Fuel consumption}$$

$$\frac{672.7 \text{ km}}{102 \text{ L}} \approx 6.6 \text{ km/L}$$

The car's fuel consumption is about 6.6 kilometers per liter.

Now find the cost of gasoline for each kilometer traveled.

$$\frac{\text{Total cost}}{\text{Distance traveled}} = \text{Cost per kilometer}$$

$$\frac{\$18.35}{672.7 \text{ km}} \approx \$.027, \text{ or } 2.7¢ \text{ per kilometer}$$

Monica's gasoline cost is about 2.7¢ for each kilometer she traveled.

exercises

Vincent Shang has an 8-cylinder full-sized car. He kept this record.

Oct.	Reading	Gasoline	Cost
1	41,850.4 km	full	- - -
10		47.5 L	$8.55
21		65.5 L	$11.79
31	42,579.9 km	54.0 L	$9.72

1. How many kilometers did Vincent travel during the month?
2. How many liters of gasoline did he buy?
3. Find his car's fuel consumption. Round your answer to the nearest tenth.
4. What was the total cost of the gasoline?
5. To the nearest tenth of a cent, find the cost of gasoline for each kilometer traveled.
6. Vincent drives about 10,000 km in a year. How much might he pay for gasoline during that time? (Hint: Multiply your answer to exercise 5 by 10,000.)

For each car, find its fuel consumption to the nearest tenth. Then find the cost of gasoline per kilometer. Round to the nearest tenth.

	Odometer reading (km)		Distance (km)	Amount of gasoline	Fuel consumption (km/L)	Total cost of gasoline	Cost per kilometer
	Oct. 1	Oct. 31					
7.	45,800.2	46,149.7	**a.**	57 L	**b.**	$11.40	**c.**
8.	62,521.3	63,069.3	**a.**	68.5 L	**b.**	$13.02	**c.**
9.	18,462.5	18,704.5	**a.**	60.5 L	**b.**	$12.40	**c.**
10.	13,520.9	13,976.9	**a.**	48 L	**b.**	$8.64	**c.**
11.	8,743.1	9,085.6	**a.**	76 L	**b.**	$15.20	**c.**
12.	38,465.0	38,883.0	**a.**	41.8 L	**b.**	$7.52	**c.**

Depreciation

The table and the graph show how the trade-in value of an "average" car can decrease, year after year. This loss in value is called **depreciation.**

The percents given in the table and the graph are based on the price of the car when it was new.

Average Trade-in Value	
After year	Percent of selling price
1	70%
2	55%
3	42%
4	33%
5	25%

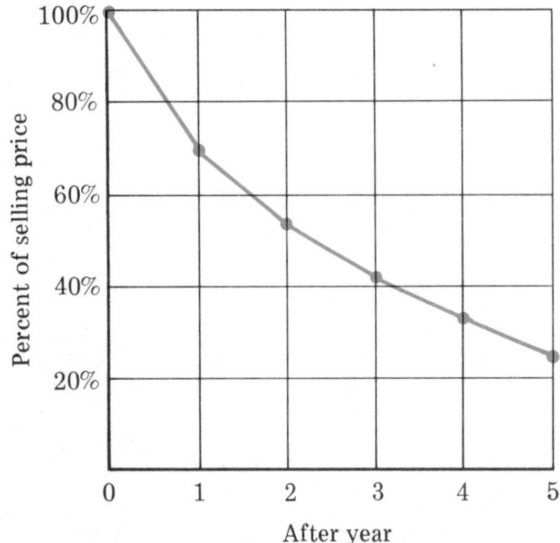

problem

Keith and Evelyn McLane bought a new \$5500 car four years ago. What is the trade-in value of the car now? How much has it depreciated?

solution

Find the trade-in value.

According to the table, the trade-in value after 4 years is 33% of the original selling price.

33% of \$5500

$.33 \times \$5500 = \$1815$ Trade-in value

Find the amount of depreciation.

\$5500	Selling price
− 1815	Trade-in value
\$3685	Depreciation

After 4 years, the trade-in value of the McLanes' car is \$1815. The car has depreciated \$3685 in 4 years.

exercises

The selling prices of ten different cars are given. For each car, find its trade-in value each year for 5 years. Use the percent table on page 152 to help you. Then subtract the trade-in value after 5 years from the selling price to find the car's depreciation after 5 years.

	Selling price	Trade-in value after					Depreciation after 5 years
		1 year	2 years	3 years	4 years	5 years	
1.	$5000	a.	b.	c.	d.	e.	f.
2.	$5300	a.	b.	c.	d.	e.	f.
3.	$5800	a.	b.	c.	d.	e.	f.
4.	$6000	a.	b.	c.	d.	e.	f.
5.	$6200	a.	b.	c.	d.	e.	f.
6.	$6600	a.	b.	c.	d.	e.	f.
7.	$7100	a.	b.	c.	d.	e.	f.
8.	$7700	a.	b.	c.	d.	e.	f.
9.	$8500	a.	b.	c.	d.	e.	f.
10.	$9000	a.	b.	c.	d.	e.	f.

Many automobile owners want to know an average loss in value for each year they own a car. They are interested in **average annual depreciation.**

problem

Julius Bennett is thinking about buying a new $6100 car and keeping it for 3 years. The car dealer estimates that the trade-in value then will be about $2550. What will be the total depreciation? What will be the average annual depreciation?

solution

Find the total depreciation.

Selling price		Trade-in value		Total depreciation
$6100	−	$2550	=	$3550

Find the average annual depreciation. Round the answer to the nearest dollar.

Total depreciation		Years owned		Average annual depreciation
$3550	÷	3	≈	$1183

exercises

Find the total depreciation and the average annual depreciation for each car. Round answers to the nearest dollar.

	Selling price	Trade-in value	Number of years owned
11.	$4000	$1680	3
12.	$4135	$1737	3
13.	$4850	$2668	2
14.	$5000	$2750	2
15.	$5650	$1865	4
16.	$5650	$1413	5
17.	$5650	$1074	6
18.	$5650	$848	7
19.	$8400	$1260	7
20.	$8400	$5880	1

A local rental agency often sells some of its cars. The price will depend partly on how much a car has depreciated. The agency bases the amount of depreciation on the age of the car in months.

If age of car is	Monthly rate of depreciation is
11 mo. or less	2.7%
12 mo. through 23 mo.	2.6%
24 mo. through 35 mo.	2.5%

This rule is used for computing the depreciation.

Monthly rate × Number of months × Original price = Total depreciation

problem

The agency has a car that was purchased 1 year 4 months ago for $5720. What is the total depreciation on this car?

solution

1 year 4 months = 16 months
The monthly rate of depreciation for 16 months is 2.6%, or .026.

$.026 \times 16 \times \$5720 \approx \$2380$ Total depreciation, rounded to nearest dollar

exercises

Use the percents given above. Find the total depreciation for each car. Round answers to the nearest dollar.

	Original price	Age of car
21.	$5720	21 months
22.	$5720	30 months
23.	$4500	9 months
24.	$4500	18 months
25.	$5200	24 months
26.	$5450	1 year 2 months
27.	$6325	1 year 7 months
28.	$6650	2 years 3 months
29.	$7000	1 year 11 months
30.	$7325	2 years 8 months
31.	$7500	1 year
32.	$8000	1 month

Automobile Mechanic

Career Cluster: Trades

Russell Brandau is a mechanic at his uncle's gas station. Most of his work involves tuning engines on a regular schedule and replacing parts that are worn out. Russell receives 40% of the charge for labor on each bill.

I HEREBY AUTHORIZE ALL REPAIR WORK AS DESCRIBED AND ALL NECESSARY REPLACEMENT OF PARTS. X Laura Red Eagle	CUSTOMER Laura Red Eagle		PHONE 555-0770	OFFICE USE ONLY
	ADDRESS 8 Angeline Dr.		CALL WHEN READY AM PM	
	MAKE	MODEL 8 cylinder, full-sized	ODOMETER 23,020	
PARTS	TIME RECEIVED 8 AM	TIME PROMISED 5 PM	WRITTEN BY Russ	
	LICENSE NO.	SERIAL NO.	DATE 11-27	

PARTS		JOB DESCRIPTION	LABOR
1 oil filter	4.95		
1 fuel filter	3.09	20,000-km Inspect.	
1 air filter	5.75	Engine tune-up	35.00
8 spark plugs	11.20	Cln. battery, replace PCV valve,	
1 set points	3.75	new air filter, gap new plugs,	
1 condenser	1.50	check distributor cap and rotor,	
		replace and gap points, adjust dwell,	
		check timing & choke, new fuel filter	
		CALL CUSTOMER IF REPAIRS NEEDED	
Total	30.24	Lube chassis	3.00

GAS, OIL, GREASE		BRANDAU'S GARAGE 4th St. & Highway A Canfield, Nebraska	
6 L oil @ 1.10	6.60	TOTAL LABOR	38.00
		TOTAL PARTS	
		GAS, OIL, GREASE	
		OTHER	
Total	6.60	TOTAL AMOUNT	

problem

Laura Red Eagle brought in her car for a 20,000-km inspection. What is the total amount of her bill? How much will Russell receive?

solution

Record the totals from the sections of the bill. Then add.

TOTAL LABOR	38.00
TOTAL PARTS	30.24
GAS, OIL, GREASE	6.60
OTHER	
TOTAL AMOUNT	74.84

The total amount of Laura's bill is $74.84.

Find 40% of the charge for labor.

40% of $38

$.40 \times \$38 = \$15.20$

Russell will receive $15.20.

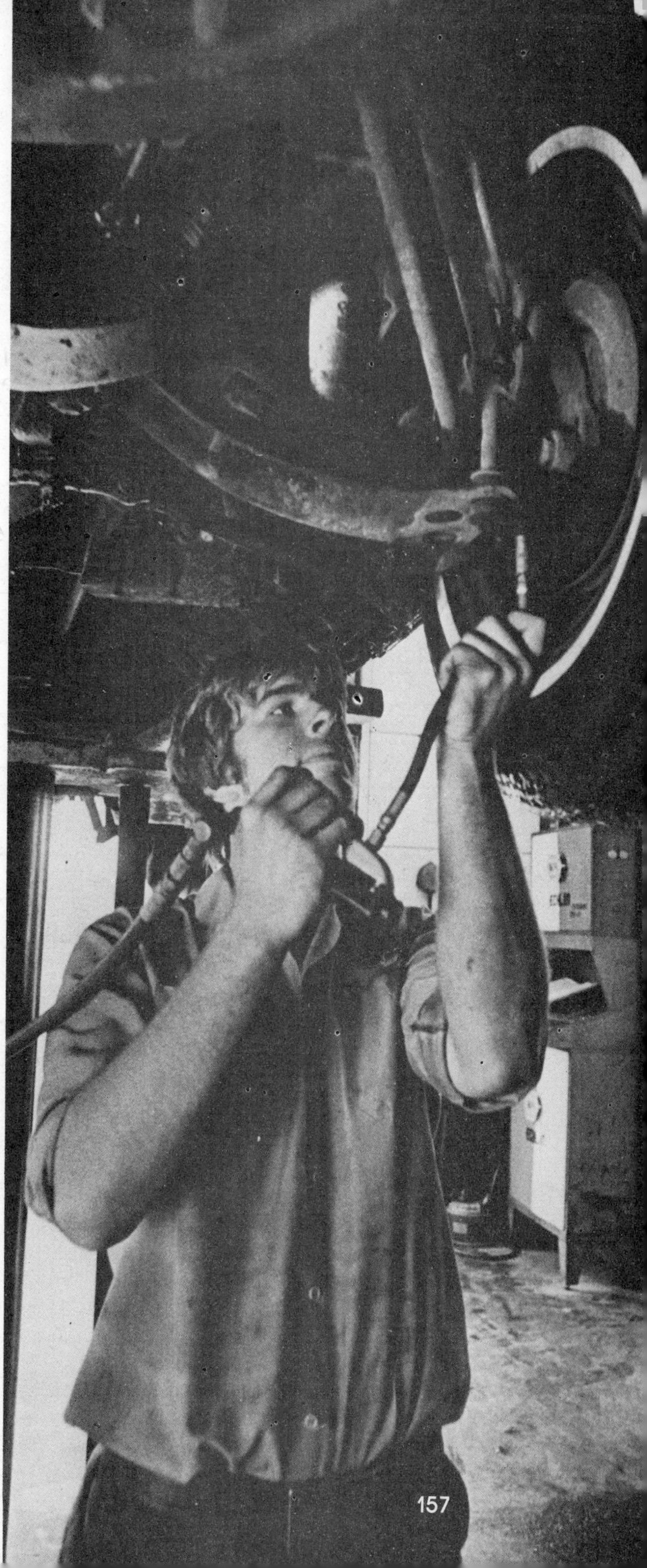

exercises

The work on Duane Beatty's car is done. Find the total for each section of his bill.

1.

JOB DESCRIPTION	LABOR
10,000 km tuneup	25.00
Put on 4 snow tires	6.00

2.

PARTS	
Oil filter	4.95
Gasket	.20

3.

GAS, OIL, GREASE	
5 L oil @ 1.10	5.50
Grease	2.00

4. What is the total amount of Duane's bill?
5. How much will Russell receive? (Find 40% of the charge for labor.)
6. Vicky Pamos's bill is for labor only. What is the total amount?

JOB DESCRIPTION	LABOR
aim headlights	6.40
adjust rear brakes	4.75
check ignition timing	7.50

7. How much will Russell receive from this bill?

Russell encourages customers to check their automobile-owner's manual to find out when parts should be replaced. The manual might contain a list like this.

Part	Replace every
Shock absorbers	30,000 km
Muffler/ Exhaust system	30,000 km
Brake-drum linings	30,000 km
Wheel cylinders	65,000 km
Carburetor	100,000 km

Find the total amount of each bill for replacing worn-out parts.

8. *Labor*

Reline drum brakes	$7.50
Make brake adjustment	$5.00
Replace front brake pads	$6.00
Check fluid in both master cylinders	no charge

Parts

2-wheel relining set	$13.00
2 pr. brake pads	$15.00

9. *Labor*

Replace muffler and tailpipe	$22.50

Parts

Muffler	$33.15
Pipe	$9.90
Clamps	$2.60
Hanger	$11.53
Hanger	$3.36

10. *Labor*
Replace front, rear shock absorbers $24.00

Parts
2 heavy-duty front shocks w/fittings $24.98
2 heavy-duty rear shocks w/fittings $24.98

11. Find the total amount charged for labor in the three bills in exercises 8-10.

12. How much will Russell receive from these three bills?

Many people keep records of all of their bills during the year. How much did each of these people spend last year on maintenance and repair?

13. Laura Red Eagle

Jan.	$6.25	June	$34.50
Mar.	$17.80	Aug.	$61.42
Apr.	$10.82	Dec.	$50.00

14. Duane Beatty

Feb.	$91.88	Aug.	$25.25
July	$16.10	Nov.	$70.04

15. Vicky Pamos

Jan.	$10.75	Aug.	$83.33
Feb.	$4.50	Sept.	$65.07
Mar.	$61.44	Nov.	$8.00
June	$25.00	Dec.	$90.21

change of pace

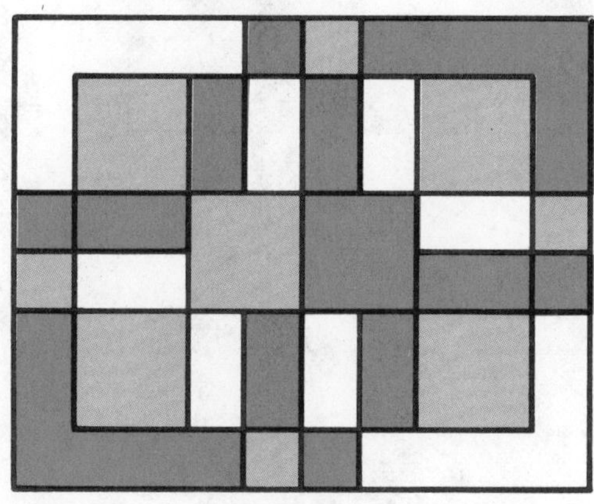

There are more than 30 squares in this picture. See if you can find them all.

Automobile Liability Insurance

If you injured someone with your car and the court decided that you owed that person $35,000, could you pay? Most people could not. Therefore, they buy **liability insurance.** They pay **premiums** to an insurance company, which agrees to pay certain accident costs.

Liability insurance has two parts. **Bodily injury insurance** protects you financially if someone else is injured by your car. **Property damage insurance** protects you if your car damages someone's property.

Many states require you to carry a minimum amount of liability insurance, such as "10/20/10" coverage. This means that in any one accident, the insurance company pays:

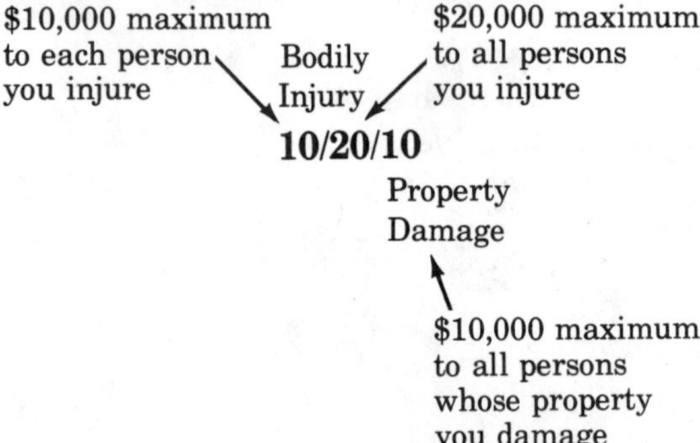

The premium that you pay for liability insurance depends on things like

- your age
- where you live
- how much you drive
- your driving record

These tables show how to figure annual premiums for drivers in a certain area. The basic rates given are for teenaged drivers. Other age groups have different basic rates.

Bodily Injury Insurance

Coverage	*Annual Premium*
10/20	Basic rate: Male $166 Female $95
25/50	Basic rate × 1.20
50/100	Basic rate × 1.33
100/300	Basic rate × 1.46
250/500	Basic rate × 1.56

Property Damage Insurance

Coverage	*Annual Premium*
10	Basic rate: Male $109 Female $60
25	Basic rate + $2
50	Basic rate + $3
100	Basic rate + $4

problem

Gloria Morales is 18. She wants to buy liability insurance with 50/100/25 coverage. What will be her annual premium?

solution

Find the premium for 50/100 coverage for bodily injury.

$95.00	Basic rate for female
× 1.33	Factor for 50/100
$126.35	Premium for bodily injury

Find the premium for $25,000 coverage for property damage.

$60.00	Basic rate for female
+ 2.00	Additional amount for $25,000
$62.00	Premium for property damage

Find the sum.

$126.35	Premium for bodily injury
+ 62.00	Premium for property damage
$188.35	Annual premium

Gloria will pay an annual premium of $188.35 for 50/100/25 liability insurance.

exercises

If your liability insurance is 25/50/10, what is the maximum the insurance company will pay

1. to each person you injure?
2. to all persons you injure?
3. to persons whose property you damage?

Find the premium that Gloria Morales would pay for bodily injury coverage of:

4. 25/50
5. 50/100
6. 100/300
7. 250/500
8. 10/20

What would Gloria pay for the following coverages in liability insurance?

9. 25/50/25
10. 50/100/50
11. 100/300/100
12. 250/500/100
13. 10/20/10

Gloria's brother Paul is 19. Find the annual premium he would pay for each amount of liability insurance.

14. 10/20/10
15. 25/50/25
16. 50/100/50
17. 100/300/100

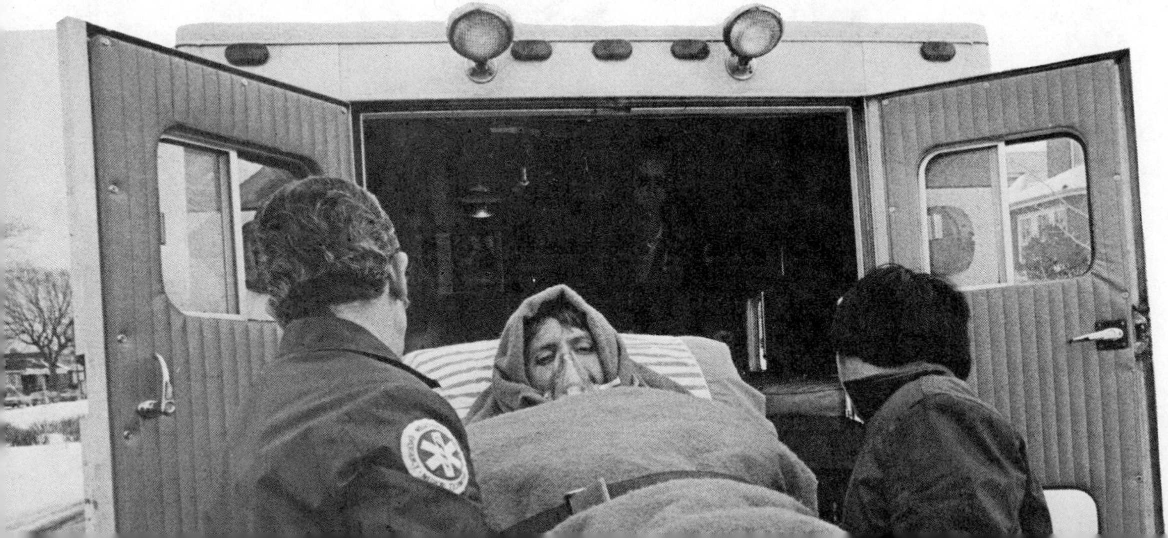

Automobile Collision and Comprehensive Insurance

Liability insurance is only one part of a total automobile insurance program. Many automobile owners also buy insurance to protect their cars. This kind of coverage is usually required if you expect to get an auto loan.

Collision insurance pays for repairs on your car in case of an accident.

Comprehensive insurance pays for repairs due to fire, theft, vandalism, or acts of nature, like floods.

To help figure the premium, an insurance company puts your car in a certain class, depending on its age and the equipment it has. You can have a lower premium if you agree to pay the first $100 of each repair bill. This feature is a **$100 deductible.** Other deductibles usually are available.

Annual Premiums for Collision and Comprehensive Insurance					
		Collision premium for		Comprehensive premium for	
Car	Driver	$50 ded	$100 ded	No ded	$50 ded
Class B	Teen female	$115	$85	$22	$10
	Teen male	$220	$160	$45	$20
	Married over 25	$60	$45	$20	$9
Class C	Teen female	$130	$95	$27	$13
	Teen male	$250	$185	$60	$26
	Married over 25	$65	$53	$26	$11
Class F	Teen female	$185	$140	$55	$25
	Teen male	$350	$260	$115	$52
	Married over 25	$100	$75	$50	$22

problem

Gloria Morales has a class C car. What would be her total annual premium for collision insurance with $100 deductible and comprehensive insurance with no deductible?

solution

Use the table on page 162. The car is "Class C." The driver is "Teen female" since Gloria is 18.

Find the collision premium.

Gloria's premium for "Collision $100 ded" is $95.

Find the comprehensive premium.

Gloria's premium for "Comprehensive No ded" is $27.

Find the total premium.

$95	Collision premium
+ 27	Comprehensive premium
$122	Total annual premium

exercises

In each exercise, find the total premium for collision and comprehensive insurance. Use the table on page 162.

	Driver	Class	Collision		Comprehensive		Total premium
			Deductible	Premium	Deductible	Premium	
	Teen female	C	$100	$95	None	$27	$122
1.	Teen male	C	$100	a.	None	b.	c.
2.	Married over 25	C	$100	a.	None	b.	c.
3.	Teen female	B	$50	a.	$50	b.	c.
4.	Teen male	B	$50	a.	$50	b.	c.
5.	Married over 25	B	$50	a.	$50	b.	c.
6.	Married over 25	F	$100	a.	$50	b.	c.
7.	Teen female	F	$100	a.	$50	b.	c.
8.	Teen male	F	$100	a.	$50	b.	c.
9.	Teen male	F	$50	a.	None	b.	c.
10.	Married over 25	B	$100	a.	$50	b.	c.

Annual Expenses

Gregory Brent, age 32, bought a new 6-cylinder mid-sized car 3 years ago. He financed the car with a two-year loan. This record shows his annual expenses.

	First year	Second year	Third year
Distance traveled	16,700 km	16,000 km	15,000 km
Depreciation	$1530.00	$765.00	$663.00
Fixed Costs			
Loan payments	$1870.92	$1870.92	—
Insurance			
Liability	$140.00	$150.00	$162.00
Collision/Comp	$77.00	$80.00	$70.00
License and fees	$40.00	$40.00	$40.00
Garage, tolls, parking	$200.00	$224.00	$224.00
Variable Costs			
Gas	$396.62	$436.15	$435.88
Repair, maintenance	$108.50	$130.39	$270.65
Radial tires	—	$120.85	—

problem

Find Greg's cost of operating his car for the first year. Then find his cost per kilometer traveled.

solution

Depreciation is stated.

$1530.00

Find the fixed costs.

$$\begin{array}{r} \$1870.92 \\ 140.00 \\ 77.00 \\ 40.00 \\ +\ \ 200.00 \\ \hline \$2327.92 \end{array}$$

Find the variable costs.

$$\begin{array}{r} \$396.62 \\ +\ \ 108.50 \\ \hline \$505.12 \end{array}$$

Find the total cost for the year.

$1530.00 + $2327.92 + $505.12 = $4363.04

Find the cost per kilometer traveled.

$4363.04 ÷ 16,700 ≈ $.261, or about 26.1¢ per kilometer

exercises

Use Greg's record for the second year. Find these amounts.

1. Depreciation
2. Fixed costs
3. Variable costs
4. Total cost for the year
5. Number of kilometers traveled
6. Cost per kilometer. Round the answer to the nearest tenth of a cent.
7. In the second year, which expense decreased?
8. What new expense did Greg have?

Use Greg's record for the third year. Find these amounts.

9. Depreciation
10. Fixed costs
11. Variable costs
12. Total cost for the year
13. Number of kilometers traveled
14. Cost per kilometer. Round the answer to the nearest tenth of a cent.
15. Why is the cost during the third year so much lower?

Byron Douglas and Christina Bookhultz are neighbors. One year ago, each of them bought a used car. They kept a record of their expenses. They also wrote these "driver profiles."

Name:	Christina Bookhultz	Byron Douglas
Age:	19	19
Locale:	Large city	Large city
Driving record for last 3 years:	2 minor accidents	2 minor accidents
Age of car:	3rd year	3rd year
Class of car:	C	F
Distance traveled	8000 km	10,000 km
Depreciation	$650.00	$840.00
Fixed Costs		
Loan payments	$745.20	$740.00
Insurance		
100/300/25 liability	$250.88	$441.70
Collision $100 ded	$118.75	$325.00
Comprehensive $50 ded	$16.25	$52.00
License, fees	$35.00	$45.00
Variable Costs		
Gas	$256.13	$410.91
Repairs, maintenance	$350.00	$326.02

Find these amounts for Christina.

16. Total cost for the year

17. Number of kilometers traveled

18. Cost per kilometer. Round the answer to the nearest tenth of a cent.

Find these amounts for Byron.

19. Total cost for the year

20. Number of kilometers traveled

21. Cost per kilometer. Round the answer to the nearest tenth of a cent.

22. How much did Christina pay for insurance for the year?

23. If she had not had the accidents, her premium would have been $311.95. How much extra did she have to pay because of her driving record?

24. How much did Byron pay for insurance for the year?

25. Without any accidents, Byron would have paid $665.36 for insurance. How much extra did he have to pay because of his driving record?

CALCULATOR EXERCISES

A car's fuel consumption usually gets worse if you drive faster or turn on the air conditioning. The table gives the fuel consumption rates of 7 different cars.

Fuel Consumption

	Without air conditioning					With air conditioning				
	Speed in km/h					Speed in km/h				
Car	48	64	80	96	112	48	64	80	96	112
	Kilometers per liter					Kilometers per liter				
T	9.16	8.53	8.12	7.58	7.08	7.89	7.78	7.56	7.37	6.91
U	10.06	10.45	8.70	6.30	5.70	7.83	7.75	6.67	5.88	4.63
V	9.73	8.25	8.62	7.56	6.33	8.94	7.40	7.32	7.37	5.70
W	7.76	8.50	6.94	6.70	5.79	6.87	7.15	6.93	5.98	5.59
X	8.64	8.50	7.44	6.87	6.32	7.15	7.13	6.82	6.19	5.68
Y	7.28	7.31	6.85	6.34	5.58	6.92	7.04	6.61	6.13	5.42
Z	7.79	8.20	6.64	6.04	5.42	7.30	7.82	6.18	5.28	4.63

At each speed, find the average of the fuel consumption rates of the 7 cars when the air conditioning is not used.

1. 48 km/h
2. 64 km/h
3. 80 km/h
4. 96 km/h
5. 112 km/h

At each speed, find the average of the fuel consumption rates of the 7 cars when the air conditioning is used.

6. 48 km/h
7. 64 km/h
8. 80 km/h
9. 96 km/h
10. 112 km/h

Use the fuel consumption rates for cars without air conditioning. Complete the table to find how much more gasoline is needed to drive at 80 km/h than at 64 km/h. Round to the nearest hundredth of a percent.

	Car	64 km/h rating (a)	80 km/h rating (b)	Change due to speed ($c = a - b$)	Percent more gasoline needed ($d = c \div b$)
	T	8.53	8.12	.41	5.05%
11.	Y	**a.**	**b.**	**c.**	**d.**
12.	Z	**a.**	**b.**	**c.**	**d.**
13.	W	**a.**	**b.**	**c.**	**d.**
14.	X	**a.**	**b.**	**c.**	**d.**
15.	U	**a.**	**b.**	**c.**	**d.**

Alternatives to Owning a Car

Some people choose not to own a car because they can use **public transportation**—buses, subways, trains, and taxicabs.

problem

Ruth Steele lives 35 km from her work in the city. She takes a bus to and from the train station in her town for $.25 each way. Ruth buys a monthly train ticket for $43.90. She walks to her office from the train station in the city. Find Ruth's cost of getting to and from work for one month. Assume that each month has 20 working days.

solution

Find the monthly cost of the bus.

Ruth takes the bus twice a day. Therefore, she takes 20 × 2, or 40, bus rides each month.

Cost of each trip		Number of trips		Bus cost per month
$.25	×	40	=	$10.00

The monthly cost of the train is given as $43.90.

Find the total monthly cost.

$10.00	Bus
+ 43.90	Train
$53.90	Total cost

It costs Ruth $53.90 per month to travel to and from work.

exercises

For exercises 1-6, find the monthly cost of traveling to and from work. Assume that each month has 20 working days.

1. $.25 bus fare each way
   $45.60 monthly train ticket
2. $65.50 monthly train ticket
   $2.50 taxicab fare each way
3. $.50 bus fare each way
   $.10 bus transfer each way
4. $.40 bus fare each way
   $.15 subway transfer each way
5. $.45 subway fare each way
   $.10 subway transfer each way
6. $2.00 per week to neighbor for ride to and from bus stop
   $.75 fare each way for express bus
7. Brett Bauman lives in one town and works in another. He takes two buses, one for $.60 each way and the other for $.75 each way. Find his monthly cost of getting to and from work.
8. Find Brett's cost for one year.
9. Brett travels about 24,000 km each year, to and from work. How much does he pay per kilometer?
10. Last year Brett drove his car to and from work. His annual expenses were about $2700. Divide $2700 by 24,000. How much did he pay per kilometer to get to and from work?

Another alternative to owning a car is **leasing** a car. A person pays a monthly fee to use a car. The car must be turned in at the end of the lease. A table that shows typical monthly leasing fees is given below.

Monthly leasing fees				
Model	12 mo.	24 mo.	30 mo.	36 mo.
Compact	$195	$147	$138	$135
Mid-sized	$212	$158	$148	$145
Full-sized	$258	$189	$178	$175

For exercises 11-22, multiply the monthly fee by the number of months to find the cost for leasing each car.

	Model	Number of months
11.	Compact	12
12.	Compact	24
13.	Compact	30
14.	Compact	36
15.	Mid-sized	12
16.	Mid-sized	24
17.	Mid-sized	30
18.	Mid-sized	36
19.	Full-sized	12
20.	Full-sized	24
21.	Full-sized	30
22.	Full-sized	36

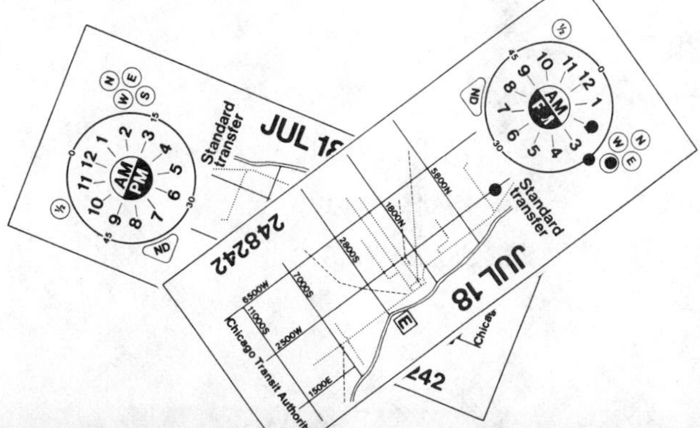

skills tune-up

Adding whole numbers and decimals, pages 6-7

1. 11 + 28 + 13
2. 6 + 14 + 57
3. 98 + 35 + 24
4. 46 + 30 + 72
5. 73 + 51 + 65
6. 84 + 48 + 71
7. 43 + 36 + 56 + 97
8. 83 + 9 + 21 + 45
9. 78 + 66 + 84 + 92
10. 232 + 101 + 367
11. 421 + 555 + 756
12. 459 + 870 + 508
13. 224 + 788 + 554
14. 7.2 + 3.46
15. 4.1 + 8.75
16. 29.24 + 12.63
17. 19.36 + 40.15
18. .5 + .7 + .6
19. 5.7 + 4.6 + 8.57
20. .06 + 1.08 + .19
21. 8.91 + 5.67 + 7.02
22. 8.78 + 5.9 + 4.38
23. .79 + .52 + .13 + .24
24. 5.81 + 4.76 + 4.49
25. 5.674 + 2.17 + .06
26. 3.01 + 4.2 + 5.6 + 8.7

Multiplying decimals, pages 10-11

1. .2 × .9
2. .4 × .5
3. .06 × .6
4. .03 × .7
5. .05 × .06
6. .11 × .04
7. .008 × .03
8. .06 × .011
9. 400 × .8
10. 700 × .6
11. 120 × .03
12. .05 × 900
13. .007 × 800
14. 400 × .001
15. .006 × .005
16. .003 × .009
17. 7000 × .0012
18. 2.1 × 6.8
19. 7.83 × 4.4
20. 5.2 × 8.23
21. 13.8 × .026
22. 8.367 × 9.72
23. 14.65 × 2.408
24. 3.72 × .4031
25. 46.093 × .136
26. .0028 × 5.673

Renaming fractions and mixed numbers, pages 14-15

Write as a mixed number.

1. $\frac{9}{4}$ **10.** $\frac{45}{8}$
2. $\frac{17}{5}$ **11.** $\frac{21}{16}$
3. $\frac{3}{2}$ **12.** $\frac{32}{24}$
4. $\frac{23}{6}$ **13.** $\frac{19}{8}$
5. $\frac{13}{6}$ **14.** $\frac{32}{6}$
6. $\frac{10}{7}$ **15.** $\frac{27}{15}$
7. $\frac{14}{3}$ **16.** $\frac{37}{12}$
8. $\frac{11}{2}$ **17.** $\frac{67}{9}$
9. $\frac{52}{12}$ **18.** $\frac{42}{28}$

Write as a fraction.

19. $1\frac{3}{8}$ **28.** $6\frac{3}{10}$
20. $3\frac{2}{3}$ **29.** 5
21. $2\frac{5}{6}$ **30.** 12
22. $7\frac{3}{4}$ **31.** $4\frac{7}{12}$
23. $5\frac{1}{5}$ **32.** $2\frac{3}{16}$
24. $2\frac{7}{8}$ **33.** $8\frac{6}{7}$
25. $9\frac{1}{2}$ **34.** $5\frac{9}{10}$
26. $6\frac{4}{5}$ **35.** $7\frac{1}{12}$
27. $3\frac{5}{9}$ **36.** $4\frac{8}{11}$

Chapter 8

review

Finding gasoline costs, pages 150-151

Daniel drove 1200 km during August. He bought 218 liters of gasoline, which cost $41.42.

1. Find his car's fuel consumption. Round the answer to the nearest tenth.
2. To the nearest tenth of a cent, find the cost of gasoline for each kilometer that Daniel traveled.

Depreciation, pages 152-155

3. Isabel bought a new $5600 car 3 years ago. What is the trade-in value of the car now? (Use the guideline that after 3 years, the trade-in value is 42% of the original selling price.)
4. How much has Isabel's car depreciated?

Automobile mechanic, pages 156-159

5. On a repair bill, the charge for labor is $18.00. The charge for parts is $17.25. The mechanic will get 45% of the labor charge. What is the total amount of the bill? How much will the mechanic receive?

Automobile liability insurance, pages 160-161

6. Gordon is 18. How much is his annual premium for liability coverage of 25/50/10? (Use the tables on page 160.)

Automobile collision and comprehensive insurance, pages 162-163

7. Miyoshi, age 17, has a class C car. She is buying collision insurance with $50 deductible and comprehensive insurance with $50 deductible. How much is her total premium? (Use the table on page 162.)

Annual expenses, pages 164-166

Joyce Jensen drove 15,000 km last year. She recorded these expenses for her car during the year:

Depreciation	$1380.00
Fixed costs	$2267.15
Variable costs	$485.33

8. Find the total cost for the year.
9. Find Joyce's cost per kilometer. Round the answer to the nearest tenth of a cent.

Alternatives to owning a car, pages 168-169

10. Harley takes the bus and the train to and from work. Bus fare is $.25 each way. His monthly train ticket is $35.10. Find Harley's monthly cost. (Assume that there are 20 working days in the month.)

Chapter 8

test

Annette drove 900 km during July. She bought 173 liters of gasoline, which cost $32.87.

1. Find her car's fuel consumption. Round the answer to the nearest tenth.

2. To the nearest tenth of a cent, find the cost of gasoline for each kilometer that Annette traveled.

3. Howard Chinn bought a new $5900 car 3 years ago. What is the trade-in value of the car now? (Use the rule that after 3 years, the trade-in value is 42% of the original selling price.)

4. How much has the car depreciated?

5. On a repair bill, the charge for labor is $12.00, and the charge for parts is $36.71. The mechanic will get 45% of the labor charge. What is the total amount of the bill? How much will the mechanic receive?

6. Elvina is 19. How much is her annual premium for liability coverage of 25/50/10? (Use the tables on page 160.)

7. Nick, age 17, has a class B car. He is buying collision insurance with $100 deductible and comprehensive insurance with $50 deductible. Find his total premium. (Use the table on page 162.)

Hector Lopez drove 15,000 km last year. He recorded these expenses for his car during the year:

Depreciation	$850.00
Fixed costs	$1745.09
Variable costs	$693.72

8. Find the total cost for the year.

9. Find Hector's cost per kilometer. Round the answer to the nearest tenth of a cent.

10. LaVonda takes the bus and the train to and from work. Bus fare is $.35 each way. Her monthly train ticket is $47.95. Find LaVonda's monthly cost. (Assume that there are 20 working days in the month.)

Chapter 9

Travel

Some people travel in their jobs; others travel for leisure and recreation. Travel agencies can assist you with making plans for a trip.

Finding Distance and Traveling Time

On this map of Pennsylvania, distances are given in kilometers. The distance between two "pointers" is shown in red. 323

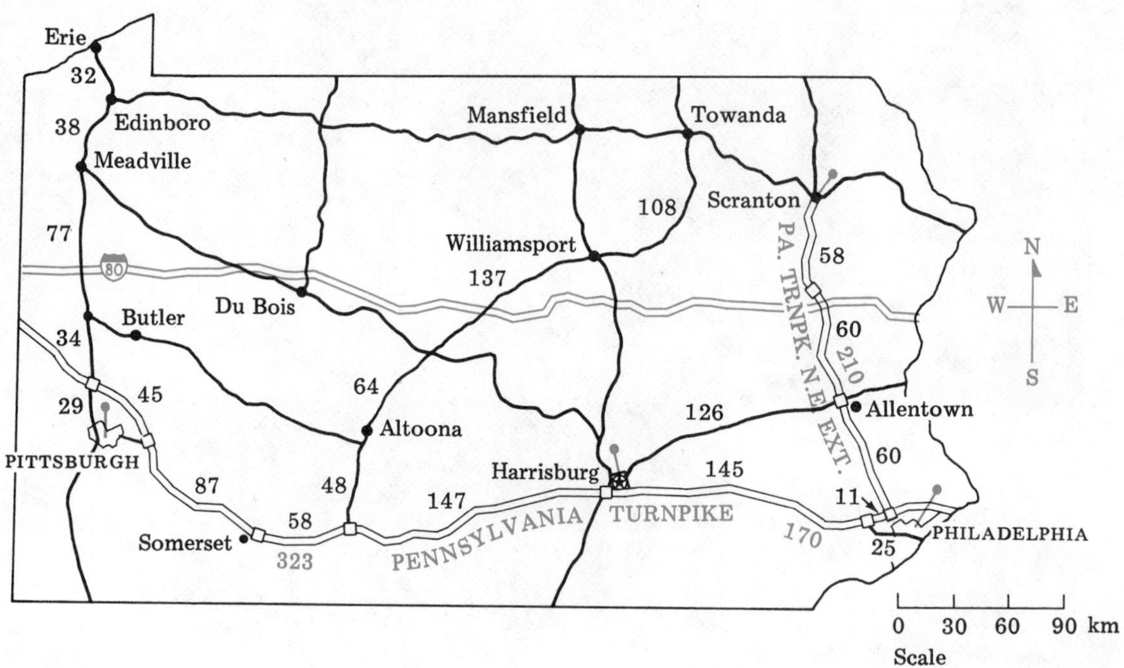

problem

How far is it from Altoona to Williamsport? At a rate of 80 km/h, how long will this trip take?

solution

Add the distances given on the map.

64 km + 137 km = 201 km

Find the traveling time. Round to the nearest half hour.

Distance	Rate	Time
201 km ÷	80 km/h ≈	2.5 h

exercises

Find the distance of each route. Then find the traveling time to the nearest half hour. Use a rate of 80 km/h.

1. Altoona to Williamsport to Towanda
2. Altoona to Somerset
3. Somerset to Harrisburg
4. Scranton to Allentown to Harrisburg
5. Philadelphia to Pittsburgh
6. Pittsburgh to Erie
7. Philadelphia to Erie through downtown Pittsburgh

If you do not need to know the exact number of kilometers, you can measure to find the straight distance.

problem

Cathy and Charlie Burdic plan to drive from Altoona to Butler to visit some friends. What is the straight distance between Altoona and Butler?

solution

The distance is not given on the map, so use the scale. Mark off segments on a card. Label the segments with the scale of the map.

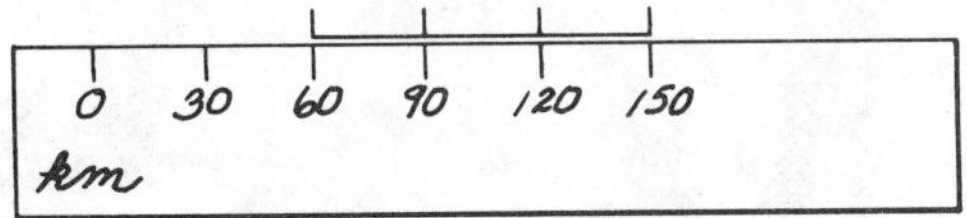

Measure the distance between Altoona and Butler. It is about halfway between 120 and 150, or 135.

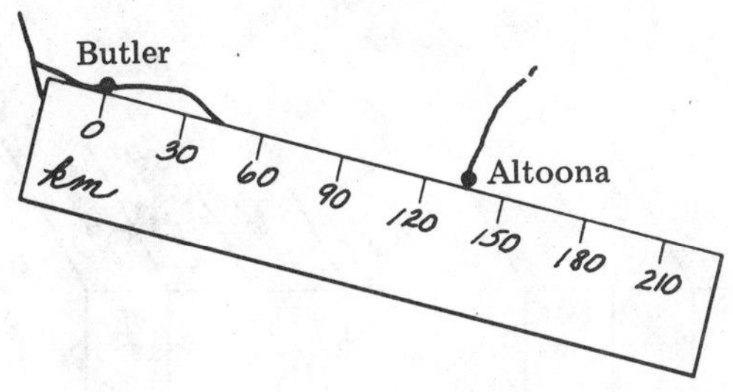

The straight distance between Altoona and Butler is about 135 kilometers.

exercises

Measure to find the straight distance along each of these routes.

8. Meadville to Du Bois
9. Mansfield to Towanda
10. Towanda to Scranton
11. Du Bois to Harrisburg
12. Mansfield to Harrisburg
13. The route north from Du Bois and east to Mansfield
14. Length of Interstate Highway 80 across the state of Pennsylvania

For each route, use the numbers on the map to find the distance. Then measure to find the straight distance.

	Route	Computed distance	Straight distance
15.	Williamsport to Towanda	**a.**	**b.**
16.	Pittsburgh to Erie	**a.**	**b.**
17.	Meadville to Edinboro	**a.**	**b.**

Find the straight distance of each route by measuring. Then find the traveling time to the nearest half hour. Use a rate of 80 km/h.

18. Edinboro to Mansfield
19. Williamsport to Harrisburg
20. Towanda to Edinboro

Reading a Distance Chart

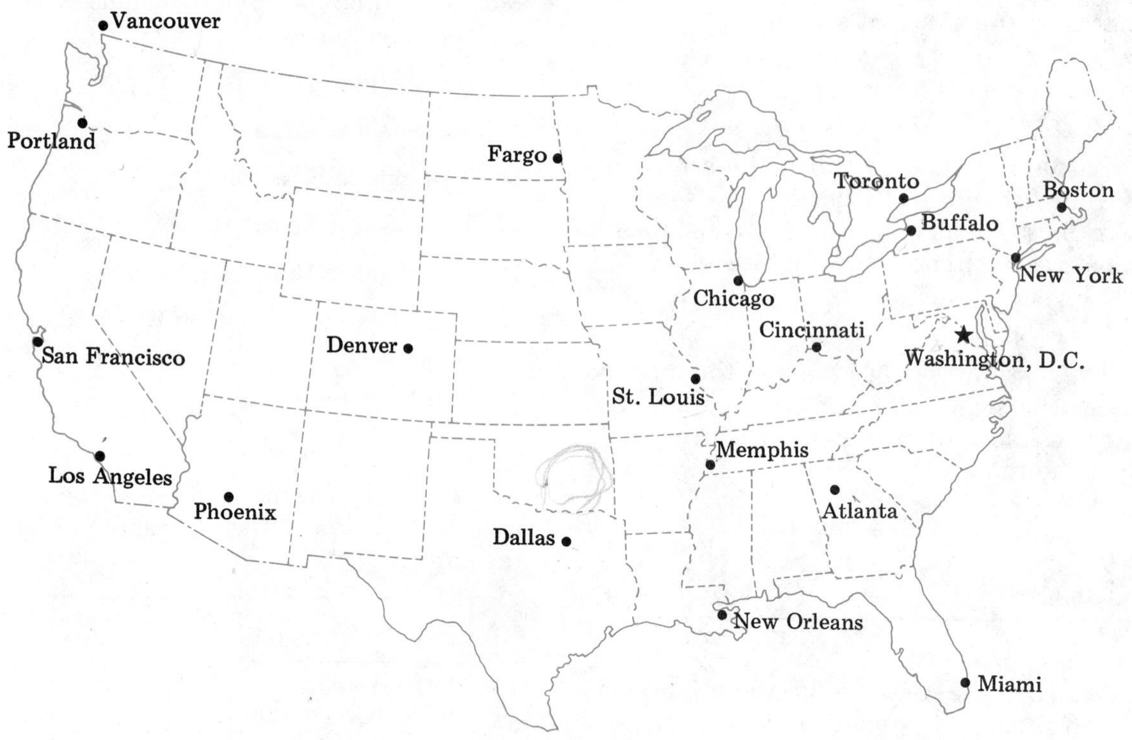

	Dallas	Denver	Fargo	Los Angeles	Phoenix	Portland	San Francisco
Chicago	1510	1642	1060	3397	2827	3437	3521
Dallas		1265	1790	2274	1647	3318	2860
Denver	1265		1453	1874	1322	2073	2044
Fargo	1790	1453		3121	2784	2565	3021
Memphis	755	1706	1711	2940	2371	3818	3487
New Orleans	806	2071	2385	3090	2463	4179	3674
Phoenix	1647	1332	2784	627		2053	1281
Portland	3318	2073	2565	1603	2053		1079
St. Louis	1050	1392	1310	3003	2406	3408	3440

Distances in the West (kilometers)

	Atlanta	Buffalo	Chicago	Cincinnati	Memphis	New Orleans	St. Louis
Atlanta		1413	1140	753	590	834	892
Boston	1726	739	1571	1389	2161	2510	1916
Buffalo	1413		839	690	1490	2013	1166
Cincinnati	753	690	474		785	1323	545
Miami	1073	2308	2221	1827	1640	1416	1971
New York	1392	592	1335	1024	1842	2182	1550
Washington	1032	600	1108	802	1479	1855	1297

Distances in the East (kilometers)

If you do not have a map with much information about distances, you can refer to a distance chart.

The chart on page 176 has two sections, East and West. Chicago, St. Louis, Memphis, and New Orleans are in both sections.

problem

Gene Papiri is moving from Boston to Dallas. He will drive to Dallas by way of Memphis. How many kilometers will he travel?

solution

Gene is traveling from an eastern city to a western city. Look in the "East" section. The distance between Boston and Memphis is 2161 km.

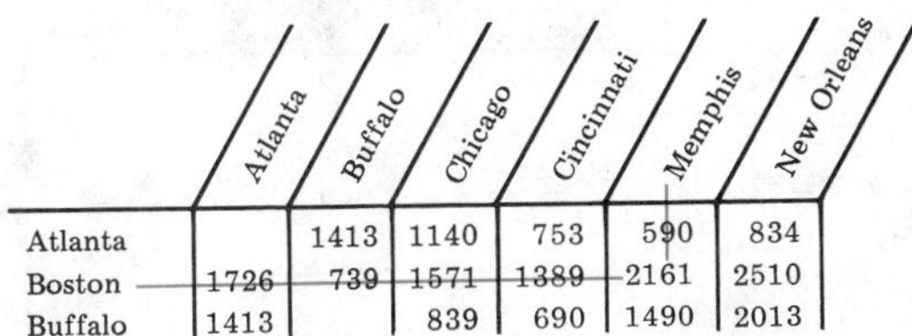

	Atlanta	Buffalo	Chicago	Cincinnati	Memphis	New Orleans
Atlanta		1413	1140	753	590	834
Boston	1726	739	1571	1389	2161	2510
Buffalo	1413		839	690	1490	2013

Look in the "West" section. The distance between Memphis and Dallas is 755 km.

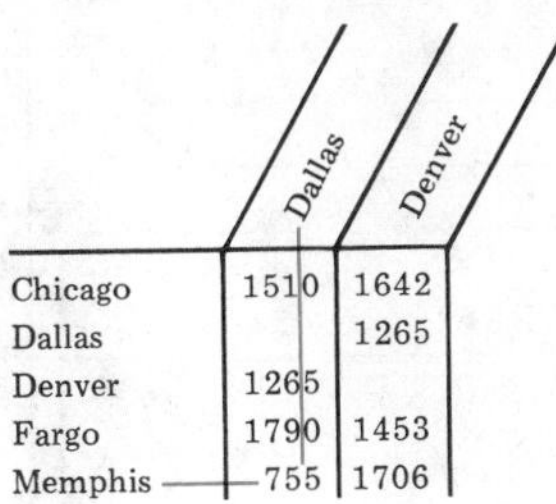

	Dallas	Denver
Chicago	1510	1642
Dallas		1265
Denver	1265	
Fargo	1790	1453
Memphis	755	1706

Find the total distance.

2161 km	Boston to Memphis
+ 755 km	Memphis to Dallas
2916 km	Total distance

exercises

Find the distance along each route.

1. Washington, D.C. to St. Louis to San Francisco
2. Miami to New Orleans to Phoenix
3. Cincinnati to Chicago to Fargo
4. New York to Memphis to Los Angeles
5. Portland to St. Louis to Atlanta
6. Dallas to St. Louis to Buffalo
7. Dallas to Memphis to Buffalo
8. Which route from Dallas to Buffalo is shorter?

Use only one section of the chart for each route.

9. New Orleans to Los Angeles to Portland
10. Buffalo to Atlanta to Miami
11. Vancouver, British Columbia, is about 515 km north of Portland. Find the distance from New Orleans to Los Angeles to Portland to Vancouver.
12. Toronto, Ontario, is about 165 km north of Buffalo. Find the distance from Toronto to Buffalo to Atlanta to Miami.

Lillian Barton is a regional sales manager who will travel this route: New York to Atlanta to Memphis to Cincinnati to Chicago to New York.

13. How far will she travel?
14. If she drives at an average rate of 80 km/h, about how many hours will she spend driving? Round to the nearest half hour.

Expenses on the Road

Most people like to know ahead of time how much expense they might have when they take a trip. Estimates can be made of expenses for gasoline, food, lodging, and other miscellaneous costs.

problem

Amy and Alex Thorson are driving 1600 km from Los Angeles to Portland, Oregon. Their car's fuel consumption is about 7.8 km/L. They will stay in motels two nights for about $25 per night. They estimate that 10 meals (5 each for 2 people) will cost about $4 each. Tolls will be about $3.50, and Alex is adding $1 for a telephone call. Find the grand total of these expenses.

solution

Find the total of each of the four categories: gasoline, food, lodging, and other. Then add.

Estimated Expenses

Gasoline

Distance — Fuel consumption — Liters

1600 km ÷ 7.8 km/L ≈ 205 L

Liters — Cost per liter — Total gas

205 L × $.20 = $41.00

Food

Cost per meal (with tip) $4.00

No. of meals (5 × 2 people) × 10

Total food $40.00

Lodging

Cost per night $25

No. of nights × 2

Total lodging $50

Other

(Tolls, telephone, sightseeing, gifts, etc.)

tolls $3.50

telephone $1.00

+$____

Total other $4.50

Grand total $135.50

exercises

For exercises 1-4, find these costs. Round the amount of gasoline to the nearest liter. Assume that gasoline costs $.20 per liter.

a. Total gas
b. Total food
c. Total lodging
d. Total other
e. Grand total

1. Tomorrow, Clifford White Feather will drive from Chicago to Minneapolis, a distance of 665 km, to attend a convention. His car's fuel consumption is about 8 km/L. Lunch will cost about $4.00.

2. Lucinda Beran plans to drive 500 km from Pittsburgh to Philadelphia. She will buy about $5 in food to eat on the way. She will stay overnight at a budget motel for about $13.00. Her car's fuel consumption is about 9 km/L. A friend has told her to allow about $10 for tolls.

3. Mr. and Mrs. Robb and their 4 sons have rented a motorhome to sleep and eat in as they drive from Miami to Fort Worth, Texas. They will stop 4 nights on the 2300-km trip. The nightly cost for lodging consists of $65, based on the cost of renting, plus an average fee of $7 for each campsite. The total cost for food will be about $100 for groceries. The Robbs are allowing $15 for tolls. Fuel consumption will be about 3 km/L.

4. When the Thorsons drive back from Portland to Los Angeles, they will bring their daughter and Amy's parents with them. There will be 25 meals instead of 10. The nightly motel cost will be about $50 because they will need two rooms. Other expenses should stay about the same.

There are 2 people in the Thorsons' car on their drive to Portland and 5 people on the trip back to Los Angeles.

5. Use the solution on page 178. Find the cost per person for the trip to Portland.

6. Find the cost per person for the trip back to Los Angeles.

Air Travel

When you take an airplane from one city to another, usually there are several different fares available. This summary gives some of the service and the fares for flights out of Chicago.

FARE SUMMARY from Chicago to							
Fare Code	Denver	Houston	Los Angeles	Miami	Minneapolis/ St. Paul	New Orleans	New York/ Newark
One Way							
F	$152	$154	$256	$182	$75	$138	$127
Y	$95	$96	$157	$114	$50	$89	$82
K	$85		$141				
FN	$95	$96	$157	$114			$82
YN	$76	$77	$126	$91			$66
KN	$68		$113				
Round Trip							
YHE40	$161	$163	$267	$194	$85	$151	$139
YLE40	$152	$154	$251	$182	$80	$142	$131

Fares include Federal Transportation Tax. All fares and service subject to change.

Explanation of codes

F—First Class
Y—Coach
K—Economy

FN—Night First Class
YN—Night Coach
KN—Night Economy

Children's fare (ages 2-11) for above: $\frac{2}{3}$ of adult fare

YHE40—Coach Excursion. Not available on all flights. Reservation and round-trip ticket required 14 days before departure. 7-day minimum stay; 30-day maximum. Fare applies June 1 through Sept. 14 (to Florida: Dec. 19 through April 30).

YLE40—Same as above but fare applies Sept. 15 through May 31 (to Florida: May 1 through Dec. 18).

Children's fare (ages 2-11) for above: One-way adult coach (Y) fare

problem

Daphne Evans and her children, ages 8 and 14, want to fly from Chicago to Houston for no more than $225. Can they fly night coach for this amount?

solution

The code for night coach is YN. The table shows that the one-way YN fare to Houston is $77. Daphne and the older child will each pay full fare. The 8-year-old will pay $\frac{2}{3}$ of full fare.

$\frac{2}{3} \times \$77 \approx \$52$ Rounded to nearest dollar

$77	Daphne's fare
77	Fare for 14-year-old
+ 52	Fare for 8-year-old
$206	Total one-way fare

The total fare, $206, is less than $225. The Evanses can fly night coach.

exercises

Find the total one-way fare from Chicago. Round each child's fare to the nearest dollar.

1. One adult flying coach to New York
2. Four adults flying coach to New York
3. One adult and two children, ages 10 and 15, flying night coach to Denver
4. Two adults and three children, ages 3, 5, and 8, flying economy to Los Angeles
5. Two adults and three children, ages 4, 7, and 10, flying first class to Los Angeles

To find the cost of each of the following round trips, first find the total one-way fare. Then multiply by 2. Round each child's fare to the nearest dollar.

6. One adult flying night first class to Miami and returning
7. One adult and one child, age 7, flying first class to Minneapolis and returning

Deane and Orris Folsom have just arrived in New Orleans. They will fly back to Chicago in 8 days.

8. The Folsoms used the YLE40 fare. How much did it cost for two people?
9. What would be the regular coach fare for two adults, round trip?
10. How much money did they save?

Renting a Car

Deane and Orris Folsom are vacationing this week in New Orleans. They decided to rent a car for a few days. The cost consists of a time charge plus a distance charge. The cost of gasoline is extra.

Class of car	Daily rate	Cost per kilometer
Compact	$16	$.12
Mid-sized	$17	$.13
Full-sized	$18	$.14
Station wagon	$21	$.15

problem

The Folsoms rented a mid-sized car for 3 days. They have just returned the car, and the clerk at the agency has computed the distance driven as 401 km. What will the Folsom's rental cost be?

solution

Find the time charge.

Number of days		Daily rate		Time charge
3	×	$17	=	$51.00

Find the distance charge.

Distance driven		Cost per kilometer		Distance charge
401	×	$.13	=	$52.13

Find the rental cost.

$51.00	Time charge
+ 52.13	Distance charge
$103.13	Rental cost

The Folsoms' rental cost will be $103.13.

exercises

In exercises 1-8, use the rates in the table to find the rental cost.

1. Mid-sized car
   Rented 3 days
   Driven 500 km
2. Mid-sized car
   Rented 7 days
   Driven 975 km
3. Full-sized car
   Rented 2 days
   Driven 500 km
4. Full-sized car
   Rented 1 day
   Driven 42 km
5. Compact car
   Rented 6 days
   Driven 1137 km
6. Mid-sized car
   Rented 1 day
   Driven 217 km
7. Station wagon
   Rented 3 days
   Driven 850 km
8. Compact car
   Rented 3 days
   Driven 850 km
9. How are the rentals in exercises 7 and 8 alike?
10. How much more did the station wagon cost?

CALCULATOR EXERCISES

Complete the table. In each exercise, find the number of kilometers by subtracting. Then use the rental rates given on page 182.

	Class	Odometer Start	Odometer End	Distance driven	Distance charge	Number of days	Time charge	Rental cost
1.	Mid-sized	6,285	7,113	a.	b.	7	c.	d.
2.	Mid-sized	11,247	11,697	a.	b.	4	c.	d.
3.	Full-sized	9,505	10,049	a.	b.	4	c.	d.
4.	Full-sized	8,377	8,424	a.	b.	1	c.	d.
5.	Station wagon	30,621	31,000	a.	b.	3	c.	d.
6.	Station wagon	27,926	28,555	a.	b.	3	c.	d.

The rental agency has this special rate.

COMPACT GETAWAY SPECIAL

7 days w/1600 km . . .$125

Each day over 7 — *$18*

Each km over 1600 — *$.20*

For $125, a customer can rent a car for as long as 7 days and drive it 1600 km.

However, if you keep the car longer or drive it further, there are extra charges. If you rent for 10 days and drive 2000 km, you are charged for 3 days (10 − 7) and for 400 km (2000 − 1600).

$125	Basic charge
54	Extra time (3 × $18)
+ 80	Extra distance (400 × $.20)
$259	Rental cost

Find the rental cost by using the Compact Getaway Special rate.

7. Rent for 3 days; drive 1400 km
8. Rent for 10 days; drive 1700 km
9. Rent for 10 days; drive 1200 km
10. Rent for 9 days; drive 2054 km
11. Rent for 5 days; drive 1961 km
12. Rent for 8 days; drive 737 km
13. Rent for 7 days; drive 2700 km
14. What is the cost under the plan on page 182 if you rent a compact for 7 days and drive 2700 km?
15. Use your answers to exercises 13 and 14. Which plan costs less? How much less?

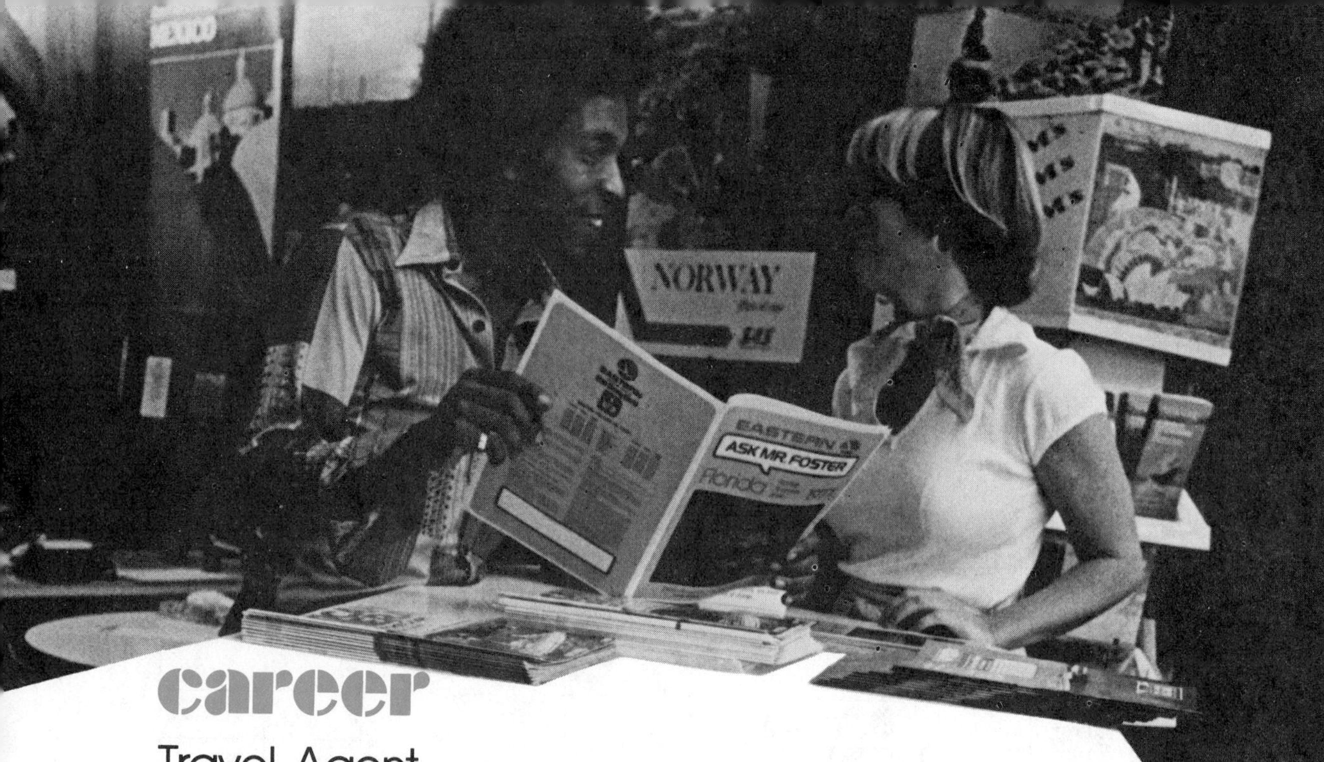

career

Travel Agent

Career Cluster: Business Contact

Gordon Wicks is a travel agent at the Walker-Wilson Travel Agency. He always reminds his customers that each method of travel has some advantages.

Gordon prepared this chart for a trip from Denver to San Francisco.

One-way costs, per person		Denver to San Francisco	
	BUS	TRAIN	AIR
Distance Time	2132 km 30 h	2214 km 30 h	1548 km 2.5 h
Adult fare	$60.45	Coach $87.50 Roomette $138.50 (1 person) Bedroom $133.50 (2 people) each	F $157 Y $98 FN $98 YN $78
Children's fare (ages 2-11)	$\frac{1}{2}$ adult fare	$\frac{1}{2}$ adult fare	$\frac{2}{3}$ adult fare
Meals, snacks	About $20	About $20	No charge
Transportation to downtown area	None	None	$2-$8

problem

Harriet Kaplan and her daughter, age 10, plan to take a bus from Denver to San Francisco. About how much will their traveling expenses be?

solution

Use the chart on page 184. A child's fare is $\frac{1}{2}$ the adult fare.

$\frac{1}{2} \times \$60.45 \approx \$30$ Rounded to nearest dollar

\$60.45	Harriet's fare
30.00	Daughter's fare
20.00	Food for two people
+ 20.00	
\$130.45	Traveling expenses

Their traveling expenses will be about \$130.45.

exercises

Find the traveling expenses for one adult going from Denver to San Francisco.

1. By bus
2. By train in a roomette
3. By air, coach. Allow \$2 for shuttle bus to downtown hotel.
4. By air, first class. Allow \$2 for shuttle bus to downtown hotel.

Find the traveling expenses for two adults and one child, age 8, traveling from Denver to San Francisco. Round each child's fare to the nearest dollar.

5. By bus
6. By train in coach seats
7. By air, coach. Allow \$8 for a taxi for all three people.
8. By air, first class. Allow \$8 for a taxi for all three people.

Virginia Chan, age 19, will fly night coach to San Francisco. Her cousin will pick her up at the airport. When she takes a bus back to Denver, Virginia will take some food with her. Her meal costs will be about \$12. Find her expenses:

9. To San Francisco
10. Back to Denver
11. For both parts of her trip

George Gallion has to attend a funeral in San Francisco tomorrow. He cannot leave Denver until tomorrow morning.

12. What method of travel should he use?
13. Find the round-trip coach fare.
14. Mr. and Mrs. Garcia, Lydia, age 14, and Alma, age 10, would pay \$467.50 for two bedrooms on the train from San Francisco to Denver. How much can they save on their train fares by using this Family Plan? Round each partial fare to the nearest dollar.

    First parent: Full fare (Bedroom)
    Other parent: $\frac{3}{4}$ full fare
    Children ages 12-21: $\frac{3}{4}$ full fare
    ages 2-11: $\frac{3}{8}$ full fare

skills tune-up

Dividing decimals, pages 12-13

Find the quotient to the nearest thousandth.

1. $23.7 \div 4$
2. $84.9 \div 7$
3. $16.31 \div 29$
4. $32.38 \div 34$
5. $4.017 \div 65$
6. $5.994 \div 78$
7. $.0089 \div .13$
8. $.0016 \div .44$
9. $.8 \div 6.2$
10. $6.3 \div 7.8$
11. $16.86 \div 8.3$
12. $12.54 \div 4.3$
13. $.396 \div .07$
14. $.642 \div .08$
15. $51 \div .3$
16. $72 \div .9$
17. $1.8 \div 3.45$
18. $3.2 \div 5.17$
19. $7.14 \div 6.04$
20. $9.59 \div 8.03$
21. $.0601 \div 9.88$
22. $.717 \div .363$
23. $.374 \div .186$
24. $.6819 \div .021$
25. $.4206 \div .053$

Adding fractions and mixed numbers, pages 18-19

1. $\frac{1}{3} + \frac{3}{4}$
2. $\frac{1}{10} + \frac{2}{5}$
3. $\frac{5}{6} + \frac{1}{2}$
4. $\frac{3}{5} + \frac{1}{15}$
5. $\frac{1}{2} + \frac{4}{7}$
6. $\frac{3}{10} + \frac{1}{2}$
7. $\frac{8}{9} + \frac{5}{12}$
8. $5\frac{1}{6} + \frac{7}{8}$
9. $\frac{9}{10} + 3\frac{1}{6}$
10. $4\frac{2}{9} + \frac{3}{4}$
11. $4\frac{4}{5} + 3\frac{8}{15}$
12. $6\frac{2}{3} + 9\frac{7}{12}$
13. $5\frac{4}{9} + 2\frac{7}{18}$
14. $3\frac{1}{2} + 1\frac{5}{8}$
15. $2\frac{3}{5} + 4\frac{1}{3}$
16. $3\frac{1}{6} + 7\frac{9}{10}$
17. $4\frac{5}{16} + 3\frac{7}{8}$
18. $2\frac{1}{5} + 6\frac{3}{8}$
19. $5\frac{7}{12} + 2\frac{2}{3} + 10\frac{3}{4}$
20. $12\frac{1}{6} + 3\frac{4}{5} + 8\frac{2}{3}$

Subtracting fractions and mixed numbers, pages 18-19

1. $\frac{5}{6} - \frac{1}{3}$
2. $\frac{3}{4} - \frac{1}{2}$
3. $\frac{5}{8} - \frac{1}{4}$
4. $\frac{4}{5} - \frac{1}{3}$
5. $\frac{7}{8} - \frac{1}{6}$
6. $\frac{5}{6} - \frac{2}{3}$
7. $\frac{1}{2} - \frac{3}{7}$
8. $\frac{3}{4} - \frac{3}{10}$
9. $3 - \frac{5}{8}$
10. $12 - \frac{1}{5}$
11. $5\frac{1}{4} - 2\frac{3}{4}$
12. $8\frac{3}{8} - 2\frac{5}{8}$
13. $10 - 5\frac{2}{3}$
14. $7 - 6\frac{7}{10}$
15. $14\frac{3}{4} - 5\frac{3}{16}$
16. $15\frac{4}{5} - 8\frac{3}{4}$
17. $18\frac{3}{10} - 11\frac{5}{6}$
18. $9\frac{1}{2} - 5\frac{7}{10}$
19. $14\frac{5}{6} - 8\frac{1}{2}$
20. $17\frac{7}{10} - 8\frac{13}{15}$

Chapter 9

review

Finding distance and traveling time, pages 174-175

Deborah Canfield will drive from Allentown to Scranton. Use the map on page 174.

1. Find the distance she will drive.
2. At a rate of 80 km/h, how many hours will Deborah be driving? Round to the nearest half hour.

Reading a distance chart, pages 176-177

3. Use the chart on page 176. Find the distance from Atlanta to St. Louis to Fargo.

Expenses on the road, pages 178-179

Warren Crown will be driving from Yellowstone National Park to Grand Canyon National Park, a distance of 1260 km. His car's fuel consumption should be about 6.2 km/L because of some driving in the mountains. He is allowing $25 for meals. He will spend two nights in motels for about $20 each night.

4. To the nearest liter, find the amount of gasoline that Warren will need. At $.20 per liter, how much will the gasoline cost?
5. Find Warren's total traveling expenses.

Air travel, pages 180-181

Two adults and one child, age 6, are flying coach from Chicago to New York. Use the fare summary on page 180. Round each child's fare to the nearest dollar.

6. Find their total one-way fare.
7. The people in exercise 6 cannot use the special round-trip fares. How much will their round trip cost?

Renting a car, page 182

8. Molly Little Horse has just returned a car that she rented for 4 days. She drove 673 km. She will be charged $17 per day and $.13 per kilometer driven. Find her rental cost.

Travel agent, pages 184-185

Three adults are traveling from Denver to San Francisco. Use the chart on page 184.

9. Find their traveling expenses if they go by train in 3 roomettes.
10. Find their traveling expenses if they fly first class and share one taxi for $7.

Chapter 9

test

Esther Shigeta is driving from Pittsburgh to Meadville. Use the map on page 174.

1. Find the distance she will drive.

2. At a rate of 75 km/h, how many hours will Esther be driving? Round to the nearest half hour.

3. Use the chart on page 176. Find the distance from Phoenix to St. Louis to Washington, D.C.

Tomorrow afternoon Bonnie Butz will drive home to Syracuse, N.Y., from her school in Boston. This distance is about 505 km. She is allowing $2 for a meal at a fast-food restaurant and about $3 for tolls on the Massachusetts Turnpike. Her car's fuel consumption is about 7.2 km/L.

4. Find the amount of gasoline that Bonnie will need to the nearest liter. At $.20 per liter, how much will the gasoline cost?

5. Find Bonnie's total traveling expenses.

Two adults and one child, age 9, are flying coach from Chicago to Houston. Use the fare summary on page 180.

6. Find their total one-way fare.

7. The travelers in exercise 6 cannot use the special round-trip fares. How much will their round trip cost?

8. Lee Parks and her husband Rick have just returned a car that they rented for 5 days. They drove 500 km. They will be charged $18 per day and $.14 per kilometer driven. Find their rental cost.

Two adults are traveling from Denver to San Francisco. Use the chart on page 184.

9. Find their traveling expenses if they go by bus.

10. Find their traveling expenses if they go by train in coach seats.

Unit 3

test

Choose the best answer.

1. A used car costs $1225. The state sales tax is 5%. Find the amount of the state sales tax.

   A $245.00 C $61.25

   B $61.05 D $62.15

2. The base price of a mid-sized car is $4950. Find the sticker price of the car with the options listed. (Use the table on page 134.)

   Power steering
   Automatic transmission
   AM-FM radio
   Air conditioner
   Vinyl top

   A $6231 C $6068

   B $6131 D $6122

3. The selling price of a new car is $6720. The trade-in allowance on a used car is $685. Find the net price.

   A $6035 C $5585

   B $6062 D $7405

4. Ann made a down payment of $1200 on a new car. She is financing the car for 36 months. Her monthly payment is $114.29. Find the deferred-payment price.

   A $4114.44 C $5314.44

   B $2914.44 D $4314.44

5. Hector sold 18 cars in October. Find his bonus earnings for the month. (Use the table on page 142.)

   A $234 C $270

   B $288 D $230

6. Ben drove 528 km during August. He used 85 liters of gasoline. Find his car's fuel consumption. Round the answer to the nearest tenth.

   A 6.3 km/L C 6.4 km/L

   B 6.8 km/L D 6.2 km/L

7. Chang bought a new $5024 car 5 years ago. What is the trade-in value of the car now? (Use the rule that after 5 years, the trade-in value is 25% of the original selling price.)

   A $1261 C $1526

   B $1256 D $2612

8. Find the premium Allen would pay for bodily injury coverage of 50/100. (Use the table on page 160.)

   A $126.35 C $111.00

   B $220.78 D $242.36

9. Lucy, age 19, has a class F car. She is buying collision insurance with $50 deductible and comprehensive insurance with $50 deductible. Find her total premium. (Use the table on page 162.)

A $143 C $240

B $165 D $210

10. Kathy drove 14,000 km last year. Her total annual expenses, including depreciation, fixed costs, and variable costs, were $3920. Find her cost per kilometer.

A $.27 C $.29

B $.30 D $.28

11. Joe Red Wing takes the bus and the train to and from work. His monthly train ticket is $35.85. The bus fare is $.40 each way. Find his monthly cost. (Assume that each month has 20 working days.)

A $16.00 C $51.85

B $43.85 D $48.35

12. How long will it take to travel 362 km at a rate of 80 km/h? Round the answer to the nearest half hour.

A 4.5 h C 5 h

B 4 h D 5.5 h

13. Use the chart on page 176. Find the distance from San Francisco to Memphis to New York.

A 4863 km C 5127 km

B 5329 km D 5516 km

14. Janet will need 75 liters of gasoline for her drive home from school. At $.20 per liter, how much will the gasoline cost?

A $14.00 C $15.75

B $11.40 D $15.00

15. A rented car was driven 624 km. The cost per kilometer is $.14. What is the distance charge?

A $44.57 C $87.36

B $87.26 D $89.88

16. Two adults are traveling from Denver to San Francisco. Find their traveling expenses if they go by train in roomettes. (Use the chart on page 184.)

A $297 C $277

B $317 D $307

Mid-book

test

Choose the best answer.

1. 6.84 + 27.3 + 15.6

   A 111.3 C 49.7

   B 49.74 D 39.74

2. 27.63 − 14.8

   A 23.23 C 42.43

   B 12.93 D 12.83

3. 5.2 × 8.47

   A 44.044 C 44.44

   B 44.744 D 42.044

4. 43.68 ÷ 5.2

   A .84 C 8.4

   B .85 D 8.5

5. $1\frac{3}{8} \times 2\frac{2}{5}$

   A $4\frac{5}{7}$ C $3\frac{3}{10}$

   B $2\frac{3}{20}$ D $1\frac{13}{20}$

6. $5\frac{1}{4} + 7\frac{2}{5}$

   A $12\frac{13}{20}$ C $12\frac{3}{20}$

   B $12\frac{1}{3}$ D $12\frac{1}{10}$

7. $7\frac{2}{3} - 5\frac{3}{8}$

   A $2\frac{1}{5}$ C $2\frac{5}{24}$

   B $1\frac{7}{24}$ D $2\frac{7}{24}$

8. Write 36% as a fraction in lowest terms.

   A $\frac{7}{20}$ C $\frac{8}{25}$

   B $\frac{9}{25}$ D $\frac{3}{8}$

9. Write 17% as a decimal.

   A 17 C 1.7

   B .17 D .017

10. What number is 32% of 58?

    A 18.56 C 18.50

    B 39.44 D 18.46

11. Choose the most sensible measure for the mass of a ten-speed bicycle.

    A 57 g C 32 mg

    B 378 kg D 21 kg

12. 5468 mL = ▒ L

    A 546.8 C 5.468

    B 54.68 D .5468

13. How much time is there from 2:05 P.M. to 6:45 P.M.?

    A 8 hr. 50 min. C 4 hr. 35 min.

    B 4 hr. 50 min. D 4 hr. 40 min.

14. Luisa sells encyclopedias for a straight commission of 35%. How much did she earn on a sale of $850?

    A $297.50 C $287.50

    B $295.50 D $297.55

15. The ending balance on a bank statement is $837.25. There is one outstanding deposit of $80.68 and one outstanding check of $57.50. What is the adjusted statement balance?

A $699.07 C $814.07

B $860.43 D $756.57

16. Use the table on page 102 to find the amount of interest on $600 at 5% compounded annually for 4 years.

A $730.02 C $729.30

B $130.02 D $129.30

17. The balance after payment on a charge account is $64. The finance charge is 1.5% per month of the balance after payment. Find the amount of the finance charge.

A $.97 C $.94

B $.95 D $.96

18. The Browns need to finance $350 for a purchase. There will be 6 monthly installments of $61.78 each. Find the total paid in installments.

A $370.28 C $376.68

B $370.68 D $360.68

19. What is the amount of the finance charge for the installment plan in exercise 18?

A $26.68 C $20.68

B $10.00 D $20.28

20. A used car costs $1835. The state sales tax is 4%. Find the amount of the state sales tax.

A $74.12 C $72.40

B $73.40 D $83.40

21. John made a down payment of $1500 on a new car. He is financing the car for 24 months. His monthly payment is $130. Find the deferred-payment price of the car.

A $4620 C $4520

B $3120 D $3020

22. Find the premium Linda would pay for bodily injury coverage of 100/300. (Use the table on page 160.)

A $126.35 C $138.70

B $64.00 D $242.36

23. Warren takes the subway to and from work. The fare is $.45 each way. Find his monthly commuting cost. (Assume 20 working days in a month.)

A $9 C $8

B $18 D $16

24. Jack Myles will need 78 liters of gasoline for his trip. At $.20 per liter, how much will the gasoline cost?

A $15.00 C $16.50

B $17.40 D $15.60

unit four

Housing

Chapter 10

Renting and Decorating a Home

Chapter 11

Buying a Home

Chapter 12

Building a Home

Chapter 10

Renting and Decorating a Home

Many people rent homes and apartments. They often decorate to make these dwellings reflect their personalities.

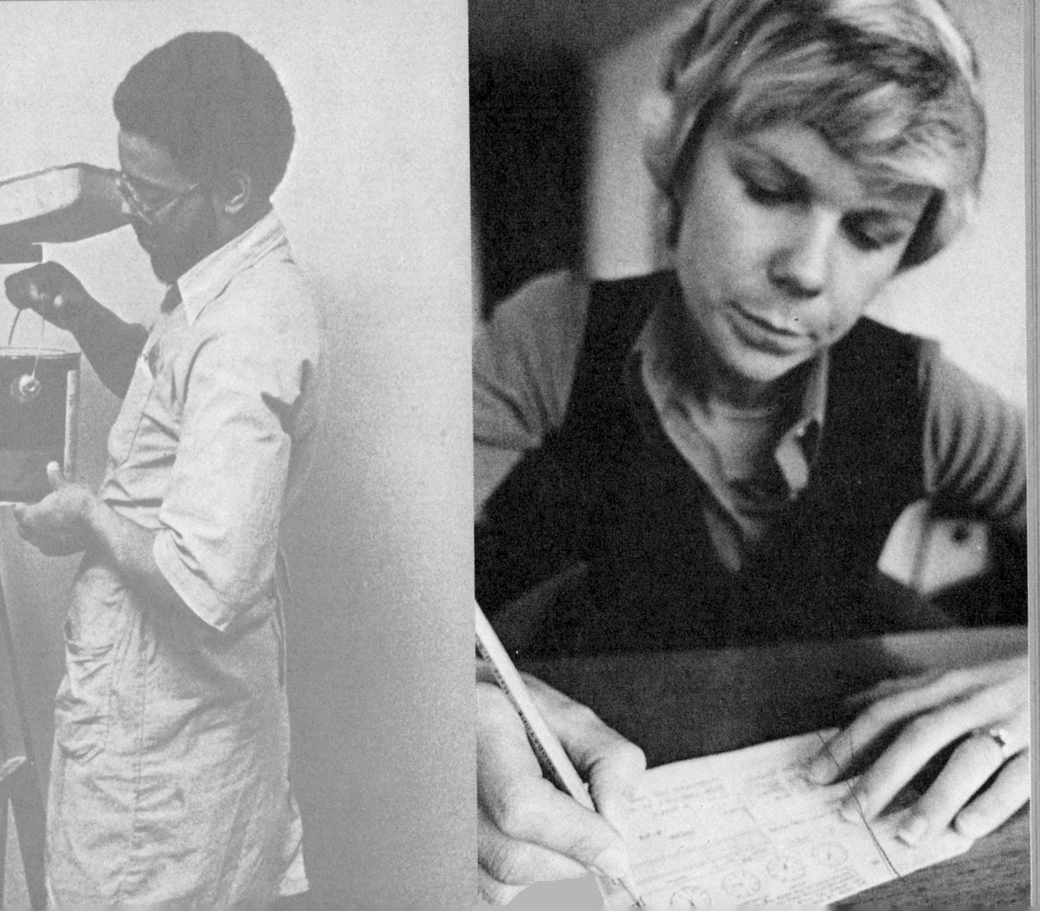

STUDIO-1 BEDROOM
$145 + $170.
LGE. studio apt. 2 1/2 rms. W. Rogers Park. AC. $190
DECOR! 5 1/2 rms appls. din rm Adults pref. $225
STUDIO, Deluxe, a/c, appls. 6031 N. Kenmore. $175.
LAWRENCE & Monticello. 2 1/2 lg. rms. mod. apt. $135.
6200 North. 2 bdrm apt. By lake and L. $270.
4700 N. Nr Lk. 4 bd, 2 ba. frplc, lge DR. $315
4350 N. ASHLAND 3 1/2 rms. $160. Util incl.
NEWTOWN-1 1/2 rms. $120; 2 1/2 rms $145.
4 rm, 3rd flr, stove, no pets, 4723 N. Hermitage
5 RMS.-Newly dec. & remod. Htd. Adult no pet $275
BEAU dec 1 bdrm exec, complete furnishings for sale.
E. ROGERS PK. nr. lake. 2 + 3 bdrm.
DE PAUL-2 bdr, ht. 2nd flr. 2235 Halsted. $225.
SANDBURG-Sublet 1 BR, crptg, balcony, $360
7 rm. Kimball & Foster. Close to shoppg, schl. Call
2 1/2 & 3 rm. apts. 7100N. Facing Lake. Reas.
5 rms 3rd flr., vicinity Irving & Kimball $220
6 ROOMS APT $135. 1437 N. Washtenaw Call
NEAR Belmont & Racine. 4 rms, 2 bdrm $140 mo.
Super dlx 1 br. immed 6120 N. Kenmore Open Sun 2-5.
- 1 br, clean-well maint. Close to transp. Cple/single:
3 rms, 2nd rear, pay own utils, stv/refr, $140.
GARDEN Apt. 4 1/2 rms. Clean. Adults pref.
Sublease lg 2 br 2b sunny apt suberb loc $410
STUDIO to Sublet Oct. 1. $243.
2 br, mod apt, compl kit, laund facils, htd. $300
Lakeview lrg remod 3 bdrm, cptd, 1038 Roscoe $325

Amount to Spend for Rent

Emily Cole and Paul Hines are investigating how much they can spend for rent when they get married. A common rule of thumb is given below.

> Do not spend more than one week's gross pay for shelter each month.

problem

Paul works 40 hours per week at $5.80 per hour. Emily is unemployed now. What is the most they should spend for renting a townhouse or an apartment?

solution

$5.80 × 40 = $232   Paul's weekly gross pay

Paul and Emily should not spend more than $232 per month for rent.

exercises

In each exercise, use the given pay rate to find the maximum amount that should be spent for rent each month. Assume a 40-hour work week.

1. $6.30 per hour
2. $4.75 per hour
3. $7.50 per hour
4. $3.80 per hour
5. $5.60 per hour
6. $10.50 per hour
7. $10,816 per year
8. $8580 per year
9. $9529 per year
10. $12,350 per year
11. $11,325 per year
12. $8850 per year

Emily and Paul read in a national survey that families who rented spent about 23% of their annual net income on shelter. This amount included utilities, such as heat, electricity, water, and sewerage.

problem

Paul's annual net income is $9421. According to the survey, what will Paul probably spend for rent each month?

solution

$.23 \times \$9421 = \$2166.83$ Expected annual rent ($23\% = .23$)

$\$2166.83 \div 12 \approx \$180.57$ Expected monthly rent

Rounded to the nearest dollar, Paul's monthly rent will probably be about $181. Notice that this amount is lower than the estimate from the rule of thumb.

exercises

Using the 23% from the survey, find the expected monthly rent for the net incomes given. Round your answers to the nearest dollar.

13. $9802

14. $7633

15. $11,468

16. $6656

17. $8185

18. $10,575

19. Emily is considering a part-time job. She would earn $3.75 per hour for 24 hours each week. Using the rule of thumb, how much could Paul and Emily spend for rent each month?

20. With both of them working, Emily and Paul estimate their net income at $12,297 the first year. According to the survey, how much would they probably spend for rent each month? (Round your answer to the nearest dollar.)

We Pay All Utilities
1, 2, & 3 Bedrooms
$185 1 Bedrm.
2 Bedroom $195
Colony Point Apts.
Bus #7 Stops At Our Door
Directions: Route 37 north
to Colony Point Drive
Mon.-Fri. 10-5; Sat. 12-4; Sun. 12-5
Equal Housing Opportunity

The Villas
- Spacious rooms
- Dishwasher, disposal
- Large closets
- Convenient to transportation, shopping, schools
- Gas heat

2 BR $210 plus elec.
Route 67 and I-21
Equal Housing Opportunity

Perfect location
with the plus-pleasure
of a full social &
recreation program.
CRANBROOK
SQUARE
Next to Cranbrook
Road Plaza
$215 Plus elec
2 B.R., one bath
Available very soon
- Shag Carpet
- Washer & Dryer
- Pool
- Tennis Courts
- Ind Controlled Heat & A/C
- All-electric Apts.

1 B.R. $204
OPEN DAILY 9-5 P.M.
SAT. & SUN. 12-6 P.M.
Equal Housing Opportunity

SUMMIT—lg. 2 bdrm.
twnhse. appl. crpt. bsmt.
$205 + util.

Selecting a Place to Live

Mike Amano and Jake Martin are planning to rent one of the two-bedroom units shown in the ads on these pages. They must consider the cost of the rent and the utilities.

Mike and Jake investigated the cost of utilities. They talked with tenants in the different buildings, and found the following facts.

- Ads that stated "plus utilities" meant the tenants paid gas heat and electricity.
- Gas heat costs about $12 per month.
- Electricity, without electric heat, costs about $15 per month.
- Electricity for an all-electric apartment costs about $30 per month.

GEORGETOWN

Country Club Living

1 & 2 Bedrm apts avail.

TENNIS

POOL

CLUBHOUSE

Your Own Washer/Dryer

Carpet thru-out

Value $189.50 plus utilities

2 BR $210

OPEN DAILY 10-6

Equal Housing Opportunity

No Security Deposit Needed

on two bedroom apts. only

1 Month's Rent Will Move You In

Meadow Green

- Carpet thru-out
- Tennis Courts
- Pool
- Playground
- Schools
- Shopping Centers
- All-elec. apts.

1 BR

$210 plus elec.

2 BR $225

OPEN DAILY 10 TO 6

Equal Housing Opportunity

750 Nichols Rd.

Modern 1 & 2 bdrm. apts. Newly dec. Tile bath, hardwd floors. 1 bdrm. from $230—2 bdrm. from $245. Gas heat. All util. included except elec. Across from tennis, golf and park. Excl. trans.

problem

What will Jake and Mike's monthly expenses be if they rent a two-bedroom unit at Georgetown Apartments?

solution

$210	Basic rental
15	Electricity
+ 12	Gas
$237	

Jake and Mike should expect to pay about $237 per month for rent and utilities.

exercises

In exercises 1–6 find the expected monthly expenses for a two-bedroom unit at each location.

1. Summit

2. 750 Nichols Road

3. Cranbrook Square

4. Meadow Green

5. Colony Point

6. The Villas

7. List all the two-bedroom units and the total monthly expenses in order. Start with the least expensive.

8. Find the difference between the least expensive and the most expensive two-bedroom units.

9. Jake and Mike decide to split the expenses on a two-bedroom apartment at Cranbrook Square. How much should each of them expect to pay every month?

career

Meter Reader

Career Cluster: Social Service

Rhonda Davis works for the electric company as a meter reader. An electric meter measures the amount of electricity used by a customer. From the readings Rhonda takes, the company can determine the number of **kilowatt-hours** used during that period. One kilowatt-hour will supply electricity to light a 100-watt light bulb for 10 hours.

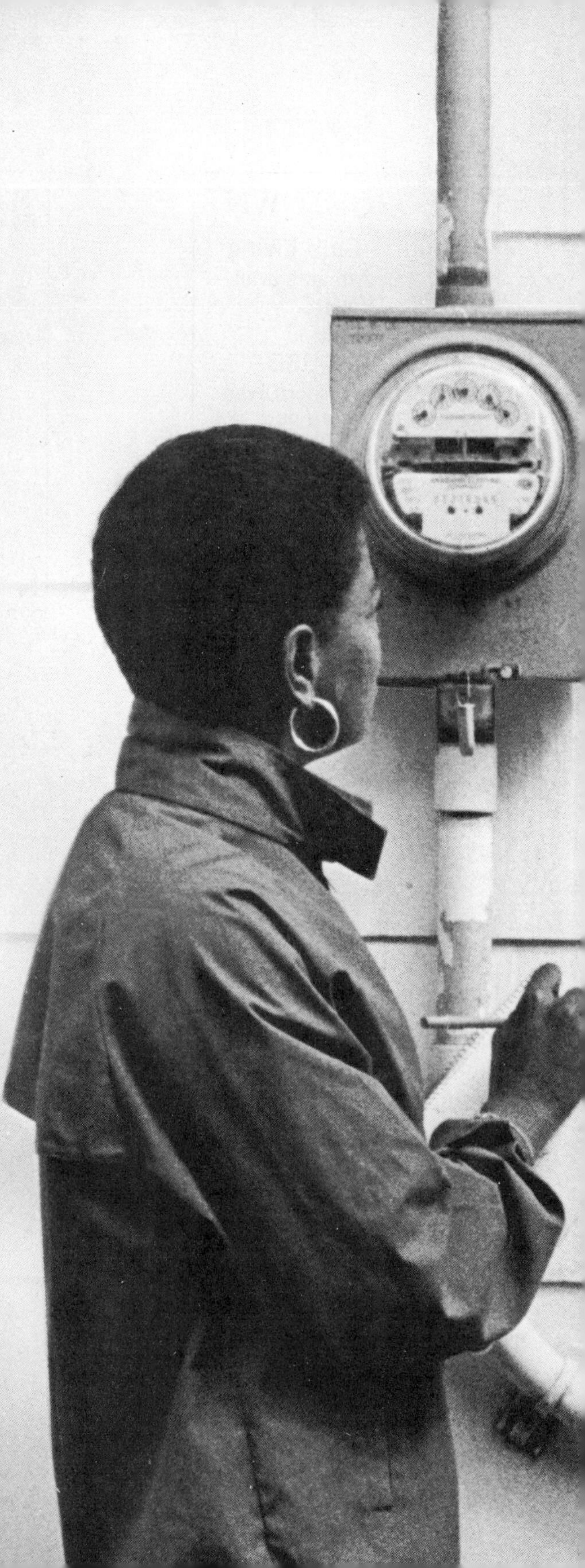

problem

What is the reading on this set of dials?

solution

Read the dials from left to right. When the hand on any dial is between two numbers, read the smaller number. When the hand is between 9 and 0, as on the 1000's dial here, think of the 0 as 10.

The reading is 29635.

exercises

Rhonda Davis read the meter at the Radows' apartment for one year. Because the Radows do not have electric heat, Rhonda read the meter every 2 months. Give the reading for each date.

1. December 1, 1976

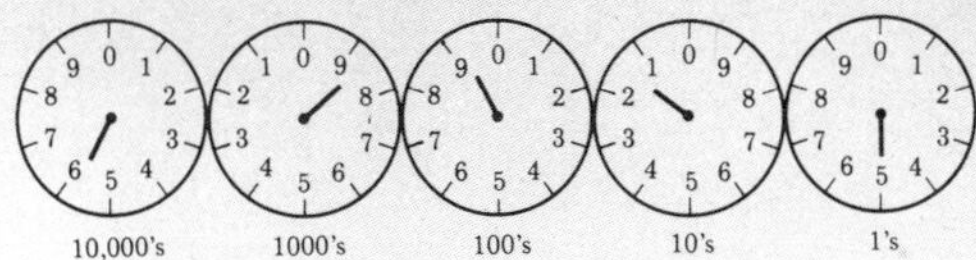

2. February 2, 1977

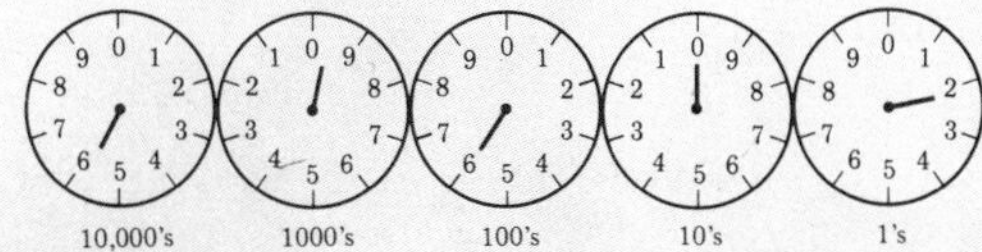

3. April 1, 1977

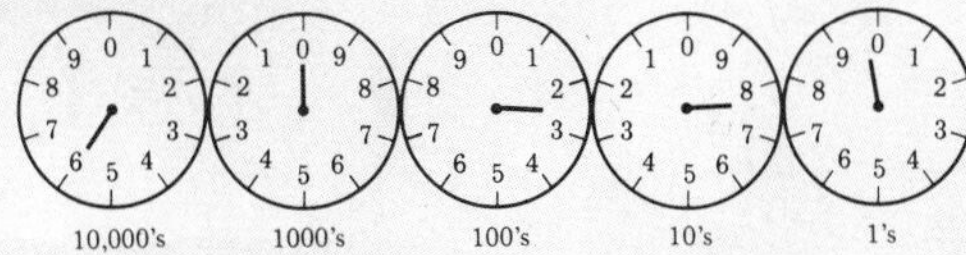

4. June 1, 1977

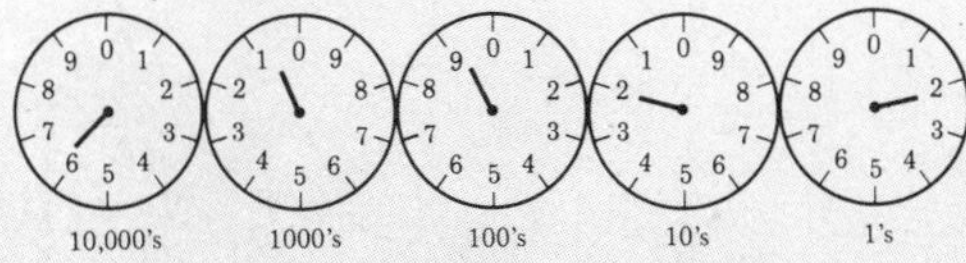

5. August 1, 1977

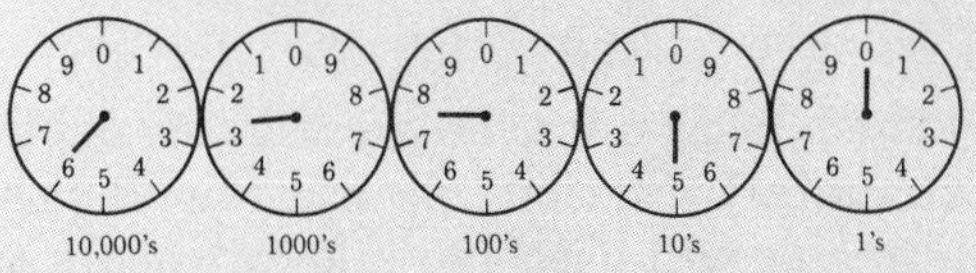

6. October 3, 1977

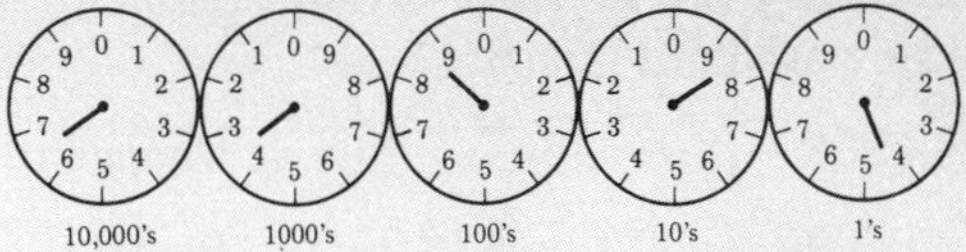

7. December 1, 1977

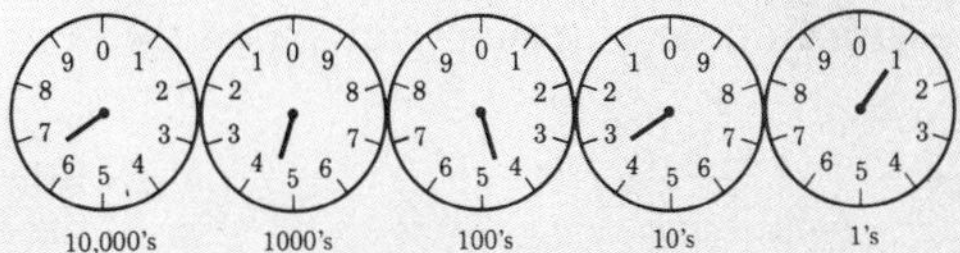

8. How many kilowatt-hours (kW • h) were used between December 1, 1976, and February 2, 1977? (Subtract the December reading from the February reading.)

9. Find the kilowatt-hours used during each of the other two-month periods.

10. In which two-month period was the electric usage greatest?

11. Give a reason why the amounts used each period vary so greatly.

CALCULATOR EXERCISES

Listed below are average amounts of electricity used annually by various electrical appliances. On the average, a freezer will use 1195 kilowatt-hours of electricity per year. In a certain area, the amount charged for electricity is 4.096¢ per kilowatt-hour. To find the cost of electricity, multiply the rate per kilowatt-hour by the number of kilowatt-hours used.

4.096¢ = $.04096 Change to dollars.

$.04096 × 1195 ≈ $48.95 Round to the nearest cent.

Find the annual cost of electricity for each appliance. The estimated cost of electricity is 4.096¢ per kilowatt-hour.

	Appliance	Estimated kilowatt-hours used annually
1.	Water heater	4219
2.	Refrigerator-freezer	1137
3.	Refrigerator-freezer (frostless)	1829
4.	Microwave oven	300
5.	Self-cleaning oven	1205
6.	Range with oven	1175
7.	Dishwasher	363
8.	Trash compactor	50
9.	Toaster	39
10.	Clothes washer (automatic)	103
11.	Clothes dryer	993
12.	Fan	43
13.	Air conditioner (window)	1389
14.	Vacuum cleaner	46
15.	Television (black and white)	362
16.	Television (color)	502
17.	Radio	86
18.	Stereo	109
19.	Sun lamp	16
20.	Shaver	1.8
21.	Electric toothbrush	0.5

22. Find the annual cost of electricity for each appliance in exercises 1–21. Use a rate of 4.187¢ per kilowatt-hour.

change of pace

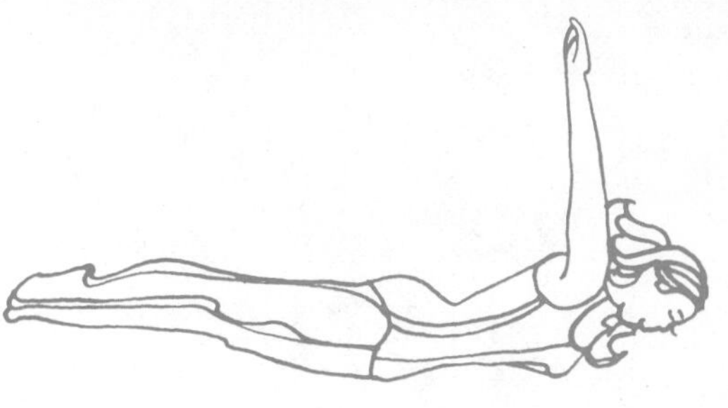

Layout

Lauren Carroll is a diver on the Harford Community College swimming team. In a swimming meet she must attempt 11 dives. Each dive has a degree of difficulty between 1 and 3. Judges rate the performance of the dive on a scale between 1 and 10.

To find Lauren's score for each dive, add the judges' scores and multiply the sum by the degree of difficulty.

Find Lauren's score for each dive.

Pike

	Dive	Position	Degree of difficulty	Judges' scores		
1.	Forward dive	Layout	1.4	3.5	4	3
2.	Back dive	Tuck	1.6	4	4.5	3
3.	Reverse somersault	Pike	1.8	6	5.5	6
4.	Inward dive	Tuck	1.2	4	4.5	4
5.	Forward dive $\frac{1}{2}$ twist	Layout	1.8	4.5	4	4.5
6.	Back $1\frac{1}{2}$ somersault	Pike	2.4	4	4.5	4
7.	Reverse somersault	Layout	2.0	2.5	2	2
8.	Inward $1\frac{1}{2}$ somersault	Tuck	2.2	5	5.5	6
9.	Forward $1\frac{1}{2}$ somer. $\frac{1}{2}$ twist	Pike	2.1	3.5	4	4
10.	Forward double somersault	Tuck	2.0	5	4.5	5
11.	Back dive 1 twist	Layout	2.1	5.5	5.5	5.5

Tuck

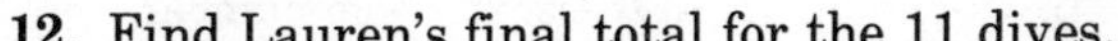

12. Find Lauren's final total for the 11 dives.

Painting an Apartment

Russell and Mattie Atkin have obtained permission from their landlord to paint their apartment. They know one liter of paint covers about 9.5 square meters ($9.5\ m^2$).

problem

The Atkins' bedroom is 4.2 meters by 3.24 meters ($4.2\ m \times 3.24\ m$). Each wall is 2.5 meters high. How many liters of paint are needed for the walls and the ceiling?

solution

Think of the four walls placed end to end.

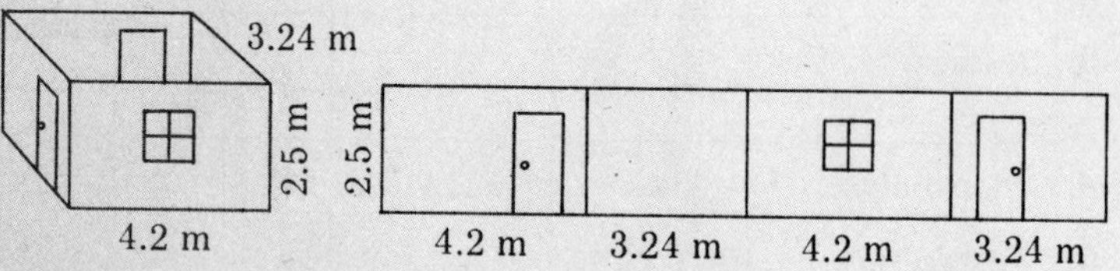

The length of this rectangle is the perimeter of the room. The width is the height of the room. The area of the walls is the perimeter times the height.

$(4.2\ m + 3.24\ m + 4.2\ m + 3.24\ m) \times 2.5\ m = 37.2\ m^2$

Find the area of the ceiling.

$4.2\ m \times 3.24\ m \approx 13.6\ m^2$ Round to the nearest tenth of a square meter.

Find the total area to be painted.

$37.2\ m^2 + 13.6\ m^2 = 50.8\ m^2$

Divide the area by 9.5 to find the number of liters of paint needed for the walls and the ceiling.

$50.8 \div 9.5 \approx 6$ Round up to the next whole number.

Mattie and Russell should buy 6 liters of paint.

exercises

Mattie and Russell did some more measuring in their apartment. They made this chart.

Room	Color	Room dimensions
Den	Sunshine gold	3.3 m × 4.1 m
Living room	Champagne	5.5 m × 3.7 m
Entrance	Champagne	1.52 m × 1.6 m
Dining room	Fern green with white ceiling	3.7 m × 3.36 m
Hallway	Fern green with white ceiling	7.54 m × 1.63 m

Complete the table below to find the number of liters of paint needed for each room. Remember each wall is 2.5 meters high. Round the areas to the nearest tenth of a square meter.

	Room	Wall area	Ceiling area	Total area to be painted	Liters of paint needed
	Bedroom	37.2 m^2	13.6 m^2	50.8 m^2	6 L
1.	Den	a.	b.	c.	d.
2.	Living room	a.	b.	c.	d.
3.	Entrance	a.	b.	c.	d.
4.	Dining room	a.	b.	——	c. Walls d. Ceiling
5.	Hallway	a.	b.	——	c. Walls d. Ceiling

6. The paint is sold in 4-liter cans. How many cans of each color are needed? (The bedroom will be painted wedgewood blue.)
7. Wall paint costs \$10.49 per can and ceiling white costs \$9.79 per can. What is the total bill for all the paint?

Ordering Wallpaper

Mary Grace Gettings wants to cover the walls of the den in her apartment with wallpaper. The clerk at the wallpaper store gave Mary Grace the following instructions for determining the amount of wallpaper to order.

- Find the total area of the walls, including all openings.
- Divide the area by 3. (There are approximately 3 square meters of paper per roll.)
- Subtract 1 roll for every 2 standard openings. (For a picture window, double doors, or any other large opening, subtract 1 roll.)

problem

Mary Grace's den is shown here. How many rolls of wallpaper should she order?

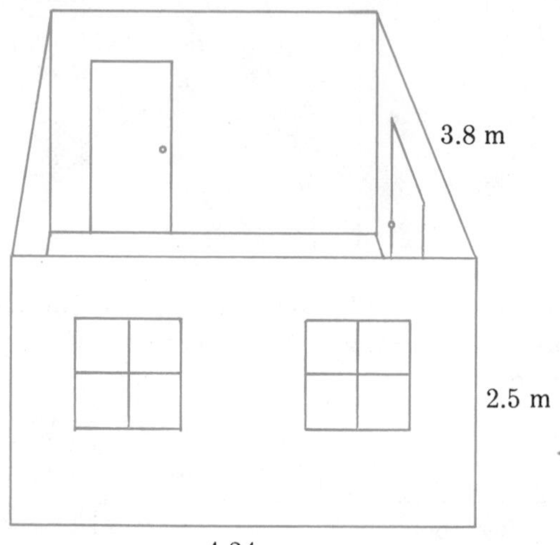

solution

The perimeter of the den is 16.08 meters. Find the area of the walls.

$16.08 \text{ m} \times 2.5 \text{ m} = 40.2 \text{ m}^2$

Find the number of rolls, including openings. Always round your answer up.

$40.2 \div 3 = 13.4 \approx 14$

Find the number of rolls to buy.

$14 - 2 = 12$ Subtract 2 rolls for 4 standard openings.

Mary Grace should order 12 rolls of wallpaper.

exercises

Mary Grace wants to paper her dining room. The length of the room is 4.8 meters and the width is 4.35 meters. All rooms are 2.5 meters high. There are three windows, one door, and a large archway in the dining room.

1. Find the area of the walls.
2. Find the number of rolls needed, including openings.
3. Find the number of rolls that should be subtracted for the openings.
4. How many rolls of wallpaper should Mary Grace order?
5. Find the cost of the paper in the dining room at $5.89 a roll.

Mary Grace's living room is 6.7 meters long and 5.5 meters wide. There are 7 standard openings.

6. Find the area of the walls.
7. Find the number of rolls of wallpaper needed, including openings.
8. Find the number of rolls that should be subtracted for the openings.
9. How many rolls of wallpaper should Mary Grace order for the living room?
10. Mary Grace wants to paper the living room for $95. What is the most she can spend for each roll?
11. Mary Grace wants to cover the bathroom walls with vinyl covering. The room is 2.8 meters long and 2.0 meters wide. The height of the wall area to be covered is 1.25 meters. How many rolls will be needed with 2 standard openings?
12. Find the cost of the vinyl covering at $10.75 a roll.

Installing Carpet Tiles

Jeff Scott rents a house and wants to put down carpet tiles in the den. His landlord will pay for the materials if Jeff installs the tiles. The carpet tiles are 30 centimeters square.

problem

Jeff's den measures 3.9 meters by 3.75 meters. How many tiles are needed for the floor?

solution

Find the number of tiles needed for the length.

$3.9 \text{ m} = 390 \text{ cm}$ Length in centimeters

$390 \div 30 = 13$ Tiles needed for the length

Find the number of tiles needed for the width.

$3.75 \text{ m} = 375 \text{ cm}$ Width in centimeters

$375 \div 30 = 12\frac{1}{2}$ Tiles needed for the width

Find the total number of tiles needed.

$13 \times 12\frac{1}{2} = 162\frac{1}{2}$ Total tiles needed

exercises

Find the number of tiles needed for the length and the width. Then find the total number of tiles needed for each room.

1. Bathroom: 2.4 m × 1.5 m
2. Bedroom: 4.2 m × 4.05 m
3. Utility room: 3.15 m × 3.3 m
4. Recreation room: 6.3 m × 4.95 m
5. Kitchen: 4.35 m × 2.85 m

problem

Jeff wants to make a design with the carpet tiles. He uses graph paper to make the design shown. A package of 10 tiles costs \$10.80. Find the cost of the black tiles.

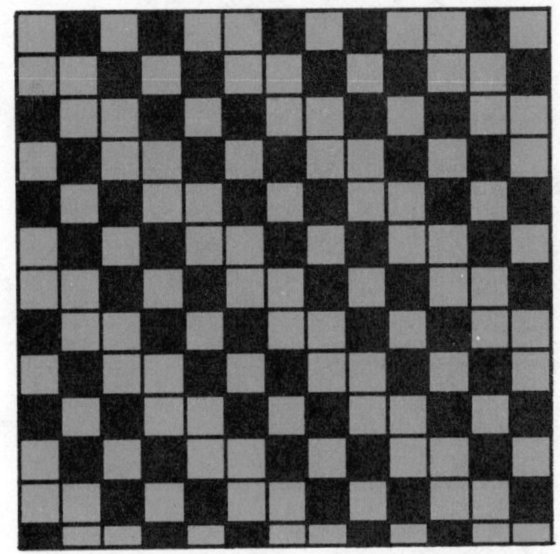

solution

Count the number of black tiles needed.

62	Full black tiles
$+ \ 2\frac{1}{2}$	5 half-tiles
$64\frac{1}{2}$	Total black tiles

Find the cost of the black tiles. If Jeff buys packages of 10 tiles, he will need 7 packages.

$7 \times \$10.80 = \$75.60$ Cost of black tiles

exercises

6. What is the cost of the red tiles for Jeff's den?

7. How much will the landlord pay for all the tiles for Jeff's den?

8. Make a regular checkerboard pattern for Jeff's recreation room on graph paper. (See exercise 4.) He wants the design in red and blue. Start in the upper left-hand corner with a blue square.

9. How many blue tiles are needed in the recreation room?

10. How many red tiles are needed in the recreation room?

The tiles for the recreation room cost \$8.90 for a box of 10.

11. What is the cost of the blue tiles?

12. What is the cost of the red tiles?

13. What is the total cost of the tiles for Jeff's recreation room?

career

Interior Designer

Career Cluster: Arts

Raul Cruz is an interior designer for Bentley's Furniture Store. He makes a **scale drawing** of Arlene Novak's living room floor. Raul shows her possible arrangements for the furniture she owns and the furniture she is buying.

problem

Raul uses a scale of 1 cm = 0.2 m. How long should the scale drawing of the living room be? The room is 4.73 meters long.

solution

Use a proportion to find the scale length.

$$\frac{1}{0.2} = \frac{n}{4.73} \begin{array}{l} \leftarrow \text{Scale length in centimeters} \\ \leftarrow \text{Actual length in meters} \end{array}$$

$1 \times 4.73 = 0.2 \times n$ Cross multiply.

$4.73 = 0.2n$

$23.65 = n$ Divide both sides by 0.2

Rounded to the nearest tenth of a centimeter, the length of the room in the scale drawing should be 23.7 cm.

exercises

For exercises 1-14, round your answers to the nearest tenth of a centimeter.

1. The living room is 3.4 m wide. How wide should the scale drawing of the room be? Use a scale of 1 cm = 0.2 m.

Find the scale dimensions for each piece of furniture. Use a scale of 1 cm = 0.2 m.

2. Sofa: 2.1 m × .86 m
3. Love seat: 1.53 m × 0.86 m
4. Chair: 0.8 m × 0.86 m
5. Cocktail table: 1.49 m × 0.58 m
6. End table: 0.65 m × 0.55 m
7. Antique desk: 1.28 m × 0.6 m

Raul made a scale drawing for another customer. He used a scale of 1 cm = 0.25 m. Find the scale dimensions for the room and each piece of furniture.

8. Bedroom: 3.6 m × 3.45 m
9. Bed: 1.95 m × 1.35 m
10. Night table: 0.57 m × 0.4 m
11. Chair: 0.65 m × 0.46 m
12. Bench: 1.08 m × 0.43 m
13. Triple dresser: 1.68 m × 0.48 m
14. Five-drawer chest: 0.9 m × 0.48 m
15. Use centimeter graph paper and the scale dimensions. Draw the outline of the bedroom in exercise 8. Allow for a closet, a window, and a door.
16. Make scale drawings of some of the furniture for the bedroom in exercises 9-14. Cut out the furniture and make an arrangement of the bedroom.

Personal Property Insurance

Lin Hong rents an apartment and carries renter's insurance. This kind of insurance covers losses or damage to personal property caused by misfortunes such as fire or theft. Lin's insurance agent gave him the information shown here. To determine depreciation, Lin needs to know the age and the replacement cost of any article lost or destroyed.

Item	Average useful years	Rate of depreciation
Athletic equipment	5	20%
Barbecue	8	12%
Bicycle	5	20%
Clock		
Electric	15	7%
Grandfather	30	3%
Furniture		
Card tables, chairs	10	10%
Children's	5	20%
Desks, tables	20	5%
Lamps	20	5%
Wood-frame (example: couch)	15	7%
Golf clubs	10	10%
Stereo	15	7%
Television	10	10%
Tools (power and hand)	20	5%
Typewriter		
Home	20	5%
Office	5	20%

problem

Lin's apartment was broken into and his typewriter was taken. The typewriter is 3 years old and will cost $175 to replace. Lin has a $50-deductible policy. How much can Lin expect to receive from the insurance company?

solution

According to the table, the rate of depreciation on Lin's typewriter is 5% of the replacement cost each year. Recall 5% = .05.

$.05 \times \$175 = \$8.75$	Depreciation for 1 year
$\$8.75 \times 3 = \$26.25$	Depreciation for 3 years
$\$175 - \$26.25 = \$148.75$	Value after depreciation
$\$148.75 - \$50 = \$98.75$	Value less amount of deductible

Lin can expect to receive $98.75 from the insurance company.

exercises

The storage area in Tom Smith's apartment building was damaged by water. The items he lost are listed below. Find the value for each item after depreciation.

Item	Replacement cost	Age (yr.)
1. Bicycle	$150	2
2. Golf clubs	$175	5
3. Barbecue	$65	1
4. Electric clock	$75	3
5. Circular saw	$85	4
6. Camping equipment	$355	2
7. Desk	$175	5

8. Tom has a $50-deductible policy. How much will he receive from the insurance company? (Subtract $50 from the total amount after depreciation.)

Donna Littlebird had a fire in her apartment. The items destroyed are listed below. Find the value for each item after depreciation.

Item	Replacement cost	Age (yr.)
9. Couch	$430	3
10. Chair	$200	2
11. Chair	$185	3
12. End table	$95	2
13. Stereo	$325	2
14. Television	$535	1
15. Lamp	$45	3

16. Donna has a $100-deductible policy. How much will she receive from the insurance company?

skills tune-up

Dividing whole numbers, pages 12–13

Find the quotient.

1. $4599 \div 9$
2. $1752 \div 6$
3. $2272 \div 7$
4. $6517 \div 7$
5. $14{,}226 \div 3$
6. $4844 \div 5$
7. $5446 \div 43$
8. $8492 \div 28$
9. $6717 \div 62$
10. $3825 \div 17$
11. $6823 \div 56$
12. $2575 \div 75$
13. $1716 \div 39$
14. $4486 \div 40$
15. $4761 \div 23$
16. $2857 \div 83$
17. $3872 \div 48$
18. $54{,}144 \div 36$
19. $61{,}356 \div 51$
20. $55{,}239 \div 73$
21. $148{,}482 \div 19$
22. $127{,}816 \div 67$
23. $381{,}451 \div 89$
24. $512{,}571 \div 615$
25. $189{,}312 \div 928$

Multiplying fractions and mixed numbers, pages 16–17

1. $\frac{5}{8} \times \frac{1}{3}$
2. $\frac{3}{4} \times \frac{1}{6}$
3. $\frac{4}{5} \times \frac{5}{14}$
4. $\frac{2}{5} \times \frac{3}{4}$
5. $\frac{5}{8} \times \frac{2}{15}$
6. $\frac{9}{16} \times 8$
7. $9 \times \frac{7}{18}$
8. $8\frac{3}{4} \times \frac{4}{7}$
9. $2\frac{1}{5} \times \frac{6}{11}$
10. $\frac{5}{18} \times 3\frac{3}{5}$
11. $4\frac{1}{6} \times \frac{3}{10}$
12. $3\frac{1}{9} \times 1\frac{4}{7}$
13. $5\frac{1}{7} \times 5\frac{1}{4}$
14. $8\frac{1}{2} \times 1\frac{1}{3}$
15. $1\frac{7}{8} \times 4\frac{4}{5}$
16. $9 \times 1\frac{3}{4}$
17. $12\frac{1}{5} \times 2$
18. $\frac{9}{14} \times \frac{7}{8} \times \frac{1}{9}$
19. $5\frac{2}{5} \times 2\frac{1}{2} \times \frac{7}{9}$
20. $6 \times 1\frac{1}{10} \times 4\frac{1}{6}$

Ratio and proportion, pages 30–31

Find the cross-products. Tell whether the ratios are equal.

1. $\frac{2}{7} \quad \frac{4}{12}$
2. $\frac{14}{18} \quad \frac{7}{9}$
3. $\frac{20}{16} \quad \frac{80}{60}$
4. $\frac{90}{2.5} \quad \frac{180}{5}$
5. $\frac{7}{9} \quad \frac{16}{16.8}$
6. $\frac{55}{3} \quad \frac{4.95}{.27}$

Solve and check.

7. $\frac{5}{9} \quad \frac{a}{54}$
8. $\frac{n}{27} = \frac{20}{9}$
9. $\frac{35}{5} = \frac{21}{c}$
10. $\frac{7}{x} = \frac{14}{9}$
11. $\frac{21.2}{14} \quad \frac{n}{3.5}$
12. $\frac{.4}{d} \quad \frac{.3}{8.1}$
13. $\frac{.7}{5.6} = \frac{50}{n}$
14. $\frac{x}{16} = \frac{10.4}{64}$

Chapter 10

review

Amount to spend for rent, pages 196–197

1. Linda earns $6.75 per hour in a 40-hour work week. Using the "week's gross pay" rule of thumb, what is the most she should spend for rent each month?

Selecting a place to live, pages 198–199

2. Sam estimates his electric bill will be about $25 per month and his gas bill will be $13 per month. If the rent for his apartment is $185, what are Sam's total monthly expenses for his apartment?

Meter reader, pages 200–201

3. Give the reading for this set of dials on an electric meter.

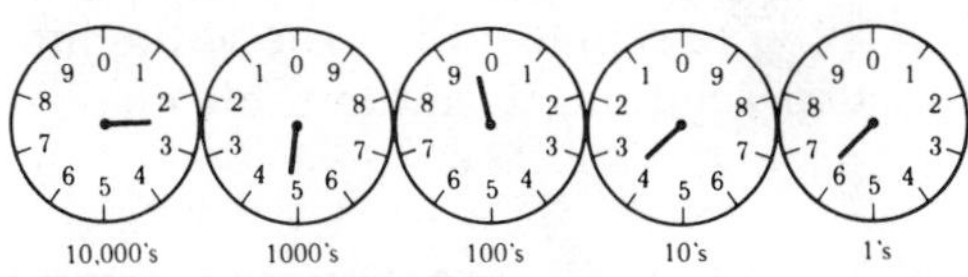

Painting an apartment, pages 204–205

4. Eleanor is going to paint the walls and the ceiling of her den. The room measures 3.7 m by 4.25 m and is 2.5 m high. Find the area to be painted. (Round each area to the nearest tenth of a square meter.)

5. How many liters of paint does Eleanor need to paint her den? (One liter covers about 9.5 m^2.)

Ordering wallpaper, pages 206–207

6. Jack wants to wallpaper his bedroom. The room measures 3.85 m by 4.3 m and is 2.5 m high. The room has 4 standard openings. Find the number of rolls of wallpaper Jack should order. (One roll of wallpaper covers about 3 m^2.)

Installing carpet tiles, pages 208–209

7. How many carpet tiles that are 30 cm square will be needed to cover a floor 5.25 meters by 4.5 meters?

Interior designer, pages 210–211

8. Using a scale of 1 cm = 0.2 m, find the scale length of a room 4.5 m long.

Personal property insurance, pages 212–213

9. Juanita carries renter's insurance. Her television set was stolen and it will cost $365 to replace. The television was 2 years old. Find the value after depreciation. (Use the table on page 212.)

10. Juanita has $100-deductible policy. How much will she receive from the insurance company?

Chapter 10

test

1. Duanne earns $11,479 per year. Using the "week's gross pay" rule of thumb, what is the most he should spend for rent each month?

2. Margo is interested in renting an apartment for $225 per month. All utilities are included except electricity. This will cost about $18 per month in her area. What are Margo's total monthly expenses for this apartment?

3. Give the reading for this set of dials on an electric meter.

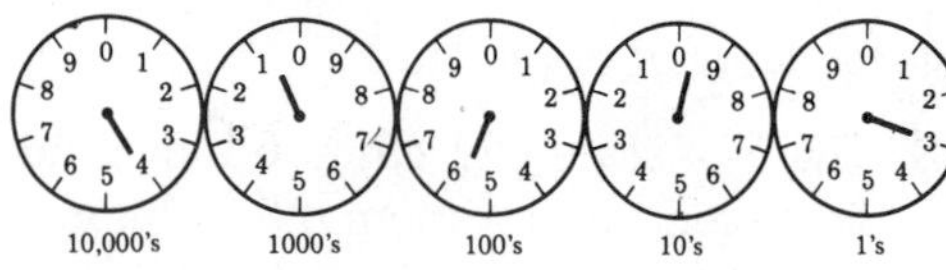

4. Marty is going to paint the walls and the ceiling of his living room. The room is 5.42 m by 3.6 m and is 2.5 m high. Find the area to be painted. (Round each area to the nearest tenth of a square meter.)

5. How many liters of paint does Marty need to paint his living room? (One liter covers about 9.5 m^2.)

6. Ana is going to wallpaper her dining room. The room measures 4.54 m by 4.6 m and is 2.5 m high. The dining room has 1 door and 1 window. Find the number of rolls of wallpaper Ana needs to order. (One roll of wallpaper covers about 3 m^2.)

7. How many carpet tiles that are 30 cm square would be needed to cover a floor 4.65 m by 3.6 m?

8. What is the scale length of a sofa that is 2.4 meters long? Use a scale of 1 cm = 0.25 m.

9. Beverly has renter's insurance. Her stereo was destroyed in a fire. The stereo was 3 years old and will cost $285 to replace. Find the value after depreciation. (Use the table on page 212.)

10. Beverly has a $50-deductible policy. How much will she receive from the insurance company?

Chapter 11

Buying a Home

Perhaps the largest single investment a person will make is the purchase of a home. What are the costs involved?

Amount to Spend for a Home

Edward and Marta Rivera are thinking of buying their own home. To determine the amount they can afford, their banker gives the following advice.

> Do not consider a house that costs more than 2.5 times your annual gross income.

problem

Edward earns $4.75 per hour in a 40-hour work week. Marta earns $950 per month. Can they consider a $47,950 home?

solution

Find the Riveras' annual gross income.

$\$4.75 \times 40 = \$190$	Edward's weekly income
$\$190 \times 52 = \$9880$	Edward's annual income
$\$950 \times 12 = \$11{,}400$	Marta's annual income
$\$9880 + \$11{,}400 = \$21{,}280$	Riveras' annual gross income

Find 2.5 times that amount.

$\$21{,}280 \times 2.5 = \$53{,}200$	Riveras' limit

The Riveras can consider this home.

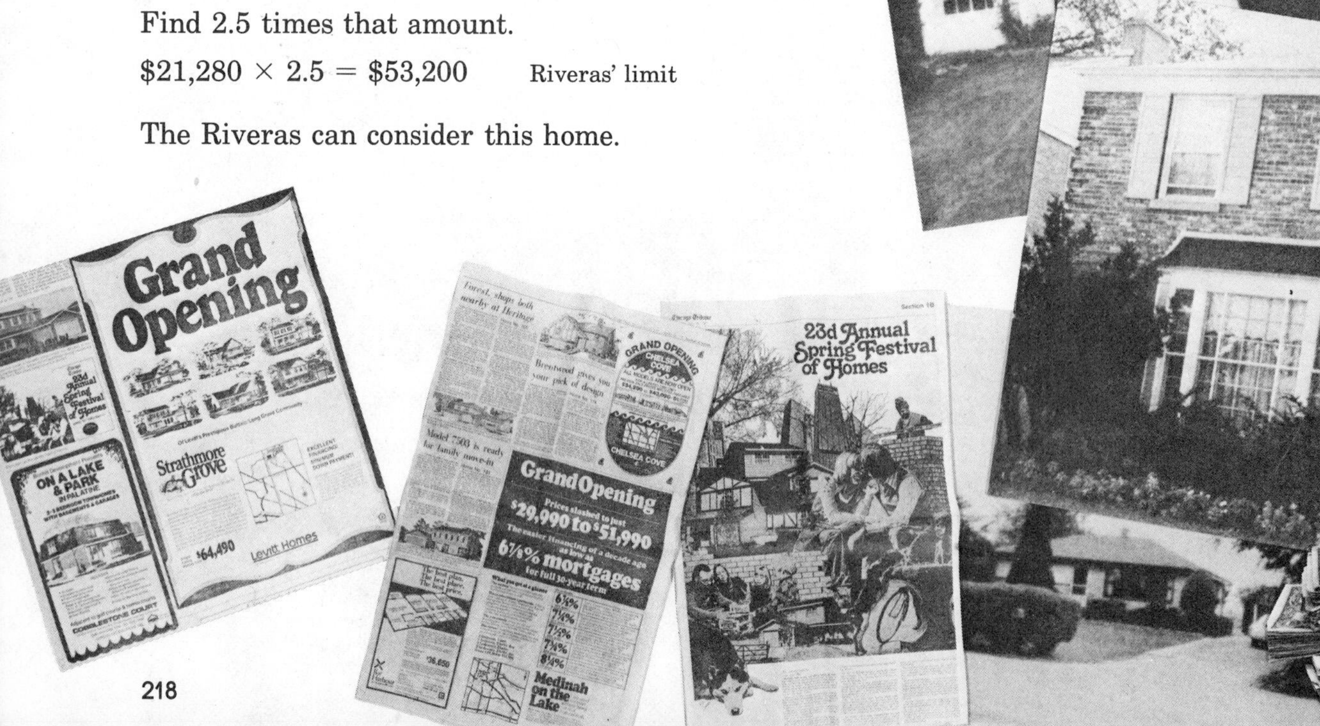

exercises

Use the general guideline to determine the greatest amount each person should spend for a home while earning the given income. Then state if each person can consider the house listed. Assume a 40-hour work week.

	Income	Cost of home
1.	$15,000 per year	$35,000
2.	$21,500 per year	$70,000
3.	$780 per month	$31,850
4.	$825 per month	$22,500
5.	$230 per week	$28,000
6.	$255 per week	$40,000
7.	$6.80 per hour	$33,500
8.	$7.50 per hour	$55,000
9.	$3.50 per hour	$35,000
10.	$12.50 per hour	$63,900

11. Tomas earns $7.65 per hour. Maria earns $525 per month. Can they consider a $58,000 home?

12. Lenny earns $3.50 per hour. Helene earns $225 per week. Can they consider a $45,600 home?

13. Anne earns $150 per week. Harvey earns $4.35 per hour. Can they consider a $40,000 condominium?

14. Barbara earns $4.25 per hour in a 20-hour work week. Frank earns $17,500 per year. Can they consider a $60,000 home?

Down Payment and Monthly Payment

Most people do not pay for a house with cash. They pay part of the purchase price right away with a down payment. They borrow the rest of the money from a lending institution. This **mortgage loan** is paid off in equal monthly payments. The table shown is used to find the monthly payment.

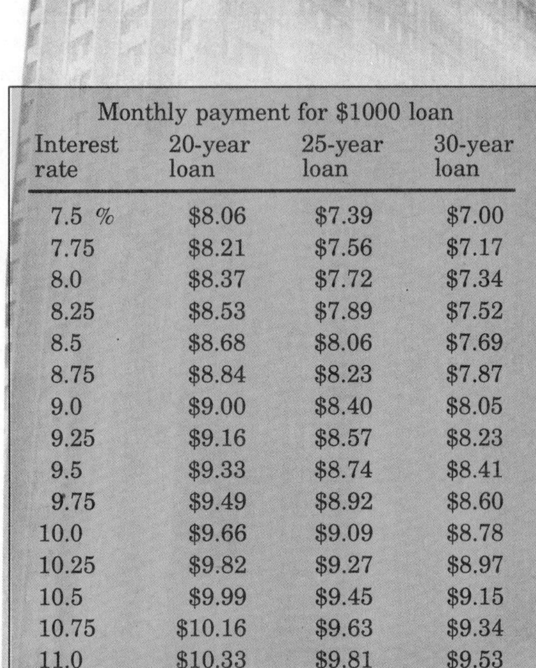

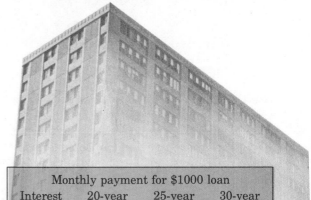

Monthly payment for $1000 loan			
Interest rate	20-year loan	25-year loan	30-year loan
7.5 %	$8.06	$7.39	$7.00
7.75	$8.21	$7.56	$7.17
8.0	$8.37	$7.72	$7.34
8.25	$8.53	$7.89	$7.52
8.5	$8.68	$8.06	$7.69
8.75	$8.84	$8.23	$7.87
9.0	$9.00	$8.40	$8.05
9.25	$9.16	$8.57	$8.23
9.5	$9.33	$8.74	$8.41
9.75	$9.49	$8.92	$8.60
10.0	$9.66	$9.09	$8.78
10.25	$9.82	$9.27	$8.97
10.5	$9.99	$9.45	$9.15
10.75	$10.16	$9.63	$9.34
11.0	$10.33	$9.81	$9.53

problem

Paula Jeffers has saved some money. She is interested in buying a condominium for $34,000. The savings and loan company told her she needs 20% of $34,000 for the down payment. She can borrow the rest of the money at 8.75% annual interest to be paid back over 25 years. How much does Paula need for the down payment? What will her monthly payment be?

solution

Find the amount of the down payment. Recall 20% = .20.

$.20 \times \$34,000 = \$6800$

Find the amount of the loan.

$\$34,000 - \$6800 = \$27,200$

Find the monthly payment. Use the table. The payment for a $1000 loan at 8.75% interest for 25 years is $8.23. Think of 27,200 as 27.2 thousands.

$\$8.23 \times 27.2 = \$223.856$

Paula's down payment is $6800. Her monthly payment will be $223.86.

exercises

Complete the table. Round the amount of the monthly payment to the nearest cent.

	Purchase price	Down payment	Amount of down payment	Amount of loan	Interest rate	Time (years)	Monthly payment
	$34,000	20%	$6800	$27,200	8.75%	25	$223.86
1.	$40,000	20%	**a.**	**b.**	8.25%	30	**c.**
2.	$40,000	10%	**a.**	**b.**	8.5%	20	**c.**
3.	$36,000	20%	**a.**	**b.**	9%	25	**c.**
4.	$36,000	30%	**a.**	**b.**	9.25%	30	**c.**
5.	$52,000	25%	**a.**	**b.**	9.5%	30	**c.**
6.	$45,000	30%	**a.**	**b.**	8.75%	30	**c.**
7.	$74,500	20%	**a.**	**b.**	9.75%	20	**c.**
8.	$62,800	25%	**a.**	**b.**	10%	25	**c.**

9. Find the difference in the amounts of the down payments for the two homes that cost $40,000. (Use the table above.)

10. Find the difference in the amounts of the down payments for the two homes that cost $36,000. (Use the table above.)

11. Find the difference in the monthly payments for these loans.
$32,700 at 9% interest for 25 years
$32,700 at 9% interest for 30 years

12. Find the difference in the monthly payments for these loans.
$38,300 at 9% interest for 25 years
$38,300 at 9.5% interest for 25 years

The purchase price of a home is $47,000.

13. Find the amount of the loan with a 10% down payment.

14. Find the amount of the loan with a 20% down payment.

15. Find the difference in the monthly payments for the loans in exercises 13 and 14 at 8.5% interest for 30 years.

Interest on a Mortgage Loan

On many home loans, people actually pay back between two and three times the amount they borrow.

problem

How much interest will be paid on a loan of $30,000 for 30 years if the annual interest rate is 8.5%?

solution

Using the method from the last lesson, you find that the monthly payment is $230.70.

Find the total number of payments.

Years		Payments per year		Total payments
30	×	12	=	360

Find the total amount repaid.

$230.70 × 360 = $83,052

Find the amount of interest.

Amount repaid		Amount borrowed		Amount of interest
$83,052	−	$30,000	=	$53,052

exercises

Complete this table. You will need to use the table on page 220 for exercises 5–7.

	Amount borrowed	Interest rate	Time (years)	Monthly payment	Total payments	Amount repaid	Amount of interest
	$30,000	8.5%	30	$230.70	360	$83,052	$53,052
1.	$30,000	8.5%	25	$241.80	**a.**	**b.**	**c.**
2.	$30,000	8.75%	30	$236.10	**a.**	**b.**	**c.**
3.	$30,000	8.75%	25	$246.90	**a.**	**b.**	**c.**
4.	$30,000	8.75%	20	$265.20	**a.**	**b.**	**c.**
5.	$25,800	9.5%	30	**a.**	**b.**	**c.**	**d.**
6.	$45,500	7.5%	20	**a.**	**b.**	**c.**	**d.**
7.	$45,500	11%	30	**a.**	**b.**	**c.**	**d.**

Use the answers you found for the table to help you with the following exercises.

8. Find the difference in the amounts of interest paid on these loans.
$30,000 at 8.75% interest for 30 years
$30,000 at 8.75% interest for 25 years

9. Find the difference in the amounts of interest paid on these loans.
$30,000 at 8.75% interest for 30 years
$30,000 at 8.75% interest for 20 years

10. Find the difference in the amounts of interest paid on these loans.
$30,000 at 8.5% interest for 25 years
$30,000 at 8.75% interest for 25 years

11. In exercises 6 and 7 you found the lowest and the highest amounts of interest shown on the mortgage table for a $45,500 loan. Find the difference between these amounts of interest.

12. In exercise 1, the amount repaid is how many times as great as the amount borrowed? (Round your answer to the nearest tenth.)

13. In exercise 2, the amount repaid is how many times as great as the amount borrowed? (Round your answer to the nearest tenth.)

Principal and Interest in a Monthly Payment

Part of each monthly payment is the interest for that month. The rest of the payment is used to reduce the principal.

problem

The Hermans are borrowing \$35,000 at 9% annual interest to be repaid over 30 years. Their monthly payment will be \$281.75. How much of their first monthly payment goes toward the principal, and how much is interest?

solution

Use the simple interest formula to find the interest for the first month.

$I = p \times r \times t$

$I = \$35{,}000 \times 9\% \times \frac{1}{12}$

$I = \$35{,}000 \times \frac{9}{100} \times \frac{1}{12}$

$I = \$262.50$

Find the amount paid on the principal the first month.

\$281.75	Monthly payment
− 262.50	Interest the first month
\$19.25	Amount paid on the principal

The first month the Hermans pay \$19.25 toward the principal and \$262.50 in interest.

To find the amount paid on the principal and the interest for the second month, you must start with the "new" principal. This is the amount of the loan that is unpaid after the first month.

\$35,000.00	Principal
− 19.25	Amount paid on principal
\$34,980.75	"New" principal

exercises

Find each amount listed.

1. The amount of interest for the second month. Use the "new" principal above. (Round your answer to the nearest cent.)
2. The amount paid on the principal the second month.
3. The "new" principal at the end of the second month.
4. The amount of interest for the third month. Use the "new" principal from exercise 3.
5. The amount paid on the principal the third month.
6. The "new" principal at the end of the third month.
7. The amount of interest for the fourth month.
8. The amount paid on the principal the fourth month.
9. The "new" principal at the end of the fourth month.

CALCULATOR EXERCISES

Many lending agencies provide their customers with an **amortization table.** It shows how each monthly payment is divided between interest and principal. Fill in the blanks in the Hermans' amortization table. Their monthly payment is $281.75.

	Herman Amortization Table			30-year loan	
	Payment number	Principal	Amount of interest	Amount paid on principal	"New" principal
	1	$35,000.00	$262.50	$19.25	$34,980.75
1.	2	$34,980.75	**a.**	**b.**	**c.**
2.	3	**a.**	**b.**	**c.**	**d.**
3.	4	**a.**	**b.**	**c.**	**d.**
4.	5	**a.**	**b.**	**c.**	**d.**
5.	6	**a.**	**b.**	**c.**	**d.**
6.	7	**a.**	**b.**	**c.**	**d.**
7.	301 (25 yr.)	$13,422.85	**a.**	**b.**	**c.**
8.	302	**a.**	**b.**	**c.**	**d.**
9.	303	**a.**	**b.**	**c.**	**d.**

Scott Lynch borrows $28,000 at 8.25% annual interest for 25 years. His monthly payment is $220.92. Fill in the blanks in Scott's amortization table.

	Lynch Amortization Table			25-year loan	
	Payment number	Principal	Amount of interest	Amount paid on principal	"New" principal
10.	1	**a.**	**b.**	**c.**	**d.**
11.	2	**a.**	**b.**	**c.**	**d.**
12.	3	**a.**	**b.**	**c.**	**d.**
13.	4	**a.**	**b.**	**c.**	**d.**

Homeowner's Insurance

Carl Meil is buying a house. The lender requires insurance so that the house is protected against any damages.

The insurance company charges an annual premium. It is based on the type of materials used to build the house, the location, and the amount the house is insured for.

Carl has several valuable articles. His insurance agent gave him the following table to determine the cost of insuring these items.

Personal property	One-year rate per $100 of value*
Jewelry	$1.35
Furs and garments trimmed with fur	$.33
Fine art not subject to breakage	$.14
Fine art subject to breakage	$.25
Cameras, projectors, etc.	$1.43
Musical instruments—amateur	$.44
Musical instruments—professional and organs	$2.75
Silverware, silver-plated ware, etc.	$.21
Stamp collections	$1.21
Coin collections	$2.20

*Only available in multiples of $100.

problem

Carl's basic premium for his homeowner's insurance is $120. He has a gold ring worth $700 and a camera worth $225 that he wants to insure separately. What is the total premium for his insurance?

solution

Rate for jewelry: $1.35 per $100
There are 7 hundreds in 700.

$\$1.35 \times 7 = \$9.45$

Rate for cameras: $1.43 per $100
Round $225 up to $300.
There are 3 hundreds in 300.

$\$1.43 \times 3 = \$4.29$

Find the total premium.

$120.00	Basic premium
9.45	Ring
+ 4.29	Camera
$133.74	Total premium

exercises

Find the annual premium for each item. Then find the total premium each person pays.

Teresa Granados pays a basic premium of $135.

1. $600 ring
2. $350 gold chain
3. $300 flute
4. $450 painting
5. Find Teresa's total premium.

Lawrence Hetter pays a basic premium of $125.

6. $975 organ
7. $325 violin
8. $250 watch
9. $800 coin collection
10. Find Lawrence's total premium.

Sam and Polly Pfaff pay a basic premium of $140.

11. $325 camera
12. $700 in silverware
13. $2300 stamp collection
14. $425 coat with fur collar
15. Find the Pfaffs' total premium.

Steve Miller is in a rock band that plays professionally. He insures his equipment as part of his homeowner's policy. Steve's basic premium is $130.

16. $325 drums
17. $150 bass guitar
18. $240 amplifier
19. $435 ring
20. Find Steve's total premium.

Many lending agencies require borrowers to pay $\frac{1}{12}$ of their annual homeowner's insurance premium every month. Find the amount each person listed below would pay for insurance each month. (Round your answers to the nearest cent.)

21. Teresa Granados
22. Lawrence Hetter
23. Sam and Polly Pfaff

Property Taxes

In most areas, the local government's chief source of income is the **property tax.** This is a tax paid each year, based upon the value of the property you own.

The local government taxes the property at a particular percentage of the current market value. This is known as the **rate of assessment.** This rate multiplied by the market value gives the **assessed valuation** of the property.

A **tax rate** is used to determine the amount of the property tax. This rate is often expressed in terms of an amount per $100 of the assessed valuation of the property.

problem

The market value of James and Lucille BearKings' condominium is $38,600. The rate of assessment in their area is 60% of the market value. The tax rate is $2.87 per $100 of assessed valuation. What is the annual property tax on the BearKings' condominium?

solution

Find the assessed valuation of the property. Recall 60% = .60.

.60 × $38,600 = $23,160

Find the property taxes.
Think of 23,160 as 231.6 hundreds.

$2.87 × 231.6 = $664.692

The BearKings' property taxes are $664.69 this year.

exercises

Complete the table. Round your answers to the nearest cent.

	Market value	Rate of assessment	Assessed valuation	Tax rate (per $100)	Property tax
	$38,600	60%	$23,160	$2.87	$664.69
1.	$37,000	50%	**a.**	$2.75	**b.**
2.	$35,000	60%	**a.**	$3.50	**b.**
3.	$48,500	50%	**a.**	$2.95	**b.**
4.	$56,700	60%	**a.**	$3.12	**b.**
5.	$42,800	60%	**a.**	$4.14	**b.**
6.	$59,900	50%	**a.**	$3.70	**b.**
7.	$45,750	30%	**a.**	$5.21	**b.**
8.	$36,900	25%	**a.**	$7.05	**b.**
9.	$48,500	30%	**a.**	$7.576	**b.**
10.	$51,700	35%	**a.**	$5.321	**b.**

11. The BearKings pay $\frac{1}{12}$ of their annual property taxes every month to the bank which holds their mortgage loan. This is to assure the payment of these taxes each year. How much do the BearKings pay for property taxes each month?

Closing Costs

Hillard and Barbara Head sign the necessary papers for the purchase of their new home. On this occasion there are fees that must be paid known as **closing costs.** The actual fees vary in different areas. Some basic closing costs paid by the buyer are listed here.

The **lawyer's fee** is often a percentage of the cost of the home. The lawyer reviews the documents of the sale.

Loan costs are usually a percentage of the amount of the loan. This covers items such as the loan application, an appraisal of the house, and a credit report on the buyer.

The **title examination fee** is often split with the seller. This involves a search into previous records of ownership of the property, to assure that no questions of rightful ownership do exist.

Taxes and government fees are often the largest portion of the closing costs. Some are listed here.

A **title transfer tax** is charged when property changes ownership. This tax is often split with the seller.

A fee for **recording** documents with government offices is often charged.

All or part of the property taxes for the rest of the year are also paid.

problem

The Heads' home cost $43,700. What is the recording fee if the Heads are charged 1.5% of the purchase price?

solution

Find 1.5% of $43,700.

$.015 \times \$43{,}700 = \$655.50$

The recording fee is $655.50.

exercises

For each buyer, find the fees listed and the total closing costs.

The Zobels: $45,000 purchase price
$36,000 loan

1. Lawyer: .75% of purchase price
2. Loan costs: 1.5% of loan
3. Title examination: $180, half paid by the Zobels
4. Title transfer: 2% of purchase price, half paid by the Zobels
5. Recording: .5% of purchase price
6. The Zobels must also pay $78.53 for property taxes this year. What are their total closing costs?

Dick Kowalski: $38,500 purchase price
$34,650 loan

7. Lawyer: .6% of purchase price
8. Loan costs: 1.25% of loan
9. Title examination: $195, 75% paid by Dick
10. Title transfer: 2% of purchase price, half paid by Dick
11. Recording: .05% of purchase price
12. Dick must also pay $663.50 for property taxes. What are his total closing costs?

The Corrins: $56,000 purchase price
$44,800 loan

13. Loan costs: 1% of loan
14. Title examination: $235, half paid by the Corrins
15. Title transfer: 2.5% of purchase price, half paid by the Corrins
16. Recording: 1.5% of purchase price
17. The Corrins must also pay $225 for their property taxes for the current year. The fee for their lawyer is $150. What are the Corrins' total closing costs?

career

Real Estate Agent

Career Cluster: Social Service

Sarah Chatfield is a real estate agent. Her job is to bring together people who want to sell property with those who want to buy property.

problem

The agency Sarah works for charges a 6% commission for selling a house. Wilma and John Guyton want to receive at least $43,000 on the sale of their home. For what price should Sarah list the Guytons' home?

solution

Let L represent the list price of the house.

The agency will receive 6% of L, or $.06L$.

List price		Commission		Amount desired by seller	
L	$-$	$.06L$	$=$	\$43,000	
$1.00L$	$-$	$.06L$	$=$	\$43,000	Write L as $1.00L$.
		$.94L$	$=$	\$43,000	$1.00L - .06L = (1.00 - .06)L$
		L	$=$	\$45,744.68	Divide both sides by .94.
		L	$\approx$	\$45,800	Round up to the nearest hundred dollars.

Sarah should list the Guytons' home for $45,800.

exercises

For what price should each house be listed? Use the commission rate given. Round answers up to the nearest hundred dollars.

	Amount desired by seller	Commission
1.	$47,800	6%
2.	$38,800	6%
3.	$52,700	7%
4.	$42,000	6%
5.	$48,500	7%

6. Suppose Sarah's agency changes the commission to 7%. For what amount should Sarah list the Guytons' house?

7. For the Guytons' house, find the difference between the list prices with a 6% commission and a 7% commission.

8. Suppose Sarah earns 4% on any house she sells. What would her earnings be on a $37,500 sale?

9. Sarah sold the Wilsons' house for $36,500, the Wheatleys' house for $58,900, and the Mitchells' house for $46,500 during a three-month period. At a 4.5% commission, what did Sarah earn for that period?

10. The Walker Real Estate Agency sold Miyoshi Tamura's house for $39,900. After the 6% commission was deducted, how much did Miyoshi receive from the sale of her house?

problem

Dave Peters is being transferred to Dallas. Sarah told him a new house, in the area he wants to live, will cost about $60,000. What can Dave expect to pay for a down payment?

solution

Sarah uses this table, prepared by the Federal Home Loan Bank Board.

Averages in Home Loans January, 1977

	New houses			Used houses		
Metropolitan area	Interest rate	Purchase price	Down payment	Interest rate	Purchase price	Down payment
Atlanta	8.74%	$53,300	23.0%	8.75%	$51,000	20.2%
Baltimore	8.74	60,100	30.5	9.00	46,700	30.1
Boston	8.55	60,900	35.0	8.65	53,500	32.5
Chicago-Northwestern Indiana	8.69	54,200	32.7	8.68	50,700	29.5
Cleveland	8.68	54,900	29.6	8.79	44,300	26.5
Dallas	8.96	56,600	19.1	9.02	54,700	18.2
Denver	8.84	55,400	24.6	8.92	52,800	25.9
Detroit	8.86	48,700	32.0	9.12	40,200	22.3
Houston	8.97	52,600	15.3	9.03	51,200	16.6
Los Angeles-Long Beach	8.99	61,200	20.4	9.12	63,500	22.5
Miami	8.48	56,300	24.2	8.49	46,900	23.6
Minneapolis-St. Paul	8.74	51,000	29.8	8.71	52,200	25.1
New York-Northeastern New Jersey	8.55	56,400	27.9	8.56	53,300	35.6
Philadelphia	8.71	48,900	29.5	9.09	43,800	26.7
St. Louis	8.90	41,300	23.5	8.98	35,100	24.5
San Francisco-Oakland	9.02	71,800	22.7	9.07	64,500	23.9
Seattle-Everett	9.12	47,200	19.4	9.15	44,900	21.1
Washington, D.C., Maryland, Virginia	8.83	59,300	20.0	8.99	58,500	26.4
U.S. average	8.80	55,000	25.5	8.90	50,400	25.1

Sarah reads 19.1% from the table. Then she finds 19.1% of $60,000.

$.191 \times \$60{,}000 = \$11{,}460$

Dave can expect to pay $11,460 for his down payment.

exercises

11. Eleanor Hesen is moving to Atlanta. She expects to buy a used home for \$55,000. What can Eleanor expect to pay for her down payment?

12. Grace and Oliver Matthews are moving to Seattle. They plan to spend \$50,000 on a new house. What can they expect to pay for a down payment?

13. Rosalee and Grayson Woodbury are being transferred to the New York area. They hope to find a house for \$58,000.

    a. What can they expect to pay for a down payment on a new house?

    b. What can they expect to pay for a down payment on a used house?

    c. Find the difference between these two amounts.

14. Mickey and Bob Moore are moving to Detroit. They ask Sarah's advice on whether to buy a new or used house. What is the difference in the average purchase prices of new and used houses in Detroit?

15. Paul Fast Wolf is moving to Denver. What is the difference in the average purchase prices of new and used homes in Denver?

16. List the cities in order based on the average purchase price of new homes. List the most expensive first.

17. List the cities in order based on the average purchase price of used homes. List the most expensive first.

18. List the areas where the average interest rate is higher for a new house than for a used house.

What is the measure of each angle? Use a straightedge (ruler, card, or edge of paper) to line up point M with the other points. Use the top scale on the protractor when one side of the angle goes through point A. Use the bottom scale when one side of the angle goes through point G. For example, ∠AME = 143° and ∠GME = 37°.

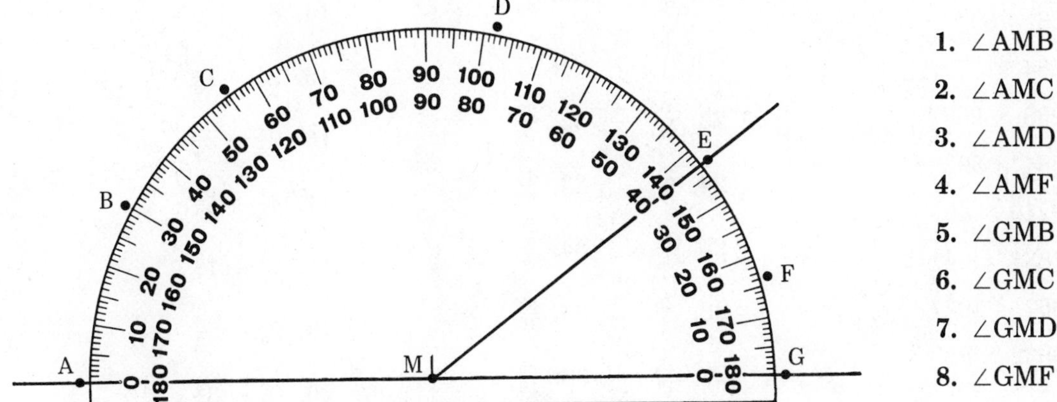

1. ∠AMB
2. ∠AMC
3. ∠AMD
4. ∠AMF
5. ∠GMB
6. ∠GMC
7. ∠GMD
8. ∠GMF

skills tune-up

Multiplying whole numbers, pages 8-9

1. 40 × 80
2. 60 × 90
3. 100 × 30
4. 200 × 500
5. 700 × 400
6. 3000 × 70
7. 50 × 9000
8. 800 × 6000
9. 7000 × 1200
10. 400 × 920
11. 250 × 700
12. 3600 × 200
13. 800 × 4300
14. 22 × 9
15. 48 × 17
16. 60 × 53
17. 7 × 291
18. 402 × 6
19. 28 × 632
20. 564 × 37
21. 268 × 808
22. 584 × 392
23. 9219 × 40
24. 2831 × 64
25. 667 × 1927
26. 5932 × 889

Renaming fractions and mixed numbers, pages 14-15

Rename in lowest terms.

1. $\frac{5}{10}$
2. $\frac{8}{12}$
3. $\frac{12}{16}$
4. $\frac{3}{15}$
5. $\frac{10}{15}$
6. $\frac{8}{16}$
7. $\frac{9}{24}$
8. $\frac{4}{16}$
9. $\frac{8}{24}$
10. $\frac{18}{24}$
11. $\frac{5}{45}$
12. $\frac{24}{36}$
13. $\frac{7}{56}$
14. $\frac{32}{40}$
15. $\frac{63}{72}$
16. $\frac{27}{54}$
17. $\frac{18}{90}$
18. $\frac{44}{66}$

Write as a mixed number.

19. $\frac{9}{2}$
20. $\frac{15}{4}$
21. $\frac{21}{6}$
22. $\frac{19}{5}$
23. $\frac{18}{12}$
24. $\frac{21}{8}$
25. $\frac{13}{2}$
26. $\frac{26}{3}$
27. $\frac{25}{10}$
28. $\frac{37}{5}$
29. $\frac{31}{8}$
30. $\frac{45}{36}$
31. $\frac{48}{11}$
32. $\frac{29}{7}$
33. $\frac{44}{33}$
34. $\frac{57}{8}$
35. $\frac{65}{10}$
36. $\frac{25}{15}$

Dividing fractions and mixed numbers, pages 16-17

1. $\frac{3}{4} \div \frac{1}{2}$
2. $\frac{1}{4} \div \frac{2}{3}$
3. $\frac{3}{8} \div \frac{1}{3}$
4. $\frac{9}{10} \div \frac{3}{4}$
5. $\frac{3}{5} \div \frac{7}{8}$
6. $\frac{7}{8} \div \frac{5}{6}$
7. $5 \div \frac{2}{3}$
8. $\frac{1}{2} \div 3$
9. $6 \div \frac{3}{8}$
10. $\frac{3}{5} \div 9$
11. $3\frac{3}{4} \div \frac{3}{5}$
12. $\frac{2}{3} \div 1\frac{1}{2}$
13. $5\frac{1}{3} \div 3$
14. $8 \div 1\frac{1}{3}$
15. $2\frac{7}{8} \div 1\frac{7}{8}$
16. $9\frac{1}{4} \div 2\frac{3}{4}$
17. $4\frac{1}{6} \div 5\frac{2}{3}$
18. $7\frac{4}{5} \div 1\frac{6}{7}$
19. $2\frac{3}{4} \div 3\frac{2}{3}$
20. $8\frac{5}{9} \div 3\frac{2}{3}$

Chapter 11

review

Amount to spend for a home, pages 218–219

1. Carol Madsen earns $7.45 per hour in a 40-hour work week. What is the greatest amount she should spend for a home? Can she consider a house costing $36,500? (Use the general guideline of 2.5 times annual income.)

Down payment and monthly payment, pages 220–221

2. Juan Espejo is buying a condominium for $48,500. He must make a 20% down payment. What is the amount of the loan after the down payment?

3. What is the monthly payment for Juan's loan if the annual interest rate is 9.25% for 25 years? (Use the table on page 220.)

Interest on a mortgage loan, pages 222–223

4. What is the total amount of interest that will be paid on a loan of $35,000 at 8.5% annual interest for 30 years? The monthly payment is $269.15.

Principal and interest in a monthly payment, page 224

5. Nancy Mikula borrows $27,000 at 8% annual interest for 25 years. What is the amount of interest she will pay the first month?

6. If Nancy's monthly payment is $208.44, what is the principal for the second month?

Homeowner's insurance, pages 226–227

7. Joyce's annual premium for her homeowner's insurance is $125. She wants to insure a watch worth $225 separately. What is the total premium for her insurance? (Use the table on page 226.)

Property taxes, pages 228–229

8. The Statens' property has a market value of $38,400. The rate of assessment in the area is 60%. The tax rate is $3.23 per $100 of assessed valuation. What is the Statens' property tax?

Closing costs, pages 230–231

9. The Condiffs paid a lawyer's fee of .5% of the purchase price of their home. What was the fee if the house cost $47,800?

Real estate agent, pages 232–235

10. Hal Parsons is a real estate agent. For what amount should he list a house so that the seller will receive at least $52,000? The commission is 6%. (Round the answer up to the nearest hundred dollars.)

Chapter 11

test

1. Paul Labe earns $6.85 per hour in a 40-hour work week. What is the greatest amount he should spend for a home? Can he consider a house that costs $42,500? (Use the general guideline of 2.5 times annual income.)

2. Elizabeth Markley is buying a home that costs $43,000. She makes a 10% down payment. What is the amount of the loan after the down payment?

3. What is Elizabeth's monthly payment if the annual interest rate is 8.75% for 30 years? (Use the table on page 220.)

4. What is the total amount of interest that will be paid on a loan of $31,500 at 9.5% annual interest for 25 years? The monthly payment is $275.31.

5. Machiko Ohira borrows $29,000 at 9% annual interest for 25 years. What is the amount of interest she will pay the first month?

6. If Machiko's monthly payment is $234.60, what is the principal for the second month?

7. Walter's basic premium for his homeowner's insurance is $130. He has a stamp collection worth $2100 that he wants to insure separately. What is the total premium for his insurance? (Use the table on page 226.)

8. The Waltons' property has a market value of $42,700. The rate of assessment in the area is 50%. The tax rate is $3.71 per $100 of assessed valuation. What is the Waltons' property tax?

9. At the Springfield Bank the recording fee is .75% of the purchase price of the home. What is the fee if a house costs $56,200?

10. Tracy Johnson sells real estate. For what amount should she list a house if the sellers hope to get at least $44,000? The real estate commission is 7%. (Round the answer up to the nearest hundred dollars.)

Chapter 12

Building a Home

Some people want to build a home to fit their needs. In making plans, they consult architects, contractors, and trade and construction workers.

career

Surveyor

Career Cluster: Technical

John Wysong is a surveyor. People who want to build a home often employ a surveyor to make a scale drawing of their property.

For his drawing, John uses the scale lengths and the **bearings** of each side of the lot. A bearing of N 81° W means to face directly NORTH and then turn WEST an angle of 81°.

problem

The bearings and lengths of the sides of a lot are N 11° W, 39 m; S 85° E, 41 m; S 8° W, 40 m; and N 80° W, 29 m. Make a drawing of the property, using a scale of 1 cm = 10 m.

solution

Diagram 1: N 11° W, 39 m

Select a starting point A. Draw a north-south line through A. Facing north from point A, mark off and draw an angle of 11° west of the north-south line. Determine the scale length of the side of the lot.

$$\frac{1}{10} = \frac{x}{39}$$

x ⟵ Scale length in centimeters

39 ⟵ Actual length in meters

$3.9 = x$

Measure 3.9 cm from point A. Label this point B.

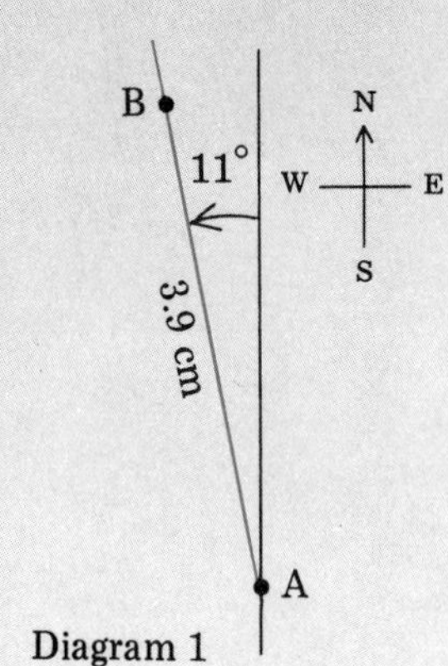

Diagram 1

Since the bearings follow around the diagram in order, the next line will come from point B.

Diagram 2: S 85° E, 41 m

Draw a north-south line through B. Facing south from point B, mark off and draw an angle of 85° east of the north-south line. Use a proportion to find the scale length of this side, 4.1 cm. Measure 4.1 cm from point B. Label this point C.

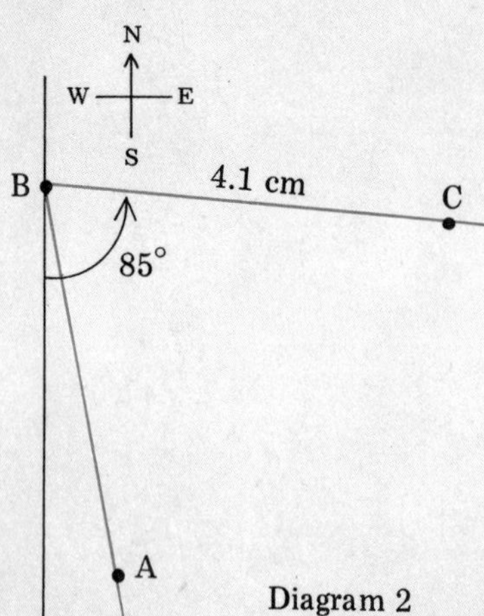

Diagram 2

Complete the last two sides as shown below. Label each side with the bearing and the actual length.

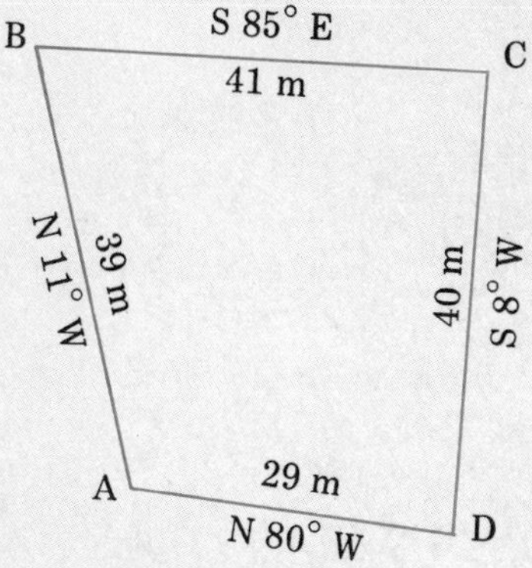

exercises

For exercises 1–8, draw an angle and one side of the lot as shown in Diagram 1. Use a scale of 1 cm = 10 m.

1. N 15° W, 20 m

2. N 87° W, 40 m

3. N 76° E, 38 m

4. N 32° E, 22 m

5. S 18° E, 54 m

6. S 65° E, 42 m

7. S 21° W, 35 m

8. S 9° W, 28 m

For exercises 9–12, draw the diagram of each lot by using the bearings and the lengths given. Use a scale of 1 cm = 10 m.

9. N 10° W, 45 m; S 80° E, 40 m; S 5° W, 44 m; and N 77° W, 27 m

10. N 20° W, 50 m; N 75° E, 53 m; S 6° W, 64 m; and N 84° W, 27 m

11. N 12° E, 42 m; N 72° E, 38 m; S 16° E, 65 m; and N 81° W, 64 m

12. N 7° E, 54 m; S 73° E, 43 m; S 17° W, 36 m; and S 81° W, 38 m

Cost of Building a Home

Diana and Miguel Vasquez want to build a home. A building contractor told them the cost is based on the size and style of home and the kind of building materials they use.

problem

Miguel and Diana decide on the one-story home shown here. They want a brick exterior. The contractor said that the house will cost about \$32 per square foot. The garage will cost about \$9.50 per square foot. What is the estimated cost of building the house with a garage?

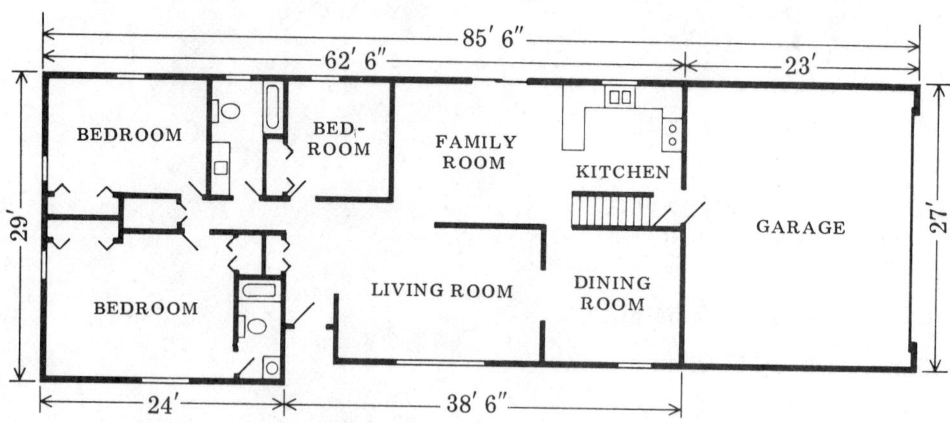

solution

To find the total area of the house, find the area of each rectangular region and add.

$24' \times 29' = 696$ sq. ft. — Area of left side

$38'\ 6'' = 38\frac{1}{2}'$

$38\frac{1}{2}' \times 27' = 1039\frac{1}{2}$ sq. ft. — Area of middle

$696 + 1039\frac{1}{2} = 1735\frac{1}{2}$

The total area of the house, rounded to the nearest square foot, is 1736 square feet.

Find the cost of the house.

$\$32 \times 1736 = \$55{,}552$

Find the area of the garage.

$23' \times 27' = 621$ sq. ft.

Find the cost of the garage.

$\$9.50 \times 621 = \$5899.50$

Find the total estimate.

$\$55{,}552.00 + \$5899.50 = \$61{,}451.50$

exercises

A two-story home usually costs less to build than a one-story home with the same living area. This is because a smaller roof is required. This house costs about $27.50 per square foot. The garage costs about $9.00 per square foot.

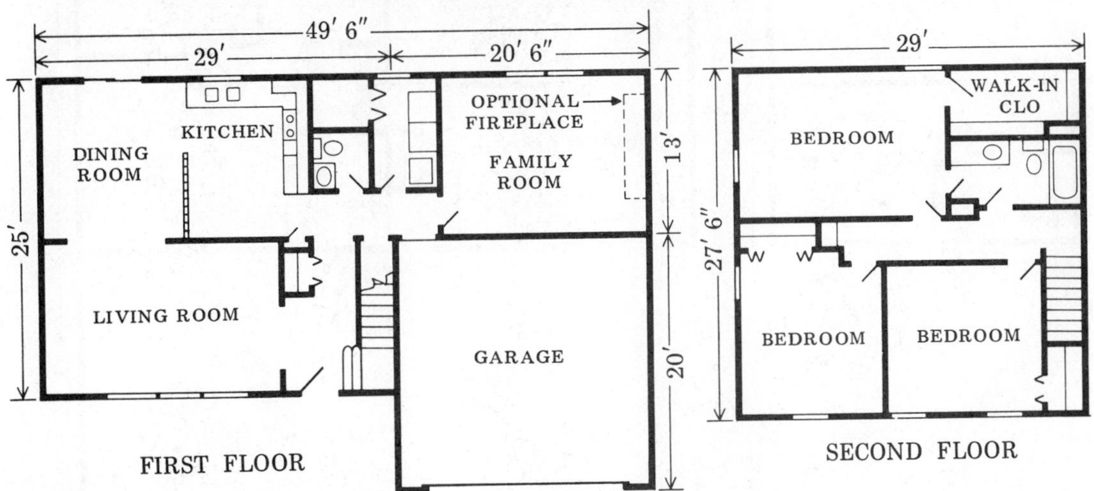

Estimate the cost of construction by finding these areas and costs.

1. Area of left side of first floor
2. Area of right side of first floor, without the garage
3. Area of second floor
4. Total area of house
5. Cost of house
6. Area of garage
7. Cost of garage
8. Total estimate

Split-level homes cost relatively less to build because much of the living space is included in the basement area. This house costs about $29 per square foot. The garage costs about $9.25 per square foot.

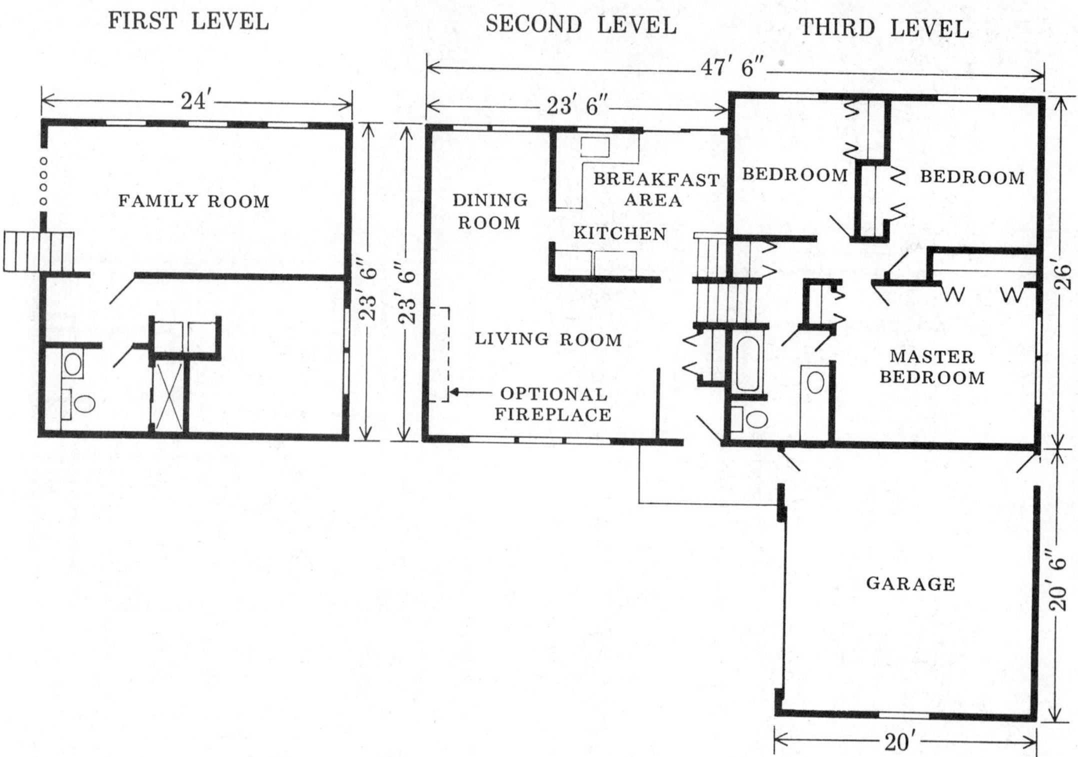

Estimate the cost of construction by finding these areas and costs.

9. Area of first level
10. Area of second level
11. Area of third level
12. Total area of house, rounded to the nearest square foot
13. Cost of house
14. Area of garage
15. Cost of garage
16. Total estimate

CALCULATOR EXERCISES

A builder is quoting the following prices for new homes. Complete the table and determine each total estimate.

	Style	Cost per square foot		Area (sq. ft.)				Estimate		
		House	Garage	First level	Second level	Third level	Garage	House	Garage	Total
	Homes built with aluminum-siding exterior									
1.	One-story	$31.50	$9.00	1750	—	—	625	a.	b.	c.
2.	Two-story	$26.50	$8.50	1000	950	—	450	a.	b.	c.
3.	Split-level	$29.00	$8.50	570	580	725	425	a.	b.	c.
	Homes built with brick exterior									
4.	One-story	$33.50	$9.50	1685	—	—	340	a.	b.	c.
5.	Two-story	$28.00	$9.00	950	1065	—	615	a.	b.	c.
6.	Split-level	$29.50	—	615	700	775	—	a.	—	b.
	Homes built with stone exterior									
7.	One-story	$37.00	$10.00	1925	—	—	585	a.	b.	c.
8.	Two-story	$29.50	—	875	925	—	—	a.	—	b.
9.	Split-level	$30.50	$9.50	430	490	675	585	a.	b.	c.
	Homes built with wood exterior									
10.	One-story	$30.00	$9.00	1875	—	—	500	a.	b.	c.
11.	Two-story	$25.50	$8.50	1050	1100	—	585	a.	b.	c.
12.	Split-level	$28.00	$8.50	650	670	580	550	a.	b.	c.

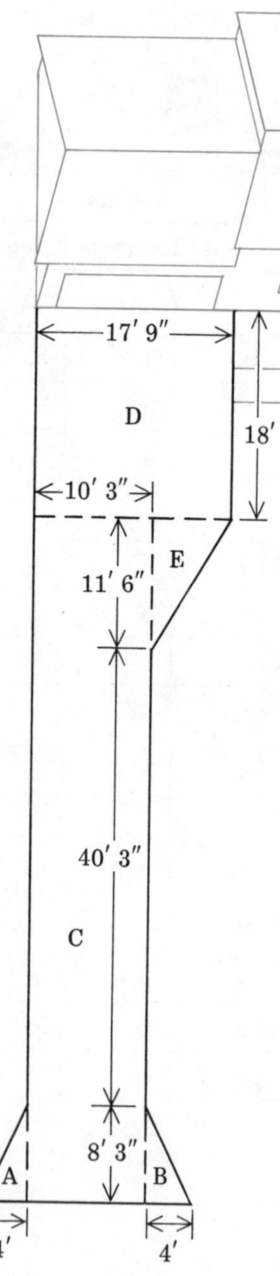

Cost of Installing a Driveway

Peter Dubois wants to install a driveway. The contractor gave him an estimate based on a price per square foot. To determine the total cost, Peter must find the area of the driveway.

The contractor told Peter that the process requires spreading and rolling coarse gravel. This costs \$.55 per square foot. Next a blacktop is applied. This costs \$.40 per square foot.

problem

Peter made the measurements as shown in the diagram. He divided the sketch into rectangles and triangles and labeled each region. What is the area of region A?

solution

The area of a triangle is $\frac{1}{2}$ times the *base* times the *height*. Recall that 8′ 3″ is $8\frac{1}{4}'$.

$A = \frac{1}{2} \times b \times h$

$A = \frac{1}{2} \times 4' \times 8\frac{1}{4}'$

$A = 16\frac{1}{2}$ sq. ft.

The area of region A is $16\frac{1}{2}$ square feet.

exercises

Find the area of each region.

1. Region B
2. Region C
3. Region D
4. Region E
5. Find the total area of the driveway. (Round the answer to the nearest square foot.)
6. Find the cost of the gravel. ($\$.55 \times$ total area)
7. Find the cost of the blacktop.
8. Find the total cost of Peter Dubois's driveway.

A sketch of Liz Kakar's driveway is shown here. Use the same costs as were used for Peter Dubois's driveway to find the cost of installing Liz's driveway.

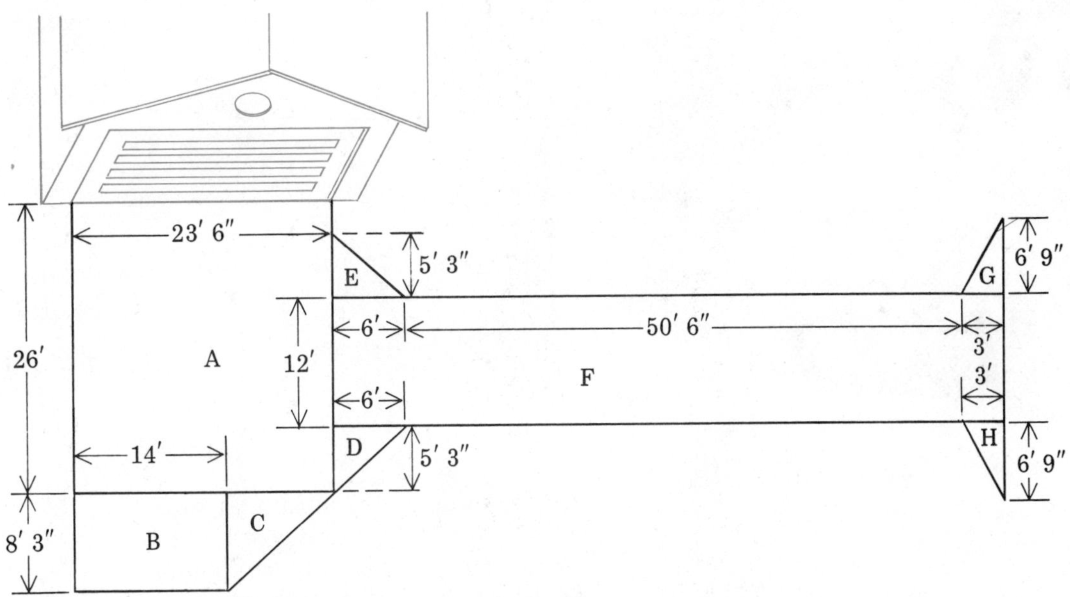

Find the area of each region.

9. Region A
10. Region B
11. Region C
12. Region D
13. Region E
14. Region F
15. Region G
16. Region H
17. Find the total area of the driveway. (Round the answer to the nearest square foot.)
18. Find the cost of the gravel.
19. Find the cost of the blacktop.
20. Find the total cost of Liz Kakar's driveway.

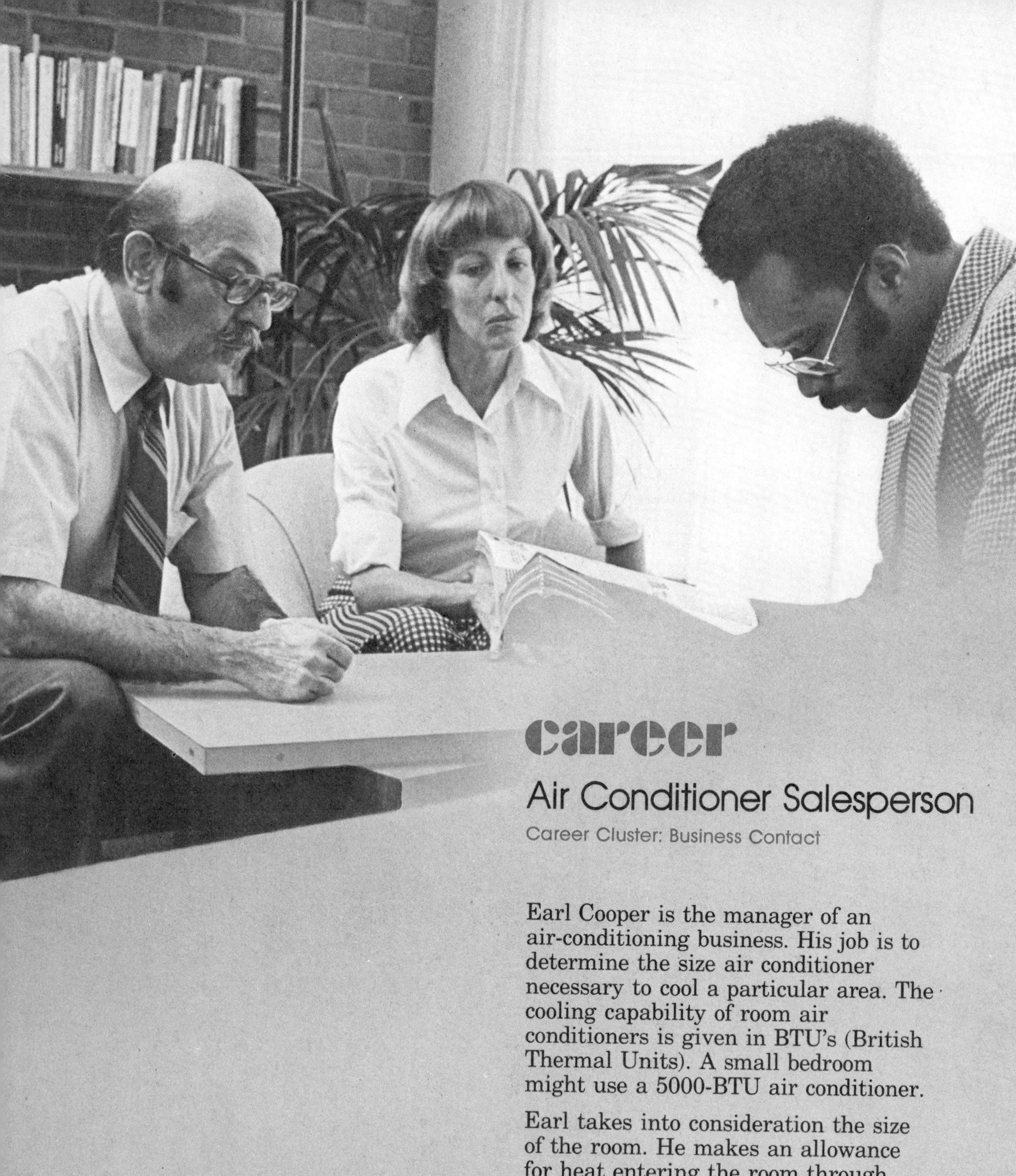

career

Air Conditioner Salesperson

Career Cluster: Business Contact

Earl Cooper is the manager of an air-conditioning business. His job is to determine the size air conditioner necessary to cool a particular area. The cooling capability of room air conditioners is given in BTU's (British Thermal Units). A small bedroom might use a 5000-BTU air conditioner.

Earl takes into consideration the size of the room. He makes an allowance for heat entering the room through doors and windows. Then he completes a form that indicates the size air conditioner needed.

problem

What is the allowance for heat entering from the windows of this room? The windows are 3′ high.

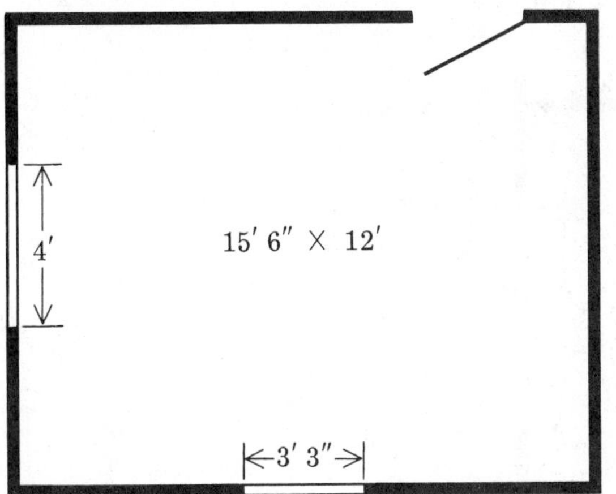

solution

Earl consults his form and realizes he must find the area of each window and then multiply by the given factor.

Find the area of the west window.

$4' \times 3' = 12$ sq. ft.

Multiply the area by the factor for a west window.

$12 \times 65 = 780$

Find the area of the south window. Recall 3′ 3″ is $3\frac{1}{4}'$.

$3\frac{1}{4}' \times 3' = 9\frac{3}{4}$ sq. ft.

Multiply the area by the factor for a south window.

$9\frac{3}{4} \times 35 = 341\frac{1}{4}$

All entries are to be rounded to the nearest whole number. Earl enters 780 and 341 on his form. Following the directions on the form, Earl enters 780 in the "Allowance" column.

HEAT SOURCE	SIZE		FACTOR		ALLOWANCE
				Enter at right only the largest figure from the column below.	
1. WINDOW DIRECTION	area				
a. west	12	sq. ft. ×	65	780	
b. east		sq. ft. ×	40		
c. south	9 3/4	sq. ft. ×	35	341	
d. north		sq. ft. ×	0		780
2. WINDOW CONSTRUCTION	area				

exercises

Jane and Richard Kirkendall live in Las Vegas. They want to air-condition several rooms in their home. Jane's diagram and notes of the family room are shown here.

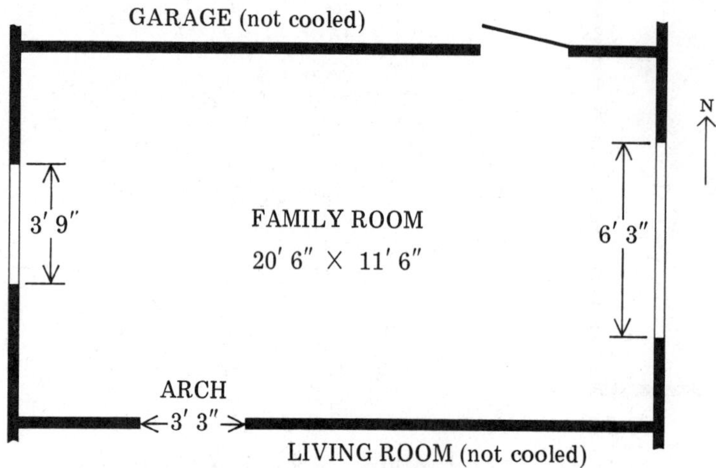

All windows are 4′ high with double-glass.
There is a bedroom above this room.
There are 4 people in the family.
Greatest wattage used is 500 watts.

Complete Earl's estimate for the Kirkendalls' family room by filling in the appropriate spaces.

HEAT SOURCE	SIZE	FACTOR		ALLOWANCE
1. WINDOW DIRECTION	area		Enter at right only the largest figure from the column below.	
a. west	______ sq. ft.	× 65	______	
b. east	______ sq. ft.	× 40	______	
c. south	______ sq. ft.	× 35	______	
d. north	______ sq. ft.	× 0	______	______
2. WINDOW CONSTRUCTION	area			
a. single-glass	______ sq. ft.	× 14		______
b. double-glass or storm windows	______ sq. ft.	× 7		______
3. OPEN DOORS AND ARCHES (between cooled and uncooled space)	width ______ ft.	× 300		______
4. WALLS	length			
a. outside walls—north side	______ ft.	× 25		______
b. outside walls—all others	______ ft.	× 45		______
	______ ft.	× 45		______
c. inside walls—between cooled and uncooled space	______ ft.	× 30		______
	______ ft.	× 30		______
5. CEILING	area			
a. insulated with attic above	______ sq. ft.	× 5		______
b. occupied space above	______ sq. ft.	× 3		______
6. PEOPLE (Use at least two people.)	______	× 600		______
7. ELECTRICAL EQUIPMENT (Use all wattage except air conditioner.)	______	× 3		______
8. SUBTOTAL				______
9. TOTAL COOLING LOAD (Multiply the subtotal by the correction factor shown on the map.)				______
10. NUMBER OF BTU'S TO BUY (Round the total cooling load to the next highest thousand.)				______

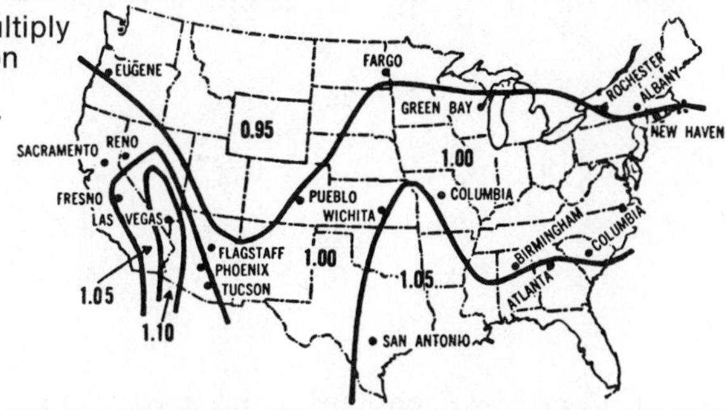

skills tune-up

Multiplying fractions and mixed numbers, pages 16–17

1. $\frac{3}{4} \times \frac{7}{12}$
2. $\frac{5}{8} \times \frac{6}{7}$
3. $\frac{4}{7} \times \frac{7}{10}$
4. $\frac{5}{6} \times \frac{3}{5}$
5. $\frac{11}{28} \times \frac{21}{22}$
6. $12 \times \frac{1}{16}$
7. $\frac{2}{7} \times 28$
8. $\frac{1}{3} \times 14$
9. $1\frac{1}{4} \times \frac{1}{2}$
10. $12\frac{1}{2} \times \frac{5}{16}$
11. $1\frac{4}{5} \times 1\frac{1}{3}$
12. $8\frac{1}{3} \times 1\frac{1}{2}$
13. $5\frac{3}{4} \times 6\frac{2}{3}$
14. $2\frac{1}{12} \times 3\frac{9}{10}$
15. $7\frac{6}{7} \times 2\frac{2}{5}$
16. $6 \times 8\frac{5}{6}$
17. $5\frac{9}{16} \times 4$
18. $\frac{1}{7} \times \frac{7}{10} \times \frac{3}{4}$
19. $\frac{1}{4} \times 6\frac{3}{5} \times \frac{10}{11}$
20. $4\frac{3}{8} \times 1\frac{1}{3} \times \frac{2}{5}$

Adding fractions and mixed numbers, pages 18–19

1. $\frac{1}{3} + \frac{5}{12}$
2. $\frac{2}{15} + \frac{2}{5}$
3. $\frac{7}{12} + \frac{5}{6}$
4. $\frac{7}{15} + \frac{1}{5}$
5. $\frac{1}{9} + \frac{5}{6}$
6. $\frac{11}{12} + \frac{2}{3}$
7. $\frac{8}{15} + \frac{2}{3}$
8. $\frac{5}{8} + \frac{5}{16}$
9. $\frac{1}{3} + 2\frac{1}{4}$
10. $4\frac{1}{8} + \frac{1}{6}$
11. $2\frac{1}{3} + 1\frac{1}{6}$
12. $2\frac{2}{5} + 6\frac{7}{20}$
13. $5\frac{7}{8} + 3\frac{1}{3}$
14. $1\frac{1}{2} + 2\frac{5}{6}$
15. $9\frac{8}{15} + 4\frac{1}{3}$
16. $2\frac{1}{6} + 5\frac{5}{8}$
17. $3\frac{13}{30} + 6\frac{7}{10}$
18. $6\frac{13}{24} + 3\frac{3}{8}$
19. $1\frac{1}{2} + 2\frac{1}{7} + 3\frac{5}{14}$
20. $11\frac{4}{5} + 6\frac{9}{10} + 9\frac{1}{2}$

Subtracting fractions and mixed numbers, pages 18–19

1. $\frac{9}{14} - \frac{1}{7}$
2. $\frac{13}{18} - \frac{2}{9}$
3. $\frac{3}{5} - \frac{1}{2}$
4. $\frac{19}{24} - \frac{1}{3}$
5. $\frac{8}{9} - \frac{13}{18}$
6. $\frac{11}{12} - \frac{1}{6}$
7. $\frac{9}{16} - \frac{3}{8}$
8. $\frac{2}{5} - \frac{7}{30}$
9. $10\frac{1}{3} - 1\frac{2}{3}$
10. $19\frac{2}{7} - 1\frac{6}{7}$
11. $3 - \frac{1}{3}$
12. $9 - \frac{1}{5}$
13. $5\frac{1}{4} - 3\frac{1}{8}$
14. $16\frac{2}{5} - 1\frac{7}{10}$
15. $7\frac{7}{9} - 4\frac{1}{6}$
16. $12\frac{2}{7} - 3\frac{11}{14}$
17. $5\frac{1}{6} - 2\frac{2}{9}$
18. $12\frac{1}{5} - 5\frac{2}{3}$
19. $6\frac{1}{12} - 4\frac{1}{4}$
20. $14\frac{1}{3} - 3\frac{4}{9}$

Chapter 12

review

Surveyor, pages 240–241

1. Draw the angle and one side of the lot. Use the bearing and length S 76° W, 42 m. Use a scale of 1 cm = 10 m.

Cost of building a home, pages 242–244

For the home shown here, find the areas of the parts listed.

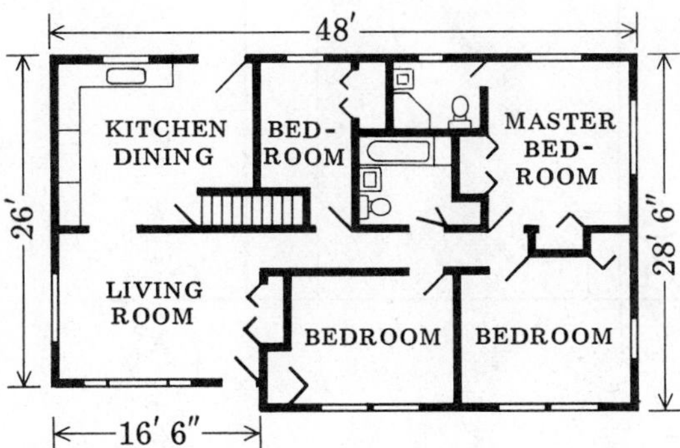

2. Area of left side
3. Area of right side
4. Find the cost estimate for this home if a builder makes a bid of $35 per square foot. (Round the total area of the house to the nearest square foot before figuring the estimate.)

Cost of installing a driveway, pages 246–247

Find the areas of the regions listed.

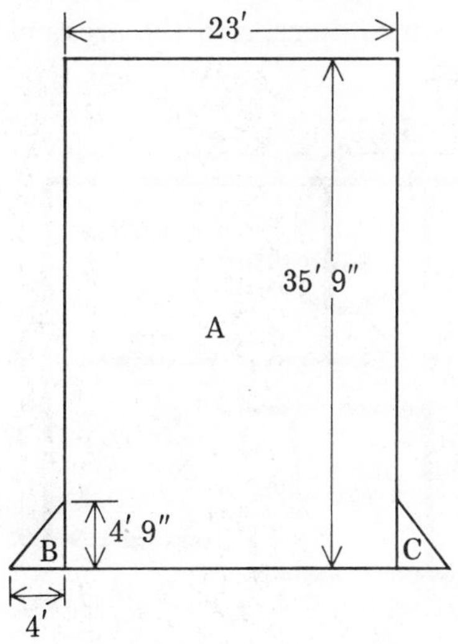

5. Region A
6. Region B
7. Find the total area of the driveway. Regions B and C are the same size. (Round your answer to the nearest square foot.)
8. A contractor will install this driveway for $.90 a square foot. What is the cost of the driveway?

Air-conditioner salesperson, pages 248–251

For exercises 9–10, use the form on page 251.

9. Find the allowance for heat entering a south window that measures 4′ 6″ by 5′.
10. Find the allowance for heat entering from an inside wall between cooled and uncooled space. The wall is 16′ 6″ long.

Chapter 12
test

1. Draw the angle and one side of the lot. Use the bearing and length N 84° E, 47 m. Use a scale of 1 cm = 10 m.

For the home shown here, find the areas of the parts listed.

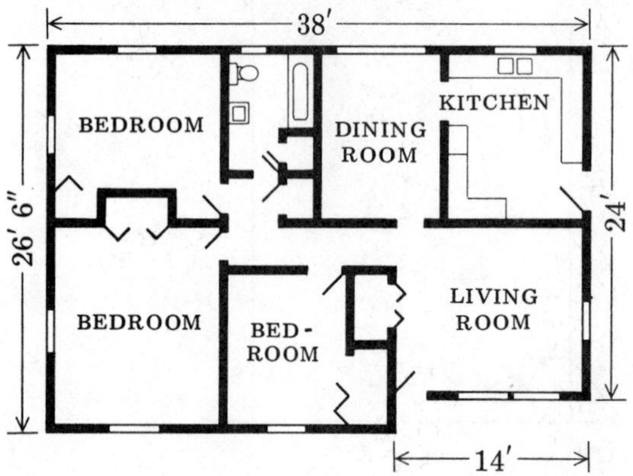

2. Area of right side
3. Area of left side
4. Find the cost estimate for this home if a builder makes a bid of $37 per square foot.

Find the areas of the regions listed.

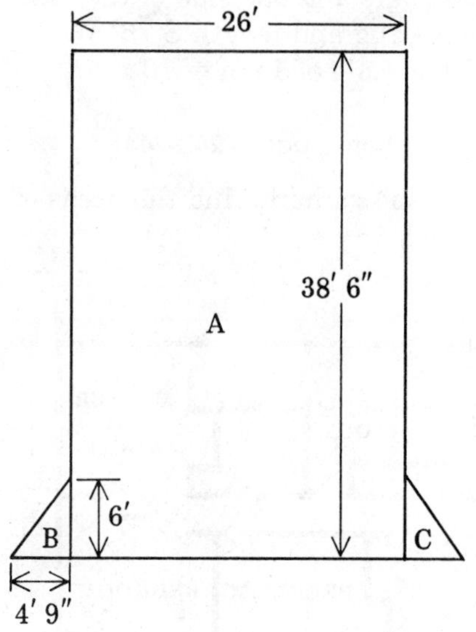

5. Region A
6. Region B
7. Find the total area of the driveway. Regions B and C are the same size. (Round your answer to the nearest square foot.)
8. A contractor will install this driveway for $.95 a square foot. What is the cost of the driveway?

For exercises 9–10, use the form on page 251.

9. Find the allowance for heat entering a single-glass window that measures 3′ 6″ by 4′.
10. Find the allowance for heat entering from an open door that is 3′ 9″ wide.

Unit 4

test

Choose the best answer.

1. Mario earns $6.45 per hour in a 40-hour work week. Using the "week's gross pay" rule of thumb, what is the most he should spend for rent each month?

   A $258 C $261

   B $251 D $248

2. Erin estimates her electric bill will be about $20 per month and her gas bill will be $16 per month. If the rent for her apartment is $205, what are Erin's expected monthly expenses for these three items?

   A $231 C $169

   B $227 D $241

3. The Tarters plan to paint the walls of their guest room. The room is 3.5 m by 5.4 m and is 2.5 m high. Find the area of the walls to be painted.

   A 44.5 m^2 C 47.25 m^2

   B 40.5 m^2 D 22.25 m^2

4. Find the number of tiles needed for the length of a room 3.9 m long. Each tile is 30 centimeters square.

   A 117 tiles C 130 tiles

   B 13 tiles D 11 tiles

5. What is the scale length for a coffee table that is 1.2 meters long? Use a scale of 1 cm = .2 m.

   A .6 cm C 6 cm

   B 2.4 cm D 24 cm

6. Stan has renter's insurance. His grandfather's clock was destroyed in a fire. The clock was 5 years old and will cost $400 to replace. The rate of depreciation is 3%. Find the value after depreciation.

   A $460 C $440

   B $360 D $340

7. Roberta earns $15,600 per year. What is the greatest amount she should spend for a home? (Use the guideline of 2.5 times annual income.)

   A $33,500 C $41,250

   B $39,000 D $36,000

8. Jerry Lajer is buying a home that costs $57,000. He makes a 20% down payment. What is the amount of the loan after the down payment?

   A $68,400 C $55,860

   B $45,600 D $37,000

9. Maria Rojas borrows $28,000 at 9% annual interest for 30 years. What is the amount of interest she will pay the first month?

A $252　　C $270

B $184　　D $210

10. Maury's basic premium for his homeowner's insurance is $135. He has a gold chain worth $300 that he wants to insure separately. What is the total premium for his insurance? (Use the table on page 226.)

A $139.05　　C $136.35

B $138.95　　D $138.05

11. Find the assessed valuation of a home with a market value of $54,000. The rate of assessment in the area is 60% of market value.

A $27,000　　C $32,400

B $21,600　　D $50,760

12. The recording fee is .5% of the purchase price of a home. What is the amount of the fee if a home costs $49,000?

A $254　　C $245

B $2450　　D $540

13. Marge Reiner sells real estate. For what amount should she list a house if the sellers hope to get at least $55,800? The real estate commission is 7%.

A $59,706　　C $57,526

B $60,000　　D $61,000

14. Find the cost of building a house with 1700 square feet. The house will cost $29.50 per square foot.

A $44,030　　C $47,200

B $48,450　　D $50,150

15. Find the area of a triangular section of a driveway. The base of the section is $7\frac{1}{2}$ ft. and the height is 4 ft.

A 15 sq. ft.　　C $28\frac{1}{2}$ sq. ft.

B $11\frac{1}{2}$ sq. ft.　　D 30 sq. ft.

16. Find the allowance for heat entering through an outside wall on the west side of a room. The wall is 15 ft. long. (Use the table on page 251.)

A 975　　C 675

B 375　　D 765

unit five

Taxes, Insurance, and Investments

Chapter 13

Income Tax

Chapter 14

Health, Life, and Retirement Insurance

Investments

Chapter 13

Income Tax

About 70 million individuals pay federal income tax in the United States each year. The taxes we pay provide money for many government services.

Finding Taxable Income

At the end of each year, employers provide a **wage and tax statement,** Form W-2, to each person they have employed. This form states the income earned and the taxes withheld for the employee during the year.

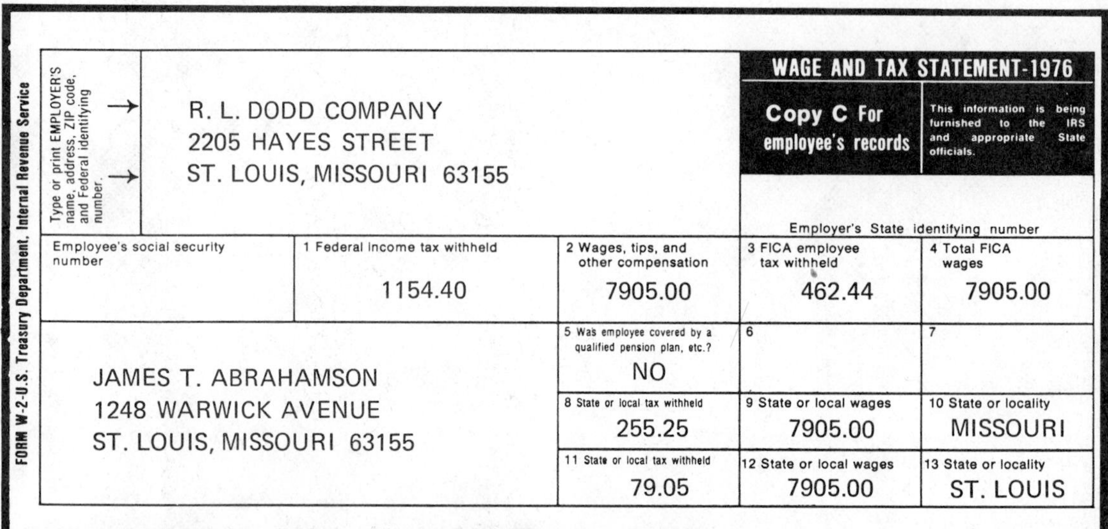

FORM W-2-U.S. Treasury Department, Internal Revenue Service

WAGE AND TAX STATEMENT-1976

Copy C For employee's records

This information is being furnished to the IRS and appropriate State officials.

Type or print EMPLOYER'S name, address, ZIP code, and Federal identifying number.

R. L. DODD COMPANY
2205 HAYES STREET
ST. LOUIS, MISSOURI 63155

Employer's State identifying number

Employee's social security number	1 Federal income tax withheld	2 Wages, tips, and other compensation	3 FICA employee tax withheld	4 Total FICA wages
	1154.40	7905.00	462.44	7905.00

	5 Was employee covered by a qualified pension plan, etc.?	6	7
JAMES T. ABRAHAMSON 1248 WARWICK AVENUE ST. LOUIS, MISSOURI 63155	NO		
	8 State or local tax withheld	9 State or local wages	10 State or locality
	255.25	7905.00	MISSOURI
	11 State or local tax withheld	12 State or local wages	13 State or locality
	79.05	7905.00	ST. LOUIS

Taxpayers use the information on the W-2 form to complete a federal **income tax return.** The tax return is an official record of money earned and amount of income tax to be paid. By April 15, the tax return must be sent to the Internal Revenue Service (IRS), along with any tax due.

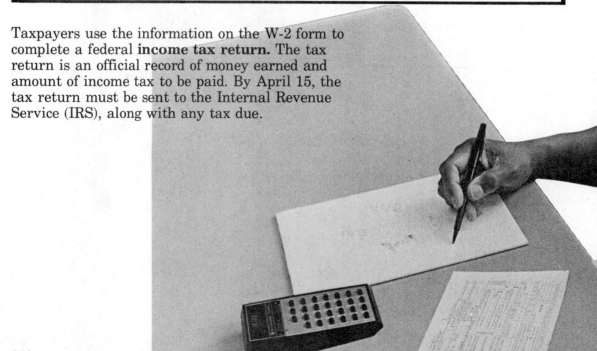

Depending upon their sources of income and personal expenses, many taxpayers may choose the **short form tax return,** Form 1040A.

To use the short form, first find **taxable income** by following these steps. You may round all amounts to the nearest dollar.

1. Find the **total income** by adding all income earned, including interest income.

2. Find the **standard deduction.** This is an allowance for certain personal expenses on which no tax is required. To figure the standard deduction, use the guidelines for the appropriate filing status.

Standard Deduction	
Single 16% of total income Minimum: $1700 Maximum: $2400	
Married filing jointly 16% of total income Minimum: $2100 Maximum: $2800	← Husband and wife use one form and combine incomes.
Married filing separately 16% of total income Minimum: $1050 Maximum: $1400	← Husband and wife use separate forms.

3. Find the **amount for exemptions** by multiplying the total number of exemptions, or dependents, by $750.

4. Use the rule below to find taxable income. If the amount computed is less than zero, the taxable income is zero.

Total income − **Standard deduction** − **Amount for exemptions** = **Taxable income**

problem

Jim Abrahamson is single. His income for this year included \$7905 in wages and \$21 in interest from a savings account. He claims 1 exemption for himself. What is his taxable income?

solution

Step 1 $\quad \$7905 + \$21 = \$7926$ — Total income

Step 2

Standard Deduction
Single
16% of total income
Minimum: \$1700
Maximum: \$2400
Married filing jointly
16% of total income
Minimum: \$2100
Maximum: \$2800
Married filing separately
16% of total income
Minimum: \$1050
Maximum: \$1400

16% of \$7926

$.16 \times \$7926 \approx \$1268$ — Rounded to the nearest dollar

Since 16% of Jim's total income is less than the minimum of \$1700, he will take a standard deduction of \$1700.

Step 3 $\quad \$750 \times 1 = \$750$ — Amount for exemptions

Step 4 $\quad \$7926 - \$1700 - \$750 = \$5476$

Jim's taxable income is \$5476.

exercises

Find each taxable income.

1. Louise Nelson
   Wages: \$2472
   Single
   1 exemption

2. Lorenzo Delgado
   Wages: \$1807
   Single
   1 exemption

3. Faith Roos
   Wages: \$11,320
   Single
   1 exemption

4. Leo Chagoya
   Wages: \$19,780
   Interest income: \$168
   Single
   1 exemption

5. Pedro and Marie Vargas
   Wages
   Husband: \$8000
   Wife: \$5791
   Interest income: \$27
   Married filing jointly
   2 exemptions

6. Darlene Hrubec
   Wages: \$7889
   Tips: \$1700
   Interest income: \$7
   Married filing separately
   2 exemptions

CALCULATOR EXERCISES

Total income − **Standard deduction** − **Amount for exemptions** = **Taxable income**

Find each taxable income.

1. Wages: $1507
Single
1 exemption

2. Wages: $2162
Interest income: $15
Single
1 exemption

3. Wages: $5023
Tips: $3056
Single
1 exemption

4. Wages: $12,050
Interest income: $77
Other income: $84
Single
1 exemption

5. Wages: $17,508
Other income: $96
Single
1 exemption

6. Wages
Husband: $8125
Wife: $0
Married filing jointly
2 exemptions

7. Wages
Husband: $5031
Wife: $6024
Married filing jointly
2 exemptions

8. Wages
Husband: $7815
Wife: $5900
Other income: $30
Married filing jointly
3 exemptions

9. Wages
Husband: $0
Wife: $14,500
Interest income: $203
Other income: $121
Married filing jointly
3 exemptions

10. Wages
Husband: $9300
Wife: $8873
Interest income: $54
Married filing jointly
4 exemptions

11. Wages: $2113
Other income: $8
Married filing separately
1 exemption

12. Wages: $5089
Married filing separately
1 exemption

13. Wages: $7602
Interest income: $98
Married filing separately
2 exemptions

14. Wages: $8621
Tips: $4331
Interest income: $75
Married filing separately
3 exemptions

15. Wages: $21,602
Interest income: $107
Other income: $85
Married filing separately
4 exemptions

Completing the Tax Return

After you compute taxable income, you can find your tax in a table. The tables are on pages 407-409.

In some years a **tax credit** is given. These are the instructions for finding the 1976 tax credit.

Tax Credit
a. Multiply \$35 by the number of exemptions.
b. Find 2% of taxable income. Maximum: \$180, or \$90 for married filing separately
The tax credit is the larger of the answers to **a** or **b.**

This credit is subtracted from the tax in the table to find the **tax required for the year.** If this difference is zero or less, the tax required is zero.

Tax from the table − **Tax credit** = **Tax required for the year**

problem

Jim Abrahamson's taxable income is \$5476. What is his tax required for the year?

solution

Find the tax from the table.

If line 15 (taxable income) is—		And you are—			
Over	But not over	Single	Married filing sepa-rately	Head of a house-hold	Married filing jointly *
		Your tax is—			
5,150	**5,200**	937	949	883	843
5,200	**5,250**	947	960	893	853
5,250	**5,300**	958	971	902	862
5,300	**5,350**	968	982	912	872
5,350	**5,400**	979	993	921	881
5,400	**5,450**	989	1,004	931	891
5,450	**5,500**	1,000	1,015	940	900
5,500	**5,550**	1,010	1,026	950	910

\$5476 is "over \$5450, but not over \$5500." Jim is single.

The tax from the table is \$1000.

Find the tax credit.

a. $\$35 \times 1 = \$35$

b. 2% of \$5476

$.02 \times \$5476 \approx \$110$ Rounded to the nearest dollar

Since \$110 is greater than \$35, Jim's tax credit is \$110.

Subtract to find the tax required for the year.

$\$1000 - \$110 = \$890$ Tax required for the year

exercises

For each exercise, find the tax required for the year. Use the tables on pages 407–409.

1. Taxable income: $17
   Single
   1 exemption
2. Taxable income: $362
   Single
   1 exemption
3. Taxable income: $802
   Single
   1 exemption
4. Taxable income: $9521
   Single
   1 exemption
5. Taxable income: $7035
   Married filing jointly
   2 exemptions
6. Taxable income: $12,522
   Married filing jointly
   3 exemptions
7. Taxable income: $19,603
   Married filing jointly
   6 exemptions
8. Taxable income: $3861
   Married filing separately
   1 exemption
9. Taxable income: $10,524
   Married filing separately
   2 exemptions

You can complete the income tax return by comparing the tax required for the year with the income tax withheld, as shown on the W-2 form.

If the amount withheld is greater, use this rule to find the **refund due the taxpayer.**

Amount withheld − **Tax required for the year** = **Refund due the taxpayer**

If the tax required is greater, use this rule to find the **balance due the IRS.**

Tax required for the year − **Amount withheld** = **Balance due the IRS**

problem

Jim Abrahamson's tax required for the year is $890. He had $1154 in federal income taxes withheld from his earnings this year. Does Jim still owe money to the IRS, or will he receive a refund? How much?

solution

The amount withheld is greater, so Jim will receive a refund.

$1154 − $890 = $264 Refund due Jim

exercises

For exercises 10-18, find the refund due the taxpayer or the balance due the IRS.

	Tax required for the year	Amount withheld
10.	$0	$67
11.	$0	$245
12.	$119	$350
13.	$217	$206
14.	$1506	$1788
15.	$1821	$1697
16.	$2981	$3015
17.	$3509	$3511
18.	$4162	$4007

Standard Deduction
Single
16% of total income
Minimum: $1700
Maximum: $2400
Married filing jointly
16% of total income
Minimum: $2100
Maximum: $2800
Married filing separately
16% of total income
Minimum: $1050
Maximum: $1400

Tax Credit
a. Multiply $35 by the number of exemptions.
b. Find 2% of taxable income. Maximum: $180, or $90 for married filing separately
The tax credit is the larger of the answers to **a** or **b.**

For exercises 19–30, find the refund due the taxpayer or the balance due the IRS. Refer to the tables above, and to those on pages 407–409.

19. Kim Leong
Total income: $4368
Single
1 exemption
Amount withheld: $385

Total income	$4368
Standard deduction	− ▒
	▒
Amount for exemptions	− ▒
Taxable income	▒
Tax from the table	▒
Tax credit	− ▒
Tax required for the year	▒
Amount withheld	$385
Tax required for the year	− ▒
Refund due the taxpayer	▒

20. Emma and Stanley Zimmer
Total income: $23,067
Married filing jointly
3 exemptions
Amount withheld: $2984

Total income	$23,067
Standard deduction	− ▒
	▒
Amount for exemptions	− ▒
Taxable income	▒
Tax from the table	▒
Tax credit	− ▒
Tax required for the year	▒
Tax required for the year	▒
Amount withheld	− $2984
Balance due the IRS	▒

21. Glen Merryman
Total income: $10,319
Single
1 exemption
Amount withheld: $1633

22. Maxine Scheetz
Total income: $3252
Single
1 exemption
Amount withheld: $187

23. Doreen Widenaur
Total income: $2460
Single
1 exemption
Amount withheld: $419

24. Rodney O'Connor
Total income: $1520
Single
1 exemption
Amount withheld: $222

25. Ed and Joy Beacham
Total income: $17,513
Married filing jointly
2 exemptions
Amount withheld: $2043

26. Lisa and Joseph Smith
Total income: $11,540
Married filing jointly
3 exemptions
Amount withheld: $780

27. May and Carl Kuehn
Total income: $13,200
Married filing jointly
5 exemptions
Amount withheld: $1310

28. Justin Hanover
Total income: $4217
Married filing separately
1 exemption
Amount withheld: $438

29. Agnes Dix
Total income: $8520
Married filing separately
1 exemption
Amount withheld: $993

30. Michael Alvarez
Total income: $12,336
Married filing separately
2 exemptions
Amount withheld: $1914

Tiger ® **By Bud Blake**

Tiger cartoon Credit: © King Features Syndicate Inc. 1977

career

Income Tax Consultant

Career Cluster: Business Contact

Helen Bankert operates a tax service business. Some of her customers use a long form to report their income tax. With this form they are allowed to list as deductions several of their personal expenses. The total of these **itemized deductions** can then be used in place of the standard deduction in computing taxable income.

Helen helps people compute their itemized deductions. Then they can compare their standard deduction with the total of their itemized deductions.

problem

One of Helen's customers is Makoto Matsubara. He is single and his total income is $18,500. His itemized deductions are listed here.

Property tax: $1200
Gasoline tax: $78
General sales tax: $157
Mortgage interest: $3121
Finance charges: $124

Which is greater, Makoto's standard deduction or the total of his itemized deductions?

solution

Find the standard deduction.

Standard Deduction
Single
16% of total income
Minimum: $1700
Maximum: $2400
Married filing jointly
16% of total income
Minimum: $2100
Maximum: $2800
Married filing separately
16% of total income
Minimum: $1050
Maximum: $1400

16% of $18,500

$.16 \times \$18,500 = \$2960$

Since 16% of Makoto's total income is greater than the maximum of $2400, he would have a standard deduction of $2400.

Find the total of his itemized deductions.

$$\begin{array}{r} \$1200 \\ 78 \\ 157 \\ 3121 \\ +\quad 124 \\ \hline \$4680 \end{array}$$ Total itemized deductions

For Makoto Matsubara, the total of his itemized deductions, $4680, is greater than his standard deduction of $2400.

exercises

In each exercise, give the standard deduction and the total of the itemized deductions. Then indicate which amount is greater.

1. Total income: $3050
   Single
   Itemized deductions
   - Gasoline tax: $43
   - General sales tax: $42
   - Finance charges: $65
   - Loan interest: $123

2. Total income: $8200
   Married filing separately
   Itemized deductions
   - State income tax: $205
   - Gasoline tax: $65
   - General sales tax: $149
   - Loan interest: $307
   - Miscellaneous deductions: $129

3. Total income: $5692
   Single
   Itemized deductions
   - State income tax: $142
   - General sales tax: $56
   - Contributions: $52
   - Allowable theft loss: $15
   - Miscellaneous deductions: $82

4. Total income: $18,300
   Married filing jointly
   Itemized deductions
   - State income tax: $800
   - Property tax: $935
   - Gasoline tax: $93
   - General sales tax: $186
   - Mortgage interest: $2300
   - Contributions: $200

5. Total income: $14,700
   Married filing jointly
   Itemized deductions
   State income tax: $368
   Gasoline tax: $77
   General sales tax: $208
   Finance charges: $157
   Loan interest: $225
   Miscellaneous deductions: $59

6. Total income: $10,540
   Single
   Itemized deductions
   Allowable medical deduction: $1315
   State income tax: $372
   Gasoline tax: $108
   General sales tax: $167
   Finance charges: $88
   Contributions: $25

7. Total income: $21,500
   Married filing jointly
   Itemized deductions
   State income tax: $940
   Property tax: $1200
   Gasoline tax: $115
   General sales tax: $197
   Mortgage interest: $1752
   Finance charges: $208
   Contributions: $100
   Allowable casualty loss: $250
   Miscellaneous deductions: $94

8. Total income: $24,184
   Married filing jointly
   Itemized deductions
   State income tax: $907
   Property tax: $846
   Gasoline tax: $138
   General sales tax: $334
   Mortgage interest: $3402
   Finance charges: $389
   Loan interest: $285
   Contributions: $400

9. Total income: $13,250
   Single
   Itemized deductions
   State income tax: $450
   Gasoline tax: $138
   General sales tax: $156
   Finance charges: $653
   Loan interest: $420
   Contributions: $232
   Miscellaneous deductions: $195

10. Total income: $12,300
    Married filing separately
    Itemized deductions
    Property tax: $620
    Gasoline tax: $48
    General sales tax: $111
    Mortgage interest: $1851
    Loan interest: $201

change of pace

Do you know what 1 billion means? Try to complete each statement with the most appropriate answer.

1. A stack of 1 billion dimes would be about as tall as

(a) 2 Empire State Buildings.

(b) 15 Empire State Buildings.

(c) 2900 Empire State Buildings.

2. One billion twin bed sheets would cover

(a) Rhode Island.

(b) Texas.

(c) Africa.

3. One billion large marshmallows could be contained in

(a) a refrigerator.

(b) a two-car garage.

(c) the Washington Monument.

4. If a small marble were magnified so that its diameter were 1 billion times as great, the marble would be about as large as

(a) a basketball.

(b) the earth.

(c) the sun.

5. If you spent 1 billion dollars at the rate of 1 dollar per minute, the money would be gone in about

(a) 1 year.

(b) 156 years.

(c) 1902 years.

How Tax Money Is Spent

Taxes are the largest source of income for the federal government. The government uses tax money to provide many services to citizens. This circle graph shows how the federal government spent its income in one year.

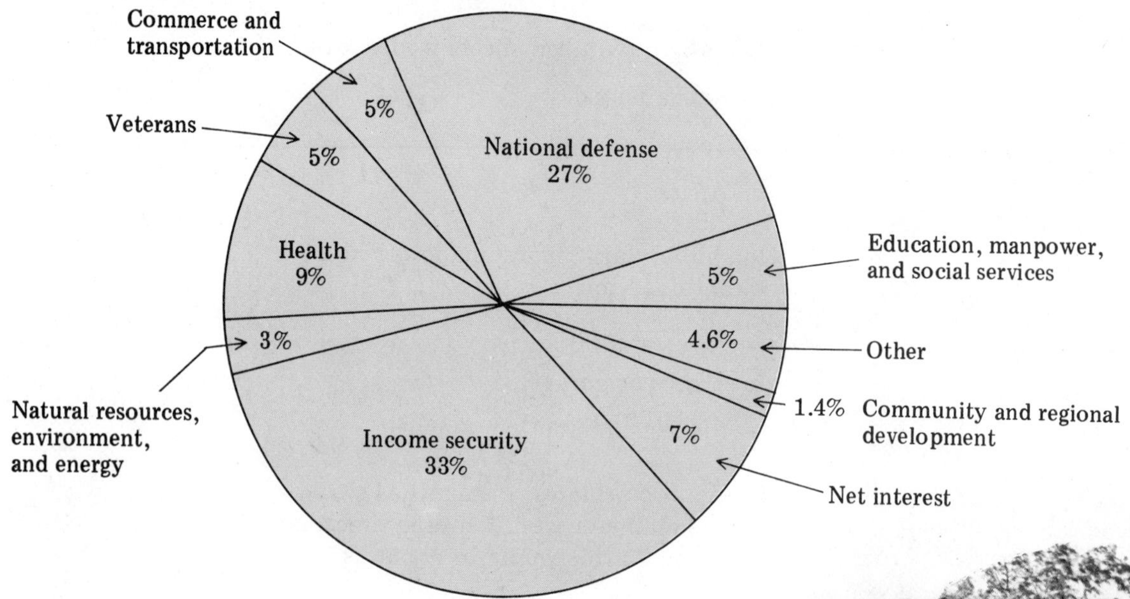

problem

If the total amount spent by the government for the year was about \$324 billion, about how much was spent for education, manpower, and social services?

solution

Find 5% of \$324 billion. Round the answer to the nearest billion dollars.

$.05 \times \$324$ billion $= \$16.2$ billion

About \$16 billion dollars was spent for education, manpower, and social services.

exercises

Use the percents shown in the circle graph. Find the amount spent by the government for each item. The total amount spent is $324 billion. Round the answers to the nearest billion dollars.

1. National defense
2. Commerce and transportation
3. Veterans
4. Health
5. Natural resources, environment, and energy
6. Income security
7. Net interest
8. Community and regional development
9. Other

problem

About $122 billion of the federal income for this year was collected in individual income taxes. What percent of the $324 billion income came from these taxes?

solution

Write an equation to find the percent. Round the answer to the nearest whole percent.

<u>%</u>	*of*	<u>total income</u>	*is*	<u>individual income taxes</u>
▒	*of*	$324 billion	*is*	$122 billion
n	$\times$	$324 billion	=	$122 billion

$$n \approx .38 = 38\%$$

exercises

Find what percent each of these items contributed to the federal income of $324 billion. Round the answers to the nearest whole percent.

10. Corporation income taxes: $40 billion
11. Social security taxes and contributions: $86 billion
12. Borrowing: $42 billion
13. Other: $34 billion
14. Make a circle graph showing the percents of each source of federal income for the year.

State Income Tax

Many states and some cities have income taxes that are similar to federal income tax. Different states include different items as income and allow varying amounts for deductions, exemptions, and credits. When taxable income has been computed, various tax rates and methods of computing the tax are used. Some are shown here.

California

Multiply taxable income by the number in the column marked (1).

Subtract the number in the column marked (2).

Mark off two decimal places from the right.

Taxable income	(1)	(2)
0–1999	1	—
2000–2999	2	2,000
3000–3499	2	2,000
3500–3999	3	5,500
4000–4499	3	5,500
4500–4999	3	5,500
5000–5999	4	10,500
6000–6499	4	10,500
6500–6999	5	17,000
7000–7499	5	17,000

Illinois

Find $2\frac{1}{2}\%$ of taxable income.

Maryland

Taxable income over	but not over	Amount of tax
$ 0	$1000	2% of taxable income
1000	2000	$20 plus 3% of amount over $1000
2000	3000	$50 plus 4% of amount over $2000
3000	—	$90 plus 5% of amount over $3000

Michigan

Find 4.37% of taxable income.

Mississippi

Find 3% of first $5000 of taxable income and 4% of taxable income over $5000.

problem

Norm Snyder lives in Maryland. His taxable income is $10,800. What is his state income tax?

solution

Norm's taxable income is greater than $3000. He must pay $90 plus 5% of the amount over $3000. Subtract to find the amount over $3000.

$10,800 − $3000 = $7800

Find 5% of $7800.

.05 × $7800 = $390

Add to find the amount of tax.

$90 + $390 = $480

problem

Liz Dietz lives in California. Her taxable income is $4720. What is her state income tax?

solution

$4720 is between $4500 and $4999. Multiply the taxable income by the number in the column marked (1).

$4720 × 3 = $14,160

Subtract the amount in the column marked (2).

$14,160 − $5500 = $8660

Mark off two decimal places from the right.

The tax is $86.60.

exercises

Use the information on page 274 to find the state income tax. Round the answers to the nearest cent.

	State	Taxable income
1.	Maryland	$895
2.	Maryland	$2560
3.	Maryland	$28,091
4.	Illinois	$3062
5.	Illinois	$9000
6.	Illinois	$35,620
7.	Michigan	$1453
8.	Michigan	$17,680
9.	Michigan	$8521
10.	Mississippi	$6792
11.	Mississippi	$21,084
12.	Mississippi	$4511
13.	California	$3782
14.	California	$6218
15.	California	$7396

skills tune-up

Rounding whole numbers and decimals, pages 4-5

Round each number to the nearest thousand, the nearest hundred, and the nearest ten.

1. 832

2. 2484

3. 555

4. 8143

5. 9602

6. 5478

7. 1071

8. 29,929

9. 603.7

10. 72,188.5

Round each number to the nearest whole number, the nearest tenth, and the nearest hundredth.

11. 7.367

12. 18.181

13. 36.912

14. 79.457

15. 783.143

16. 257.768

17. 546.801

18. 40.992

19. 59.607

20. 602.015

Subtracting whole numbers and decimals, pages 6-7

1. 78 − 26

2. 52 − 17

3. 56 − 8

4. 98 − 9

5. 42 − 37

6. 96 − 95

7. 93.7 − 45.1

8. 54.2 − 36.7

9. 68.59 − 2.39

10. 46.75 − 4.86

11. 85.62 − 16.2

12. 45.32 − 9.4

13. 15.098 − 7.46

14. 40.095 − 37.18

15. 32.317 − 21.228

16. 96.013 − 4.172

17. 8.64 − 5.325

18. 72.19 − 3.337

19. 27.2 − 26.4

20. 48.6 − 47.9

21. 4.612 − 2

22. 86.059 − 39

23. 37 − 34.5

24. 4 − .3

25. 26 − .42

26. 83 − 27.08

Writing percents, decimals, and fractions, pages 34-35

Write as a fraction in lowest terms.

1. 12%	**11.** 70%
2. 80%	**12.** 31%
3. 55%	**13.** 27%
4. 10%	**14.** 40%
5. 47%	**15.** 65%
6. 25%	**16.** 28%
7. 62%	**17.** 225%
8. 30%	**18.** 132%
9. 16%	**19.** 103%
10. 97%	**20.** 450%

Write as a percent.

21. $\frac{1}{2}$	**31.** $\frac{11}{20}$
22. $\frac{1}{5}$	**32.** $\frac{3}{8}$
23. $\frac{1}{10}$	**33.** $\frac{15}{20}$
24. $\frac{3}{4}$	**34.** $\frac{9}{16}$
25. $\frac{3}{5}$	**35.** $\frac{7}{8}$
26. $\frac{1}{4}$	**36.** $\frac{9}{40}$
27. $\frac{7}{10}$	**37.** $\frac{17}{4}$
28. $\frac{9}{20}$	**38.** $\frac{11}{2}$
29. $\frac{19}{50}$	**39.** $\frac{38}{5}$
30. $\frac{4}{25}$	**40.** $\frac{13}{8}$

Chapter 13

review

Finding taxable income, pages 260–262

1. Daisy Smurlo is single. Her income for the year includes wages of $11,250 and interest of $85. What is her standard deduction? (Use the information on page 261.)

2. Daisy Smurlo claims 1 exemption. What is her taxable income?

Completing the tax return, pages 264–267

3. Daren and Lois Gwinn's taxable income is $17,562. They are married filing a joint tax return. They claim 3 exemptions. What is their tax required for the year? (Use the tables on pages 407–409, and the information on page 264.)

4. The Gwinns had $3760 in federal income tax withheld from their earnings this year. What is their refund or their balance due the IRS?

Income tax consultant, pages 268–270

5. Mark and Britta Garcia are married filing jointly. Their total income is $18,256. What is their standard deduction? (Use the information on page 26.)

6. The Garcias' itemized deductions are listed here. Find the total.

   Property tax: $750
   Gasoline tax: $61
   General sales tax: $181
   Mortgage interest: $2548
   Loan interest: $352
   Contributions: $104
   Miscellaneous deductions: $55

7. For the Garcias, which is greater, their standard deduction or the total of their itemized deductions?

How tax money is spent, pages 272–273

8. One year federal spending totaled $268 billion. About 5% of that amount was spent on commerce and transportation. How much was spent on these items? (Round the answer to the nearest billion dollars.)

State income tax, pages 274–275

For exercises 9–10, use the information on page 274.

9. Dennis Franklin lives in Mississippi. His taxable income is $11,200. What is his state income tax?

10. Marilyn Hughes lives in California. Her taxable income is $6280. What is her state income tax?

Chapter 13

test

1. Dawn and Todd Lindskog are married filing a joint tax return. Their income for the year is $9058. What is their standard deduction? (Use the information on page 261.)

2. The Lindskogs claim 2 exemptions. What is their taxable income?

3. Huang Lee's taxable income is $4371. He is married filing separately, and claims 1 exemption. What is his tax required for the year? (Use the tables on pages 407-409, and the information on page 264.)

4. Huang Lee had $645 in federal income taxes withheld from his earnings this year. What is his refund or his balance due the IRS?

5. Jill Murphy is single. Her total income is $14,700. What is her standard deduction? (Use the information on page 261.)

6. Jill Murphy's itemized deductions are listed here. Find the total.

   Allowable medical deduction: $351
   Gasoline tax: $64
   General sales tax: $132
   Finance charges: $94
   Loan interest: $282

7. For Jill Murphy, which is greater, her standard deduction or the total of her itemized deductions?

8. One year federal spending totaled $268 billion. About 4% of that amount was spent on education, manpower, and social services. How much was spent for these items? (Round the answer to the nearest billion dollars.)

For exercises 9–10, use the information on page 274.

9. Louis Atcitty lives in Illinois. His taxable income is $9872. What is his state income tax?

10. George and Amy Batzel live in Maryland. Their taxable income is $27,052. What is their state income tax?

Chapter 14

Health, Life, and Retirement Insurance

When planning for the future, you should consider the financial security of your family. Insurance can provide money in case of unexpected medical expenses or loss of income.

Health Insurance

Because of the high cost of medical bills, many people have some type of **health insurance** that pays for part or all of their doctor and hospital bills, and the cost of medicine. This insurance is often provided by employers at large companies for their employees. The government also provides health insurance for its employees, disabled persons, and those over 65.

Many health insurance policies have a deductible amount. The insurance company pays a certain portion of the total expenses after the deductible amount is subtracted.

The person covered by the insurance policy is called the **insured.**

problem

Robert Pottinger works for a company that carries medical insurance on its employees. The insurance is a $50-deductible policy. The insurance company pays 80% of the amount after the deductible.

Robert Pottinger had surgery on his foot and was in the hospital for two days. His medical bills amounted to $715. How much did the insurance company pay? How much did Robert pay?

solution

Subtract the deductible amount.

$\$715 - \$50 = \$665$ Amount after deductible

Find 80% of $665.

$.80 \times \$665 = \$532$ Paid by insurance

Subtract the amount paid by insurance from the total bill.

$\$715 - \$532 = \$183$ Paid by Robert

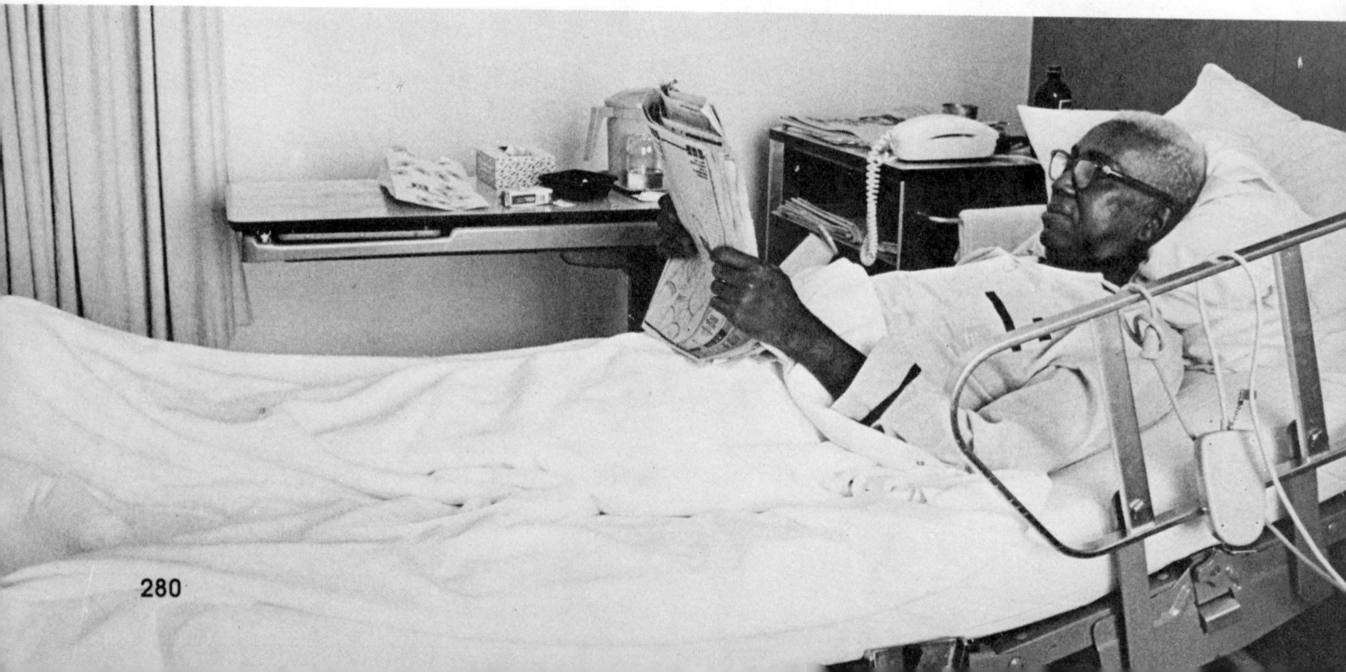

exercises

For each exercise, find the amount paid by insurance and the amount the insured pays.

	Insured	Deductible amount	Insurance pays after deductible	Medical expenses	Paid by insurance	Insured pays
	Robert Pottinger	$50	80%	$715.00	$532.00	$183.00
1.	Leonard Kaplan	$50	80%	$540.00	a.	b.
2.	Elsie Garden	0	80%	$2165.00	a.	b.
3.	Prudence Cook	$200	90%	$4100.00	a.	b.
4.	Jaime Fisher	0	90%	$2555.00	a.	b.
5.	Elliott Cartier	$150	85%	$1750.00	a.	b.
6.	Lydia Mayfair	0	85%	$4600.00	a.	b.
7.	Jake Oxx	0	75%	$2276.00	a.	b.
8.	Maxine Rice	$125	87%	$3714.00	a.	b.
9.	Art Long	$60	92%	$980.00	a.	b.
10.	Joan Fine	$40	83%	$4216.50	a.	b.

11. Malissa Greenwald has two health insurance policies. One pays her $50 for each day that she is in the hospital. The other is a $60-deductible policy. The insurance company pays 80% of all medical bills over $60. Malissa was in the hospital 10 days and her bills totaled $3305. How much did she pay?

12. Chong Sun Lee has a $90-deductible health insurance policy. After $90, the insurance company pays 75% of all medical bills including prescription medicines. Last year, Chong had $285 in doctor bills and spent $23 on prescription medicines. How much did the insurance company pay?

13. Frances Zilliox has a $70-deductible health insurance policy. She has medical bills that total $1482.70. Her insurance will pay whichever is less of these two amounts:

a. 85% of the amount after the deductible.

b. $1200

How much will Frances pay?

14. Mike Gruber has a $50-deductible health insurance policy. The insurance company pays 80% of all covered medical expenses from $50 to $2000. Above $2000, the insurance company pays 100%. Mike was in the hospital for major surgery. His medical bills amounted to $5470. How much did the insurance company pay?

Term Life Insurance

The main purpose of life insurance is to provide money for dependents of the insured person in case of death. The person named in the policy to receive the insurance money is called the **beneficiary.** The amount of money that the beneficiary would receive is the **face value** of the policy.

The least expensive type of life insurance is **term life insurance.** It is issued for a certain period of time, such as 5 or 10 years. Unless the insured dies during that time, no money is collected from the insurance company.

This table shows annual premiums for a certain 5-year term insurance policy. In this case, rates are the same for both men and women.

5-Year Term Insurance Annual Premiums per $1000			
Age	Premium	Age	Premium
15	$4.60	30	$5.95
16	4.68	31	6.06
17	4.76	32	6.17
18	4.84	33	6.28
19	4.92	34	6.39
20	5.00	35	6.50
21	5.09	36	6.62
22	5.18	37	6.74
23	5.27	38	6.86
24	5.36	39	6.98
25	5.45	40	7.10
26	5.55	41	7.23
27	5.65	42	7.36
28	5.75	43	7.49
29	5.85	44	7.62

problem

Sally Hart is 25 years old. She is buying a 5-year term insurance policy with a face value of $8000. What is her annual premium?

solution

From the table, the rate per $1000 is $5.45.

Multiply by 8 to find the annual premium for $8000.

$8 \times \$5.45 = \$43.60$ Annual premium

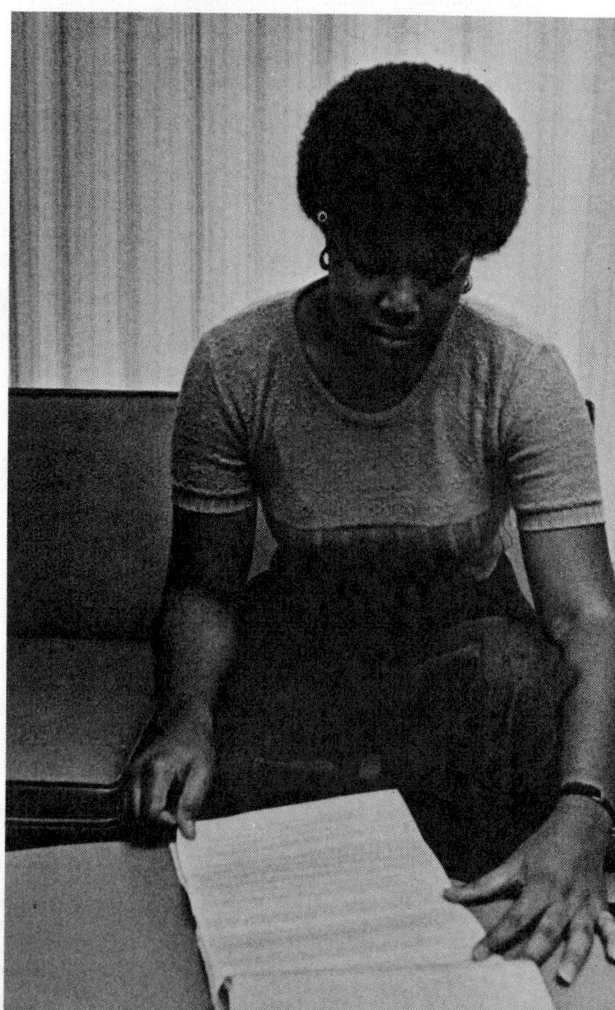

problem

Michael Dolan is 25 years old. He is buying a 5-year term insurance policy with a face value of $50,000. If Michael lives longer than five years, he will not collect any insurance. How much will he pay for insurance protection for 5 years?

solution

For age 25, the annual premium for each $1000 of term insurance is $5.45. Multiply by 50 to find the annual premium for $50,000.

$50 \times \$5.45 = \$272.50$ Annual premium

Find the total premiums for five years.

$5 \times \$272.50 = \$1362.50$ Total premiums

Michael will pay $1362.50 for 5 years of insurance protection.

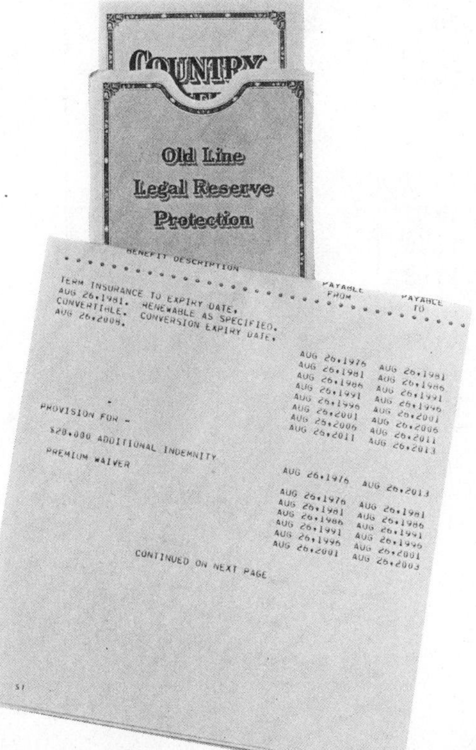

exercises

Use the table to find the annual premium for each 5-year term policy.

	Age	Face value
1.	22	$5,000
2.	22	$40,000
3.	39	$40,000
4.	43	$9,000
5.	31	$25,000
6.	18	$5,000
7.	18	$15,000
8.	40	$15,000
9.	38	$250,000
10.	15	$7,000

11. At age 30, Betty Neal can buy 10-year term insurance for $6.25 per $1000. How much will her annual premium be for a $50,000 policy?

12. At age 20, Jack Owen can buy 15-year term insurance for $5.40 per $1000. What will be his annual premium for a $25,000, 15-year term insurance policy?

For exercises 13-15, use the rates in the table on page 282.

13. Dan Mane is 27 years old. He is buying a 5-year term insurance policy with a face value of $25,000. If Dan dies after four years, how much will his beneficiary receive? How much will Dan pay for insurance for four years?

14. Ken Sawyer is 29 years old. How much 5-year term insurance (sold in multiples of $1000) can he buy for $60 a year?

15. Alice Jordan is 32 years old. How much 5-year term insurance (sold in multiples of $1000) can she buy for $75 a year?

Straight Life, Limited Payment Life, and Endowment Insurance

Besides providing financial protection in case of death, some policies have a savings plan. After premiums are paid for a certain length of time, the policy has a **cash value.** This amount of money increases as the policy gets older. The policy can be **surrendered,** or traded-in, for its cash value. Also, the insured can borrow against the cash value at very low rates of interest.

One of the most common types of life insurance that has a cash value is **straight life insurance.** For this type of insurance, the insured pays premiums for life or until a certain age, usually 65 or 70. The insurance stays in force until the insured dies.

Another type of life insurance that has a cash value is **limited payment life insurance.** This type of policy is like straight life, but the premiums are paid for only a certain time, usually 20 or 30 years. For this reason the premiums are higher than for straight life. A limited payment policy that is paid for in 20 years is called a **20-payment life insurance** policy. The insurance stays in force until the insured dies.

The most expensive type of insurance is **endowment insurance.** The premiums are paid for a definite period, usually 20 or 30 years. At the end of that time, the insured can collect the face value of the policy. When the face value is collected, the insurance is no longer in force.

This table shows premium rates for certain life insurance policies with a cash value. These types of insurance are more expensive than term insurance. Rates given are for men. For a woman, subtract 3 years from her age and use the resulting age.

Annual premiums for $1000 worth of insurance			
Age	Straight life	20-payment life	Endowment 20-year
15	$11.05	$17.42	$41.80
16	11.35	17.84	41.86
17	11.66	18.27	41.92
18	11.99	18.72	41.98
19	12.31	19.15	42.04
20	12.67	19.63	42.08
21	13.02	20.08	42.12
22	13.39	20.54	42.16
23	13.79	21.04	42.20
24	14.21	21.54	42.24
25	14.64	22.07	42.27
26	15.06	22.55	42.30
27	15.51	23.07	42.33
28	15.97	23.60	42.36
29	16.46	24.14	42.39
30	16.98	24.69	42.44
31	17.52	25.27	42.51
32	18.07	25.87	42.60
33	18.67	26.49	42.70
34	19.29	27.14	42.82

problem

Mabel Snowbird is 25 years old. She is buying $8000 worth of straight life insurance. What is her annual premium?

solution

Subtract 3 years from Mabel's age.

$25 - 3 = 22$

The annual premium for each $1000 of straight life insurance at age 22 is $13.39. Multiply by 8 to find the annual premium for $8000.

$8 \times \$13.39 = \$107.12$ Annual premium

exercises

Find the annual premium for each policy.

	Policy	Age	Sex	Face value
1.	Straight life	23	Male	$20,000
2.	Straight life	23	Female	$20,000
3.	20-year endowment	32	Male	$9,000
4.	20-payment life	32	Male	$9,000
5.	Straight life	18	Female	$15,000
6.	20-year endowment	18	Female	$15,000
7.	Straight life	34	Male	$7,000
8.	20-year endowment	26	Female	$25,000
9.	20-payment life	29	Male	$12,000
10.	20-payment life	19	Male	$12,000
11.	Straight life	20	Female	$6,000
12.	20-year endowment	15	Male	$10,000
13.	20-payment life	24	Female	$5,000
14.	20-payment life	30	Female	$14,000
15.	20-year endowment	21	Male	$30,000

This table shows the cash values for the straight life insurance policy whose premiums are given on page 284.

Cash value of straight life per $1000					
Age at issue	End of year 5	10	15	20	At age 65
15	$21	$ 77	$133	$210	$729
16	22	79	136	216	726
17	23	82	140	222	723
18	24	84	144	228	719
19	25	86	148	234	714
20	26	89	152	241	710
21	27	91	156	247	703
22	28	94	161	254	696
23	29	97	165	262	690
24	30	99	171	270	682
25	31	102	176	278	673
26	32	105	181	286	663
27	33	109	186	295	651
28	34	112	192	303	639
29	35	115	198	313	625
30	36	119	204	323	611
31	37	123	210	333	596
32	38	126	217	343	578
33	39	131	224	355	560
34	40	135	231	367	540

problem

Jethrow Williams is 20 years old. He is buying $18,000 worth of straight life insurance. What is the total amount he will pay for premiums in 15 years? What will be the cash value of his policy after 15 years?

solution

Use the table on page 284. The annual premium for each $1000 of straight life insurance at age 20 is $12.67. Multiply by 18 to find the annual premium for $18,000.

$18 \times \$12.67 = \$228.06$ Annual premium

Find the total premiums for 15 years.

$15 \times \$228.06 = \$3420.90$

Use the table at the left. The cash value after 15 years for each $1000 of a policy issued at age 20 is $152. Multiply by 18 to find the cash value for $18,000 worth of insurance.

$18 \times \$152 = \$2736$ Cash value

exercises

Use the tables on pages 284 and 286.

16. Elwood Stansfield is 28 years old. He plans to buy $8000 worth of straight life insurance. What is the total amount he will pay in premiums in 20 years?

17. What will be the cash value of Elwood's insurance in 20 years?

18. Charles Puget is 19 years old. He plans to buy $12,000 worth of straight life insurance. What is the total amount he will pay in premiums in ten years?

19. What will be the cash value of Charles's insurance in ten years?

20. Harry Kidd is 30 years old. He plans to buy $75,000 worth of straight life insurance. What will be his annual premium?

21. If Harry lives to be 65, how much will he pay in premiums?

22. When Harry is 65, what will be the cash value of his insurance?

23. Carl Russell is 23 years old. He plans to buy $40,000 worth of straight life insurance. What will be the cash value of this insurance in five years?

24. Quenten Jonas is 33 years old. He plans to buy $25,000 worth of straight life insurance. What will be the cash value of this insurance when Quenten is 65 years old?

25. Dennis Tunney is 22 years old. He plans to buy $30,000 worth of straight life insurance. What will be the cash value of this insurance when Dennis is 37 years old?

career

Insurance Office Clerk

Career Cluster: Business Detail

Roger Iverson works as a clerk for an insurance agent. Often customers prefer to pay their insurance premiums semiannually, quarterly, or monthly, instead of annually. This usually costs more per year. Roger uses this table to compute premiums.

Mode of payment	Factor
Semiannually	0.51
Quarterly	0.26
Monthly	0.0875

problem

Joan Bigelow's insurance policy has an annual premium of \$236.48. She wants to pay premiums monthly. What is the amount of her monthly premium? How much more per year will she pay?

solution

Multiply the annual premium by the factor for monthly premiums from the table. Round to the nearest cent.

$\$236.48 \times .0875 \approx \$20.69$ Monthly premium

Joan's monthly premium will be \$20.69.

Find the total of her monthly premiums for the year.

$12 \times \$20.69 = \$248.28$ Total of monthly premiums

Subtract the annual premium from the total of monthly premiums.

$\$248.28 - \$236.48 = \$11.80$

Joan will pay \$11.80 more per year if she makes monthly payments.

exercises

1. Lisa Montel pays \$342.50 annually on her straight life policy. What will be her monthly premium?
2. How much more per year will Lisa pay for monthly premiums?
3. Ollie Weathers pays an annual premium of \$149.30 for his 5-year term insurance. If he pays quarterly, how much will his quarterly premium be?
4. How much more per year will Ollie pay for quarterly premiums?
5. Jane Jansen pays a premium of \$462.80 each year for her endowment policy. What will be her semiannual premium?
6. How much more per year will Jane pay for semiannual premiums?
7. George Plain pays a premium of \$264.90 annually for his 20-payment life insurance policy. His monthly premiums would be \$23.18. What is the difference per year between paying annually and paying monthly?
8. Beth Winter pays a premium of \$316.75 annually for her endowment policy. Her quarterly premium would be \$82.36. What is the difference per year between paying annually and paying quarterly?
9. Justin Galchutt is 25 years old. He is buying a \$30,000, 20-year endowment policy. How much are Justin's annual premiums? (Use the table on page 284.)
10. What would Justin's monthly premium be?
11. Find the difference for Justin, between paying annually and paying monthly for 20 years.

CALCULATOR EXERCISES

Refer to the factors given on page 288 to help you complete these tables. In the table headings, A means annual premium, S means semiannual premium, Q means quarterly premium, and M means monthly premium.

For exercises 1–7, the last column is the yearly difference between paying premiums monthly and annually.

	A	M	$12M$	$12M-A$
	$138.12	$12.09	$145.08	$6.96
1.	172.49	a.	b.	c.
2.	254.68	a.	b.	c.
3.	127.46	a.	b.	c.
4.	229.23	a.	b.	c.
5.	148.77	a.	b.	c.
6.	89.41	a.	b.	c.
7.	124.55	a.	b.	c.

For exercises 8–14, the last column is the yearly difference between paying premiums quarterly and annually.

	A	Q	$4Q$	$4Q-A$
	$127.19	$33.07	$132.28	$5.09
8.	218.73	a.	b.	c.
9.	157.42	a.	b.	c.
10.	309.50	a.	b.	c.
11.	148.71	a.	b.	c.
12.	272.18	a.	b.	c.
13.	197.45	a.	b.	c.
14.	314.89	a.	b.	c.

For exercises 15–20, the last column is the yearly difference between paying premiums semiannually and annually.

	A	S	$2S$	$2S-A$
	$237.80	$121.28	$242.56	$4.76
15.	193.42	a.	b.	c.
16.	246.55	a.	b.	c.
17.	311.71	a.	b.	c.
18.	275.84	a.	b.	c.
19.	329.09	a.	b.	c.
20.	254.81	a.	b.	c.

This is a **perfect squared rectangle.** The rectangle is made up of squares A through J, all of different sizes. As shown, square E is 7 cm on a side. Square F is 12 cm on a side. Without measuring, find the dimensions of the other squares. What are the length and the width of the rectangle?

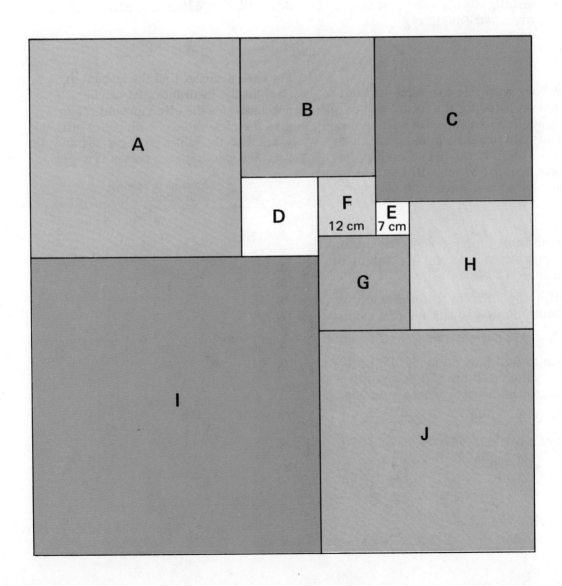

B
C
A
F
D
E
12 cm
7 cm
H
G
I
J

Choosing Insurance and Savings Plans

Many people would like to combine a program of insurance protection and long-term savings. This program is only one part of financial planning. Some things that must be considered when choosing a plan include family financial needs, earning ability now and in the future, and investments.

problem

Fred Post is 25. He can force himself to put money aside for the future by buying straight life insurance. He will be billed monthly for the insurance. How much straight life insurance can he buy for $50 per month? What will be the cash value of the insurance after 20 years?

solution

Use the table on page 284. The annual premium for each $1000 of straight life insurance is $14.64.

Multiply by .0875 to find the monthly premium. Round to the nearest cent.

$.0875 \times \$14.64 \approx \$1.28$

Divide to find how many $1000 units can be purchased for $50 per month. Round to the nearest whole number.

$\$50 \div \$1.28 \approx 39$ $1000 units

Fred can buy 39 × $1000, or $39,000, worth of straight life insurance.

Use the table on page 286. The cash value of each $1000 worth of straight life insurance after 20 years is $278.

Multiply by 39 to find the cash value of Fred's policy after 20 years.

$39 \times \$278 = \$10{,}842$ Cash value

exercises

For each exercise, find the amount of straight life insurance that can be purchased for the given amount. Then give the cash value of each policy after 20 years. Use the tables on pages 284 and 286. Assume that each person is a male.

	Age	Amount to spend each month
1.	20	$75
2.	17	$40
3.	18	$85
4.	33	$85
5.	23	$45
6.	28	$65
7.	30	$60
8.	19	$70
9.	26	$90
10.	34	$80

problem

Bob Makin wants to set aside $50 each month for insurance and savings. He decides that he needs $35,000 of term insurance for the next 20 years. The amount that is not spent for his insurance premium each month will be put in a savings account that earns 6% interest. His 20-year term insurance has an annual premium of $200. How much can Bob save each month? If Bob keeps all of his interest in the account, how much will he have in the savings account after 20 years?

solution

Multiply by .0875 to find the monthly premium for the insurance.

$.0875 \times \$200 = \$17.50$ Insurance premium

Subtract to find the amount to be put in savings each month.

$\$50 - \$17.50 = \$32.50$ Savings each month

Use this table to find the amount Bob will have in savings after 20 years.

Value of $1 invested monthly (interest compounded monthly)			
Years	5%	6%	7%
5	$ 68.01	$ 69.77	$ 71.59
10	155.28	163.88	173.08
15	267.29	290.82	316.96
20	411.03	462.04	520.93
25	595.51	692.99	810.07
30	832.26	1004.52	1219.97

At 6% interest, deposits of $1 per month for 20 years will accumulate to a value of $462.04. Multiply by 32.50 to find the value of deposits of $32.50 per month for 20 years.

$32.5 \times \$462.04 = \$15,016.30$ Savings after 20 years

exercises

11. Jeannie Pope is 20 years old. Her annual premium for $70,000 worth of 20-year term insurance is $375. How much does she pay per month for this insurance? (The factor is .0875.)

12. Jeannie spends a total of $75 per month for insurance and savings. What amount does she put in her savings account each month?

13. Jeannie's savings account pays 7% interest. The interest is added to the account monthly. If she lets the interest accumulate, how much will be in the savings account in 20 years?

14. Deke Coughlin is 20 years old. He pays a premium of $75 a month for straight life insurance. He just bought the insurance. What is the face value of Deke's policy?

15. What will be the cash value of $65,000 worth of straight life insurance in 20 years if the insurance is purchased at age 20?

Social Security Retirement Benefits

Most people in the United States are covered by social security. A portion of each person's paycheck is withheld for social security. The maximum income on which a person pays social security has been increased several times. The table gives these maximum incomes for 1951 through 1977.

When a person aged 62 or older **retires,** or stops working full-time, the government provides the person retirement benefits from the social security fund.

Year	Maximum income on which social security is paid	Glen's earnings subject to social security
1951	$3,600	
1952	3,600	
1953	3,600	
1954	3,600	
1955	4,200	
1956	4,200	
1957	4,200	
1958	4,200	
1959	4,800	$3,380
1960	4,800	3,580
1961	4,800	3,790
1962	4,800	4,020
1963	4,800	4,260
1964	4,800	4,700
1965	4,800	4,800
1966	6,600	5,450
1967	6,600	5,860
1968	7,800	6,310
1969	7,800	6,790
1970	7,800	7,300
1971	7,800	7,800
1972	9,000	8,460
1973	10,800	9,100
1974	13,200	9,790
1975	14,100	10,530
1976	15,300	13,000
1977	16,500	3,500
	Total	$122,420

problem

Glen Foness retired in 1977 at the age of 65. He was born in 1912, so his retirement benefits are based on the average amount on which he has paid social security for 19 years.

Glen's earnings subject to social security for the 19 years from 1959 through 1977 are given in the table. What is his annual retirement benefit?

solution

Divide the total earnings by 19 to find Glen's average annual income.

$\$122,420 \div 19 \approx \$6443$

Use the table on page 295 to find his monthly retirement benefit. The entry in the table closest to $6443 is $6500. At age 65, Glen's benefit is $385.10.

Multiply to find his annual benefit.

$12 \times \$385.10 = \$4621.20$ Annual benefit

Monthly retirement benefits for workers				
Average annual income	Retirement			
	at 65	at 64	at 63	at 62
$ 923 or less	$114.30	$106.80	$ 99.20	$ 91.50
$1150	139.40	130.10	120.90	111.60
1500	169.30	157.90	146.70	135.40
2000	191.40	178.70	166.00	153.20
2500	214.00	199.80	185.50	171.30
3000	236.40	220.70	205.00	189.20
3500	256.20	239.20	222.10	205.20
3750	268.50	250.70	232.80	214.80
4000	278.10	259.70	241.10	222.60
4250	290.50	271.40	252.00	232.60
4500	300.60	280.70	260.60	240.50
4750	313.00	292.10	271.40	250.50
5000	322.50	301.00	279.50	258.00
5250	334.40	312.20	289.90	267.50
5500	343.50	320.60	297.70	274.90
5750	354.90	331.40	307.70	284.10
6000	364.40	340.30	315.90	291.70
6250	373.70	348.80	323.80	298.90
6500	385.10	359.60	333.80	308.10
6750	396.10	369.70	343.40	316.90
7000	408.40	381.30	354.00	326.80
7250	420.70	392.70	364.80	336.70
7500	432.70	404.20	375.40	346.40

exercises

Find the annual benefits that will be received from social security.

	Average annual income	Age
1.	$4815	64
2.	$6300	65
3.	$5900	63
4.	$7115	62
5.	$6780	65
6.	$5420	63
7.	$4215	65
8.	$6150	62
9.	$7210	64
10.	$6983	65

11. Marie Horn earned more each year than the maximums listed in the table. To compute her benefits, she averages the maximum incomes listed for the 19 years from 1959 through 1977. What is her average annual income?

12. Marie is 65 when she retires. What amount will she receive annually from social security?

problem

Wanda Mailor retired at the age of 62 in 1975. Her average annual income was $5448. Constance Bertram retired at the age of 65 in 1978. Her average annual income was $6352. Using the table on page 295, how much did each receive per year from social security? In what year will Constance's total benefits be more than Wanda's?

solution

Using the table on page 295, at retirement Wanda's monthly benefit was $274.90.

Multiply to find her annual benefit.

$12 \times \$274.90 = \$3298.80$

Using the table on page 295, at retirement Constance's monthly benefit was $373.70.

Multiply to find her annual benefit.

$12 \times \$373.70 = \$4484.40$

The table shows the total amount received by each woman.

Year	Total Wanda received since retirement	Total Constance received since retirement
1975	$3,298.80	
1976	$6,597.60	
1977	$9,896.40	
1978	$13,195.20	$4,484.40
1979	$16,494.00	$8,968.80
1980	$19,792.80	$13,453.20
1981	$23,091.60	$17,937.60
1982	$26,390.40	$22,422.00
1983	$29,689.20	$26,906.40
1984	$32,988.00	$31,390.80
1985	$36,286.80	$35,875.20
1986	$39,585.60	$40,359.60

In 1986 Wanda will have received $39,585.60 in social security benefits. The same year Constance will have received $40,359.60. This is the year that total benefits for Constance will be more than those for Wanda.

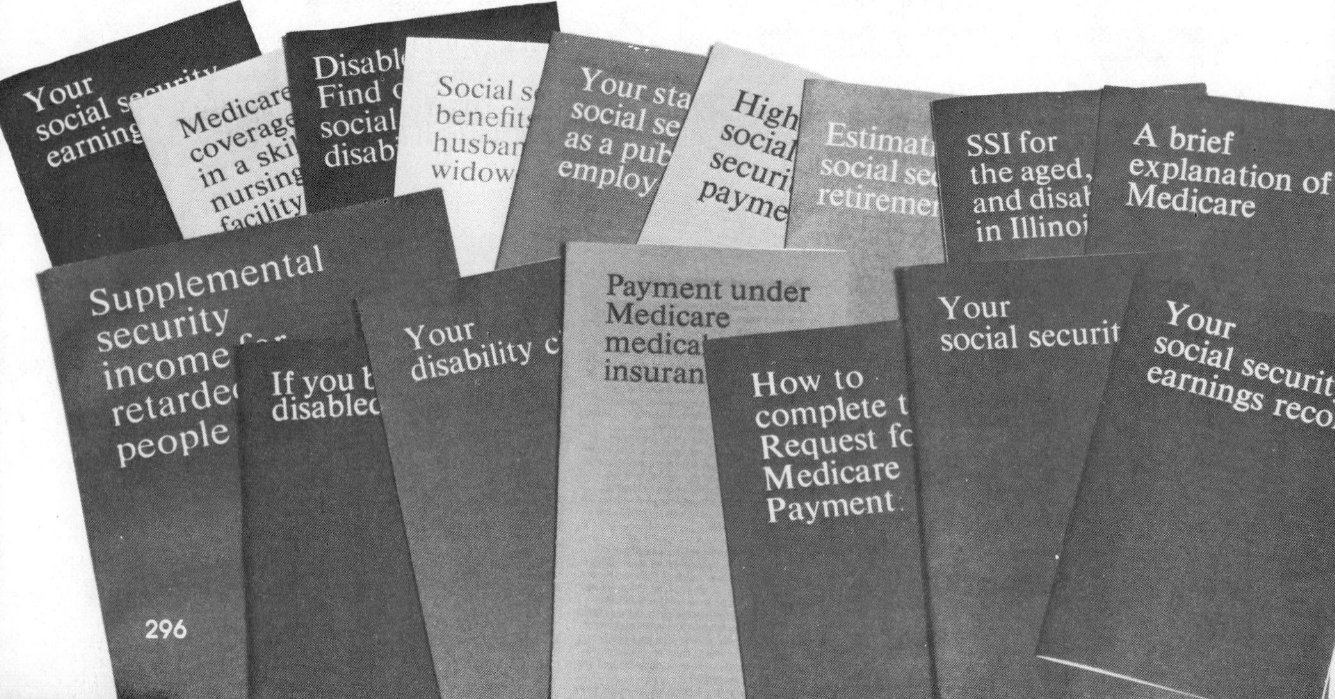

exercises

13. Judy Hank can retire when she is 63 years old and receive $433.40 per month from social security. How much is this per year?
14. If Judy waits to retire until she is 65, she will receive $472.50 per month from social security. How much is this per year?
15. If Judy retires at 63, how much will she receive from social security during the next 25 years?
16. If Judy retires at 65, how much will she receive from social security during the next 25 years?
17. Carl Talman can retire next year at age 63 and receive $305.70 per month from social security. How much is this per year?
18. If Carl waits to retire until he is 65 years old, he will receive $352.80 per month. How much is this per year?
19. Make a table to decide how many years Carl has to live to receive more total income from social security retiring at 65 than retiring at 63.
20. Rudy Aldinger retired at 65 and receives $370.30 per month from social security. If social security benefits were raised 5.8%, how much would Rudy receive each month? (Round up to the nearest ten cents.)

skills tune-up

Adding whole numbers and decimals, pages 6–7

1. 15 + 27 + 13
2. 8 + 29 + 16
3. 86 + 25 + 59
4. 48 + 27 + 89
5. 53 + 19 + 36
6. 72 + 34 + 56
7. 15 + 23 + 44 + 38
8. 5 + 98 + 57 + 36
9. 73 + 26 + 81 + 51
10. 212 + 496 + 174
11. 958 + 247 + 532
12. 650 + 135 + 286
13. 703 + 684 + 845
14. 6.8 + 3.17
15. 13.84 + 8.1
16. 22.46 + 32.32
17. 68.58 + 47.08
18. .3 + .5 + .1
19. 4.1 + 7.2 + 4.75
20. 1.86 + .17 + .76
21. 9.71 + 2.24 + 5.86
22. 4.3 + 6.59 + 1.71
23. .68 + .17 + . 59+ .05
24. 1.91 + 9.87 + 5.58
25. .46 + 7.17 + 3.639
26. 8.1 + 5.68 + 2.1 + 7.8

Multiplying whole numbers, pages 8–9

1. 35 × 40
2. 60 × 40
3. 50 × 400
4. 200 × 300
5. 600 × 350
6. 50 × 6400
7. 120 × 3500
8. 5000 × 900
9. 2000 × 6000
10. 170 × 1800
11. 100 × 680
12. 150 × 5400
13. 2000 × 170
14. 5 × 17
15. 72 × 26
16. 60 × 42
17. 734 × 4
18. 2721 × 3
19. 776 × 38
20. 17 × 2451
21. 480 × 686
22. 2184 × 143
23. 12.274 × 12
24. 30 × 4015
25. 593 × 1085
26. 901 × 6867

Percent problems, pages 36–38

1. 4% of 235 is ▒.
2. 90% of 39 is ▒.
3. 25% of 80 is ▒.
4. Find 12% of 200.
5. Find $44\frac{1}{2}$ of 4.
6. What number is 6.2% of 85?
7. What number is $1\frac{1}{4}\%$ of 7200?
8. 32% of ▒ is 256.
9. 15% of ▒ is 1.23.
10. $42\frac{1}{2}\%$ of ▒ is 17.
11. 25% of ▒ is 1.8.
12. $3\frac{3}{4}\%$ of ▒ is 7.5.
13. 83% of what number is 290.5?
14. 90 is 72% of what number?
15. 34.03 is 8.3% of what number?
16. ▒% of 84 is 21.
17. ▒% of 78 is 74.1.
18. ▒% of 20 is 2.5.
19. ▒% of 60 is 51.
20. What percent of 800 is 256?
21. 2.59 is what percent of 74?
22. 416 is what percent of 640?

Chapter 14

review

Health insurance, pages 280-281

1. Pam Rutledge has a $50-deductible health insurance policy. The insurance company pays 75% of all covered medical expenses after the deductible amount. Pam was hospitalized with an ear infection. Her medical bills amounted to $1735.25. How much did Pam pay?

Term life insurance, pages 282-283

2. Beth Stolie is 25 years old. She bought $75,000 worth of term life insurance. How much did she spend per year for the insurance? (Use the table on page 282.)

Straight life, limited payment life, and endowment insurance, pages 284-287

3. Ted Larson bought $30,000 worth of straight life insurance at age 27. What is his annual premium? (Use the table on page 284.)

4. In 20 years, what will be the cash value of Ted's insurance? (Use the table on page 286.)

Insurance office clerk, pages 288-289

5. Angela Manuel pays $384.72 annually for her insurance. How much will she pay monthly? (The factor is .0875.)

6. How much more per year will Angela pay if she pays monthly rather than yearly?

Choosing insurance and savings plans, pages 292-293

7. Andy Nissen is 27 years old. He buys a straight life insurance policy and pays a premium of $70 a month. How much insurance did he buy? Use the table on page 284. (The factor for converting from annual to monthly premiums is .0875.)

8. Jan Swan deposits $40 each month in a savings account that pays 6% interest compounded monthly. If she lets the interest accumulate, how much will be in the account after 20 years? (Use the table on page 293.)

Social security retirement benefits, pages 294-297

9. Cora Lessing was born in 1912. She retired at the age of 65. Her average annual income for the 19 years from 1958 through 1976 is $7465. What does Cora receive annually from social security? (Use the table on page 295.)

10. Jack Sanders retired at age 63. He receives $323.80 per month. How much will he receive from social security during the next 5 years?

Chapter 14

test

1. Wilma Altmann has a $60-deductible health insurance policy. The insurance company pays 80% of all medical bills after the deductible amount. Wilma broke her arm. Her medical bills amounted to $315.75. How much did the insurance company pay?

2. Alma Julliard is 30 years old. She bought $60,000 worth of term insurance. What is her annual premium? (Use the table on page 282.)

3. Russell Elliot, who is 32 years old, buys $50,000 worth of straight life insurance. How much is his annual premium? (Use the table on page 284.)

4. In 20 years, what will be the cash value of Russell's insurance? (Use the table on page 286.)

5. Belle Townsend pays $583.50 annually for her insurance. How much will she pay quarterly? (The factor is .26.)

6. How much more will Belle pay each year if she pays quarterly rather than yearly?

7. Randy Perez is 30 years old. He buys a straight life insurance policy and pays a premium of $60 a month. How much insurance did he buy? Use the table on page 284. (The factor for converting from annual to monthly premiums is .0875.)

8. Sarah Orr deposits $30 each month in a savings account that pays 7% interest compounded monthly. If she lets the interest accumulate, how much will be in the account after 20 years? (Use the table on page 293.)

9. Gwen Conway was born in 1912. She retired at the age of 65. Her average annual income for the 19 years from 1958 through 1976 is $6880. What does Gwen receive annually from social security? (Use the table on page 295.)

10. Emily Craig retired at age 64. She receives $392.70 per month. How much will she receive from social security during the next 5 years?

Chapter 15

Investments

After providing for all of their living expenses, many people decide to invest money for a profitable return.

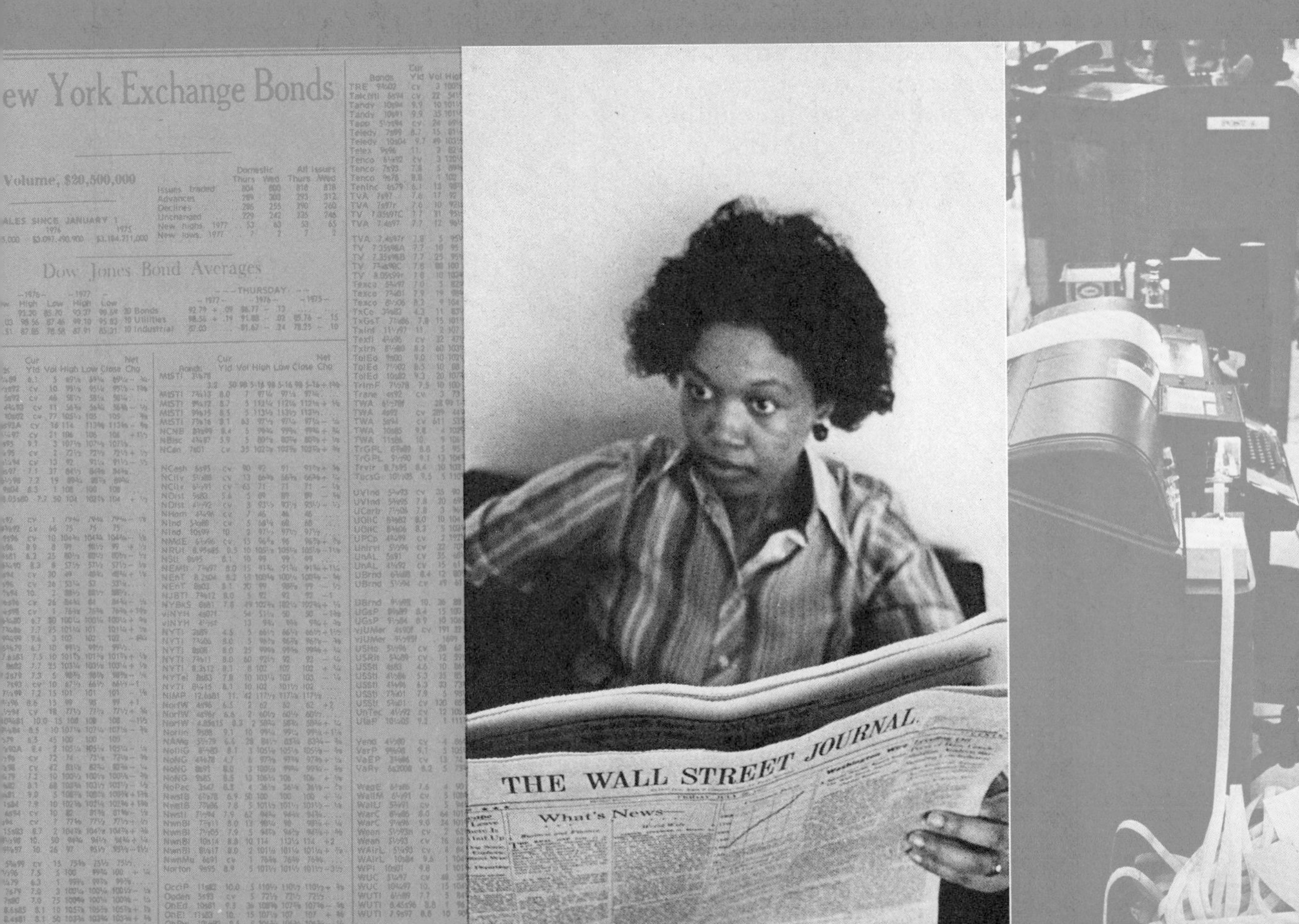

U.S. Savings Bonds— Series E

Many people use **Series E Savings Bonds** to save money regularly and develop a "savings habit." The bonds are guaranteed by the federal government. They are sold at most banks and savings institutions.

Series E Bonds can be purchased with **face values** of $25, $50, $75, $100, $200, $500, $1000, and $10,000. The cost of the bonds is 75% of their face value.

The bonds can be **redeemed,** or cashed in, any time after 2 months from the date of purchase. The amount you receive for redeeming a bond is the cost of the bond plus interest for the time you have owned it. If held to **maturity,** 5 years, the interest on the cost of the bond is 6% compounded semiannually. The redemption value of any bond is based on the redemption value of a $25 bond.

$25 Series E Savings Bond
(Issued after December 1, 1973)
Cost $18.75

	After	Redemption value is
	2 months	$18.88
	6 months	$19.13
	1 year	$19.61
	1.5 years	$20.10
	2 years	$20.60
	2.5 years	$21.14
	3 years	$21.71
	3.5 years	$22.31
	4 years	$22.97
	4.5 years	$23.67
Maturity →	5 years	$25.20
	5.5 years	$25.95
	6 years	$26.73
	6.5 years	$27.54
	7 years	$28.36
	7.5 years	$29.21
	8 years	$30.09
	8.5 years	$30.99
	9 years	$31.92
	9.5 years	$32.88
	10 years	$33.86
	15 years	$45.51
	20 years	$61.16

problem

Allan Casey wants to invest part of his earnings in a $200 Series E Savings Bond. How much will the bond cost? If he redeems the bond in 5 years, how much will he receive for it?

solution

The cost of the bond is 75% of its face value.

75% of $200

$.75 \times \$200 = \$150$ Cost of $200 bond

To find the redemption value of the bond, use the table on page 302. The redemption value of a $25 bond after 5 years is $25.20. Use a proportion to find the redemption value of the $200 bond after 5 years.

$\frac{25.20}{25} = \frac{r}{200}$ ← Redemption value (5 yr.) / ← Face value

$5040 = 25r$ Find the cross-products.

$201.60 = r$ Divide each side by 25.

Allan will receive $201.60 if he redeems the bond after 5 years.

exercises

Find the cost of these bonds.

	Number of bonds	Face value of each	Cost of 1 bond	Total cost
1.	1	$50	**a.**	——
2.	1	$75	**a.**	——
3.	3	$100	**a.**	**b.**
4.	3	$500	**a.**	**b.**
5.	6	$50	**a.**	**b.**
6.	4	$75	**a.**	**b.**
7.	3	$100	**a.**	**b.**
8.	12	$25	**a.**	**b.**
9.	2	$10,000	**a.**	**b.**
10.	20	$1000	**a.**	**b.**

Find the redemption value of each bond.

	Years owned	Face value
11.	3	$25
12.	7	$25
13.	5	$75
14.	5	$500
15.	2.5	$100
16.	9.5	$75
17.	8	$50
18.	15	$200
19.	3.5	$1,000
20.	6.5	$10,000
21.	20	$50

22. Karl just bought these Series E Savings Bonds: three $50 bonds, four $25 bonds, and three $75 bonds. What will be the total redemption value of these bonds after 10 years?

Certificates of Deposit

Most savings institutions offer their customers **certificates of deposit.** These certificates (CD's) earn higher interest rates than regular savings accounts.

Some types of certificates require a minimum deposit, usually $1000. Money invested in a CD must be left on deposit a certain length of time. If the money is withdrawn early, part of the interest is lost. In addition, the interest is recalculated using the regular savings-account rate instead of the higher CD rate. This penalty for early withdrawal is required by federal law.

Generally, the interest on a CD is compounded daily. A table for interest compounded daily is shown here.

Compound amount per $1 invested

Annual rate	Interest period			
	3 mo.	6 mo.	9 mo.	1 yr.
4.75%	1.01178	1.02370	1.03576	1.04864
5%	1.01240	1.02496	1.03768	1.05127
5.25%	1.01303	1.02623	1.03960	1.05390
5.5%	1.01365	1.02749	1.04152	1.05654
5.75%	1.01428	1.02876	1.04345	1.05918
6%	1.01490	1.03003	1.04538	1.06183
6.25%	1.01553	1.03130	1.04731	1.06449
6.5%	1.01616	1.03257	1.04925	1.06715
6.75%	1.01678	1.03384	1.05119	1.06982
7%	1.01741	1.03512	1.05314	1.07250
7.25%	1.01804	1.03640	1.05509	1.07519
7.5%	1.01866	1.03767	1.05704	1.07788
7.75%	1.01929	1.03895	1.05900	1.08057

GLENVIEW STATE BANK
CERTIFICATE OF DEPOSIT
NOT SUBJECT TO CHECK

ISSUE DATE	EXPIRATION DATE	TERM (MOS.)	SOCIAL SECURITY NO.	RATE	AMOUNT	No. 27698

NAME(S)

ADDRESS CITY STATE ZIP

HAS DEPOSITED IN THIS BANK

DOLLARS

UPON WHICH SUM THE SAID BANK WILL PAY INTEREST AT THE ANNUAL RATE AS SHOWN ABOVE FROM THIS DATE TO MATURITY, AND WILL REPAY THE LIKE AMOUNT WITH INTEREST TO THE PAYEE HEREOF FOR THE TERM SHOWN ABOVE, ON THE RETURN AND ENDORSEMENT OF THIS CERTIFICATE WHICH IS ASSIGNABLE ONLY ON THE BOOKS OF THIS BANK.

NOTWITHSTANDING THE ABOVE TERMS AND CONDITIONS, THIS CERTIFICATE MAY BE RENEWED AUTOMATICALLY FOR SUCCESSIVE PERIODS EACH EQUAL TO THE ORIGINAL TERM UNTIL THE CERTIFICATE HOLDER HEREOF SHALL PRESENT THIS CERTIFICATE FOR PAYMENT ON THE MATURITY DATE OR WITHIN TEN DAYS THEREOF OR AT THE END OF ANY SUBSEQUENT PERIOD BASED ON TERM SHOWN ABOVE. THE BANK RESERVES THE RIGHT TO CALL THIS CERTIFICATE FOR PAYMENT OR CHANGE THE RATE OF INTEREST BY SENDING WRITTEN NOTICE BY ORDINARY MAIL TO THE CERTIFICATE HOLDER AT HIS LAST KNOWN ADDRESS, AT LEAST 10 DAYS IN ADVANCE OF ANY MATURITY DATE. THIS CERTIFICATE WILL BEAR NO INTEREST AFTER MATURITY DATE SUBSEQUENT TO PROPER NOTICE OF CALL BY THE BANK.

NON-NEGOTIABLE
AUTOMATICALLY RENEWABLE

INTEREST DISPOSITION
☐ CAPITALIZED
☐ MAIL CHECK EVERY ____ MONTH(S)
☐ DEPOSIT TO ☐ SAVINGS ☐ CHECKING ACCOUNT NO. ______

Glenview STATE Bank
800 Waukegan Rd./1825 Glenview Rd./U.S. Naval Air Station/Glenview, Illinois 60025.

AUTHORIZED SIGNATURE

⑈027698⑈ ⑆5901⑉3030⑆

problem

Millie Yuma inherited $2000. Since she already has a savings account, she decided to invest this money in a 3-year certificate of deposit that earns 6.5% interest compounded daily.

Millie agrees to leave her money on deposit for the full 3 years. The bank agrees to send her a check for the interest each year. How much interest will Millie receive at the end of each year?

solution

The factor from the table for 6.5% interest compounded daily for 1 year is 1.06715.

Amount invested		Factor from the table		Compound amount
$2000	×	1.06715	=	$2134.30

$2134.30	Compound amount
− 2000.00	Amount invested
$ 134.30	Interest

The bank will send Millie a check for $134.30 each year.

exercises

Find the amount of interest earned on each certificate of deposit.

	Amount invested	Annual rate	Interest period	Factor from the table	Compound amount	Interest
	$2000	6.5%	1 yr.	1.06715	$2134.30	$134.30
1.	$1000	7%	1 yr.	a.	b.	c.
2.	$5000	6%	1 yr.	a.	b.	c.
3.	$10,000	7.75%	1 yr.	a.	b.	c.
4.	$3000	7.25%	6 mo.	a.	b.	c.
5.	$4000	6.25%	6 mo.	a.	b.	c.
6.	$2000	6.75%	3 mo.	a.	b.	c.
7.	$2000	7.5%	3 mo.	a.	b.	c.

8. Gail bought a $1000, 4-year CD that earns 7.5% interest compounded daily. She will receive an interest check every year. How much interest will she receive each year?

9. Gail withdrew her money at the end of 1 year. She received only 9 months interest at the regular savings rate of 5.25% compounded daily. Find the amount of interest she was paid on her $1000 deposit.

10. How much interest did Gail lose this year by withdrawing her money?

One method that people may use to compare certificates of deposit is to find the **annual yield** of each CD. In order to get the most interest, choose a CD with the highest annual yield.

$$\text{Annual yield} = \frac{\text{Amount earned in 1 yr.}}{\text{Amount invested}}$$

Annual yield is usually expressed as a percent.

problem

Millie's $2000 CD earned $134.30 in interest each year. What is the annual yield of this investment?

solution

$$\text{Annual yield} = \frac{\text{Amount earned in 1 yr.}}{\text{Amount invested}}$$

$$\text{Annual yield} = \frac{\$134.30}{\$2000}$$

$$\text{Annual yield} = .06715 \approx 6.72\%$$

The annual yield is 6.72%, rounded to the nearest hundredth of a percent.

exercises

Find the annual yield for each certificate of deposit. Round to the nearest hundredth of a percent.

	Amount invested	Annual rate	Interest paid	Amount earned in 1 year	Annual yield
	$2000	6.5%	$134.30 each year	$134.30	6.72%
11.	$1000	7.5%	$72.50 each year	$72.50	a.
12.	$2000	5.75%	$118.36 each year	$118.36	a.
13.	$5000	6.25%	$322.45 each year	$322.45	a.
14.	$1000	7.5%	$35.12 every 6 mo.	a.	b.
15.	$2000	5.75%	$57.52 every 6 mo.	a.	b.
16.	$5000	6.25%	$156.50 every 6 mo.	a.	b.
17.	$2000	5.75%	$28.56 every 3 mo.	a.	b.
18.	$5000	6.25%	$77.65 every 3 mo.	a.	b.

19. Which has the higher annual yield, a $1000 CD at 6% that earns $61.83 each year, or a $2000 CD at 6% that earns $60.06 every 6 months?

20. Which has the higher annual yield, a $1000 CD at 7.5% that earns $77.88 each year, or a $5000 CD at 7% that earns $362.50 each year?

CALCULATOR EXERCISES

The grandparents of a child born this year bought the baby a $2500 CD that earns 7.75% interest compounded daily. They plan to leave the $2500 and the interest it earns in the CD until the child graduates from high school. Complete the table to find the value of the CD 18 years from now. Round all answers to the nearest cent.

	Year	Amount invested	Factor from the table	Compound amount
	1	$2500	1.08057	$2701.43
1.	2	$2701.43	1.08057	**a.**
2.	3	**a.**	1.08057	**b.**
3.	4	**a.**	1.08057	**b.**
4.	5	**a.**	1.08057	**b.**
5.	6	**a.**	1.08057	**b.**
6.	7	**a.**	1.08057	**b.**
7.	8	**a.**	1.08057	**b.**
8.	9	**a.**	1.08057	**b.**
9.	10	**a.**	1.08057	**b.**
10.	11	**a.**	1.08057	**b.**
11.	12	**a.**	1.08057	**b.**
12.	13	**a.**	1.08057	**b.**
13.	14	**a.**	1.08057	**b.**
14.	15	**a.**	1.08057	**b.**
15.	16	**a.**	1.08057	**b.**
16.	17	**a.**	1.08057	**b.**
17.	18	**a.**	1.08057	**b.**

18. Subtract the original $2500 invested from the final compound amount (exercise 17b) to find the amount of interest this CD will earn in 18 years.

19. Study the answers you computed for the column labeled "compound amount." How many years does it take for the $2500 to double in value? To triple in value?

20. This CD earned $201.43 in interest the first year. If the interest had been withdrawn each year, the total interest earned by this CD in 18 years would have been $201.43 × 18. Find this amount.

Common Stock

Another way that people invest their money is to buy **shares** of **common stock.** The holder of common stock is a partial owner of the company that issues the stock. If the company makes a profit during the year, it may pay **dividends,** part of the profits, to its stockholders.

To buy stocks, you can go to a **broker.** The broker buys and sells stocks for you, and can give you advice about which stocks may be good investments. You will pay the broker a commission, a fee for his services, each time you buy or sell stocks.

The current prices of many stocks are listed each day in the financial section of most newspapers. Part of one listing is shown.

1	2		3	4	5	6	7
	Div	PE	Sales 100	Hi	Low	Close	Net Chg.
				— A —	A —		
ACF Ind	1.80	7	17	32¾	32⅜	32⅜	− ⅜
AJ Indust		7	301	4½	4⅜	4⅜	− ⅛
AMF Inc	1.24	10	1143	19⅛	18⅞	19⅛	+ ⅛
APLCorp	1	5	8	14½	14½	14½	....
ARASv	1.20	13	50	50⅛	49⅛	49¾	+ ⅝
ASALtd	.80	..	373	23⅛	22¾	22¾	+ ⅛
ATOInc	.28	5	79	9¼	9	9⅛	+ ⅛
AbbtLab	.88	16	541	48	46⅝	48	+ ⅝
AcmeClv	.50	13	49	8⅞	8½	8⅝	....
AdmDg	.04	5	70	3	2⅞	3	+ ⅛
AdmEx	.91e	..	44	12	11¾	12	+ ¼
AdmsMillis		7	33	4⅛	3⅞	4⅛	+ ¼
Addrssg	.10e	16	326	11¾	11¼	11½	+ ⅛
AetnaLf	1.20	9	1188	35	34⅝	34⅞	+ ¼
Aquirre Co		93	6	9¼	9¼	9¼	− ⅛
Ahmans	.22	7	106	17	16⅞	16⅞	....
Aileen Inc		63	85	3¼	3	3⅛	+ ⅛
AirProd	.20	14	569	31⅞	30½	31⅝	+ ⅞
AirbnFrt	.60	12	39	13¼	13⅛	13¼	+ ¼
AircoInc	1.15	6	20	28⅝	28¼	28⅝	+ ½
Akzona	1.20	11	238	14	13⅞	14	+ ⅛
AlaGas	1.28	7	19	15	14⅞	15	+ ⅛

1 An abbreviation for the name of the stock.

2 *Div* Dividends paid in the last year. For example, 1.80 means $1.80 per share was paid in dividends in the last year.

3 *Sales 100* Hundreds of shares sold today. 17 means 1700 shares were sold today.

4 *Hi* The highest price paid for a share today. $32\frac{3}{4}$ means $32\frac{3}{4}$ dollars, or $32.75.

5 *Low* The lowest price paid today.

6 *Close* The last price paid today.

7 *Net Chg.* Net change. The amount by which today's closing price is different from yesterday's closing price. For example, $-\frac{3}{8}$ means that today's closing price was $\frac{3}{8}$ of a dollar, or $.375, per share lower than yesterday's closing price.

problem

Sandy MacKay bought 25 shares of stock for $35.375 per share. She paid a commission of $21.50. What was the total amount Sandy invested?

solution

$35.375	Cost per share
× 25	Number of shares
$884.375 ≈ $884.38	Cost of stock

$884.38	Cost of stock
+ 21.50	Commission paid
$905.88	Total amount invested

exercises

Find the total amount invested.

	Number of shares	Cost per share	Commission paid
1.	45	$4.125	$8.25
2.	90	$15.25	$28.00
3.	50	$10.375	$15.00
4.	20	$35.25	$18.50
5.	70	$28.875	$36.50
6.	100	$63.625	$79.25
7.	200	$58.875	$140.00
8.	150	$26.25	$57.50
9.	60	$103.375	$76.00
10.	120	$100.50	$148.61

problem

Sandy sold her 25 shares of stock several months after she bought them. The sale price was $36.875 per share. She paid a commission of $22. What was the profit or loss on the $905.88 that Sandy had invested?

solution

Find the amount that Sandy received from the sale of her stock.

$36.875	Sale price per share
× 25	Number of shares
$921.875 ≈ $921.88	Amount of sale

$921.88	Amount of sale
− 22.00	Commission paid
$899.88	Received from sale

Since Sandy received less from the sale of her stock than she had invested, she had a loss.

$905.88	Amount invested
− 899.88	Received from sale
$ 6.00	Loss

exercises

Find the amount received from the sale of these stocks.

	Number of shares	Sale price per share	Commission paid
11.	20	$7.625	$7.50
12.	30	$29.25	$21.50
13.	50	$43.375	$38.50
14.	70	$80.125	$70.50
15.	100	$31.875	$50.75
16.	50	$116.25	$72.50
17.	100	$126.75	$136.00
18.	60	$21.375	$26.75
19.	10	$57.50	$16.00
20.	200	$10.50	$51.30

Find the profit or loss on these stock investments. The sale price given is the price per share of stock.

		Sale of Stock		
	Amount invested	No. of shares	Sale price	Commission paid
21.	$715	80	$8.875	$18.75
22.	$116	20	$5.625	$6.75
23.	$2320	40	$63.50	$43.00
24.	$740	50	$15.75	$20.00
25.	$1150	100	$13.375	$29.50
26.	$5950	100	$57.625	$74.00
27.	$1484	60	$27.25	$31.25
28.	$320	10	$32.125	$11.00
29.	$6880	200	$41.00	$107.75
30.	$23,420	200	$118.25	$236.00

problem

Craig invested $550 in 30 shares of stock. During the following year, the company paid dividends of $1.20 per share. What was the annual yield on Craig's investment?

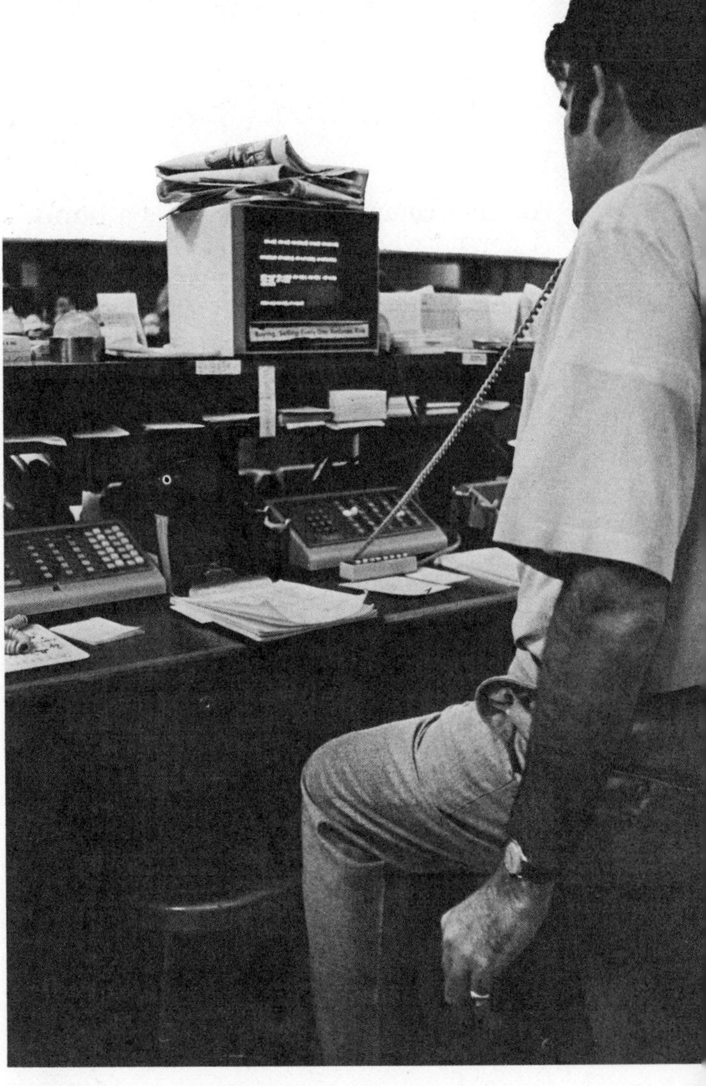

solution

Find the amount he received in dividends during the year.

$ 1.20	Dividends per share
× 30	Number of shares
$36.00	Amount of dividends

Find the annual yield.

$$\text{Annual yield} = \frac{\text{Amount earned in 1 yr.}}{\text{Amount invested}}$$

$$\text{Annual yield} = \frac{\$36}{\$550}$$

$$\text{Annual yield} \approx .06545 \approx 6.55\%$$

The annual yield is 6.55%, rounded to the nearest hundredth of a percent.

exercises

Find the annual yield on these stock investments. Round to the nearest hundredth of a percent.

	Amount invested	Number of shares	Dividends per share	Amount of dividends	Annual yield
	$550	30	$1.20	$36.00	6.55%
31.	$2100	40	$3.00	a.	b.
32.	$6400	100	$4.20	a.	b.
33.	$4000	150	$1.06	a.	b.
34.	$3100	100	$2.15	a.	b.
35.	$7000	210	$1.72	a.	b.

Bonds

Another common investment is a **bond.** A person who buys a bond is loaning money to the company or government agency that issued the bond. As with any loan, the borrower pays interest to the lender.

Bonds are generally issued with face values of $1000. Interest is paid on the face value of the bond. Usually, the company issuing the bonds wants to borrow the money for a long period of time—15, 20, or even 30 years or more. If the lenders, the owners of the bonds, want to get their money back before the end of this time, they must sell the bonds to another investor. Bond brokers handle these purchases and sales.

Like stocks, bonds vary in price. Some $1000 bonds cost less than $1000. Some cost more than $1000. The price is determined by many factors, including the interest rate, the date of maturity of the bond, and the stability of the company issuing the bond.

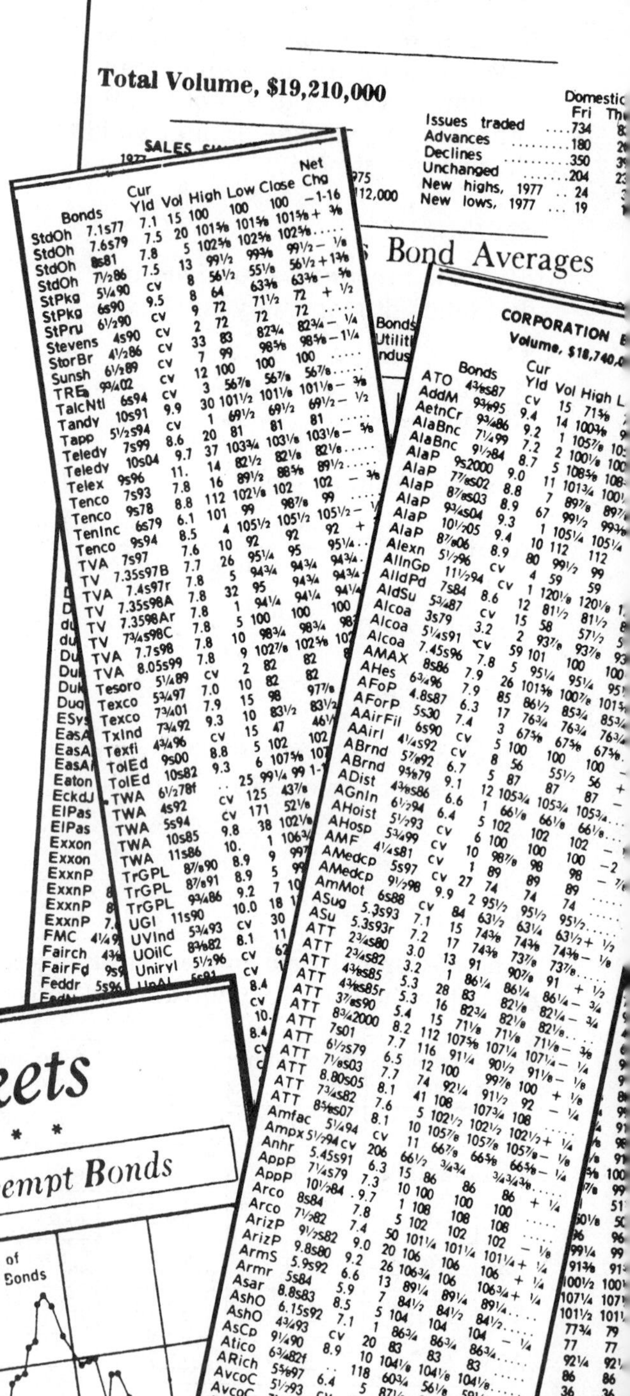

problem

Joel bought a $1000 bond that pays 6.7% interest and matures in 1998. The cost, including the broker's commission, was $860. What is the annual yield on Joel's investment?

solution

The interest is paid on the face value of the bond. Find the amount of interest paid each year.

6.7% of $1000

$.067 \times \$1000 = \$67.00$ Interest

Find the annual yield.

$$\text{Annual yield} = \frac{\text{Amount earned in 1 yr.}}{\text{Amount invested}}$$

$$\text{Annual yield} = \frac{\$67}{\$860}$$

$$\text{Annual yield} \approx .0779 = 7.79\%$$

The annual yield is 7.79%, rounded to the nearest hundredth of a percent.

exercises

Find the annual yield of these bond investments. Round to the nearest hundredth of a percent.

	Maturity date	Face value	Interest rate	Amount of interest	Cost, including commission	Annual yield
	1998	$1000	6.7%	$67.00	$860	7.79%
1.	1988	$1000	11%	a.	$1100	b.
2.	1988	$1000	6.5%	a.	$880	b.
3.	1994	$1000	10%	a.	$1005	b.
4.	1997	$1000	7%	a.	$840	b.
5.	1983	$1000	3.9%	a.	$870	b.
6.	1983	$1000	8.4%	a.	$1040	b.
7.	2000	$1000	11.6%	a.	$1130	b.
8.	2001	$1000	7.6%	a.	$920	b.
9.	1991	$1000	4.5%	a.	$720	b.
10.	1991	$1000	10.25%	a.	$1070	b.

career

Investment Counselor

Career Cluster: Business Contact

Carla Reyes is an investment counselor. She helps people decide how to invest their money.

Melinda Collier is planning to invest money for the first time. Carla encourages her to learn about **mutual funds.**

A mutual fund combines the money of many investors to buy a large variety of stocks and bonds. These investments are chosen by the fund's professional investment managers. The money that the fund earns from its investments is paid to the shareholders as dividends.

The value of one share of a mutual fund is the seller's price. It is the amount that an investor would receive by selling one share back to the fund.

The amount that a new investor would have to pay to buy a share of a mutual fund sometimes includes a sales charge, or **load.** Thus, the buyer's price is the value of a share (the seller's price) plus the sales charge.

Mutual funds that do not have a sales charge are called **no-load** (NL) mutual funds. For these funds, the buyer's price is the same as the seller's price.

The current prices of many funds are listed in the financial section of many daily newspapers.

problem

Melinda decided to study two mutual funds, the AB Mutual Fund and the DX Mutual Fund. How much would 50 shares of each fund cost?

solution

Use the listing shown at the right. The AB fund is a no-load fund. The buyer's and seller's prices are both $10.86 per share.

$\$10.86 \times 50 = \$543$ Cost of 50 shares of AB

The DX Mutual Fund has a sales charge. The buyer's price is $10.90 per share.

$\$10.90 \times 50 = \$545$ Cost of 50 shares of DX

MUTUAL FUNDS

Name	Sell	Buy
AB Mut. F.	10.86	NL
AE Fund	13.05	14.26
BG Inv.	11.01	12.00
DX Mut. F.	9.97	10.90
GV Fund	7.63	8.34
Fin. Pln.	4.50	NL
HTH Grp.	12.12	13.25
Jay Fund	19.91	NL
MBT Grp.	5.79	NL
New Inv.	19.53	21.23
Park Fd.	24.97	NL
Va. Fund	4.01	NL

exercises

Use the listing above to find the cost of these mutual fund shares.

	Shares bought	Mutual fund	Buy price	Total cost
1.	5	Jay Fund	**a.**	**b.**
2.	20	New Inv.	**a.**	**b.**
3.	15	AE Fund	**a.**	**b.**
4.	50	Va. Fund	**a.**	**b.**
5.	75	Fin. Pln.	**a.**	**b.**
6.	40	BG Inv.	**a.**	**b.**
7.	12	GV Fund	**a.**	**b.**
8.	21	MBT Grp.	**a.**	**b.**
9.	16	Park Fd.	**a.**	**b.**
10.	30	HTH Grp.	**a.**	**b.**

11. How much would you receive if you sold 50 shares of the GV Fund back to the fund?

12. How much would you receive if you sold 40 shares of the Jay Fund back to the fund?

13. What is the sales charge on each share of DX Mutual Fund?

14. What is the sales charge on each share of the HTH Grp. fund?

15. How many shares of the Fin. Pln. fund can be bought for $500? Round to the nearest ten-thousandth.

16. How many shares of the BG Inv. fund can be bought for $500? Round to the nearest ten-thousandth.

skills tune-up

Rounding whole numbers and decimals, pages 4-5

Round each number to the nearest thousand, the nearest hundred, and the nearest ten.

1. 718

2. 654

3. 3492

4. 6136

5. 9358

6. 4772

7. 56,201

8. 2815

9. 999.9

10. 50,743.3

Round each number to the nearest whole number, the nearest tenth, and the nearest hundredth.

11. 5.627

12. 12.195

13. 47.458

14. 81.603

15. 376.286

16. 140.438

17. 764.971

18. 99.182

19. 68.019

20. 417.905

Dividing decimals, pages 12-13

Find the quotient to the nearest thousandth.

1. $18.2 \div 6$

2. $77.9 \div 9$

3. $34.15 \div 38$

4. $10.37 \div 23$

5. $8.094 \div 89$

6. $2.835 \div 54$

7. $.0026 \div .11$

8. $.0074 \div .47$

9. $.6 \div 2.7$

10. $4.6 \div 7.2$

11. $14.12 \div 5.1$

12. $10.27 \div 8.5$

13. $.291 \div .08$

14. $.578 \div .06$

15. $48 \div .6$

16. $72 \div .3$

17. $9.6 \div 2.05$

18. $4.15 \div 8.31$

19. $1.04 \div 2.66$

20. $2.49 \div 8.01$

21. $.4773 \div 2.61$

22. $.614 \div .549$

23. $.941 \div .427$

24. $.4816 \div .031$

25. $.7082 \div .029$

Ratio and proportion, pages 30-31

Find the cross-products. Tell whether the ratios are equal.

1. $\frac{3}{5}$ $\frac{2}{3}$

2. $\frac{5}{12}$ $\frac{15}{36}$

3. $\frac{4}{7}$ $\frac{2}{9}$

4. $\frac{6}{1.8}$ $\frac{3}{.9}$

5. $\frac{30.6}{100}$ $\frac{1.8}{6}$

6. $\frac{3}{3.98}$ $\frac{5}{5.98}$

Solve and check.

7. $\frac{7}{8} = \frac{21}{a}$

8. $\frac{5}{3} = \frac{c}{21}$

9. $\frac{36}{n} = \frac{12}{21}$

10. $\frac{d}{6} = \frac{4}{5}$

11. $\frac{.25}{1} = \frac{6}{x}$

12. $\frac{3.5}{a} = \frac{.07}{.2}$

13. $\frac{.56}{.07} = \frac{y}{2}$

14. $\frac{n}{4.9} = \frac{1.2}{2.1}$

Chapter 15

review

U. S. Savings Bonds – Series E, pages 302-303

1. What is the cost of a $75 Series E Savings Bond?
2. What is the redemption value of a $75 bond after 6 years? (Use the table on page 302.)

Certificates of deposit, pages 304-306

3. Dana Evans bought a $4000 CD that earns 6.75% interest compounded daily. She receives an interest check every three months. How much interest does she receive every 3 months? (Use the table on page 304.)
4. Stan Larsen has a $3000 CD that earns $46.59 in interest every 3 months. What is the annual yield on Stan's investment? Round to the nearest hundredth of a percent.

Common stock, pages 308-311

5. Ellen Drake bought 70 shares of stock for $53.375 per share. She paid a commission of $54. What was the total amount Ellen invested?
6. Ronald Moy sold 50 shares of stock for $63.625 per share. He paid a commission of $49. How much did Ronald receive from the sale?
7. Ronald's original investment was $3000. What was the profit or loss on his investment?
8. Kirk invested $800 in 30 shares of stock. During the following year, he was paid dividends of $1.25 per share. What was the annual yield on his investment? Round to the nearest hundredth of a percent.

Bonds, pages 312-313

9. Rita bought a $1000 bond that matures in the year 2016. It pays 8.25% interest. She paid $1020 for the bond. What is the annual yield on her investment? Round to the nearest hundredth of a percent.

Investment counselor, pages 314-315

10.

MUTUAL FUNDS

Name	Sell	Buy
RV Fund	14.85	NL
Est. Grp.	12.20	14.00

Use the listing above to find the total cost of buying 20 shares of the RV Fund.

Chapter 15

1. What is the cost of a $500 Series E Savings Bond?

2. What is the redemption value of a $100 Series E Savings Bond after 5 years? (Use the table on page 302.)

3. Grant bought a $2000 CD that earns 7.5% interest compounded daily. How much interest will he receive at the end of 1 year? (Use the table on page 304.)

4. Marcia has a $2000 CD that earns $145 in interest each year. What is the annual yield on her investment?

5. Edgar bought 20 shares of stock for $48.50 per share. He paid a commission of $23. What was his total investment?

6. Jeannie sold 100 shares of stock for $15.75 per share. She paid a commission of $31. How much did she receive from the sale?

7. Jeannie's original investment was $1560. What was the profit or loss on her investment?

8. Jill invested $500 in 10 shares of stock. During the following year, she was paid dividends of $4.10 per share. What was the annual yield on Jill's investment?

9. Carlos bought a $1000 bond that pays 5% interest per year. He paid $600 for the bond. What is the annual yield on his investment? Round to the nearest hundredth of a percent.

10. MUTUAL FUNDS

Name	Sell	Buy
Ntl. Inv.	27.10	NL
QA Fund	7.50	8.14

Use the listing above to find the total cost of buying 30 shares of the QA Fund.

Unit 5

Choose the best answer.

1. Curtis Lee is single. His total income for this year is $14,850. Use the following information to find his standard deduction.

   Standard Deduction – Single
   16% of total income
   Minimum: $1700
   Maximum: $2400

   A $2400 **C** $2326
   B $2376 **D** $1700

2. Adam had $2857 in federal income taxes withheld from his earnings this year. His tax required for the year is $2194. Find the refund due Adam or the balance due the IRS.

   A $663 due IRS **C** $743 due IRS
   B $663 refund **D** $743 refund

3. The Bermans' itemized deductions are listed here. Find the total.

   General sales tax: $183
   Gasoline tax: $102
   Loan interest: $257
   Miscellaneous deductions: $76

   A $608 **C** $618
   B $518 **D** $609

4. One year, federal spending totaled $281 billion. About 3% of that amount was spent on natural resources, environment, and energy. How much was spent on these items? (Round the answer to the nearest billion dollars.)

   A $8 billion **C** $9 billion
   B $65 billion **D** $84 billion

5. Lynn Lawson's taxable income is $17,200. The state where she lives computes state income tax by finding 4% of taxable income. What is Lynn's state income tax?

   A $588 **C** $508
   B $788 **D** $688

6. Cristina Sanchez has a $100-deductible health insurance policy. The insurance company pays 85% of all costs after the deductible amount. Cristina broke her leg. Her medical bills totaled $380. How much did the insurance company pay?

   A $238 **C** $142
   B $323 **D** $280

7. Tim Kelly is 36 years old. He wants to buy $30,000 worth of term life insurance. What will be his annual premium? (Use the table on page 282.)

   A $195.00 **C** $198.60
   B $202.20 **D** $238.32

8. Paul Prokop, who is 22 years old, wants to buy $15,000 worth of straight life insurance. What will be his annual premium? (Use the table on page 284.)

   A $195.30 C $294.58

   B $206.85 D $200.85

9. Felicia McBride pays $168 annually for her insurance. How much will she pay semiannually? (The factor is .51.)

   A $55.68 C $85.68

   B $85.60 D $81.68

10. Sophie Taglia was born in 1912. She retired at the age of 65. Her average annual income for the 19 years from 1958 through 1976 is $7238. What does Sophie receive annually from social security? (Use the table on page 295.)

    A $4900.80 C $4712.40

    B $5192.40 D $5048.40

11. Find the cost of a $50 Series E Savings Bond. (The cost is 75% of face value.)

    A $12.50 C $28.50

    B $37.50 D $42.50

12. Chad bought a $3000 certificate of deposit that pays 7% interest compounded daily. How much interest will he receive at the end of 1 year? (Use the table on page 304.)

    A $217.50 C $3217.50

    B $225.60 D $225.57

13. Mary Ellen sold 80 shares of stock for $24.75 per share. She paid a commission of $36. How much did she receive from the sale?

    A $1944 C $2016

    B $2904 D $2160

14. Wes invested $600 in 40 shares of stock. During the following year, he was paid dividends of $3.70 per share. Find the total amount that Wes received in dividends during the year.

    A $222 C $148

    B $55 D $452

15. Jolana bought a $1000 bond that pays 4% interest per year. The cost, including the broker's commission, was $500. What is the annual yield on her investment?

    A 7% C 12.5%

    B 4% D 8%

16. DJR Mutual Fund is a no-load fund. The current selling price is $14.07 per share. Find the cost of buying 60 shares of DJR Mutual Fund.

    A $882.60 C $8826.40

    B $844.20 D $8442.20

unit six

Purchasing and Budgeting

Buying Food

Chapter 17

Buying, Making, and Renting Goods

Budgeting

Chapter 16

Buying Food

The cost of food is an ever-increasing expense. It is necessary for consumers to shop carefully by planning meals and comparing costs.

career

Dietitian

Career Cluster: Health

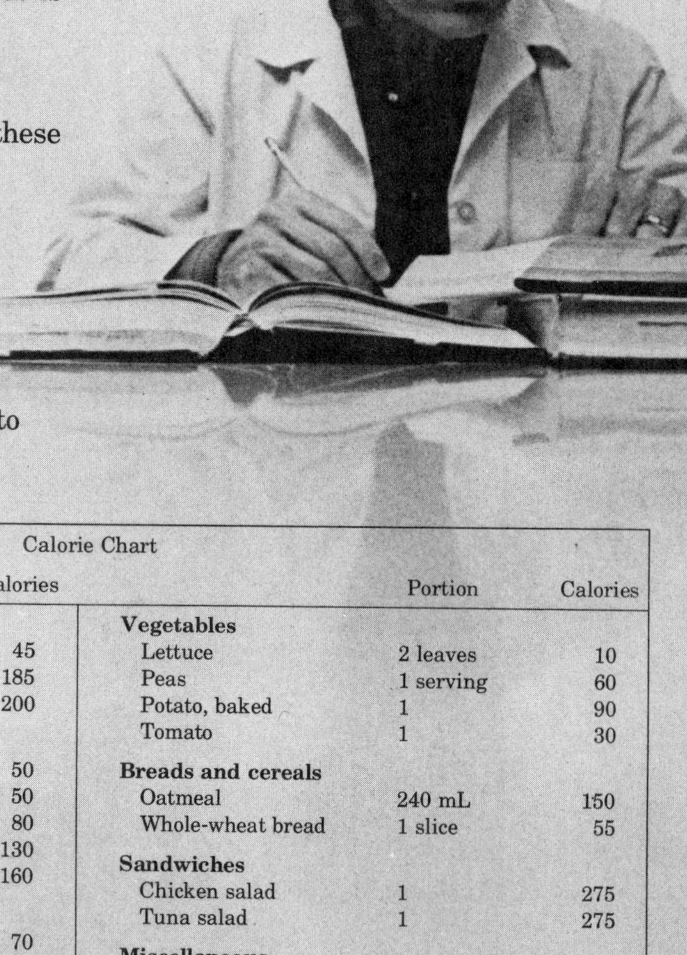

Henry Robinson is a dietitian. His job is to help people plan nutritious, well-balanced meals.

When Henry writes meal plans for people, he takes into consideration these four main food groups.

- Meat, poultry, eggs, and fish
- Milk and dairy products
- Fruits and vegetables
- Breads and cereals

He also uses a calorie chart. A portion of one is shown below. A **calorie** is a heat unit that is used to express the fuel value of foods.

Calorie Chart

	Portion	Calories
Meat, poultry		
Bacon	1 slice	45
Chicken, broiled	1 piece	185
Meat loaf	1 slice	200
Dairy products and eggs		
Butter	1 pat	50
Cottage cheese	55 g	50
Egg, poached	1	80
Ice cream	100 g	130
Milk	240 mL	160
Fruits		
Apple	1	70
Grapefruit	$\frac{1}{2}$	55
Orange juice	120 mL	55
Peaches, canned	1 serving	100

	Portion	Calories
Vegetables		
Lettuce	2 leaves	10
Peas	1 serving	60
Potato, baked	1	90
Tomato	1	30
Breads and cereals		
Oatmeal	240 mL	150
Whole-wheat bread	1 slice	55
Sandwiches		
Chicken salad	1	275
Tuna salad	1	275
Miscellaneous		
French dressing	15 mL	60
Vegetable soup	240 mL	80

problem

Henry is writing meal plans for Roy Benson. Roy has to reduce before wrestling season starts. Because of Roy's age, height, and size, Henry determines that Roy should not exceed 1800 calories per day. Find the number of calories in the breakfast that Henry has planned for Roy.

Monday breakfast

$\frac{1}{2}$ grapefruit
240 mL oatmeal
120 mL milk
2 slices bacon

solution

Find the number of calories in each item. Then add to find the total.

55 cal.	Grapefruit
150 cal.	Oatmeal
80 cal.	Milk (160 ÷ 2)
+ 90 cal.	Bacon (45 × 2)
375 cal.	

Monday's breakfast contains 375 calories.

exercises

Find the number of calories in each meal.

1. Monday lunch

   240 mL vegetable soup
   $\frac{1}{2}$ tomato
   240 mL milk
   1 tuna salad sandwich

2. Monday dinner

   2 pieces broiled chicken
   1 serving canned peaches
   1 serving peas
   240 mL milk
   100 g ice cream

3. Tuesday breakfast

   120 mL orange juice
   2 poached eggs
   1 slice whole-wheat toast
   1 pat butter
   240 mL milk

4. Tuesday lunch

   1 chicken salad sandwich
   55 g cottage cheese
   240 mL milk
   1 apple

5. Tuesday dinner

   2 slices meat loaf
   1 baked potato
   4 leaves of lettuce
   15 mL French dressing
   240 mL milk

6. Find the total number of calories planned for Monday.

7. Find the total number of calories planned for Tuesday.

Calorie Usage

Jed Horton's doctor gave him information about the number of calories used for certain activities. Jed kept track of how long he did each activity one day. Then he completed the table below.

Activity	Calories used per kilogram of mass each hour	Number of hours spent one day
Sleeping	0.9	7.5
Sitting quietly reading, writing, talking on the telephone, watching TV, attending classes	1.8	9.5
Light exercise walking slowly, playing the piano, typing, driving a car	2.4	4.3
Moderate exercise bicycling 8 km per hour, walking briskly, bowling, playing catch	3.9	.5
Active exercise dancing, doing calisthenics, playing Ping-Pong, raking leaves	5.7	.6
Very active exercise jogging 8 km per hour, swimming, playing tennis	10.1	1.6
	Total hours	24.0

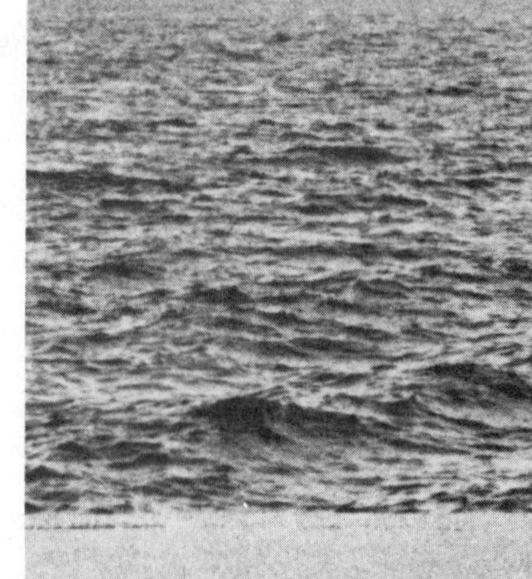

problem

How many calories did Jed use while sleeping? His mass is 73 kilograms.

solution

Multiply the factor for sleeping by Jed's mass.

$0.9 \times 73 = 65.7$ Calories used for one hour of sleeping

Multiply the number of calories used in one hour by the number of hours Jed slept. Round the answer to the nearest whole number.

$65.7 \times 7.5 \approx 493$ Calories used for sleeping 7.5 hours

exercises

For exercises 1-5, find the number of calories Jed used in each activity listed in the chart. Round the answers to the nearest whole number.

1. Sitting quietly
2. Light exercise
3. Moderate exercise
4. Active exercise
5. Very active exercise
6. Find the total number of calories Jed used on that day. (Include the calories used for sleeping.)

Find the number of calories used by Betty Granville for each activity listed. The number of hours Betty spent on each activity in one day is given. Her mass is 63 kilograms. Round the answers to the nearest whole number.

7. Sleeping, 8.0 hours
8. Sitting quietly, 10.4 hours
9. Light exercise, 2.7 hours
10. Moderate exercise, 1.2 hours
11. Active exercise, 1.4 hours
12. Very active exercise, .3 hour
13. Find the total number of calories used by Betty on that day.
14. To slim down, Betty is trying to use up more calories than she consumes. Betty consumed 1375 calories. She used how many more calories than she consumed?

Grocery Shopping

Jaime and Alicia Lorenzo plan their weekly menus before they shop. From these menus the Lorenzos make a shopping list. This helps them to buy only the items they need. They use ads in the newspaper to find the cost of what they want to buy.

problem

Bananas cost \$.64 per kilogram (\$.64/kg). Find the cost of 1.3 kilograms of bananas.

solution

$.64	Cost per kilogram
× 1.3	Number of kilograms
$.832 ≈ $.84	Always round the answer up to the next whole cent.

problem

Beef gravy mix is marked 3/\$1.00. This means 3 packages cost \$1.00. How much would 2 packages of gravy mix cost?

solution

Find the cost of 1 package.

$$\begin{array}{r} .33 \\ 3\overline{)1.00} \\ -9 \\ \hline 10 \\ -9 \\ \hline 1 \end{array}$$

When there is a remainder, round the answer up to the next whole cent.

One package of gravy mix costs \$.34. Therefore, 2 packages cost \$.34 × 2, or \$.68.

When Jaime and Alicia shop they often compare prices to determine the best buys. When two items are the same size, the better buy is the less expensive item.

problem

Which is the better buy?

Peanut butter
  Large jar: 300 grams for $.78
  Family-size jar: 600 grams for $1.48

solution

The family size contains twice as much as the large jar.

You would have the same amount of peanut butter if you bought either 1 family-size jar or 2 large jars.

Find the cost of 2 large jars.

$\$.78 \times 2 = \$1.56$

In 2 large jars, 600 grams of peanut butter cost $1.56.
In 1 family-size jar, 600 grams of peanut butter cost $1.48.

The family size is less expensive. It is the better buy.

exercises

Find the cost of the items listed. Round the answers up to the next whole cent.

1. 1.2 kg of apples at $1.54/kg
2. 3 cans of pears at $.58 each
3. 0.5 kg of steak at $4.25/kg
4. 2 cans of peas at 5/$2.00
5. 2 bottles of salad dressing at 3/$2.00
6. 3 packages of pudding at 4/$1.50
7. 2 cans of fruit drink at $.62 each
8. 3 cans of pork and beans at 2/$.89

For exercises 9-12, list the item that is the better buy.

9. Ketchup—small: 200 g for $.35
   large: 400 g for $.68
10. Vinegar—large: 500 mL for $.31
   family: 1000 mL for $.56
11. Mayonnaise—large: 450 g for $.93
   family: 900 g for $1.87
12. Tea bags—small: 15 tea bags for $.54
   large: 45 tea bags for $1.49

These are the items on the Lorenzos' grocery list. For each item, find its cost if the Lorenzos choose the better buy. Round answers up to the next whole cent.

13.	Bacon, 1 package	Name brand $1.93/pkg.	Store brand $1.89/pkg.
14.	Chicken, 1.4 kg	Whole $1.21/kg	Cut-up $1.43/kg
15.	Ground beef for hamburgers, 1.5 kg	Prepackaged $2.55/kg	1.5-kilogram box of frozen patties $4.15
16.	Milk, 4 L	2-liter carton $.87	4-liter carton $1.75
17.	Eggs, 2 dozen	Large $.85/dozen	Medium $.72/dozen
18.	Bread, 2 loaves	Name brand $.56 each	Store brand 3/$1.60
19.	Orange juice, frozen concentrate, 600 g	150-gram can $.52	300-gram can $.93
20.	Tuna fish, 1 can	Name brand $1.55 each	Store brand 2/$3.00
21.	Green beans, 2 cans	Name brand 4/$1.25	Store brand $.33 each
22.	Corn flakes, 500 g	250-gram box $.46	500-gram box $.83
23.	Frozen chopped broccoli, 600 g	300-gram box $.47	600-gram box $.98
24.	Lettuce, 2 heads	$.65 each	2/$1.25
25.	Potatoes, 5 kg	2.5-kilogram bag $1.47	$.75/kg
26.	Onions, 1.5 kg	1.5-kilogram bag $1.25	$.78/kg

27. Find the total cost for the Lorenzos' shopping list.

28. When the Lorenzos checked out of the grocery store, their total bill with tax was $24.87. What was their change from $40?

CALCULATOR EXERCISES

Another way to compare prices is to find the **unit price** of an item. This is the price per unit of measure. The item with the lower unit price is the better buy. Some stores have unit prices marked on the shelves.

To find the unit price of an item, divide the price by the number of grams or milliliters.

Fruit cocktail

825-gram can for $1.25

$1.25 \div 825 \approx .0015 \longrightarrow .15¢/g$

225-gram can for $.45

$.45 \div 225 = .002 \longrightarrow .2¢/g$

The 825-gram can costs .15¢/gram. The 225-gram can costs .2¢/gram. The 825-gram can is a better buy.

Find the unit price of each item. Write the answers to the nearest hundredth of a cent. List the item that is the better buy.

1. Chili sauce
340-gram bottle for $.59
570-gram bottle for $.93

2. Raisins
85-gram box for $.37
312-gram box for $.95

3. Applesauce
285-gram jar for $.33
675-gram jar for $.62

4. Mustard
300-gram jar for $.34
450-gram jar for $.58

5. Apple juice
590-milliliter bottle for $.47
950-milliliter bottle for $.69

6. Peaches
450-gram can for $.67
908-gram can for $1.23

7. Barbecue sauce
950-milliliter bottle for $.89
1240-milliliter bottle for $1.29

8. Tomato juice
535-milliliter can for $.34
Individual serving cans (total 957 mL) for $.84

9. Fruit drink
2-liter bottle (liquid) for $.99
Dry mix that will make 11 liters for $2.05

10. Noodles
.5-kilogram box for $.49
.9-kilogram box for $.83

Meatcutter

Career Cluster: Trades

Ella Guercio is a meatcutter. At her butcher shop, she sells separate cuts of meat. She also sells **sides of beef.** A side of beef is half of all of the meat obtained from the animal. This amount of meat would feed a family for several months.

Ella includes the cost of freezing and wrapping the meat in the price she quotes for a side of beef. Her price is given as an amount per kilogram before butchering. There is a loss during butchering due to trimming away fat, discarding bone, and normal shrinkage. This loss is usually between 20% and 30%.

problem

The mass of a side of beef is 135 kg. The loss during butchering is 28%. The price of the side of beef is $1.83 per kilogram before butchering. Find the amount of usable meat. Find the cost per kilogram of usable meat.

solution

Find the cost of the side of beef.

$135 \times \$1.83 = \$247.05$ Cost

To find the amount of usable meat, first find the loss during butchering.

28% of 135 kg

$.28 \times 135 = 37.8$ kg Loss

$$\begin{array}{rl} 135.0 \text{ kg} & \text{Before butchering} \\ - \ 37.8 \text{ kg} & \text{Loss} \\ \hline 97.2 \text{ kg} & \text{Usable meat} \end{array}$$

Find the cost per kilogram of usable meat.

$\$247.05 \div 97.2 \approx \$2.54$ Rounded to the nearest cent

The cost per kilogram of usable meat is $2.54.

exercises

Complete the table. Round the answers to the nearest cent.

	Before butchering	Price per kilogram	Cost	Loss	Amount of usable meat	Cost per kilogram of usable meat
	135 kg	$1.83	$247.05	28%	97.2 kg	$2.54
1.	130 kg	$1.80	a.	30%	b.	c.
2.	145 kg	$1.90	a.	26%	b.	c.
3.	125 kg	$1.66	a.	24%	b.	c.
4.	155 kg	$1.92	a.	29%	b.	c.
5.	165 kg	$1.75	a.	25%	b.	c.

Comparing Meat Prices

Ned Vargo is interested in buying a side of beef. He wants to compare the cost of buying separate cuts of meat each week with the cost of buying the side of beef.

Ned has this table showing the cuts of meat obtained from a side of beef. The table also shows the amount of each cut that will be obtained. This amount is given as a percent of the side of beef.

Cut of meat	Percent of side of beef
Ground beef	11.1%
Round steak	11.0%
Stew meat	10.3%
Chuck blade roast	8.9%
Sirloin steak	8.3%
Rib roast	6.1%
Chuck arm roast (boneless)	5.8%
Porterhouse, T-bone, and club steaks	5.1%
Rump roast (boneless)	3.3%
Brisket (boneless)	2.1%
Flank steak	.5%
Kidney	.3%
Total usable cuts	72.8%
Waste (fat, bone, shrinkage)	27.2%
Total	100.0%

problem

How many kilograms of ground beef can Ned expect from a 140-kilogram side of beef? The current price for ground beef in a grocery store is $2.39 per kilogram. Using this price, find the value of the ground beef obtained from the side of beef.

solution

According to the table, 11.1% of the side of beef will be ground beef.

$.111 \times 140 \text{ kg} \approx 15.5 \text{ kg}$ Rounded to the nearest tenth

Find how much this amount of ground beef would cost in the grocery store.

$15.5 \times \$2.39 \approx \$37.05$ Rounded to the nearest cent

The side of beef should yield about 15.5 kilograms of ground beef. This amount of ground beef would cost $37.05 in the grocery store.

exercises

Complete the table. The mass of the side of beef is 140 kilograms. Round the answers to the nearest tenth of a kilogram or to the nearest cent.

	Cut of meat	Amount obtained	Current price per kilogram	Value at the current price
	Ground beef	15.5 kg	$2.39	$37.05
1.	Round steak	**a.**	$3.99	**b.**
2.	Stew meat	**a.**	$2.89	**b.**
3.	Chuck blade roast	**a.**	$1.79	**b.**
4.	Sirloin steak	**a.**	$4.39	**b.**
5.	Rib roast	**a.**	$3.49	**b.**
6.	Chuck arm roast (boneless)	**a.**	$2.89	**b.**
7.	Porterhouse, T-bone, club steaks	**a.**	$5.49	**b.**
8.	Rump roast (boneless)	**a.**	$3.99	**b.**
9.	Brisket (boneless)	**a.**	$2.79	**b.**
10.	Flank steak	**a.**	$4.19	**b.**
11.	Kidney	**a.**	$1.09	**b.**

12. What is the total value of all of the cuts of meat from the side of beef?

13. The price of the 140-kilogram side of beef is $1.85 per kilogram before butchering. What is the cost of the side of beef?

14. Ned does not have room to store a side of beef at home. He can rent a locker to store the beef for $8.25 per month. What is the cost of renting a locker for 6 months?

15. Find the total cost of the side of beef and the locker rental for six months.

16. What is the difference between the total cost of the side of beef, including the locker rental, and the total value of the beef at the current store prices?

Comparing Meal Costs

There are alternatives to preparing and eating meals at home. Many people choose to eat in restaurants or purchase prepared foods and carry-out meals.

When eating at a restaurant, most people give the waiter or waitress a **tip** for serving the food. This is usually between 10% and 20% of the bill, depending on the service.

problem

Irene and Stan Tyrrell want to compare the cost of eating in a restaurant with the cost of having the same dinner at home. They recently had fish dinners at a restaurant. The bill was \$12.35, and they left a 15% tip. Preparing the meal at home costs \$6.25. What is the difference in cost between eating out and eating at home?

solution

Find the amount of the tip.

At a restaurant, many people compute the tip mentally. To do this, they think 15% = 10% + 5%.

First, round the amount of the bill to the nearest dollar.

$12.35 ⟶ $12.00

Find 10% of $12.00.

.10 × $12.00 = $1.20

Since 5% is $\frac{1}{2}$ of 10%, find $\frac{1}{2}$ of $1.20.

$\frac{1}{2}$ × $1.20 = $.60

Then add.

$1.20	10% of bill
+ .60	5% of bill
$1.80	Tip (15% of bill)

Find the total cost at the restaurant.

$12.35	Bill
+ 1.80	Tip
$14.15	Total cost

Find the difference in the costs of the two meals.

$14.15	Restaurant
− 6.25	Home
$ 7.90	

The meal costs $7.90 more at the restaurant.

exercises

Find the total cost for two people for each meal listed.

1. Pizza carry-out

Pizza with sausage, mushrooms, onions, and green pepper	$5.75
Beverage at home	$.15 per person

2. Pizza prepared at home

Package for sausage pizza mix	$1.35
Mushrooms	$.52
Onions	$.09
Green pepper	$.23
Beverage	$.15 per person

3. Pizza at a restaurant

Dinner for two	$6.85
Beverage	$.45 per person

Include a 15% tip.

4. Find the difference in the total costs of the most expensive and the least expensive pizza dinners.

5. Beef stew prepared at home

Frozen beef stew	$1.55 per person
Salad	$.40 per person
Beverage	$.15 per person

6. Beef stew prepared at home

Beef	$1.45
Potatoes	$.30
Carrots	$.06
Salad	$.40 per person
Beverage	$.15 per person

7. Beef stew dinner at a restaurant

Dinner for two	$8.45
Beverage	$.35 per person

Include a 20% tip.

8. Find the difference in the total costs of the most expensive and the least expensive beef stew dinners.

skills tune-up

Multiplying decimals, pages 10-11

1. .6 × .5

2. .1 × .7

3. .03 × .3

4. .08 × .2

5. .07 × .05

6 ..06 × .07

7. .001 × .04

8. .09 × .011

9. 200 × .6

10. 800 × .8

11. 600 × .03

12. .05 × 120

13. .003 × 400

14. 500 × .011

15. .005 × .008

16. .007 × .004

17. 6000 × .0011

18. 4.3 × 9.7

19. 2.84 × 3.9

20. 6.7 × 3.02

21. 14.1 × .035

22. 4.635 × 3.64

23. 18.41 × 6.018

24. 5.38 × .9729

25. 32.852 × .418

26. .892 × .0034

Dividing fractions and mixed numbers, pages 16-17

1. $\frac{1}{2} \div \frac{5}{8}$

2. $\frac{2}{3} \div \frac{3}{4}$

3. $\frac{3}{8} \div \frac{9}{16}$

4. $\frac{2}{3} \div \frac{1}{6}$

5. $\frac{7}{8} \div \frac{2}{5}$

6. $\frac{3}{5} \div \frac{6}{7}$

7. $6 \div \frac{3}{4}$

8. $\frac{1}{8} \div 2$

9. $10 \div \frac{5}{8}$

10. $\frac{4}{5} \div 3$

11. $2\frac{1}{4} \div \frac{9}{10}$

12. $\frac{2}{3} \div 1\frac{1}{5}$

13. $5\frac{7}{8} \div 2$

14. $9 \div 1\frac{5}{7}$

15. $1\frac{1}{8} \div 1\frac{5}{16}$

16. $3\frac{3}{5} \div 2\frac{1}{4}$

17. $2\frac{7}{10} \div 1\frac{3}{5}$

18. $9\frac{3}{8} \div 1\frac{7}{8}$

19. $7\frac{1}{4} \div 2\frac{1}{2}$

20. $5\frac{5}{8} \div 5\frac{5}{6}$

Percent problems, pages 36-38

1. 5% of 25 is ▒.

2. 20% of 30 is ▒.

3. $7\frac{1}{2}$% of 200 is ▒.

4. 8.5% of 55 is ▒.

5. Find $3\frac{1}{2}$% of 500.

6. Find 15% of 4.

7. What number is 5.5% of 60?

8. What number is 35% of 24?

9. 25% of ▒ is 1.8.

10. 6.75% of ▒ is 3.78.

11. 2% of ▒ is .56.

12. $4\frac{1}{2}$% of ▒ is 9.

13. 5% of what number is 1.85?

14. 40% of what number is 60?

15. 15 is $12\frac{1}{2}$% of what number?

16. ▒% of 36 is 27.

17. ▒% of 70 is 66.5.

18. ▒% of 30 is 7.5.

19. ▒% of 5.98 is 2.99.

20. What percent of 60 is 45?

21. What percent of 68 is 17?

22. 54 is what percent of 80?

Chapter 16

review

Dietitian, pages 324-325

1. Find the number of calories in this meal. (Use the table on page 324.)

   Breakfast
   120 mL orange juice
   2 slices whole-wheat toast
   2 pats butter
   2 slices bacon

Calorie usage, pages 326-327

2. Angela's mass is 62 kilograms. She went bicycling for 2.5 hours. At 3.9 calories per kilogram per hour, how many calories did she use? (Round the answer to the nearest whole number.)

Grocery shopping, pages 328-330

3. Find the cost of 2 cans of beans at 3/$.89. (Round the answer up to the next whole cent.)

4. List the item that is a better buy.

   Salad oil—large: 700 mL for $1.31
   family: 1400 mL for $2.65

Meatcutter, pages 332-333

5. The mass of a side of beef is 160 kilograms. The price is $1.75 per kilogram before butchering. What is the cost of the side of beef?

6. There is a 28% loss during butchering. Find the amount of usable meat in the 160-kilogram side of beef.

7. What is the cost per kilogram of usable meat? (Round the answer to the nearest cent.)

Comparing meat prices, pages 334-335

8. How many kilograms of sirloin steak can Mark expect from a 130-kilogram side of beef? 8.3% of the side of beef will be sirloin steak. (Round the answer to the nearest tenth of a kilogram.)

9. The current price for sirloin steak in the grocery store is $4.59 per kilogram. How much would Mark pay for the sirloin steak in exercise 8 at the grocery store? (Round the answer to the nearest cent.)

Comparing meal costs, pages 336-337

10. Find the total cost of this meal for two people.

    Chicken dinner at a restaurant
    Dinner for two $7.35
    Beverage $.45 per person
    Include a 15% tip.

Chapter 16

test

1. Find the number of calories in this meal. (Use the table on page 324.)

   Dinner
   2 slices meat loaf
   1 serving canned peaches
   55 g cottage cheese
   1 serving peas
   240 mL milk

2. Stu's mass is 78 kilograms. He went swimming for 1.2 hours. At 10.1 calories per kilogram per hour, how many calories did he use? (Round the answer to the nearest whole number.)

3. Find the cost of 0.5 kg of pork chops at $3.95/kg. (Round the answer up to the next whole cent.)

4. List the item that is the better buy.

   Jelly—small: 300 g for $.65
   large: 600 g for $1.23

5. The mass of a side of beef is 150 kilograms. The price is $1.80 per kilogram before butchering. What is the cost of the side of beef?

6. There is a 25% loss during butchering. Find the amount of usable meat in the 150-kilogram side of beef.

7. What is the cost per kilogram of usable meat for the side of beef in exercises 5 and 6?

8. How many kilograms of round steak can Nancy expect from a 160-kilogram side of beef? 11% of the side of beef will be round steak.

9. The current price for round steak in the grocery store is $4.10 per kilogram. How much would Nancy pay for the round steak in exercise 8 at the grocery store?

10. Find the total cost of this meal for two people.

    Steakburger dinner at a restaurant
    Dinner for two $5.65
    Beverage $.40 per person
    Include a 10% tip.

Chapter 17

Buying, Making, and Renting Goods

The purchasing power of the dollar continues to be reduced by inflation. Wise consumers cope with inflation by using their own ingenuity.

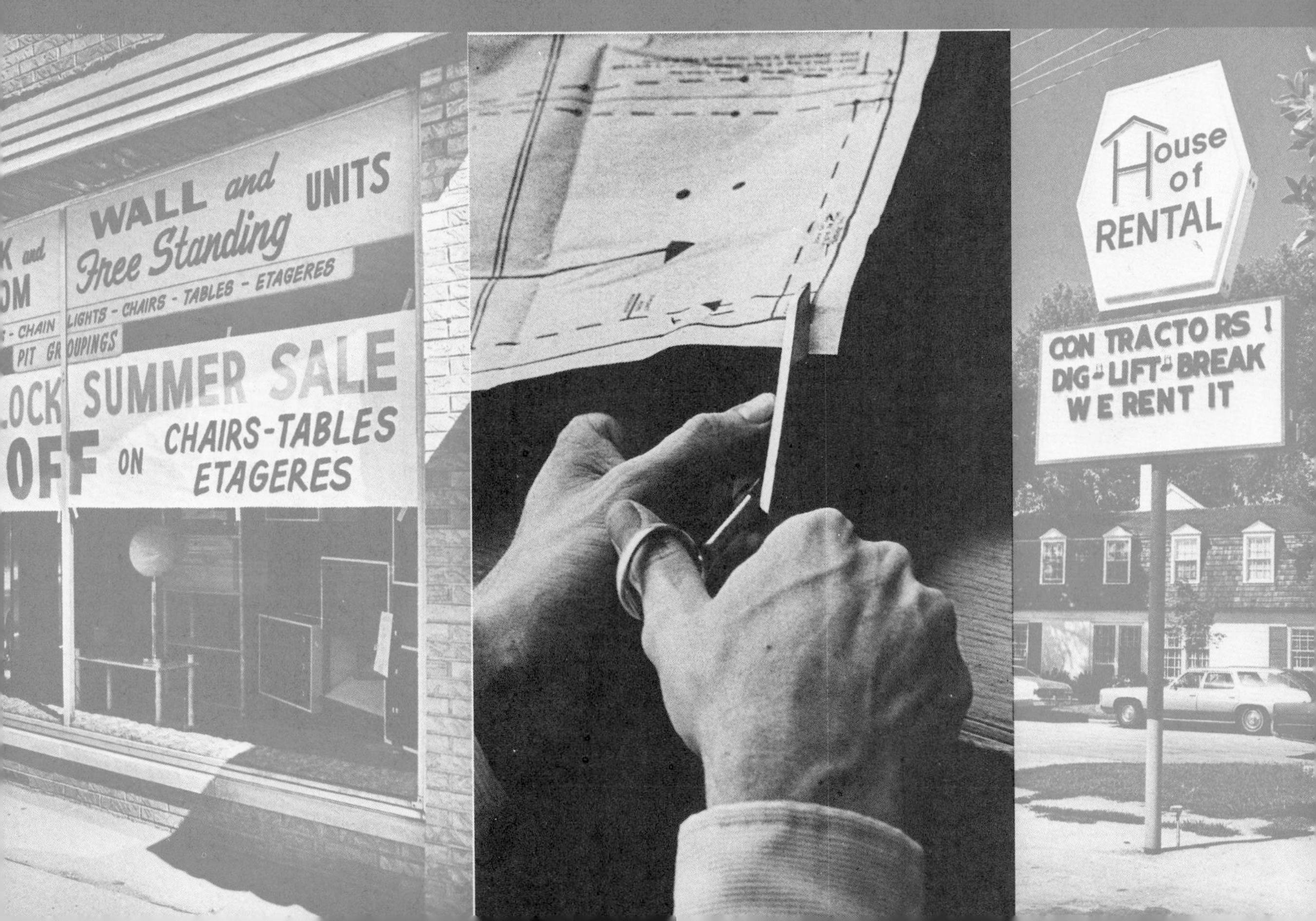

Catalog Buying

Dave and Diane Tomlinson buy many items through catalogs. They can look through the catalogs at home and make purchasing decisions together.

When people buy from a catalog, they usually pay shipping and handling charges. A cost table for packages shipped by parcel post is shown.

Shipping and Handling Charges for Orders Shipped by Parcel Post				
Shipping weight	Local zone	Zones 1 & 2	Zone 3	Zone 4
1 oz. to 8 oz.	$.45	$.52	$.52	$.54
9 oz. to 15 oz.	.83	.88	.88	.88
1 lb. to 2 lb.	.95	1.05	1.10	1.30
2 lb. 1 oz. to 3 lb.	1.00	1.20	1.25	1.40
3 lb. 1 oz. to 4 lb.	1.05	1.30	1.40	1.61
4 lb. 1 oz. to 5 lb.	1.10	1.38	1.50	1.73
5 lb. 1 oz. to 6 lb.	1.14	1.45	1.58	1.84
6 lb. 1 oz. to 7 lb.	1.20	1.53	1.68	1.96
7 lb. 1 oz. to 8 lb.	1.24	1.61	1.77	2.07

problem

Diane wants to buy the 3-piece pantsuit and blouse shown here. She wants the pantsuit in brown and the blouse in beige, both in size 10. The sales tax in her state is 4%. She lives in zone 3. Fill in the order form for Diane's outfit.

[A] **3-PIECE PANTSUIT**—Versatile wool pantsuit with patch pockets. Colors: camel, red, navy, brown. Sizes: misses 6, 8, 10, 12, 14, 16
Wt. 1 lb. 12 oz.
P24-0163 .... $65.95

[B] **BLOUSE**—Supple, polyester knit blouse, long sleeve, button front, tie at neck, machine washable. Colors: white, beige. Sizes: misses 6, 8, 10, 12, 14, 16
Wt. 6 oz.
S37-9254 .... $18.49

solution

Fill in the order form.

Item	Catalog number	How many	Size	Color	Price for one	Total price	Shipping weight lb.	oz.
Pantsuit	P24-0163	1	10	brown	$65.95	$65.95	1	12
Blouse	S37-9254	1	10	beige	18.49	18.49		6

			Total lb.	Total oz.
	Total for goods	84.44		
4% of $84.44 (rounded) →	Tax	3.38		
For 2 lb. 2 oz. in zone 3 →	Shipping and handling	1.25	2	2
Add to find the total →	AMOUNT ENCLOSED	$89.07		

exercises

Dave wants to buy the outfit shown below in the rust color. He needs the shirt in size large. For the slacks, he needs the waist 32″ and the inseam medium.

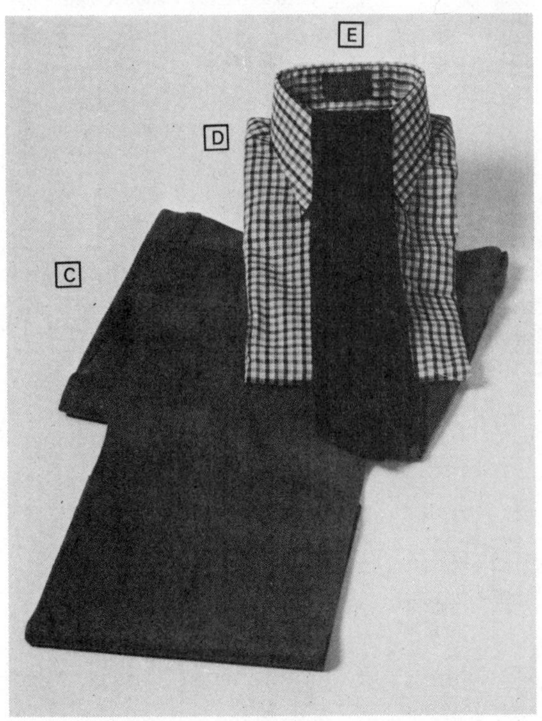

C **SLACKS**—Quality tailored dress slacks. 100% polyester. Machine wash, tumble dry. Colors: navy, rust, brown, gray.

Waist (inches)	30, 31, 32, 34, 36, 38
Inseam (inches)	S($29\frac{1}{2}$), M(31), L(33)

Wt. 1 lb. 5 oz.
F7-2407 . . . .$18.95

D **SHIRT**—Durable oxford cloth shirt of 60% cotton-40% polyester. Long sleeve, 7-button front. Machine wash, tumble dry. Colors: navy, rust, brown, gray. Sizes: S, M, L, XL
Wt. 10 oz.
H8-4371 . . . .$12.89

E **TIE**—100% polyester, 4″ wide. Colors: navy, rust, brown, gray
Wt. 6 oz.
J9-5637 . . . .$6.85

1. What is the total cost of the goods?
2. What is the amount of the tax if the tax is 4% of the cost of the goods?
3. What is the total weight of the goods?
4. What are the shipping and handling costs for zone 3?
5. What is the total amount Dave must enclose with his order?

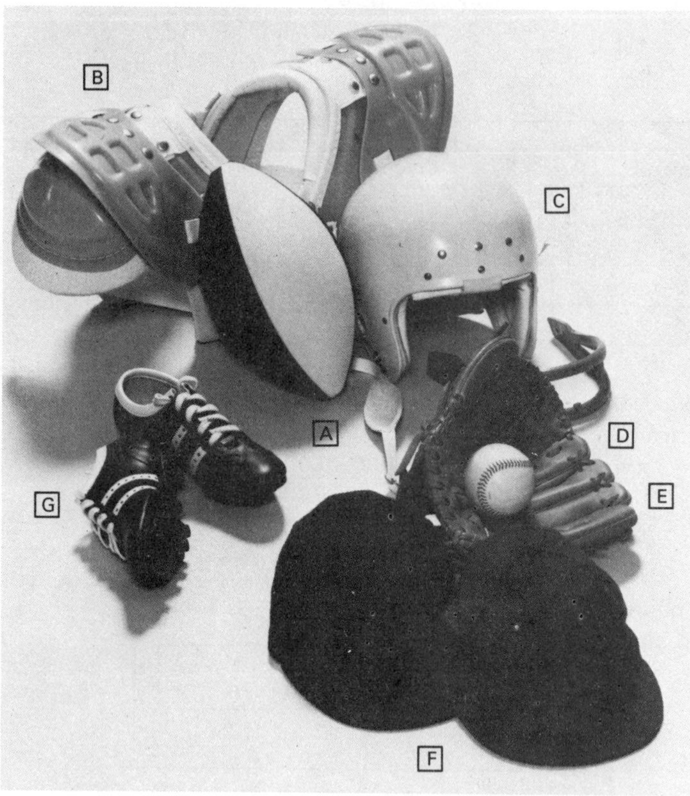

[A] **FOOTBALL**—Genuine cowhide-leather football. Official size. Tee included. Wt. 1 lb. 7 oz.
M 430-4562 . . . .$10.99

[B] **SHOULDER PADS**—Durable construction. 100% nylon covering. Sizes: S(26-28), M(28-30), L(30-32)
Wt. 2 lb. 2 oz.
P 232-9851 . . . .$15.99

[C] **HELMET**—Fully padded for maximum protection. Chin strap and face guard included. White only. Sizes: S($6\frac{1}{4}$-$6\frac{1}{2}$), M($6\frac{5}{8}$-7), L($7\frac{1}{8}$-$7\frac{3}{8}$). Wt. 2 lb. 1 oz.
R 342-6917 . . . .$17.99

[D] **FIELDER'S GLOVE**—Large pocket with tough lacing across the top. Cowhide outside, leather lining. For right-handed throwers.
Wt. 13 oz.
V 516-4392 . . . .$9.99

[E] **BASEBALL**—Little League approved. Rugged horsehide cover, nylon stitching, cork center. Wt. 7 oz.
W 916-7342 . . . .$4.99

[F] **BASEBALL CAP**—Just like they use in the big league. Colors: navy, red, gold, green. Sizes: S, M, L. Wt. 5 oz.
Y 327-8420 . . . .$2.89

[G] **SPORT SHOES**—Black leather uppers, white stripes, padded ankle collar. 13 molded cleats. Medium width. Black only. Sizes: 1-10 Wt. 1 lb. 15 oz.
T 829-3901 . . . .$6.79

Clarence wants to buy a football, a helmet (size M), and shoulder pads (size M).

6. What is the total cost of the goods?
7. The tax is 5% of the cost of the goods. Find the amount of the tax.
8. What is the total weight of the goods?
9. Use the table on page 342 to find the shipping and handling costs. Clarence lives in the local zone.
10. What is the total amount Clarence must enclose with his order?

Nancy wants to buy a baseball, a fielder's glove, a cap (red, size L), and a pair of sport shoes (size 8).

11. What is the total cost of the goods?
12. The tax is 6% of the cost of the goods. Find the amount of the tax.
13. What is the total weight of the goods?
14. Use the table on page 342 to find the shipping and handling costs. Nancy lives in zone 4.
15. What is the total amount Nancy must enclose with her order?

CALCULATOR EXERCISES

Complete this order form for office supplies.

	Name of item	Quantity	Catalog number	Unit price	Total price	Number per box	Weight each box	Total weight
							LB. OZ.	LB. OZ.
	Portfolios	200	3-47A	$.96	$192.00	10	1 4	25 0
1.	Legal ruled pads	180	5-62X	$.35	**a.**	12	1 6	**b.**
2.	Payroll record pads	50	9-51C	$.45	**a.**	10	2 8	**b.**
3.	Requisition pads	72	7-13R	$.40	**a.**	12	1 12	**b.**
4.	Letter openers	24	1-34T	$1.59	**a.**	12	2 14	**b.**
5.	Legal-size envelopes	7 boxes	8-21B	$9.32	**a.**	——	3 13	**b.**
6.	Staplers	25	2-63F	$5.65	**a.**	5	4 7	**b.**
7.	Pencils	288	6-40D	$1.35/doz.	**a.**	12	7	**b.**
8.	Pens	96	6-37Y	$3.17/doz.	**a.**	12	15	**b.**
	9.	Total for goods			**a.**	Total		**b.**
	10.	Tax (5%)			**a.**			
	11.	Shipping charges ($.07/lb.)			**a.**			
	12.	TOTAL			**a.**			

50 years ago

Guess how long a typical factory worker had to work to earn the price of a new car.

Today

Guess how long a typical factory worker has to work to earn the price of a new car.

Sewing Costs

The members of the Aberdeen High School a Capella Choir want outfits to wear for their performances. They decided on vests for the girls and matching ties for the boys. The school is unable to purchase the outfits, but is willing to pay for the materials if some of the members will make the vests and the ties.

The choir is made up of 32 girls and 21 boys. There are seven girls who wear size 8, ten who wear size 10, eleven who wear size 12, and four who wear size 14.

The patterns show the number of yards of material necessary for various sizes and different widths of material.

Vest (to be lined)		Yards required			
Width of fabric	sizes	8	10	12	14
35″ or 36″		$1\frac{1}{8}$	$1\frac{1}{8}$	$1\frac{1}{4}$	$1\frac{1}{4}$
44″ or 45″		$\frac{3}{4}$	$\frac{3}{4}$	$\frac{3}{4}$	1
54″		$\frac{5}{8}$	$\frac{3}{4}$	$\frac{3}{4}$	$\frac{3}{4}$
Vest lining—Purchase same amount of 35″, 36″, 44″, 45″, or 54″ fabric.					

Tie (one size) 5″ wide	
35″ or 36″, 44″ or 45″	$\frac{3}{4}$ yd.
Tie lining—Purchase same amount of 35″, 36″, 44″, or 45″ material.	

problem

If the fabric selected for the vests is 36″ wide, how many yards are needed for 7 vests, size 8?

solution

Find the row on the chart for 36″ fabric. In the column for size 8, find $1\frac{1}{8}$. This is the number of yards of material needed for 1 vest.

Find the number of yards needed for 7 vests.

$7 \times 1\frac{1}{8} = 7 \times \frac{9}{8} = \frac{63}{8} = 7\frac{7}{8}$ yd.

The fabric needed for 7 vests, size 8, is $7\frac{7}{8}$ yd.

exercises

1. How many yards of 36″ fabric are needed for 10 vests, size 10?
2. How many yards of 36″ fabric are needed for 11 vests, size 12?
3. How many yards of 36″ fabric are needed for 4 vests, size 14?
4. How many yards of 36″ fabric are needed for 21 ties?
5. What is the total number of yards needed for the vests and the ties? (Remember that there are 4 sizes of vests.)
6. At $4.80 a yard, what is the cost of fabric for the vests and ties?
7. At $1.60 a yard, what is the cost of lining for the vests and the ties?
8. Patterns for each size vest cost $1.25. The choir members decide that they should buy 2 for each size. What is the cost of the vest patterns?
9. The pattern for the tie costs $.95. The choir members decide that they should buy 4 tie patterns. What is the cost of the tie patterns?
10. Eight buttons are required for each vest. How many buttons are needed for all the vests?
11. There are six buttons in a package. How many packages of buttons are needed?
12. If each package costs $1.35, what is the total cost of the buttons?
13. Thread costs $.45 per spool. The choir members need 12 spools. What is the cost of the thread?
14. What is the total cost of all materials (fabric, lining, patterns, buttons, and thread)?
15. If the fabric store gives a 15% discount to the school, what is the cost of the materials? (Round the answer to the nearest cent.)
16. If the choir members pay for the materials with eighteen $20 bills, how much change would they receive?
17. The ready-made vests that the choir members like cost $16.79 each. The ties cost $3.50 each. Find the total cost if ready-made vests and ties were bought for the choir.
18. How much was saved by having the choir members make the outfits?

Seasonal Sales

Barbara and Jim King were discussing some of the items that they plan to buy during the coming year. They have a chart that gives the best month for buying certain items. A portion of the chart is shown here.

JANUARY	FEBRUARY	MARCH	APRIL
Men's coats Dresses Shoes Books Linens	Men's shirts Furniture Curtains	Spring clothes Winter coats Hosiery Laundry appliances	Dresses Infants' wear Men's suits

MAY	JUNE	JULY	AUGUST
Handbags Linens	Dresses Summer clothes and fabrics Building materials T V sets	Bathing suits Handbags Infants' wear Men's shirts Shoes	Women's coats Men's coats School clothes

SEPTEMBER	OCTOBER	NOVEMBER	DECEMBER
Furniture Paint Hardware	Hosiery School clothes	Dresses Men's suits	Women's coats Shoes

Value! 19″ diag. color TV.
Large-screen portable is ideal for family viewing. UHF/VHF antennas, AFC. Solid state.
299.88

Save $100
Cozy corner group, guest room all in 1.
199.88 Reg. 299.95
Easy-care olefin cover. Light birch vinyl veneered table; hidden, convenient storage.

Save 25%
Little boys' long sleeve sweatshirts
2.99 Reg. 3.99
We've got his number. Machine wash. Acrylic/cotton. 2-8.

32% off.
Comfortable crew socks for men.
2 pr. $1 Reg. 74¢ pr.
Soft, long-wearing acrylic/nylon. In fashion tones. 10-13.

problem

Jim needs a new coat. The regular price of the coat that Jim wants is $75.99. During the best months he can get a 15% discount. What are the best months for buying men's coats? What will be the sale price of the coat?

solution

To find the discount, find 15% of $75.99

$.15 \times \$75.99 \approx \$11.40$ Rounded to the nearest cent

Find the sale price of the coat.

$75.99	Regular price
− 11.40	Amount of discount
$64.59	Sale price

The best months for buying men's coats are January and August. With the discount, Jim's coat will cost $64.59.

exercises

For each exercise, list the best month(s) to buy each item. Then find the amount of the discount, rounded to the nearest cent, and the sale price of the item.

	Item	Best months to buy	Regular price	Discount	Amount of discount	Sale price
	Men's coat	January, August	$75.99	15%	$11.40	$64.59
1.	Shoes	a.	$18.00	15%	b.	c.
2.	Paint	a.	$9.85	20%	b.	c.
3.	Clothes dryer	a.	$259.95	25%	b.	c.
4.	TV set	a.	$689.95	15%	b.	c.
5.	Bedroom set	a.	$569.95	20%	b.	c.
6.	Sheets	a.	$9.99	30%	b.	c.
7.	Handbag	a.	$17.50	15%	b.	c.
8.	Curtains	a.	$7.47	25%	b.	c.
9.	Bathing suit	a.	$26.30	35%	b.	c.
10.	Dress	a.	$48.00	40%	b.	c.

Craft Supplies

Lorraine Olson enjoys making latch-hook rugs. She makes them for herself and as gifts for friends and relatives. These rugs are made by knotting short strands of yarn onto a mesh canvas backing with a latch hook.

The canvas mesh can be purchased with the design printed on it. The yarn is often purchased separately. Yarn is priced in the following way.

7 or more packages (same color)	$.49 each
1-6 packages (same color)	$.59 each

problem

Find the total cost of materials for the rug titled "Tennis." The canvas mesh costs $5.00. The yarn needed for this rug is given below.

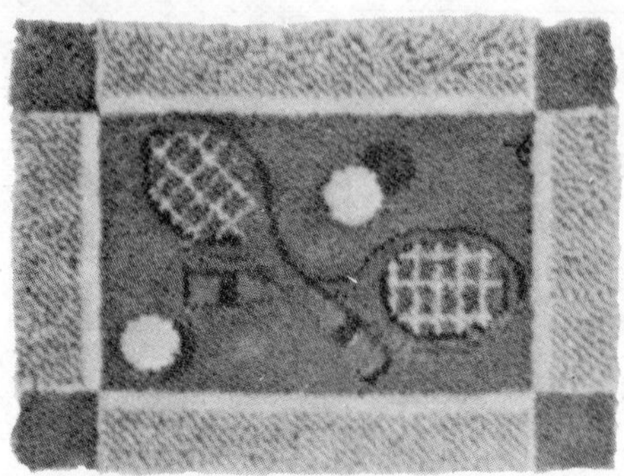

15 green
8 vanilla
2 bronze
1 dark brown
1 bright orange
1 spear green

solution

There are 15 green and 8 vanilla, or 23 packages of yarn at $.49 each. Find the cost of this yarn.

23 × $.49 = $11.27

There are 2 bronze, 1 dark brown, 1 bright orange, and 1 spear green, or 5 packages of yarn at $.59 each. Find the cost of this yarn.

5 × $.59 = $2.95

Find the total cost of materials.

$5.00	Canvas mesh
11.27	$.49 yarn
+ 2.95	$.59 yarn
$19.22	

The total cost of materials is $19.22.

exercises

Find the total cost of materials for each latch-hook rug listed. The cost of the canvas mesh is given. Use the prices for yarn given on page 350.

1. Impressions

   22 red
   16 wine
   12 black
   7 beige
   canvas
   mesh: $10

2. Spring/Autumn Leaves

   14 white
   9 spear green
   3 apple green
   3 avocado
   3 acid green
   1 green
   canvas mesh: $4

3. Whirls

   11 dark brown
   8 sky blue
   8 slate
   6 henna
   6 beige
   canvas
   mesh: $10

4. French Provincial

   16 red
   12 white
   6 black
   6 spear green
   4 yellow
   2 lilac
   canvas mesh: $8

The picture above shows a table top design made from mosaic tiles. Juan has the pattern for the design and the instructions for making it. The materials needed are listed below.

Tiles

Color	Amount	Cost per lb.
Buff	1 lb.	$1.40
Beige	1 lb.	1.40
Lt. brown	1 lb.	1.40
Gray	1 lb.	1.40
Dark gray	1 lb.	1.40
Brown	1 lb.	1.40
Burnt umber	2 lb.	1.40
Opaque black	2 lb.	1.80
Terra cotta	2 lb.	1.80
Sienna	5 lb.	1.40

Other materials

1 mosaic tile adhesive	$2.65/can
1 silicone grout	1.60/bottle
2 lb. special grout	.65/lb.
1 tile grout coloring	1.65/jar
1 pair mosaic tile nippers	6.35/pair
1 cement spreader	1.10/each

5. Find the total cost of the tiles.

6. Find the total cost of all materials for the mosaic table top.

Do-It-Yourself Project

Bob and Joan Sarkisian found the plans and a list of materials for a shed in a do-it-yourself magazine.

Most of the materials on the list are referred to by their size. A 2″ × 4″ × 10′ is a board 2 inches thick, 4 inches wide, and 10 feet long.

Bob and Joan can purchase lumber in two ways. They can buy lumber by the **linear foot.** They pay an amount of money for each foot in the length of the board, regardless of width and thickness. Some prices are quoted in board feet. A **board foot** is the amount of lumber in a board 1 inch thick, 1 foot wide, and 1 foot long.

Nails are also referred to by their size. A 2-penny nail (2d), for example, is 1″ long. A 20d nail is 4″ long.

problem

Find the cost of two boards, each 2″ × 6″ × 14′, at $.30/board foot.

solution

Find the number of board feet in one 2″ × 6″ × 14′ board. Recall, 6 inches is $\frac{1}{2}$ foot.

Thickness (inches)		Width (feet)		Length (feet)		Board feet
2	×	$\frac{1}{2}$	×	14	=	14

Find the number of board feet in two 2″ × 6″ × 14′ boards.

2 × 14 = 28 board feet

Multiply the total board feet by the unit price to find the cost.

28 × $.30 = $8.40

The cost of these two boards is $8.40.

exercises

Find the cost of each item for the storage shed.

	Description	Size	Amount required	Unit price	Cost
	Ridge beam	2″ × 6″ × 14′	2	$.30/board foot	$8.40
1.	Galvanized nails	3d 6d	$\frac{1}{2}$ lb. 5 lb.	$.60/lb.	**a.** **b.**
2.	Common nails	10d 16d 20d	$3\frac{1}{2}$ lb. 7 lb. 3 lb.	$.45/lb.	**a.** **b.** **c.**
3.	Hinges	Heavy steel T-hinge	2 pairs	$2.75/pair	**a.**
4.	Anchor bolts	$\frac{1}{2}$″ × $5\frac{1}{2}$″	8	$.50 each	**a.**
5.	Plywood	$\frac{1}{2}$″ × 4′ × 8′	28 sheets	$14/sheet	**a.**
6.	Concrete for pad		1.6 cubic yards	$30/cu. yd.	**a.**
7.	Roofing	Shingles	180 sq. ft.	$19/100 sq. ft.	**a.**
8.	Gravel for pad		3100 lb.	$5/ton	**a.**
9.	Door trim and doorway	1″ × 4″ × 10′ 1″ × 4″ × 8′ 1″ × 4″ × 7′	2 4 7	$.16/linear foot	**a.** (2 × 10 × $.16) **b.** **c.**
10.	Battens	1″ × 3″ × 7′ 1″ × 3″ × 10′	40 2	$.07/linear foot	**a.** **b.**
11.	Door stop	1″ × 2″ × 4′ 1″ × 2″ × 7′	1 2	$.05/linear foot	**a.** **b.**
12.	Framing and forms for concrete	2″ × 2″ × 6′ 2″ × 8″ × 12′ 2″ × 4″ × 8′ 2″ × 4″ × 4′ 2″ × 4″ × 10′ 2″ × 4″ × 12′ 2″ × 4″ × 14′	6 4 8 1 11 5 24	$.30/board foot	**a.** **b.** **c.** **d.** **e.** **f.** **g.**

13. Find the total cost of materials for the storage shed.

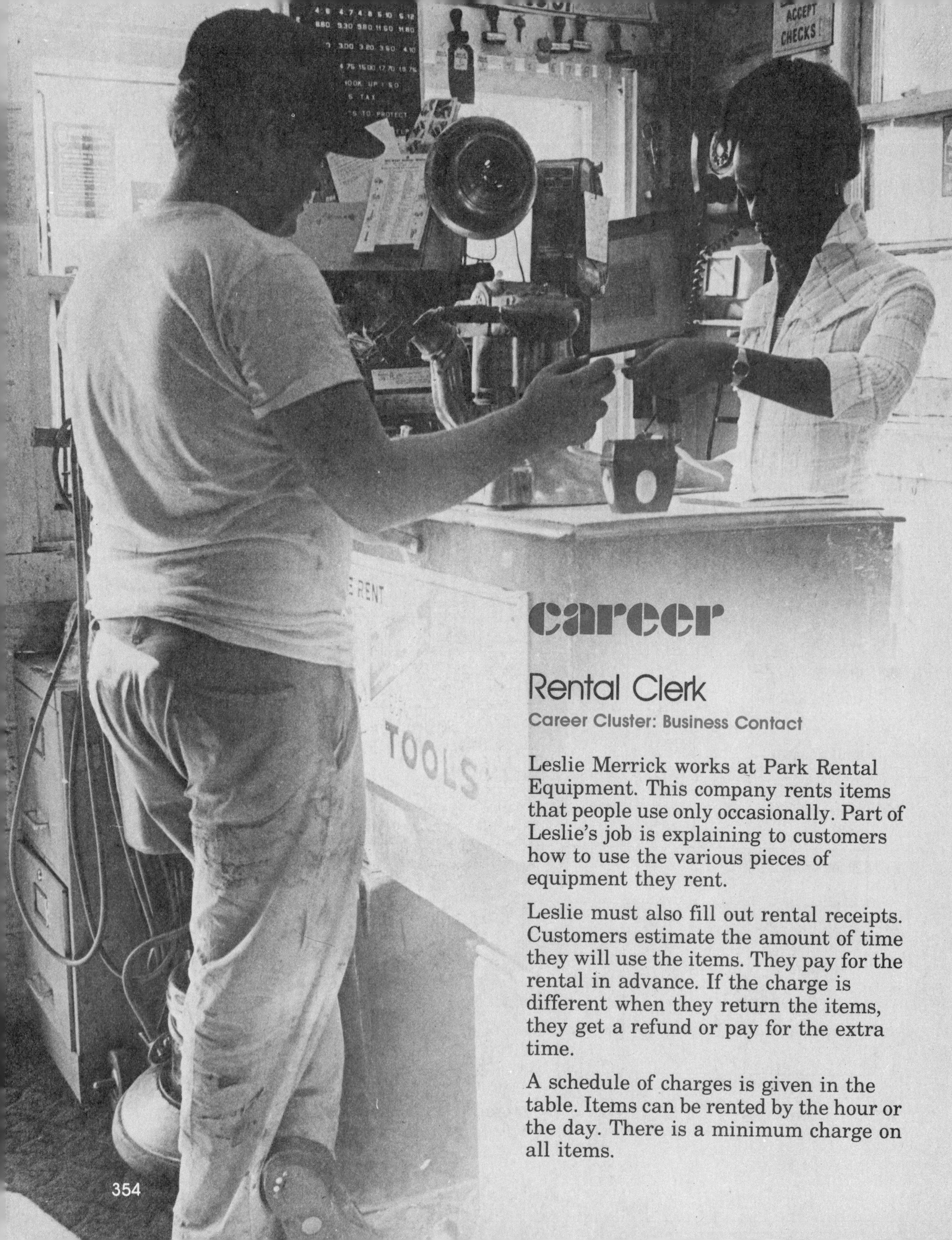

career

Rental Clerk

Career Cluster: Business Contact

Leslie Merrick works at Park Rental Equipment. This company rents items that people use only occasionally. Part of Leslie's job is explaining to customers how to use the various pieces of equipment they rent.

Leslie must also fill out rental receipts. Customers estimate the amount of time they will use the items. They pay for the rental in advance. If the charge is different when they return the items, they get a refund or pay for the extra time.

A schedule of charges is given in the table. Items can be rented by the hour or the day. There is a minimum charge on all items.

Item	Minimum charge	Hourly rate	Daily rate
Circular saw	$4.50	$1.50	$9.00
$\frac{3}{8}''$ drill	$3.00	$1.00	$6.00
Disc sander	$3.75	$1.25	$7.50
Hand-belt sander	$6.00	$2.00	$12.00
Jigsaw	$3.75	$1.25	$7.50
Car polisher	$5.25	$1.75	$10.50
Chain saw	$10.50	$3.50	$21.00
Rug shampooer	$4.50	$1.50	$9.00
Rug steamer	$12.00	$4.00	$24.00
Floor scrubber	$5.25	$1.75	$10.50
Floor sander	$6.75	$2.25	$13.50
Extension ladder	$4.50	$1.50	$9.00
Tiller	$12.75	$4.25	$25.50
Lawn aerator	$3.75	$1.25	$7.50

problem

Elliott Deutsch wants to rent a disc sander. Find the cost of renting the sander one day for $6\frac{1}{2}$ hours.

solution

Round the hours *up* to the next full hour.

$6\frac{1}{2}$ hours $\longrightarrow$ 7 hours

Find the cost of 7 hours' rental.

$\$1.25 \times 7 = \$8.75$

At the hourly rate, Elliott would pay $8.75. However, since he will use the sander for only one day, he will be charged the daily rate of $7.50.

exercises

Find the cost of renting each item for the hours given. Use the daily rate or the minimum charge if needed.

	Item	Time
1.	Chain saw	4 hours
2.	Floor scrubber	$5\frac{1}{2}$ hours
3.	Extension ladder	$3\frac{1}{2}$ hours
4.	$\frac{3}{8}''$ drill	7 hours
5.	Rug steamer	9 hours
6.	Lawn aerator	$8\frac{1}{2}$ hours
7.	Floor sander	$7\frac{1}{2}$ hours
8.	Jigsaw	1 hour
9.	Circular saw	2 hours
10.	Hand-belt sander	$2\frac{1}{2}$ hours

11. Fred uses a tiller 2 days per year. If a tiller costs about $450, how many years could he rent one at the daily rate and still pay less than if he bought one?

12. The price of a rug shampooer is $59. It takes Kazuko one day to shampoo her rugs and she does this twice a year. In how many years will the rental cost exceed the purchase price of the shampooer?

13. A car polisher costs $35 to buy. How many hours could Jan rent it at the hourly rate and still pay less than if she buys it?

14. If Jan uses the car polisher about eight hours per year, how many years could she rent it at the hourly rate before the rental is more than the cost?

skills tune-up

Dividing whole numbers, pages 12–13

Find the quotient.

1. $8752 \div 4$
2. $3201 \div 9$
3. $6217 \div 7$
4. $5476 \div 2$
5. $1552 \div 8$
6. $6950 \div 6$
7. $2581 \div 61$
8. $3815 \div 79$
9. $8388 \div 12$
10. $5430 \div 94$
11. $4347 \div 38$
12. $7607 \div 53$
13. $6023 \div 87$
14. $7644 \div 26$
15. $2798 \div 98$
16. $5120 \div 64$
17. $2307 \div 31$
18. $28{,}293 \div 52$
19. $89{,}402 \div 28$
20. $88{,}788 \div 42$
21. $273{,}889 \div 23$
22. $424{,}003 \div 77$
23. $847{,}178 \div 69$
24. $840{,}189 \div 209$
25. $177{,}123 \div 787$

Adding fractions and mixed numbers, pages 18–19

1. $\frac{2}{15} + \frac{4}{5}$
2. $\frac{6}{7} + \frac{9}{14}$
3. $\frac{1}{8} + \frac{7}{12}$
4. $\frac{1}{14} + \frac{6}{7}$
5. $\frac{2}{3} + \frac{1}{6}$
6. $\frac{1}{3} + \frac{5}{8}$
7. $\frac{5}{12} + \frac{5}{6}$
8. $\frac{1}{4} + \frac{1}{60}$
9. $\frac{1}{6} + \frac{8}{9}$
10. $\frac{1}{4} + 5\frac{1}{6}$
11. $7\frac{7}{15} + \frac{1}{3}$
12. $2\frac{9}{10} + 2\frac{7}{30}$
13. $5\frac{2}{3} + 2\frac{1}{2}$
14. $6\frac{4}{7} + 11\frac{3}{7}$
15. $14\frac{7}{9} + 6\frac{1}{18}$
16. $9\frac{1}{3} + 7\frac{2}{5}$
17. $4\frac{1}{24} + 2\frac{2}{3}$
18. $2\frac{4}{15} + 8\frac{3}{5}$
19. $9\frac{1}{20} + \frac{1}{2} + 8\frac{4}{5}$
20. $6\frac{1}{2} + 4\frac{2}{5} + 7\frac{1}{10}$

Subtracting fractions and mixed numbers, pages 18–19

1. $\frac{5}{6} - \frac{1}{2}$
2. $\frac{2}{3} - \frac{8}{15}$
3. $\frac{7}{8} - \frac{1}{6}$
4. $\frac{7}{9} - \frac{11}{36}$
5. $\frac{2}{3} - \frac{5}{8}$
6. $\frac{4}{5} - \frac{11}{15}$
7. $\frac{1}{3} - \frac{5}{21}$
8. $\frac{10}{21} - \frac{1}{7}$
9. $17 - 2\frac{6}{7}$
10. $7 - 1\frac{1}{4}$
11. $4 - \frac{1}{2}$
12. $11\frac{31}{48} - 7\frac{37}{48}$
13. $10 - \frac{3}{5}$
14. $4 - \frac{2}{3}$
15. $5\frac{1}{3} - 5\frac{1}{8}$
16. $16\frac{7}{10} - 8\frac{1}{2}$
17. $34\frac{1}{8} - 26\frac{17}{24}$
18. $21\frac{1}{6} - 17\frac{7}{30}$
19. $26\frac{3}{8} - 9\frac{13}{24}$
20. $11\frac{1}{6} - 9\frac{13}{15}$

Chapter 17

review

Catalog buying, pages 342-344

> **AM-FM RADIO**—100% solid state chassis with 3-inch speaker. Built-in AM, telescoping FM antennas. Operates on AC cord or 4 optional "C" batteries. Black plastic case with handle. Wt. 2 lb. 10 oz.
> S 5-398 .... $28.95

Kaye Kwail wants to buy 2 AM-FM radios from the catalog for gifts.

1. What is the total cost of the goods?
2. The tax is 5% of the cost of the goods. Find the amount of the tax. Round the answer to the nearest cent.
3. What is the total weight of the goods?
4. Use the table on page 342 to find the shipping and the handling costs. Kaye lives in zone 2.
5. What is the total amount Kaye must enclose with her order?

Sewing costs, pages 346-347

6. If $1\frac{1}{4}$ yards of fabric are needed to make one vest, how much fabric is needed to make 9 vests?

Seasonal sales, pages 348-349

7. TV sets are often on sale in June. The regular price of a certain model is $345. What is the sale price with a 15% discount?

Craft supplies, pages 350-351

8. Yarn costs $.51 per package for 1-6 packages of the same color. It costs $.49 per package for 7 or more of the same color. Find the total cost of these packages of yarn.

   30 white
   10 yellow
   4 blue

Do-it-yourself project, pages 352-353

9. Find the cost of four boards, each 2″ × 6″ × 10′, at $.30/board foot.

Rental clerk, pages 354-355

10. Find the cost of renting a car polisher for $4\frac{1}{2}$ hours at $1.75 per hour.

Chapter 17

test

> **SWEATER**—100% wool. Pull-over style with ribbed neckline, wrist, and bottom edge. Long sleeve, raglan shoulder. Machine wash warm, tumble dry low. Colors: navy, brown, light blue, yellow, red. Sizes: S, M, L, XL. Wt. 15 oz.
> Q 5-391 ....$18.75

George Wright wants to buy 2 sweaters from the catalog.

1. What is the total cost of the goods?

2. The tax is 4% of the cost of the goods. Find the amount of the tax.

3. What is the total weight of the goods?

4. Use the table on page 342 to find the shipping and the handling costs. George lives in zone 1.

5. What is the total amount George must enclose with his order?

6. If $\frac{3}{4}$ yard of fabric is needed to make one necktie, how much fabric is needed to make 7 ties?

7. Men's suits are often on sale in November. The regular price of one suit is $115. Find the sale price of the suit with a 20% discount.

8. What is the cost of 7 pounds of mosaic tiles at $1.80 per pound?

9. Find the cost of three boards, each 1″ × 4″ × 8′, at $.16/linear foot.

10. Find the cost of renting a tiller for 5 hours at $4.25 per hour.

Chapter 18

Budgeting

In order to manage income and expenses, it is important to make a budget. You can learn to make better use of your money and live within your means by following a financial plan.

Analyzing Spending Habits

A **budget** is an organized spending plan. It helps people control spending so that they will have enough money to pay all bills. The first step in making a budget is analyzing current spending habits.

The chart below can be used to organize records of **variable monthly expenses.** These are the spending categories that usually occur every month, but in different amounts.

Variable monthly expenses	
Food	$____
Car: Gas, oil, tolls	$____
Other transportation	$____
Telephone	$____
Entertainment, recreation	$____
Personal spending	$____
Gifts, contributions	$____
Other	
a. ____	$____
b. ____	$____
Miscellaneous	$____
TOTAL	$____

problem

Jenny Brown is a high school student. After school and on weekends, she drives to her part-time job. Her spending records for the four weeks in one month are shown. How did Jenny organize her spending records? What was her total expense for food this month?

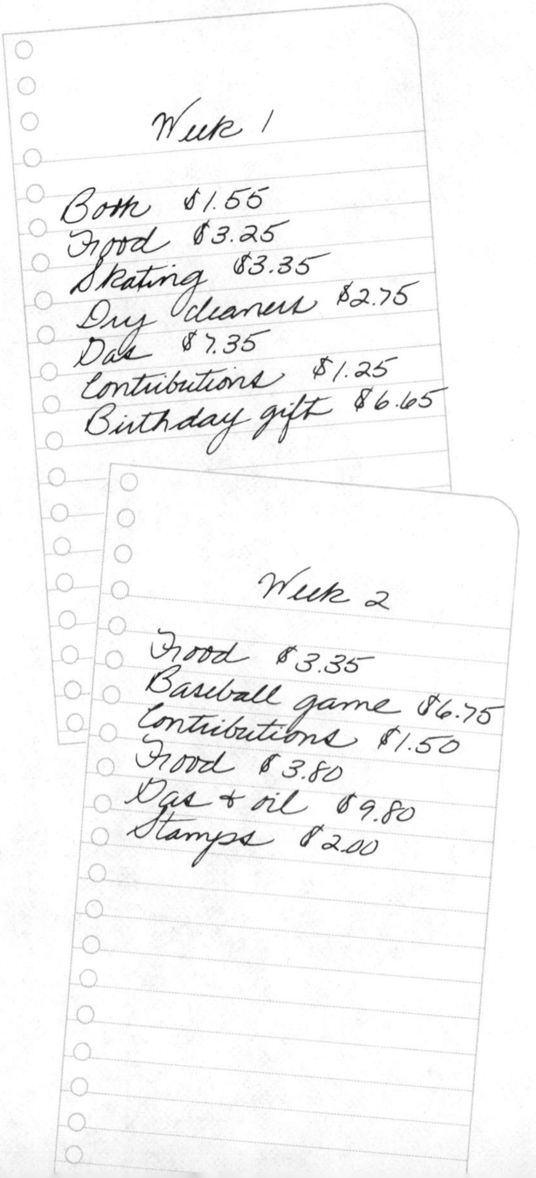

Week 1

Book $1.55
Food $3.25
Skating $3.35
Dry cleaners $2.75
Gas $7.35
Contributions $1.25
Birthday gift $6.65

Week 2

Food $3.35
Baseball game $6.75
Contributions $1.50
Food $3.80
Gas + oil $9.80
Stamps $2.00

Week 3

Food $3.55
Notebook paper $1.89
Pencils $.39
Collection for flowers $1.00
Gas $4.25
Magazines $2.50
Soccer match $6.75
Food $2.75
Contributions $1.50
Gas $6.15

Week 4

Movie $3.00
Food $3.15
Batteries $2.29
Contributions $.75
Bowling $4.85
Food $3.25
Gas $7.30

solution

Jenny compared her spending with the items in the chart on page 360. She decided to use these categories:

Food
Car: Gas, oil, tolls
Entertainment, recreation
Gifts, contributions
Miscellaneous (all other spending)

She added her food expenses for the four weeks.

$3.25	Week 1
3.35 3.80	Week 2
3.55 2.75	Week 3
3.15 + 3.25	Week 4
$23.10 ≈ $23	Total, rounded to the nearest dollar

exercises

Complete Jenny's record of spending for the month. Round each answer to the nearest dollar.

	Variable monthly expenses	
	Food	$ 23
1.	Car: Gas, oil, tolls	$____
	Other transportation	$____
	Telephone	$____
2.	Entertainment, recreation	$____
	Personal spending	$____
3.	Gifts, contributions	$____
	Other	
	a. ____________	$____
	b. ____________	$____
4.	Miscellaneous	$____
5.	TOTAL	$____

Jerry and Tina Ortega are a young working couple. Tina takes a train to work. Jerry is in a car pool and drives every fourth week. They each have a personal spending allowance of $75 per month from which they buy their personal items and lunches. Jerry and Tina eat in restaurants several times a month. When discussing their spending, they decided to list their restaurant expenses as "Entertainment, recreation."

The record of their spending for one month is shown below.

Groceries $15.75
Bowling $8.75
Recreation —
(eating out) $10.45
Contributions $4.00
Gas $4.30
Groceries $11.63
Newspapers $5.73
Miscellaneous $10.38
Allowances —
Jerry $75
Tina $75
Miscellaneous $4.26
Shirt laundry $8.17
Groceries $24.50
Contributions $5.00
Miscellaneous $1.75
Concert $10.00
Recreation —
(eating out) $8.45
Phone $15.88

Groceries $22.18
Gas/oil $7.65
Miscellaneous $5.18
Groceries $8.93
Plant (gift) $7.80
Miscellaneous $.59
Commuter ticket $43.70
Groceries $18.75
Recreation —
(eating out) $14.70
Shirt laundry $7.24
Gas $12.25
Groceries $9.77
Miscellaneous $2.04
Tolls $4.60
Dry cleaners $3.55
Groceries $3.14
Movie $3.50
Recreation
(eating out) $6.30
Miscellaneous $7.45

Use the chart to organize the Ortegas' record of their variable expenses. Round each answer to the nearest dollar.

	Variable monthly expenses	
6.	Food	$____
7.	Car: Gas, oil, tolls	$____
8.	Other transportation	$____
9.	Telephone	$____
10.	Entertainment, recreation	$____
11.	Personal spending	$____
12.	Gifts, contributions	$____
	Other	
13.	a. Clothes care	$____
14.	b. Newspapers	$____
15.	Miscellaneous	$____
16.	TOTAL	$____

The Peterson family's variable expenses for one month are listed below. Sid Peterson is in a car pool and drives every third week. His wife Lucy walks to her part-time job. The Peterson children, Frank and Jill, are junior high school students.

The Petersons decided to list separately the cost of the children's school lunches and Sid's lunches. All other eating costs are included under "Food." Each family member has an allowance for personal spending.

Food $32.16
Gas $5.80
Phone $22.18
Museum $5.25
School lunches $6.30
Sid's lunches $15.40
Miscellaneous $2.68
allowances
Sid $25 Frank $10
Lucy $25 Jill $10
Food $57.64
Gift $9.73
School lunches $6.35
Gas $6.25
Sid's lunches $16.80
amusement Park $29.60
Food $15.10

School lunches $5.75
Miscellaneous $2.45
Sid's lunches $17.10
Gas + oil $9.00
Food $71.31
School lunches $5.90
Miniature golf $10
Food $16.53
Miscellaneous $1.58
Food $55.49
Gas $6.70
Sid's lunches $15.65
School lunches $2.85
Miscellaneous $5.33
Food $58.74
Contributions $15
Food $21.85

Use the chart to organize the Petersons' record of their variable expenses. Round each answer to the nearest dollar.

	Variable monthly expenses	
17.	Food	$____
18.	Car: Gas, oil, tolls	$____
	Other transportation	$____
19.	Telephone	$____
20.	Entertainment, recreation	$____
21.	Personal spending	$____
22.	Gifts, contributions	$____
	Other	
23.	a. School lunches	$____
24.	b. Sid's lunches	$____
25.	Miscellaneous	$____
26.	TOTAL	$____

Budgeting Variable Expenses

Records of variable monthly expenses can be used to make a budget. One way to do this is to keep records for several months and average the amounts spent for each item. This average amount becomes the **amount budgeted.**

problem

Jenny Brown's 3-month spending records show that she has spent \$23, \$18, and \$20 for food. How much should she allow in her budget for food for one month?

solution

Find the average amount spent for food.

$\$23 + \$18 + \$20 = \$61$

$\$61 \div 3 \approx \$20.33$

Rounded to the nearest dollar, the amount budgeted for food should be \$20.

exercises

Complete the chart to find the amount that Jenny should budget for each of her variable expenses. Round each amount to the nearest dollar.

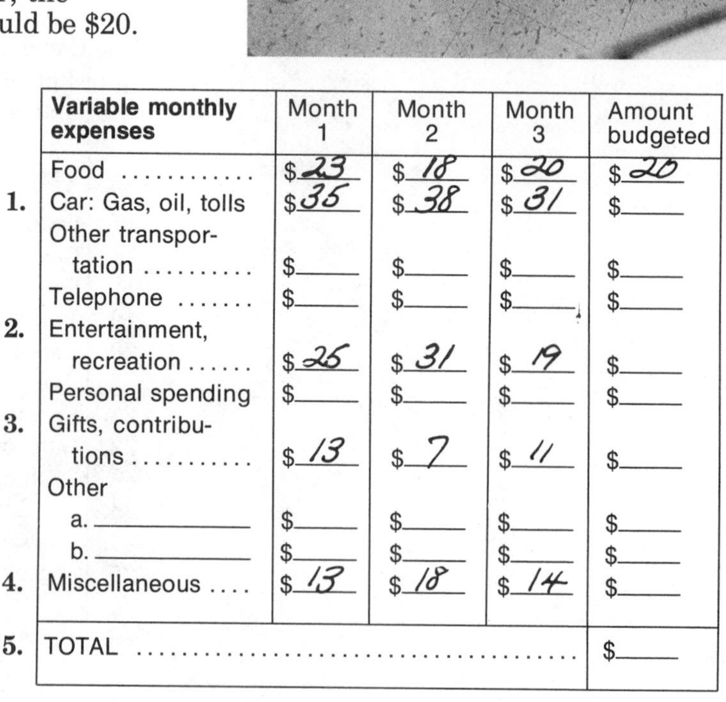

	Variable monthly expenses	Month 1	Month 2	Month 3	Amount budgeted
	Food	\$23	\$18	\$20	\$20
1.	Car: Gas, oil, tolls	\$35	\$38	\$31	\$____
	Other transportation	\$____	\$____	\$____	\$____
	Telephone	\$____	\$____	\$____	\$____
2.	Entertainment, recreation	\$26	\$31	\$19	\$____
	Personal spending	\$____	\$____	\$____	\$____
3.	Gifts, contributions	\$13	\$7	\$11	\$____
	Other				
	a. ____________	\$____	\$____	\$____	\$____
	b. ____________	\$____	\$____	\$____	\$____
4.	Miscellaneous	\$13	\$18	\$14	\$____
5.	TOTAL				\$____

The Ortegas' 3-month record of their variable expenses is shown. Complete the chart to find the amount they should budget for each item. Round each amount to the nearest dollar.

	Variable monthly expenses	Month 1	Month 2	Month 3	Amount budgeted
6.	Food	$115	$128	$116	$____
7.	Car: Gas, oil, tolls	$29	$32	$30	$____
8.	Other transportation	$44	$44	$44	$____
9.	Telephone	$16	$13	$16	$____
10.	Entertainment, recreation	$62	$85	$92	$____
11.	Personal spending	$150	$150	$150	$____
12.	Gifts, contributions	$17	$15	$14	$____
	Other				
13.	a. Clothes care	$19	$14	$20	$____
14.	b. Newspapers	$6	$6	$6	$____
15.	Miscellaneous ...	$32	$27	$15	$____
16.	TOTAL				$____

The Petersons' 3-month record of their variable expenses is shown. Complete the chart to find the amount they should budget for each item. Round each amount to the nearest dollar.

	Variable monthly expenses	Month 1	Month 2	Month 3	Amount budgeted
17.	Food	$329	$315	$331	$____
18.	Car: Gas, oil, tolls	$28	$18	$21	$____
	Other transportation	$____	$____	$____	$____
19.	Telephone	$22	$19	$20	$____
20.	Entertainment, recreation	$45	$49	$55	$____
21.	Personal spending	$70	$70	$70	$____
22.	Gifts, contributions	$25	$50	$30	$____
	Other				
23.	a. School Lunches	$27	$29	$33	$____
24.	b. Sid's Lunches	$65	$60	$70	$____
25.	Miscellaneous ...	$12	$30	$17	$____
26.	TOTAL				$____

Making a Budget

Budget sheet for Jenny Brown

Monthly take-home pay $ 435

Variable monthly expenses

Food	$ 20
Car: Gas, oil, tolls	$ 35
Other transportation	$
Telephone	$
Entertainment, recreation	$ 25
Personal spending	$
Gifts, contributions	$ 10
Other	
a.	$
b.	$
Miscellaneous	$ 15
TOTAL	$ 105

Fixed monthly expenses

Rent or mortgage Rm + board	$ 100
Car payment	$ 70
Installment payments	
a.	$
b.	$
c.	$
Savings	
a. Savings account	$ 25
b.	$
c.	$
Other	
a.	$
b.	$
c.	$
TOTAL	$

Annual expenses

Car insurance	$ 485
Car repairs	$ 200
License plates	$ 18
City registration	$ 10
Property taxes	$
Homeowner's or renter's insurance	$
Home repairs	$
Electric bills	$
Water, garbage, sewerage bills	$
Heating, cooking gas	$
Life insurance	$
Medical, dental bills	$ 85
Clothing	$ 450
Clubs, professional organizations	$
Vacation	$
Other	
a. Training program tuition	$ 80
b.	$
c.	$
TOTAL	$
Reserved monthly— (TOTAL ÷ 12)	$

MONTHLY SPENDING PLAN

Total variable expenses	$
Total fixed expenses	$
Reserved for annual expenses	$
Unexpected expenses, estimation errors	$
SPENDING TOTAL	$

Besides variable monthly expenses, two other types of expenses must be included in a budget. **Fixed monthly expenses** require the same amount to be paid every month. Rent payments and car payments are examples of fixed monthly expenses.

Annual expenses are all expenses that do not occur every month. The electric bill, for example, might come every two months; the bill for car insurance, every six or twelve months. Money must be set aside in the monthly spending plan to allow for annual expenses.

problem

Jenny Brown will be working full-time after she graduates from high school this month. To plan her spending, she made the budget shown on page 366.

Jenny thinks that her variable expenses will remain the same. Her budgeted amounts for variable expenses are listed.

Jenny's fixed monthly expenses include \$100 to her parents for room and board. Her other fixed expenses and all of her annual expenses are also listed.

What is the total of Jenny's annual expenses? How much should she reserve each month to pay annual expenses?

solution

Add the amounts listed under "Annual expenses" on the budget sheet. The total is \$1328.

Divide by 12 to find the amount that must be reserved each month to pay these expenses.

$\$1328 \div 12 \approx \$111$ Rounded to the nearest dollar

Jenny must reserve \$111 each month to pay her annual expenses.

exercises

Many of Jenny's budget entries are only estimates. Therefore, she budgets 4% of her monthly take-home pay for "Unexpected expenses and estimation errors."

Complete Jenny's monthly spending plan. Round each item to the nearest dollar.

	MONTHLY SPENDING PLAN	
1.	Total variable expenses	\$______
2.	Total fixed expenses	\$______
	Reserved for annual expenses	\$ 111
3.	Unexpected expenses, estimation errors 4% of pay	\$______
4.	SPENDING TOTAL	\$______

5. If the spending total is greater than the monthly take-home pay, the budget must be revised. Does Jenny need to revise her budget?.

Complete this budget sheet for Jerry and Tina Ortega.

Budget sheet for *Jerry & Tina Ortega*

Monthly take-home pay $ *1285*

Variable monthly expenses

Food	$ *120*
Car: Gas, oil, tolls	$ *30*
Other transportation	$ *44*
Telephone	$ *15*
Entertainment, recreation	$ *80*
Personal spending	$ *150*
Gifts, contributions	$ *15*
Other	
a. *Clothes care*	$ *18*
b. *Newspapers*	$ *6*
Miscellaneous	$ *25*
TOTAL	$ *503*

Fixed monthly expenses

	Rent or mortgage	$ *240*
	Car payment	$ *112*
	Installment payments	
	a. *Furniture*	$ *45*
	b.	$
	c.	$
	Savings	
	a. *Savings account*	$ *150*
	b.	$
	c.	$
	Other	
	a.	$
	b.	$
	c.	$
6.	TOTAL	$

Annual expenses

	Car insurance	$ *330*
	Car repairs	$ *150*
	License plates	$ *35*
	City registration	$ *15*
	Property taxes	$
	Homeowner's or renter's insurance	$ *65*
	Home repairs	$
	Electric bills	$ *180*
	Water, garbage, sewerage bills	$
	Heating, cooking gas	$
	Life insurance	$ *420*
	Medical, dental bills	$ *100*
	Clothing	$ *500*
	Clubs, professional organizations	$
	Vacation	$ *400*
	Other	
	a. *Magazine subscriptions*	$ *20*
	b.	$
	c.	$
7.	TOTAL	$
8.	Reserved monthly—(TOTAL ÷ 12)	$

MONTHLY SPENDING PLAN

9.	Total variable expenses	$
10.	Total fixed expenses	$
11.	Reserved for annual expenses	$
	Unexpected expenses, estimation errors	$ *40*
12.	SPENDING TOTAL	$

13. Does this budget need to be revised?

Make a budget sheet like the one on page 366. Use it to write a budget for the Peterson family. Include the following information.

(a) Sid and Lucy have a total take-home pay of $1670 per month.

(b) The Petersons' budgeted amounts for variable monthly expenses are: food, $325; car, $22; telephone, $20; entertainment, $50; personal spending, $70; gifts, $35; school lunches, $30; Sid's lunches, $65; and miscellaneous expenses, $20.

(c) The Petersons' fixed monthly expenses include the following: mortgage payment, $224; car payment, $120; Series E Bond (savings), $37.50; mutual fund (savings), $25; and savings account, $50.

(d) The Petersons' annual expenses include these insurance costs: car insurance, $235; homeowner's insurance, $160; and life insurance, $498. They budget $150 for car repairs, $18 for license plates, and $10 for city registration of their car.

They pay $850 each year in personal property taxes, and estimate their home repair and maintenance costs to be $650 per year. In addition, they budget $300 for electricity, $425 for heating and cooking gas, and $225 for water and garbage collection bills.

They estimate their medical and dental bills to be $782 per year and their clothing bills to be $1990 per year. They belong to a recreation club and pay annual dues of $170. They budget $100 per year for newspaper and magazine subscriptions.

Complete a monthly spending plan for the Petersons.

	MONTHLY SPENDING PLAN	
14.	Total variable expenses	$_____
15.	Total fixed expenses	$_____
16.	Reserved for annual expenses	$_____
	Unexpected expenses, estimation errors	$ 25
17.	SPENDING TOTAL	$_____

18. Does the Petersons' budget need to be revised?

Find the perimeter of this figure.

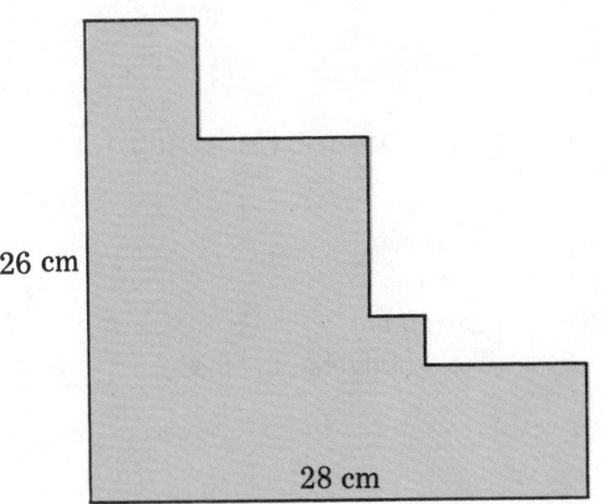

Adjusting Budgets

Once a budget has been made, any change in expenses or income will require a change in the budget. Sometimes income can be increased to pay for increased expenses. Generally, however, income cannot be increased. In order to pay for new expenses, other expenses have to be reduced.

problem

Jenny Brown would like to move into an apartment with two friends. She must adjust her budget from page 366 to decide if she can afford this change.

The three friends plan to allow $150 per month for groceries. In addition, Jenny will have to spend about $10 for food to make her lunches for work. She also wants to allow $20 per month for eating out. What should be the new amount that Jenny budgets for food?

solution

Find Jenny's share of the grocery expense.

$\$150 \div 3 = \$50$

Find the total amount budgeted for food.

$50	Groceries
10	Lunches
+ 20	Eating out
$80	Total budgeted for food

exercises

Make a budget sheet like the one on page 366. Use it to write a new budget for Jenny. Round amounts to the nearest dollar.

Variable monthly expenses
Record the new amount budgeted for food and make these additional changes in Jenny's budget from page 366.

1. She will be driving farther to work. Increase the amount for gas $5. What will be the new amount budgeted?
2. The telephone bill for the apartment is about $25 per month. The three friends will share this expense equally. What will be Jenny's share of this expense?
3. All of her other variable expenses will remain the same. What will be the new total of Jenny's variable monthly expenses?

Fixed monthly expenses
Make these changes in Jenny's budget from page 366.

4. The rent for the apartment, including heat, is $270 per month. What amount should Jenny budget for her share of the rent expense?
5. Jenny will have to buy some furniture. She will have installment payments of $15 and $25 each month. What will be her total expense for installment payments for furniture?
6. All of her other fixed monthly expenses will remain the same. What will be her new total of fixed monthly expenses?

Annual expenses
Make these changes in Jenny's budget from page 366.

7. Jenny will need to buy renter's insurance for her personal property. Her semiannual premium will be $25. What will be her annual expense for renter's insurance?
8. The electric bill for the apartment is usually about $30 every two months. What is the annual cost of electricity for the apartment? What will be Jenny's share of this expense?
9. All of her other annual expenses will remain the same. What will be the new total of Jenny's annual expenses?
10. How much should she reserve each month to pay her annual expenses?

Complete the new monthly spending plan.

MONTHLY SPENDING PLAN	
Total variable expenses	$______
Total fixed expenses	$______
Reserved for annual expenses	$______
Unexpected expenses, estimation errors	$17
11. SPENDING TOTAL	$______

12. Can Jenny afford to move into the apartment with her friends?
13. In 8 months, Jenny will complete her training program in night school. She will then be eligible for a promotion. The new job would give her an annual take-home pay of about $6600. What would be her monthly take-home pay?
14. Will Jenny be able to afford the move if she gets the promotion?

Tina Ortega wants to go to college full-time. Many changes in the Ortegas' budget will result from moving to an apartment on the college campus. Tina and Jerry must decide if they can pay her college expenses and all of their living expenses with only Jerry's take-home pay.

Make a budget sheet. Use it and the Ortegas' budget from page 368 to write a new budget for Tina and Jerry. Round all amounts to the nearest dollar.

Variable monthly expenses
Find the new amount budgeted for these variable expenses.

15. Increase the car expenses $10 per month because Jerry will have to drive farther to work.

16. Tina will not be commuting. Eliminate the amount for "Other transportation."

17. Cut $60 from the recreation budget.

18. Cut $95 from the budget for personal spending.

19. Cut gifts and contributions in half. They will eliminate gifts to each other and buy other gifts carefully.

20. Jerry will do the ironing. Eliminate the amount for "Clothes care."

21. Cut $10 from the amount for miscellaneous expenses.

22. All other variable expenses will remain the same. What will be the new total of their variable expenses?

Fixed monthly expenses
Find the new amount budgeted for these fixed monthly expenses.

23. The rent for the new apartment, including utilities, will be $70 per month less than their current rent.

24. The furniture will be paid for before they move. Eliminate this payment.

25. They will not budget any money for savings.

26. All other fixed expenses will remain the same. What will be the new total of their fixed monthly expenses?

Annual expenses
Find the new amount budgeted for these annual expenses.

27. Increase the amount for car repairs $50.

28. Utilities are included in the rent. Eliminate the amount for electric bills.

29. Cut the medical budget in half. They will use the college's health care plan.

30. Cut $300 from the clothing budget.

31. Eliminate the vacation budget.

32. Cut 50% from the amount for magazines.

33. Tina's college costs will include $520 for tuition, $120 for fees, and $150 for books. List the total college costs under "Other."

34. All other annual expenses will remain the same. What will be the new total of their annual expenses?

35. How much should they reserve each month to pay their annual expenses?

36. Jerry and Tina will allow $15 per month for unexpected expenses. What will be their new spending total?

37. Jerry's take-home pay will be $755 per month. Will the Ortegas be able to pay all of the expenses in their revised budget?

CALCULATOR EXERCISES

The Peterson family would like to take a long vacation before the children finish high school. To do this, they will have to begin saving now.

The Petersons decided that they could make changes in their variable and annual expenses. Many of the changes will result from having a family garden to cut food costs.

Make a budget sheet like the one on page 366. Use it to revise the Peterson family's variable and annual expenses from the exercises on page 369. The budget changes are listed below. Find the new amount budgeted for each item. Round to the nearest dollar.

Variable monthly expenses

1. They will use produce from the garden. Cut 9% from the monthly food budget.
2. The children will earn their spending money from part-time jobs. Cut $20 from the personal spending budget.
3. The children will take their lunches to school. Cut 80% from the school lunch budget.
4. Sid will take his lunches to work. Cut 85% from the amount budgeted for Sid's lunches.
5. All other variable expenses will remain the same. What will be the new total of their variable monthly expenses?

Annual expenses

6. Cut 20% from the clothing budget. They will use self-service dry cleaning, make clothes, and buy at the end-of-season sales.
7. There will be new annual expenses of $25 for gardening supplies and $25 for canning supplies. List the total as "Gardening costs" under "Other."
8. All other annual expenses will remain the same. What will be the new total of their annual expenses?
9. Since this is a new budget, the Petersons decided to increase the amount budgeted for unexpected expenses and estimation errors to $35. What will be their new monthly spending total?
10. How much less is this new spending total than the total in their budget from page 369?
11. The Petersons will have to save at least $180 per month in order to vacation in Australia. Have they cut their budget enough to be able to afford this trip?
12. The Petersons will have to save at least $135 per month in order to vacation in Canada. Have they cut their budget enough to be able to afford this trip?

career

Economist

Career Cluster: Science

Tony Bartlett is an economist. As part of his work, he determines the portion of gross income that an "average" family spends for different items in its budget.

Tony's figures can be used to show in a general way what it costs an average family to maintain a standard of living. Tony made the bar graph on page 375 to show the ways in which urban families of four spend their gross incomes. Averages for low-, middle-, and high-income families are shown on the graph.

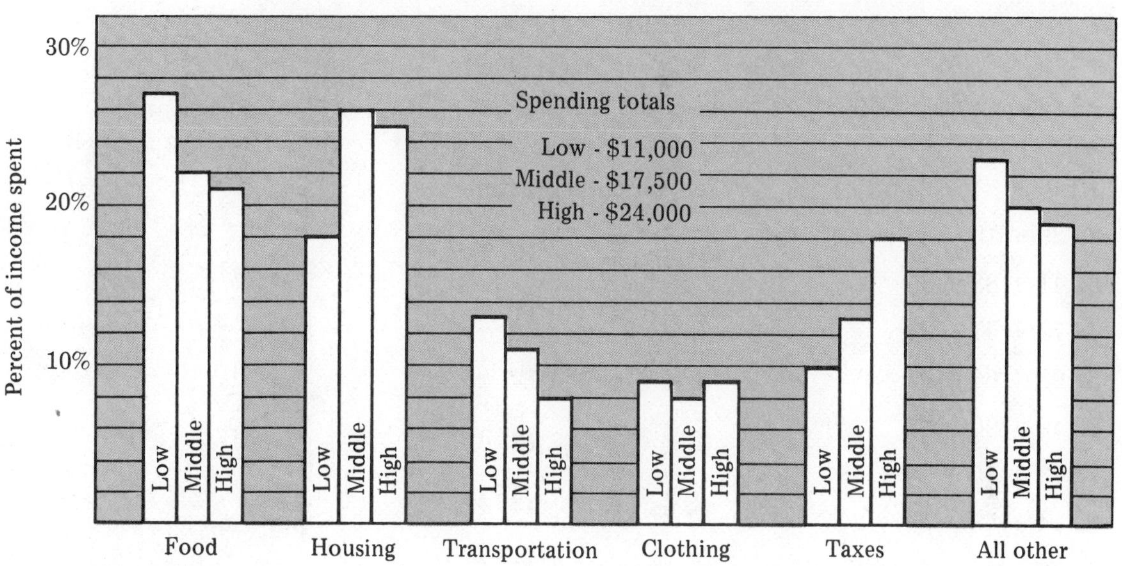

problem

What amount did an average low-income family spend for food?

solution

Find the section of the graph labeled "Food." The bar for low-income families shows that 27% of their total spending was for food. The total spending for the low-income family is $11,000.

27% of $11,000

$.27 \times \$11{,}000 = \$2970$

An average low-income family spent $2970 for food during the year.

exercises

Find the amount spent by an average family for each item.

	Item	Income Level		
		Low	Middle	High
1.	Food	$2970	a.	b.
2.	Housing	a.	b.	c.
3.	Transportation	a.	b.	c.
4.	Clothing	a.	b.	c.
5.	Taxes	a.	b.	c.

skills tune-up

Adding whole numbers and decimals, pages 6-7

1. 16 + 31 + 25
2. 29 + 13 + 8
3. 41 + 83 + 37
4. 72 + 57 + 24
5. 98 + 66 + 35
6. 49 + 90 + 87
7. 23 + 45 + 76 + 58
8. 14 + 78 + 54 + 26
9. 76 + 48 + 29 + 80
10. 779 + 101 + 331
11. 639 + 817 + 193
12. 400 + 893 + 247
13. 224 + 364 + 190
14. 2.6 + 5.14
15. 14.26 + 3.81
16. 35.14 + 17.08
17. 16.95 + 81.66
18. .21 + .37 + .16
19. 6.7 + 8.5 + 2.65
20. .74 + 3.09 + .07
21. 9.36 + 8.67 + 2.04
22. 4.34 + 1.72 + 9.5
23. .89 + .07 + .34 + .26
24. 5.02 + 1.17 + 6.83
25. .08 + 4.289 + 6.13
26. 7.6 + 1.89 + 3.7 + 6.6

Renaming fractions and mixed numbers, pages 14-15

Tell which is greater.

1. $\frac{3}{4}$ $\frac{5}{8}$
2. $\frac{2}{3}$ $\frac{8}{9}$
3. $\frac{3}{5}$ $\frac{3}{4}$
4. $\frac{3}{8}$ $\frac{1}{3}$
5. $\frac{1}{2}$ $\frac{5}{9}$
6. $\frac{5}{12}$ $\frac{3}{8}$
7. $\frac{7}{9}$ $\frac{5}{6}$
8. $\frac{2}{5}$ $\frac{1}{2}$
9. $\frac{5}{9}$ $\frac{7}{12}$
10. $\frac{3}{5}$ $\frac{7}{10}$
11. $\frac{1}{2}$ $\frac{3}{7}$
12. $\frac{5}{6}$ $\frac{7}{8}$
13. $\frac{1}{3}$ $\frac{3}{10}$
14. $\frac{3}{8}$ $\frac{5}{16}$
15. $\frac{3}{4}$ $\frac{5}{6}$
16. $\frac{7}{12}$ $\frac{1}{2}$
17. $\frac{1}{4}$ $\frac{3}{8}$
18. $\frac{5}{11}$ $\frac{3}{5}$

Rename in lowest terms.

19. $\frac{2}{8}$
20. $\frac{6}{10}$
21. $\frac{2}{4}$
22. $\frac{3}{9}$
23. $\frac{9}{12}$
24. $\frac{4}{6}$
25. $\frac{12}{24}$
26. $\frac{5}{15}$
27. $\frac{21}{24}$
28. $\frac{15}{18}$
29. $\frac{9}{36}$
30. $\frac{28}{40}$
31. $\frac{45}{72}$
32. $\frac{36}{48}$
33. $\frac{24}{30}$
34. $\frac{6}{63}$
35. $\frac{66}{88}$
36. $\frac{14}{42}$

Dividing fractions and mixed numbers, pages 16-17

1. $\frac{1}{4} \div \frac{1}{3}$
2. $\frac{4}{9} \div \frac{2}{7}$
3. $\frac{2}{5} \div \frac{2}{3}$
4. $\frac{5}{7} \div \frac{5}{8}$
5. $\frac{1}{10} \div \frac{2}{3}$
6. $\frac{12}{25} \div \frac{4}{15}$
7. $5 \div \frac{5}{8}$
8. $\frac{4}{15} \div 8$
9. $7 \div \frac{3}{4}$
10. $\frac{15}{16} \div 3$
11. $5\frac{3}{5} \div \frac{4}{5}$
12. $\frac{3}{8} \div 2\frac{1}{3}$
13. $1\frac{4}{5} \div 15$
14. $12 \div 3\frac{3}{4}$
15. $1\frac{3}{5} \div 2\frac{2}{3}$
16. $8\frac{1}{6} \div 1\frac{2}{5}$
17. $3\frac{3}{5} \div 4\frac{1}{5}$
18. $6\frac{7}{8} \div 1\frac{5}{6}$
19. $1\frac{5}{7} \div 5\frac{1}{4}$
20. $3\frac{3}{10} \div 4\frac{2}{5}$

Chapter 18

review

Analyzing spending habits, pages 360-363

Bus tokens $4.50	Food $3.30
Food $7.80	Stamps $2.60
Movie $4.50	Bus tokens $4.50
Books $7.15	Dance $10.00
Miscellaneous $2.45	Food $8.50
Taxi fare $2.85	Art exhibit $3.50
Ball game $3.50	

Use the spending record above. Round each answer to the nearest dollar.

1. Find the total expense for transportation.
2. Find the total expense for entertainment and recreation.

Budgeting variable expenses, pages 364-365

3. Use the 3-month spending record that is given. Find the amount that should be budgeted for this variable expense. Round to the nearest dollar.

	Month 1	Month 2	Month 3	Amount budgeted
Food	$30	$45	$50	$____

4. The budgeted amounts for Rae's variable monthly expenses are: food, $15; car, $20; extertainment, $20; gifts, $7; and miscellaneous, $10. What is the total of Rae's variable monthly expenses?

Making a budget, pages 366-369

5. The total of Rae's annual expenses is $328. To the nearest dollar, how much should she reserve each month to pay her annual expenses?
6. Rae's fixed expenses include $25 for savings and $18 to repay a loan from her parents. What is the total of Rae's fixed monthly expenses?

Complete a monthly spending plan for Rae.

MONTHLY SPENDING PLAN

Total variable expenses ...... $____

Total fixed expenses .... $____

Reserved for annual expenses .... $____

Unexpected expenses, estimation errors .... $ 5

7. SPENDING TOTAL .... $____

8. Rae's take-home pay is $150 per month. Does her budget need to be revised?

Adjusting budgets, pages 370-372

9. The Springer family currently budgets $58 per month for car expenses. If Mr. Springer joins a car pool, he can cut this expense in half. What will be the new amount budgeted for car expenses?

Economist, pages 374-375

10. In one area, an average family spends 23.5% of its income for housing. If the family's income is $16,600 per year, what is the amount spent for housing?

Chapter 18

test

Gas $8.20	Gift $8.75
Food $3.55	Charity $4.00
Album $6.15	Gas & oil $7.90
Miscellaneous $3.27	Food $7.83
Tennis $7.50	Haircut $4.75
Food $2.30	Books $6.30
Gas $4.25	

Use the spending record above. Round each answer to the nearest dollar.

1. Find the total expense for food.

2. Find the total expense for gas, oil, and tolls.

3. Use the 3-month spending record that is given. Find the amount that should be budgeted for this variable expense.

	Month 1	Month 2	Month 3	Amount budgeted
Telephone	$18	$23	$19	$______

4. The budgeted amounts for Larry's variable monthly expenses are: food, $25; car, $30; entertainment, $35; gifts, $8; and miscellaneous, $10. What is the total of Larry's variable monthly expenses?

5. The total of Larry's annual expenses is $675. To the nearest dollar, how much should he reserve each month to pay his annual expenses?

6. Larry's fixed expenses are $85 per month for his car payment and $35 per month for savings. What is the total of Larry's fixed monthly expenses?

Complete a monthly spending plan for Larry.

MONTHLY SPENDING PLAN

Total variable expenses	$______
Total fixed expenses	$______
Reserved for annual expenses	$______
Unexpected expenses, estimation errors	$ 5
7. SPENDING TOTAL	$______

8. Larry's take-home pay is $290 per month. Does his budget need to be revised?

9. The James family budgets $1825 annually for clothes. Mr. and Mrs. James hope to save $350 annually by making many of their clothes. What should be the new amount budgeted for clothes?

10. One survey indicated that an average family spends 29% of its income for food. If the family income is $10,500 per year, what amount is spent for food?

Unit 6

test

Choose the best answer.

1. Find the number of calories in 3 slices of bacon if 1 slice has 45 calories.

A 48 **C** 135

B 125 **D** 15

2. Rene's mass is 66 kilograms. She went bowling for 1.4 hours. At 3.9 calories per kilogram per hour, how many calories did she use? (Round the answer to the nearest whole number.)

A 360 **C** 361

B 230 **D** 240

3. Find the cost of 1 can of pineapple at 5 cans/$2.00.

A $.50 **C** $.10

B $.40 **D** $.25

4. Find the amount of usable meat in a 200-kilogram side of beef. There is a 23% loss during butchering.

A 177 kg **C** 46 kg

B 23 kg **D** 154 kg

5. Find the number of kilograms of rib roast that Casey can expect from a 150-kilogram side of beef. 6% of the side of beef will be rib roast.

A 90 kg **C** 80 kg

B 8 kg **D** 9 kg

6. Find the total cost of this meal for two people.

Shrimp dinner at a restaurant
Dinner for two $12.00
Beverages $.50 per person
Include a 15% tip.

A $14.95 **C** $14.38

B $13.00 **D** $15.05

7. Use the table on page 342 to find the shipping and handling charges for an order weighing 3 lb. 7 oz. Use zone 2.

A $1.05 **C** $1.40

B $1.20 **D** $1.30

8. If $2\frac{1}{4}$ yd. of fabric is needed to make one blouse, how much fabric is needed to make two blouses?

A $4\frac{1}{16}$ yd. **C** $4\frac{1}{4}$ yd.

B $4\frac{1}{2}$ yd. **D** $4\frac{1}{8}$ yd.

9. Laundry appliances are often on sale in March. The regular price of a clothes washer is $300. What is the sale price with a 15% discount?

   A $270 C $245

   B $255 D $285

10. What is the cost of 9 pounds of mosaic tile at $1.80 per pound?

   A $15.60 C $16.20

   B $16.60 D $20.00

11. Find the cost of renting a rug shampooer for 6 hours at $4.50 per hour.

   A $28.00 C $26.50

   B $27.50 D $27.00

12. Find the total expense for recreation and entertainment for one month. Round the answer to the nearest dollar.

Rock concert	$6.00
Hockey game	$8.75
Bowling	$4.35

   A $19 C $18

   B $20 D $17

13. A 3-month spending record is given for gas, oil, and tolls. Find the amount that should be budgeted for this variable expense.

Month 1	$28
Month 2	$31
Month 3	$28

   A $30 C $29

   B $28 D $31

14. The total of Leslie's annual expenses is $465. To the nearest dollar, how much should she reserve each month to pay her annual expenses?

   A $46 C $39

   B $38 D $47

15. The Storc family budgets $1500 annually for vacations. They hope to save $325 annually by driving instead of flying to their destination. What should be the new amount budgeted for vacations?

   A $1185 C $1275

   B $1175 D $1825

16. One survey indicates that an average family spends 22% of its income on housing. If the family income is $13,200 per year, what amount is spent for housing?

   A $2904 C $3036

   B $2706 D $2872

End-of-book

test

Part A **Chapters 1-9**

Choose the best answer.

1. $8.56 + 21.7 + 3.19$

A 13.92 **C** 33.45

B 30.26 **D** 33.54

2. $3\frac{3}{5} \times \frac{2}{3}$

A $2\frac{2}{5}$ **C** $1\frac{11}{15}$

B $1\frac{3}{5}$ **D** $5\frac{2}{5}$

3. Solve. $\frac{5}{9} = \frac{35}{h}$

A $h = 19$ **C** $h = 63$

B $h = 128$ **D** $h = 33$

4. What number is 15% of 80?

A 68 **C** 48

B 13 **D** 12

5. Choose the most sensible measure for the length of a dollar bill.

A 16 mm **C** 16 m

B 16 cm **D** 16 km

6. Add 4 hours 35 minutes to 3 hours 20 minutes.

A 1 hr. 35 min. **C** 7 hr. 15 min.

B 1 hr. 55 min. **D** 7 hr. 55 min.

7. Floyd earns $4.75 per hour as a bank teller. What is his gross pay for working a 35-hour week?

A $167.25 **C** $146.25

B $166.05 **D** $166.25

8. The weekly gross pay earned by Patty O'Brian is $147. Her deductions are $23.80 for federal income taxes and $8.59 for social security. What is Patty's net pay?

A $114.61 **C** $123.20

B $32.39 **D** $138.41

9. Lisa is depositing checks in these amounts: $15.46, $184.35, and $3.50. If she wants $70 in cash, how much will she deposit in her account?

A $203.31 **C** $133.31

B $476.62 **D** $129.81

10. Ramon Ruiz had a balance of $924.35 in his checking account. He wrote a check for $87.12. Find the new balance.

A $1011.47 **C** $963.23

B $837.23 **D** $847.23

11. A savings account of $850 earns 6% simple interest. Find the amount of interest the account will earn in 6 months.

A $51.00 **C** $25.50

B $875.50 **D** $306.00

12. Find the amount of the monthly payment on a level-payment loan of $800 at 12% for 6 months. (Use the table on page 406.)

A $137.64 **C** $138.83

B $138.04 **D** $138.00

13. A used car costs $1360. The state sales tax is 6%. Find the amount of the state sales tax.

A $78.60 **C** $81.66

B $81.60 **D** $91.60

14. The selling price of a new car is $4856. The trade-in allowance on a used car is $1327. Find the net price.

A $3529 **C** $3531

B $6183 **D** $3528

15. Tony Rizzo drove 630 km during June. He bought 95 liters of gasoline. Find his car's fuel consumption. Round the answer to the nearest tenth.

A 6.4 km/L **C** 6.6 km/L

B 6.5 km/L **D** 6.7 km/L

16. Alice drove 13,000 km last year. Her total annual expenses, including depreciation, fixed costs, and variable costs, was $3510. Find the cost per kilometer.

A $.26 **C** $.28

B $.29 **D** $.27

17. How long will it take to travel 450 km at a rate of 80 km/h? Round the answer to the nearest half hour.

A 4.5 hr. **C** 5.5 hr.

B 5 hr. **D** 6 hr.

18. Use the chart on page 176. Find the distance from Cincinnati to Memphis to Phoenix.

A 3694 km **C** 3156 km

B 3569 km **D** 3248 km

Part B Chapters 10-18

Choose the best answer.

1. Kevin earns $5.65 per hour in a 40-hour work week. Using the "week's gross pay" rule of thumb, what is the most he should spend for rent each month?

   A $262 C $226

   B $141 D $222

2. The Krafts plan to paint the walls of their den. The room is 4.2 m by 5.8 m and is 2.5 m high. Find the area of the walls.

   A 60.9 m^2 C 50 m^2

   B 25 m^2 D 69.72 m^2

3. Marilyn's stereo was stolen. The value of the stereo after depreciation is $316. Marilyn has a $100-deductible policy for renter's insurance. How much will Marilyn receive from the insurance company?

   A $416 C $306

   B $216 D $400

4. A home costs $61,000. What is the amount of the mortgage loan after a 25% down payment?

   A $45,750 C $15,250

   B $59,475 D $44,750

5. The assessed valuation of a home is $28,300. The tax rate is $3.60 per $100 of assessed valuation. Find the annual property tax on this home.

   A $856.80 C $643.00

   B $1018.80 D $1015.20

6. Find the cost of building a house with 2100 square feet. The house will cost $26.50 per square foot.

   A $53,760 C $57,750

   B $79,245 D $55,650

7. The amount for exemptions in computing federal income tax is $750 for each exemption. Karen Trent claims 3 exemptions. Find her total amount for exemptions.

   A $2250 C $747

   B $250 D $753

8. Rhonda had $783 in federal income taxes withheld from her earnings this year. Her tax required for the year is $972. Find the refund due Rhonda or the balance due the IRS.

   A $211 due IRS C $189 due IRS

   B $211 refund D $189 refund

9. Greg Miller's taxable income is $9847. His state income tax is 3% of taxable income. What is Greg's state income tax?

A $296.22 C $294.41

B $284.61 D $295.41

10. Diane Gorski has a $50-deductible health insurance policy. The insurance company pays 80% of all costs after the deductible amount. Diane's medical bills totaled $1636. How much did the insurance company pay?

A $1308.80 C $1348.80

B $1268.80 D $1300.80

11. Find the cost of a $200 Series E Savings Bond. (The cost is 75% of face value.)

A $125 C $275

B $150 D $114

12. Eric bought a $4000 certificate of deposit that pays 6.5% interest compounded daily. How much interest will he receive at the end of 1 year? (Use the table on page 304.)

A $4268.60 C $4257.96

B $257.96 D $268.60

13. Find the cost of 1 can of tomato sauce at 6 cans/$1.50.

A $.25 C $.90

B $.20 D $.30

14. Find the total cost of this meal.

Lasagna dinner for two $8.50
Beverages $.40 per person
Include a 10% tip.

A $9.79 C $10.20

B $9.30 D $10.35

15. Find the cost of $4\frac{1}{2}$ yards of fabric at $3.20 per yard.

A $14.40 C $13.44

B $16.38 D $10.35

16. The regular price of a sofa is $450. What is the sale price with a 20% discount?

A $90 C $360

B $430 D $428

17. A 3-month spending record for food is given. Find the amount that should be budgeted for this variable expense.

Month 1	$82
Month 2	$79
Month 3	$88

A $82 C $249

B $83 D $88

18. The total of Harold's annual expenses is $637. To the nearest dollar, how much should he reserve each month to pay his annual expenses?

A $54 C $56

B $57 D $53

Skills File

Tables

skills file

Rounding whole numbers and decimals, pages 4-5

Round each number to the nearest thousand and the nearest hundred.

1. 637
2. 924
3. 501
4. 809
5. 718
6. 576
7. 1386
8. 6827
9. 5906
10. 8391
11. 3674
12. 4102
13. 2416
14. 9383
15. 7561
16. 5234
17. 2776
18. 9643
19. 7084
20. 1867
21. 5425
22. 9536
23. 2021
24. 4771
25. 8698
26. 3124
27. 96,932
28. 20,248
29. 43,036
30. 39,601
31. 84,853
32. 50,626
33. 67,359
34. 11,707
35. 30,858
36. 68,475
37. 26,391
38. 94,033
39. 74,906
40. 56,521
41. 68,072
42. 91,468
43. 80,925
44. 13,797
45. 52,385
46. 25,013
47. 47,203
48. 79,619
49. 605.8
50. 523.7
51. 892.1
52. 701.4
53. 1281.2
54. 8456.3
55. 5074.8
56. 4832.5
57. 91,736.6
58. 70,454.2
59. 35,487.3
60. 29,818.7

Round each number to the nearest whole number and the nearest hundredth.

61. 3.493
62. 2.662
63. 8.088
64. 4.255
65. 1.792
66. 7.534
67. 5.824
68. 6.106
69. 9.415
70. 3.015
71. 2.059
72. 5.379
73. 6.738
74. 9.386
75. 2.801
76. 8.148
77. 1.252
78. 9.683
79. 4.928
80. 5.747
81. 62.293
82. 37.109
83. 94.014
84. 29.675
85. 68.256
86. 40.322
87. 37.894
88. 81.547
89. 55.008
90. 78.753
91. 26.378
92. 59.668
93. 90.544
94. 11.935
95. 72.482
96. 84.807
97. 65.068
98. 37.075
99. 20.367
100. 84.711
101. 912.049
102. 305.254
103. 745.923
104. 689.742
105. 567.605
106. 268.866
107. 193.249
108. 530.194
109. 808.351
110. 659.083
111. 446.502
112. 563.867
113. 880.921
114. 337.274
115. 671.413
116. 100.895
117. 466.059
118. 739.573
119. 248.341
120. 574.185

skills file

Adding whole numbers and decimals, pages 6-7

1. 23 +56

2. 17 +31

3. 65 +18

4. 27 +43

5. 84 +56

6. 77 +28

7. 12 33 +41

8. 42 16 +31

9. 18 7 +65

10. 21 36 + 3

11. 23 35 +14

12. 48 23 +26

13. 81 40 +25

14. 50 65 +94

15. 89 57 +31

16. 26 44 +78

17. 11 42 30 +12

18. 23 11 32 +20

19. 45 3 22 +14

20. 14 35 7 +41

21. 63 47 85 +90

22. 56 48 70 +62

23. 153 +438

24. 371 +265

25. 203 +978

26. 783 +609

27. 35 343 +261

28. 404 360 + 82

29. 330 475 +108

30. 283 316 +257

31. 625 884 +589

32. 745 134 +978

33. 8.4 +3.56

34. 9.2 +4.63

35. 5.27 +8.9

36. 4.39 +1.17

37. 7.08 +6.75

38. 18.37 +25.04

39. .3 .1 +.4

40. .2 .8 +.7

41. 2.6 1.9 +3.5

42. 7.6 6.38 +3.4

43. 5.71 1.5 +4.2

44. 7.9 9.4 +2.83

45. 3.52 9.1 +8.36

46. 6.1 1.31 +5.07

47. 4.85 8.04 +6.2

48. 5.46 8.01 + .63

49. 4.67 .82 +9.05

50. 3.69 1.27 +8.45

51. 7.02 6.01 +9.48

52. 8.52 1.04 +3.07

53. 2.71 .43 1.02 +3.56

54. 8.29 3.48 .76 +7.05

55. 3.108 5.72 +4.06

56. 1.01 3.707 +6.32

57. 9.68 2.19 +4.452

58. 2.8 8.1 7.53 +5.4

59. 1.72 4.6 5.4 +3.9

60. 9.7 8.2 1.5 +3.04

61. .13 .285 9.47 + .39

62. 7.35 .61 6.473 +4.06

63. 5.26 9.19 .48 + .606

skills file

Subtracting whole numbers and decimals, pages 6-7

1. 87 −53	**15.** 865 −621	**29.** 57.9 −13.6	**43.** 46.02 −35.5	**57.** 56.714 −23.4	**71.** 20.05 −18.164
2. 49 −38	**16.** 283 −191	**30.** 28.4 − 5.7	**44.** 87.26 −59.8	**58.** 15.673 − 8.8	**72.** 68.7 −41.436
3. 53 − 5	**17.** 924 −577	**31.** 35.3 − 8.8	**45.** 28.537 −14.216	**59.** 47.206 −22.4	**73.** 17.1 − 8.863
4. 74 − 9	**18.** 358 −149	**32.** 74.8 −26.5	**46.** 49.817 − 8.649	**60.** 85.061 −39.4	**74.** 83.7 − 5.625
5. 63 −57	**19.** 708 −314	**33.** 17.5 −16.9	**47.** 85.271 − 3.625	**61.** 90.225 −73.9	**75.** 92.8 −17.066
6. 26 −17	**20.** 150 −129	**34.** 36.47 −21.35	**48.** 32.045 −18.637	**62.** 92.7 −51.43	**76.** 50.3 −36.218
7. 80 −37	**21.** 413 −186	**35.** 64.08 − 3.89	**49.** 54.306 −39.271	**63.** 25.8 − 3.31	**77.** 80.71 −49
8. 50 −19	**22.** 3884 −1267	**36.** 28.01 −24.35	**50.** 70.427 −27.299	**64.** 91.2 − 5.67	**78.** 93.28 −57
9. 94 −69	**23.** 7946 −2871	**37.** 96.14 −48.59	**51.** 41.825 −20.51	**65.** 80.7 −62.19	**79.** 83.721 −26
10. 41 −25	**24.** 8124 − 315	**38.** 6.06 − .97	**52.** 94.347 −56.17	**66.** 50.1 −17.06	**80.** 56.004 −49
11. 76 −47	**25.** 5463 − 872	**39.** 40.14 −39.57	**53.** 15.939 − 1.87	**67.** 9.47 − .254	**81.** 27 − 6.3
12. 96 −17	**26.** 9017 −1815	**40.** 73.85 −31.4	**54.** 60.803 −26.21	**68.** 83.12 −74.538	**82.** 84 −59.5
13. 81 −73	**27.** 6207 −4334	**41.** 32.52 − 8.9	**55.** 87.528 −18.04	**69.** 18.75 − 6.672	**83.** 63 −21.84
14. 62 −15	**28.** 5001 −3745	**42.** 54.07 − 6.1	**56.** 58.241 − 3.19	**70.** 95.03 −32.671	**84.** 55 − 7.39

skills file

Multiplying whole numbers, pages 8-9

1. 20×80
2. 60×30
3. 70×40
4. 10×90
5. 50×20
6. 60×50
7. 30×70
8. 900×40
9. 200×90
10. 500×60
11. 700×10
12. 400×30
13. 800×50
14. 600×20
15. 800×900
16. 500×700
17. 600×100
18. 700×200
19. 400×600
20. 100×800
21. 300×300
22. 6000×90
23. 3000×80
24. 4000×10
25. 9000×50
26. 7000×70
27. 1000×40
28. 5000×80
29. 9000×100
30. 4000×400
31. 1000×700
32. 2000×300
33. 7000×900
34. 3000×500
35. 8000×200
36. 530×100
37. 400×250
38. 1200×600
39. 1100×800
40. 4100×300
41. 2000×7400
42. 2900×8000
43. 32×3
44. 14×8
45. 43×2
46. 70×5
47. 66×4
48. 89×7
49. 513×6
50. 241×9
51. 604×8
52. 708×2
53. 857×5
54. 983×4
55. 52×13
56. 34×22
57. 40×67
58. 82×80
59. 28×74
60. 57×39
61. 349×42
62. 612×33
63. 507×86
64. 801×45
65. 428×67
66. 723×96
67. 3246×17
68. 1472×40
69. 9053×80
70. 5416×26
71. 6923×35
72. 7672×54
73. 642×533
74. 471×319
75. 257×306
76. 803×142
77. 643×718
78. 978×535
79. 6926×416
80. 7158×247
81. 5904×832
82. 9268×107
83. 5296×308
84. 2087×546

skills file

Multiplying decimals, pages 10-11

1. .3 × .7
2. .9 × .5
3. .1 × .8
4. .6 × .4
5. .5 × .2
6. .8 × .7
7. .04 × .9
8. .01 × .3
9. .07 × .5
10. .02 × .6
11. .09 × .9
12. .05 × .8
13. .008 × .6
14. .002 × .2
15. .006 × .1
16. .005 × .3
17. .008 × .5
18. .007 × .6
19. .09 × .02
20. .04 × .01
21. .03 × .08
22. .07 × .07
23. .06 × .05
24. .09 × .11
25. .004 × .07
26. .001 × .02
27. .005 × .05
28. .003 × .06
29. .008 × .04
30. .009 × .07
31. .004 × .003
32. .005 × .001
33. .009 × .008
34. .003 × .009
35. 800 × .3
36. 400 × .2
37. 200 × .07
38. 800 × .08
39. .006 × 900
40. .004 × 600
41. .0011 × 7000
42. .0005 × 4000
43. 37 × .8
44. 15 × .3
45. .36 × 52
46. .49 × 27
47. 5.8 × .3
48. 2.3 × .4
49. 7.5 × 1.2
50. 1.6 × 6.8
51. 3.7 × 3.6
52. 2.4 × 8.9
53. 6.43 × 1.9
54. 4.97 × 2.3
55. 5.08 × 3.4
56. 7.07 × 6.8
57. 2.51 × 7.4
58. 4.52 × 8.7
59. 17.3 × .214
60. .639 × 92.7
61. .471 × 36.2
62. 87.3 × .007
63. 20.6 × .603
64. 59.2 × .778
65. 7.49 × .31
66. 6.41 × .27
67. 2.38 × .64
68. 4.02 × .57
69. 8.13 × .06
70. 3.85 × .78
71. 5.814 × 6.29
72. 7.32 × .841
73. 1.93 × .478
74. 2.737 × 5.03
75. 8.054 × 2.81
76. 9.176 × 7.84
77. .124 × .362
78. .703 × .819
79. 3.762 × .105
80. 8.051 × .368
81. 4.695 × .732
82. 2.597 × .986
83. .0072 × .659
84. .0093 × .728

skills file

Dividing whole numbers, pages 12-13

1. $3\overline{)765}$
2. $2\overline{)983}$
3. $7\overline{)821}$
4. $9\overline{)846}$
5. $5\overline{)388}$
6. $7\overline{)4136}$
7. $6\overline{)8723}$
8. $4\overline{)1273}$
9. $3\overline{)4391}$
10. $8\overline{)2476}$
11. $5\overline{)31954}$
12. $4\overline{)12734}$
13. $2\overline{)51370}$
14. $7\overline{)50633}$
15. $9\overline{)45127}$
16. $6\overline{)172536}$
17. $3\overline{)367124}$
18. $4\overline{)279503}$
19. $6\overline{)706487}$
20. $8\overline{)256318}$
21. $7\overline{)300429}$
22. $13\overline{)1538}$
23. $30\overline{)4286}$
24. $23\overline{)1288}$
25. $42\overline{)5862}$
26. $36\overline{)8417}$
27. $75\overline{)3435}$
28. $40\overline{)3393}$
29. $26\overline{)7210}$
30. $39\overline{)8114}$
31. $57\overline{)3591}$
32. $63\overline{)6207}$
33. $81\overline{)7342}$
34. $38\overline{)2053}$
35. $53\overline{)5096}$
36. $92\overline{)7954}$
37. $27\overline{)8342}$
38. $66\overline{)3308}$
39. $51\overline{)6009}$
40. $88\overline{)2816}$
41. $94\overline{)5526}$
42. $67\overline{)2004}$
43. $14\overline{)17236}$
44. $31\overline{)42921}$
45. $43\overline{)22184}$
46. $22\overline{)39378}$
47. $56\overline{)42185}$
48. $72\overline{)65929}$
49. $37\overline{)20555}$
50. $17\overline{)83424}$
51. $68\overline{)65438}$
52. $49\overline{)86047}$
53. $84\overline{)31765}$
54. $76\overline{)57810}$
55. $28\overline{)94613}$
56. $91\overline{)85736}$
57. $18\overline{)13290}$
58. $52\overline{)39728}$
59. $77\overline{)26952}$
60. $87\overline{)90508}$
61. $59\overline{)27126}$
62. $61\overline{)56235}$
63. $98\overline{)60403}$
64. $16\overline{)181457}$
65. $21\overline{)664713}$
66. $33\overline{)986264}$
67. $12\overline{)726583}$
68. $44\overline{)869389}$
69. $71\overline{)375534}$
70. $86\overline{)261379}$
71. $46\overline{)920417}$
72. $73\overline{)868716}$
73. $97\overline{)482582}$
74. $64\overline{)173696}$
75. $82\overline{)294379}$
76. $93\overline{)500372}$
77. $65\overline{)380049}$
78. $123\overline{)18372}$
79. $262\overline{)27671}$
80. $695\overline{)86368}$
81. $304\overline{)84512}$
82. $737\overline{)68254}$
83. $162\overline{)32012}$
84. $40\overline{)26107}$
85. $738\overline{)63872}$
86. $282\overline{)76446}$
87. $870\overline{)40653}$
88. $376\overline{)68808}$
89. $564\overline{)55364}$
90. $920\overline{)37032}$
91. $656\overline{)23209}$
92. $541\overline{)576324}$
93. $263\overline{)198745}$
94. $147\overline{)724838}$
95. $454\overline{)476224}$
96. $862\overline{)633461}$
97. $506\overline{)345092}$
98. $627\overline{)602753}$
99. $313\overline{)920369}$
100. $204\overline{)863446}$
101. $854\overline{)767755}$
102. $470\overline{)230042}$
103. $926\overline{)470283}$
104. $781\overline{)532931}$
105. $939\overline{)307005}$

skills file

Dividing decimals, pages 12-13

Find the quotient to the nearest thousandth.

1. 7)36.8
2. 3)56.3
3. 9)28.7
4. 6)40.9
5. 3)22.6
6. 4)72.3
7. 8)90.1
8. 7)13.2
9. 6)47.9
10. 9)58.3
11. 14)43.72
12. 41)37.21
13. 70)56.42
14. 23)30.86
15. 66)52.04
16. 90)17.62
17. 37)74.27
18. 54)58.02
19. 62)10.36
20. 89)24.79

21. 16)5.338
22. 82)2.397
23. 60)4.712
24. 54)7.084
25. 74)8.354
26. 33)3.206
27. 97)6.523
28. 1.3).6
29. 8.5).2
30. 3.4).9
31. 2.9).8
32. 6.7).5
33. 9.2).4
34. 3.2)7.7
35. 7.4)1.3
36. 2.8)4.6
37. 6.1)9.2
38. 9.5)4.1
39. 8.3)7.2
40. 5.9)2.8

41. 4.1)98.26
42. 7.4)36.09
43. 5.2)61.73
44. 4.8)27.21
45. 6.3)48.05
46. 2.7)50.19
47. 9.6)78.23
48. .65).132
49. .24).309
50. .17).905
51. .41).286
52. .93).526
53. .57).217
54. .19).8274
55. .25).0145
56. .64).3092
57. .38).9103
58. .51).8367
59. .98).5005
60. .73).6419

61. .3)52
62. .7)13
63. .6)76
64. .9)96
65. .7)48
66. .3)79
67. .9)67
68. 3.13)5.7
69. 2.49)7.6
70. 1.93)9.3
71. 7.02)6.9
72. 4.05)2.7
73. 8.33)4.2
74. 6.19)4.77
75. 1.72)3.59
76. 2.98)5.38
77. 7.02)7.46
78. 4.01)8.64
79. 9.32)6.01
80. 6.97)4.08

81. 3.24).4178
82. 9.38).5735
83. 2.98).3182
84. 6.07).2379
85. 1.69).5205
86. 8.43).7024
87. 7.36).0951
88. .426).198
89. .376).215
90. .082).517
91. .604).069
92. .753).501
93. .275).843
94. .142).4357
95. .035).6172
96. .406).0349
97. .718).7024
98. .659).3406
99. .008).9347
100. .123).0009

skills file

Renaming fractions and mixed numbers, pages 14-15

Tell which is greater.

1. $\frac{1}{2}$ $\frac{1}{4}$
2. $\frac{1}{3}$ $\frac{4}{9}$
3. $\frac{1}{4}$ $\frac{1}{3}$
4. $\frac{7}{8}$ $\frac{1}{2}$
5. $\frac{1}{6}$ $\frac{1}{4}$
6. $\frac{1}{3}$ $\frac{1}{5}$
7. $\frac{1}{6}$ $\frac{1}{8}$
8. $\frac{4}{5}$ $\frac{3}{4}$
9. $\frac{5}{8}$ $\frac{2}{3}$
10. $\frac{3}{8}$ $\frac{3}{4}$
11. $\frac{2}{3}$ $\frac{3}{5}$
12. $\frac{5}{6}$ $\frac{7}{8}$
13. $\frac{1}{3}$ $\frac{3}{11}$
14. $\frac{3}{4}$ $\frac{5}{8}$
15. $\frac{7}{10}$ $\frac{4}{7}$
16. $\frac{3}{4}$ $\frac{13}{16}$
17. $\frac{7}{9}$ $\frac{3}{5}$
18. $\frac{5}{12}$ $\frac{9}{16}$

Rename in lowest terms.

19. $\frac{3}{6}$
20. $\frac{6}{24}$
21. $\frac{3}{15}$
22. $\frac{6}{18}$
23. $\frac{5}{20}$
24. $\frac{6}{8}$
25. $\frac{10}{12}$
26. $\frac{16}{24}$
27. $\frac{7}{14}$
28. $\frac{3}{24}$
29. $\frac{12}{21}$
30. $\frac{32}{36}$
31. $\frac{15}{45}$
32. $\frac{18}{20}$
33. $\frac{9}{15}$
34. $\frac{30}{35}$
35. $\frac{44}{66}$
36. $\frac{21}{27}$
37. $\frac{24}{30}$
38. $\frac{15}{18}$
39. $\frac{25}{40}$
40. $\frac{21}{48}$
41. $\frac{16}{80}$
42. $\frac{12}{32}$
43. $\frac{25}{75}$
44. $\frac{18}{81}$
45. $\frac{28}{42}$
46. $\frac{54}{63}$
47. $\frac{49}{56}$
48. $\frac{48}{64}$

Write as a mixed number.

49. $\frac{10}{3}$
50. $\frac{5}{2}$
51. $\frac{9}{4}$
52. $\frac{24}{5}$
53. $\frac{19}{6}$
54. $\frac{37}{8}$
55. $\frac{27}{5}$
56. $\frac{73}{9}$
57. $\frac{38}{7}$
58. $\frac{18}{10}$
59. $\frac{29}{18}$
60. $\frac{45}{10}$
61. $\frac{23}{7}$
62. $\frac{18}{4}$
63. $\frac{19}{12}$
64. $\frac{59}{6}$
65. $\frac{43}{3}$
66. $\frac{63}{8}$
67. $\frac{87}{7}$
68. $\frac{56}{24}$
69. $\frac{109}{5}$
70. $\frac{75}{4}$
71. $\frac{63}{15}$
72. $\frac{123}{10}$
73. $\frac{49}{2}$
74. $\frac{67}{9}$
75. $\frac{56}{5}$

Write as a fraction.

76. $1\frac{2}{3}$
77. $3\frac{1}{4}$
78. $8\frac{1}{5}$
79. $2\frac{3}{4}$
80. $4\frac{1}{10}$
81. $9\frac{1}{3}$
82. $3\frac{5}{8}$
83. $5\frac{1}{5}$
84. $7\frac{1}{6}$
85. $6\frac{3}{7}$
86. $9\frac{7}{8}$
87. $8\frac{2}{3}$
88. $5\frac{9}{10}$
89. $7\frac{6}{7}$
90. $9\frac{5}{6}$
91. $5\frac{7}{12}$
92. $3\frac{5}{11}$
93. $6\frac{8}{9}$
94. $7\frac{5}{12}$
95. $4\frac{3}{16}$
96. $12\frac{3}{4}$
97. $30\frac{3}{5}$
98. $42\frac{1}{2}$
99. $15\frac{2}{3}$
100. $17\frac{1}{10}$
101. $14\frac{1}{8}$
102. $25\frac{3}{4}$
103. $21\frac{2}{3}$
104. $16\frac{4}{5}$
105. $85\frac{3}{4}$

skills file

Multiplying fractions and mixed numbers, pages 16-17

1. $\frac{1}{2} \times \frac{1}{8}$

2. $\frac{1}{3} \times \frac{4}{5}$

3. $\frac{3}{5} \times \frac{1}{4}$

4. $\frac{1}{4} \times \frac{1}{2}$

5. $\frac{2}{3} \times \frac{1}{6}$

6. $\frac{1}{2} \times \frac{5}{8}$

7. $\frac{3}{7} \times \frac{1}{3}$

8. $\frac{1}{4} \times \frac{8}{9}$

9. $\frac{4}{5} \times \frac{3}{8}$

10. $\frac{5}{9} \times \frac{3}{5}$

11. $\frac{2}{3} \times \frac{7}{8}$

12. $\frac{9}{10} \times \frac{5}{6}$

13. $\frac{5}{8} \times \frac{2}{3}$

14. $\frac{3}{4} \times \frac{8}{9}$

15. $\frac{5}{6} \times \frac{7}{10}$

16. $\frac{4}{5} \times \frac{15}{16}$

17. $\frac{8}{9} \times \frac{9}{16}$

18. $\frac{2}{3} \times \frac{5}{6}$

19. $\frac{7}{8} \times \frac{4}{7}$

20. $\frac{8}{15} \times \frac{3}{4}$

21. $\frac{5}{12} \times \frac{2}{5}$

22. $\frac{8}{11} \times \frac{3}{8}$

23. $\frac{2}{3} \times \frac{6}{7}$

24. $\frac{3}{14} \times \frac{7}{18}$

25. $\frac{15}{16} \times \frac{2}{3}$

26. $\frac{2}{7} \times \frac{3}{5}$

27. $\frac{1}{2} \times 15$

28. $\frac{3}{4} \times 28$

29. $7 \times \frac{1}{8}$

30. $\frac{2}{3} \times 21$

31. $15 \times \frac{1}{3}$

32. $\frac{1}{6} \times 50$

33. $\frac{1}{4} \times 56$

34. $\frac{4}{9} \times 24$

35. $45 \times \frac{7}{10}$

36. $\frac{4}{5} \times 20$

37. $\frac{1}{8} \times 72$

38. $\frac{4}{5} \times 100$

39. $36 \times \frac{5}{6}$

40. $\frac{3}{8} \times 52$

41. $\frac{7}{10} \times 48$

42. $350 \times \frac{4}{5}$

43. $\frac{1}{2} \times 1\frac{1}{2}$

44. $\frac{4}{7} \times 1\frac{2}{5}$

45. $1\frac{1}{5} \times \frac{1}{2}$

46. $\frac{2}{5} \times 4\frac{3}{8}$

47. $3\frac{1}{2} \times \frac{6}{7}$

48. $\frac{2}{3} \times 1\frac{5}{16}$

49. $2\frac{1}{4} \times \frac{2}{3}$

50. $1\frac{3}{8} \times \frac{8}{11}$

51. $\frac{9}{10} \times 1\frac{1}{4}$

52. $\frac{5}{6} \times 2\frac{1}{3}$

53. $6\frac{2}{3} \times \frac{3}{5}$

54. $5\frac{1}{4} \times \frac{1}{6}$

55. $\frac{3}{5} \times 3\frac{1}{7}$

56. $15\frac{3}{4} \times \frac{5}{9}$

57. $2\frac{4}{5} \times \frac{5}{18}$

58. $1\frac{2}{3} \times 2\frac{1}{5}$

59. $2\frac{1}{2} \times 3\frac{1}{3}$

60. $1\frac{1}{3} \times 3\frac{3}{4}$

61. $1\frac{5}{8} \times 1\frac{1}{7}$

62. $2\frac{1}{6} \times 1\frac{1}{2}$

63. $1\frac{1}{8} \times 5\frac{1}{3}$

64. $4\frac{4}{5} \times 1\frac{3}{8}$

65. $2\frac{1}{3} \times 3\frac{1}{2}$

66. $1\frac{3}{4} \times 2\frac{2}{3}$

67. $4\frac{1}{5} \times 7\frac{1}{7}$

68. $2\frac{2}{5} \times 3\frac{8}{9}$

69. $1\frac{2}{7} \times 2\frac{1}{3}$

70. $1\frac{1}{4} \times 2\frac{2}{9}$

71. $5\frac{1}{4} \times 1\frac{2}{3}$

72. $3\frac{3}{5} \times 4\frac{4}{9}$

73. $2\frac{1}{2} \times 9\frac{1}{5}$

74. $8\frac{3}{4} \times 1\frac{3}{7}$

75. $2\frac{1}{12} \times 2\frac{2}{15}$

76. $5\frac{1}{2} \times 3\frac{1}{6}$

77. $6\frac{3}{5} \times 2\frac{7}{9}$

78. $5\frac{5}{16} \times 4\frac{4}{15}$

79. $3 \times 1\frac{1}{2}$

80. $5\frac{1}{4} \times 3$

81. $1\frac{1}{8} \times 12$

82. $3\frac{2}{3} \times 9$

83. $6 \times 1\frac{7}{8}$

84. $5\frac{1}{6} \times 4$

85. $4\frac{1}{2} \times 4$

86. $9 \times 1\frac{5}{6}$

87. $4\frac{1}{3} \times 24$

88. $8 \times 1\frac{1}{12}$

89. $7\frac{2}{3} \times 4$

90. $\frac{2}{5} \times \frac{1}{2} \times \frac{1}{3}$

91. $\frac{3}{4} \times \frac{8}{9} \times \frac{9}{10}$

92. $\frac{3}{5} \times \frac{2}{7} \times 1\frac{2}{3}$

93. $3\frac{1}{8} \times \frac{2}{3} \times \frac{4}{5}$

94. $\frac{1}{9} \times 5\frac{1}{4} \times \frac{2}{7}$

95. $\frac{1}{2} \times 3\frac{1}{5} \times 1\frac{3}{4}$

96. $2\frac{1}{2} \times \frac{7}{10} \times 1\frac{3}{7}$

97. $4\frac{1}{8} \times 1\frac{3}{5} \times \frac{2}{3}$

98. $\frac{2}{3} \times \frac{3}{8} \times 5$

99. $\frac{5}{6} \times 3 \times \frac{4}{15}$

100. $\frac{3}{16} \times 2\frac{1}{3} \times 4$

101. $10 \times \frac{4}{5} \times 3\frac{1}{12}$

102. $3\frac{4}{5} \times 8 \times \frac{5}{16}$

103. $1\frac{3}{4} \times 2\frac{2}{3} \times 5$

104. $8 \times 6\frac{1}{4} \times 5\frac{1}{2}$

105. $2\frac{13}{16} \times 8 \times 1\frac{4}{9}$

skills file

Dividing fractions and mixed numbers, pages 16-17

1. $\frac{1}{2} \div \frac{2}{3}$

2. $\frac{3}{4} \div \frac{1}{2}$

3. $\frac{3}{5} \div \frac{1}{5}$

4. $\frac{1}{5} \div \frac{1}{3}$

5. $\frac{1}{4} \div \frac{1}{2}$

6. $\frac{4}{9} \div \frac{1}{3}$

7. $\frac{1}{10} \div \frac{1}{8}$

8. $\frac{3}{4} \div \frac{9}{10}$

9. $\frac{2}{3} \div \frac{4}{9}$

10. $\frac{2}{5} \div \frac{2}{3}$

11. $\frac{4}{7} \div \frac{6}{7}$

12. $\frac{5}{6} \div \frac{1}{2}$

13. $\frac{3}{10} \div \frac{4}{5}$

14. $\frac{1}{6} \div \frac{2}{5}$

15. $\frac{3}{4} \div \frac{7}{8}$

16. $\frac{2}{3} \div \frac{3}{4}$

17. $\frac{3}{10} \div \frac{5}{7}$

18. $\frac{1}{2} \div \frac{7}{8}$

19. $\frac{2}{7} \div \frac{4}{9}$

20. $\frac{5}{8} \div \frac{2}{3}$

21. $\frac{9}{16} \div \frac{5}{8}$

22. $\frac{1}{9} \div \frac{2}{3}$

23. $\frac{5}{12} \div \frac{5}{8}$

24. $\frac{3}{4} \div \frac{4}{5}$

25. $\frac{5}{9} \div \frac{2}{3}$

26. $\frac{4}{5} \div \frac{4}{7}$

27. $\frac{7}{8} \div \frac{1}{6}$

28. $\frac{3}{11} \div \frac{3}{8}$

29. $\frac{2}{5} \div \frac{3}{4}$

30. $\frac{7}{8} \div \frac{2}{3}$

31. $\frac{9}{16} \div \frac{5}{7}$

32. $\frac{1}{4} \div 2$

33. $\frac{3}{5} \div 3$

34. $\frac{2}{3} \div 2$

35. $\frac{1}{2} \div 3$

36. $\frac{3}{4} \div 5$

37. $\frac{5}{6} \div 2$

38. $\frac{3}{8} \div 6$

39. $\frac{9}{10} \div 3$

40. $\frac{4}{5} \div 10$

41. $\frac{8}{9} \div 12$

42. $\frac{7}{12} \div 4$

43. $6 \div \frac{1}{2}$

44. $5 \div \frac{2}{3}$

45. $3 \div \frac{3}{8}$

46. $1 \div \frac{3}{4}$

47. $4 \div \frac{4}{5}$

48. $8 \div \frac{4}{7}$

49. $2 \div \frac{4}{5}$

50. $7 \div \frac{1}{4}$

51. $10 \div \frac{5}{8}$

52. $8 \div \frac{3}{5}$

53. $9 \div \frac{6}{7}$

54. $\frac{1}{3} \div 1\frac{1}{9}$

55. $\frac{1}{2} \div 1\frac{1}{4}$

56. $\frac{3}{4} \div 7\frac{1}{2}$

57. $\frac{2}{5} \div 2\frac{3}{5}$

58. $\frac{3}{8} \div 3\frac{1}{2}$

59. $7\frac{1}{2} \div \frac{1}{2}$

60. $1\frac{1}{8} \div \frac{5}{6}$

61. $3\frac{3}{4} \div \frac{3}{8}$

62. $8\frac{1}{3} \div \frac{1}{6}$

63. $6\frac{2}{3} \div \frac{15}{16}$

64. $8\frac{1}{4} \div 3$

65. $2\frac{2}{3} \div 3$

66. $5\frac{1}{4} \div 7$

67. $3\frac{1}{5} \div 8$

68. $9\frac{1}{3} \div 7$

69. $8\frac{3}{4} \div 14$

70. $4 \div 1\frac{2}{3}$

71. $6 \div 1\frac{1}{8}$

72. $10 \div 4\frac{3}{8}$

73. $25 \div 3\frac{1}{3}$

74. $7 \div 2\frac{1}{2}$

75. $56 \div 1\frac{3}{5}$

76. $1\frac{7}{8} \div 3\frac{1}{3}$

77. $7\frac{1}{2} \div 1\frac{1}{2}$

78. $3\frac{7}{8} \div 1\frac{1}{4}$

79. $4\frac{1}{2} \div 2\frac{2}{5}$

80. $6\frac{2}{3} \div 7\frac{1}{2}$

81. $3\frac{3}{5} \div 2\frac{1}{4}$

82. $6\frac{1}{4} \div 2\frac{1}{2}$

83. $8\frac{2}{3} \div 2\frac{1}{6}$

84. $4\frac{1}{6} \div 3\frac{3}{4}$

85. $3\frac{1}{3} \div 2\frac{1}{12}$

86. $1\frac{1}{4} \div 7\frac{1}{2}$

87. $10\frac{1}{2} \div 1\frac{3}{4}$

88. $2\frac{7}{8} \div 1\frac{5}{8}$

89. $2\frac{3}{5} \div 3\frac{9}{10}$

90. $4\frac{2}{3} \div 1\frac{1}{6}$

91. $2\frac{4}{5} \div 1\frac{3}{4}$

92. $8\frac{2}{3} \div 2\frac{3}{5}$

93. $6\frac{3}{4} \div 4\frac{1}{2}$

94. $3\frac{1}{8} \div 1\frac{1}{3}$

95. $2\frac{3}{8} \div 1\frac{1}{2}$

96. $3\frac{3}{4} \div 1\frac{2}{3}$

97. $4\frac{1}{2} \div 2\frac{1}{4}$

98. $10\frac{1}{2} \div 2\frac{1}{3}$

99. $2\frac{2}{7} \div 5\frac{1}{3}$

100. $5\frac{5}{6} \div 1\frac{5}{9}$

101. $9\frac{1}{3} \div 2\frac{2}{5}$

102. $13\frac{3}{4} \div 1\frac{2}{3}$

103. $4\frac{9}{10} \div 2\frac{11}{12}$

104. $16\frac{2}{3} \div 2\frac{3}{11}$

105. $12\frac{3}{5} \div 1\frac{1}{7}$

skills file

Adding fractions and mixed numbers, pages 18-19

1. $\frac{3}{4} + \frac{3}{8}$
2. $\frac{1}{6} + \frac{1}{3}$
3. $\frac{1}{2} + \frac{1}{5}$
4. $\frac{2}{3} + \frac{1}{4}$
5. $\frac{1}{2} + \frac{3}{4}$
6. $\frac{7}{9} + \frac{1}{3}$
7. $\frac{1}{5} + \frac{2}{3}$
8. $\frac{5}{9} + \frac{1}{2}$
9. $\frac{1}{4} + \frac{1}{6}$
10. $\frac{7}{10} + \frac{1}{4}$
11. $\frac{1}{6} + \frac{3}{8}$
12. $\frac{1}{2} + \frac{4}{7}$
13. $\frac{2}{3} + \frac{1}{2}$
14. $\frac{3}{5} + \frac{7}{8}$
15. $\frac{8}{15} + \frac{1}{3}$
16. $\frac{1}{2} + \frac{7}{10}$
17. $\frac{9}{16} + \frac{3}{4}$
18. $\frac{1}{2} + \frac{5}{6}$
19. $\frac{7}{8} + \frac{2}{3}$
20. $\frac{5}{6} + \frac{3}{10}$
21. $\frac{8}{15} + \frac{4}{5}$
22. $\frac{7}{15} + \frac{9}{10}$
23. $\frac{11}{18} + \frac{5}{6}$
24. $\frac{1}{9} + \frac{7}{12}$
25. $2\frac{1}{8} + \frac{1}{4}$
26. $3\frac{1}{6} + \frac{1}{3}$
27. $8\frac{1}{2} + \frac{3}{8}$
28. $1\frac{1}{5} + \frac{3}{7}$
29. $7\frac{3}{10} + \frac{1}{6}$
30. $1\frac{3}{4} + \frac{1}{2}$
31. $5\frac{2}{3} + \frac{3}{4}$
32. $3\frac{5}{8} + \frac{2}{3}$
33. $4\frac{1}{2} + \frac{3}{5}$
34. $3\frac{5}{16} + \frac{7}{8}$
35. $12\frac{9}{10} + \frac{3}{5}$
36. $16\frac{1}{5} + \frac{5}{6}$
37. $2\frac{1}{6} + 5\frac{5}{6}$
38. $1\frac{1}{2} + 3\frac{3}{10}$
39. $4\frac{1}{2} + 1\frac{2}{3}$
40. $6\frac{3}{4} + 7\frac{5}{8}$
41. $5\frac{1}{6} + 8\frac{2}{9}$
42. $5\frac{3}{4} + 6\frac{1}{3}$
43. $7\frac{7}{16} + 4\frac{3}{8}$
44. $2\frac{7}{8} + 6\frac{5}{6}$
45. $5\frac{1}{6} + 8\frac{1}{2}$
46. $9\frac{2}{3} + 2\frac{7}{9}$
47. $5\frac{1}{7} + 3\frac{2}{3}$
48. $4\frac{1}{2} + 3\frac{3}{5}$
49. $6\frac{1}{4} + 2\frac{4}{5}$
50. $5\frac{1}{6} + 9\frac{3}{10}$
51. $9\frac{4}{5} + 3\frac{1}{2}$
52. $3\frac{6}{7} + 4\frac{1}{2}$
53. $7\frac{3}{4} + 8\frac{5}{12}$
54. $9\frac{4}{9} + 9\frac{3}{4}$
55. $8\frac{2}{3} + 5\frac{7}{10}$
56. $4\frac{11}{12} + 3\frac{1}{4}$
57. $7\frac{1}{2} + 2\frac{1}{3}$
58. $8\frac{8}{9} + 5\frac{5}{18}$
59. $16\frac{1}{3} + 2\frac{1}{6}$
60. $15\frac{3}{8} + 9\frac{3}{16}$
61. $1\frac{5}{8} + 2\frac{5}{8} + \frac{7}{8}$
62. $4\frac{2}{3} + 6\frac{1}{6} + \frac{1}{2}$
63. $4\frac{1}{2} + \frac{4}{5} + \frac{3}{5}$
64. $5\frac{5}{8} + 2\frac{1}{2} + \frac{7}{16}$
65. $3\frac{1}{12} + 2\frac{1}{3} + 5\frac{1}{6}$
66. $7\frac{11}{16} + 5\frac{1}{8} + 4\frac{1}{4}$
67. $3\frac{1}{2} + 5\frac{1}{8} + 6\frac{1}{4}$
68. $4\frac{4}{15} + 1\frac{5}{6} + 2\frac{1}{2}$

skills file

Subtracting fractions and mixed numbers, pages 18-19

1. $\frac{1}{2} - \frac{1}{4}$
2. $\frac{7}{8} - \frac{3}{4}$
3. $\frac{3}{5} - \frac{1}{2}$
4. $\frac{5}{6} - \frac{1}{3}$
5. $\frac{3}{4} - \frac{1}{5}$
6. $\frac{1}{2} - \frac{2}{5}$
7. $\frac{2}{3} - \frac{1}{4}$
8. $\frac{9}{10} - \frac{1}{2}$
9. $\frac{5}{8} - \frac{1}{2}$
10. $\frac{3}{5} - \frac{1}{10}$
11. $\frac{1}{3} - \frac{1}{12}$
12. $\frac{7}{10} - \frac{1}{2}$
13. $\frac{7}{9} - \frac{1}{3}$
14. $\frac{3}{4} - \frac{3}{10}$
15. $\frac{4}{5} - \frac{1}{6}$
16. $\frac{2}{3} - \frac{3}{8}$
17. $\frac{9}{10} - \frac{5}{6}$
18. $\frac{3}{4} - \frac{7}{12}$
19. $\frac{7}{8} - \frac{1}{6}$
20. $\frac{4}{5} - \frac{2}{3}$
21. $\frac{6}{7} - \frac{1}{2}$
22. $\frac{5}{6} - \frac{7}{10}$
23. $\frac{3}{4} - \frac{9}{16}$
24. $\frac{11}{12} - \frac{1}{8}$
25. $\frac{3}{7} - \frac{1}{5}$
26. $\frac{3}{4} - \frac{2}{3}$
27. $\frac{9}{16} - \frac{3}{8}$
28. $\frac{5}{12} - \frac{1}{6}$
29. $5 - \frac{3}{10}$
30. $2 - \frac{1}{2}$
31. $1 - \frac{4}{5}$
32. $7 - \frac{3}{4}$
33. $3 - \frac{1}{6}$
34. $6 - \frac{3}{7}$
35. $9 - \frac{2}{3}$
36. $10 - \frac{7}{8}$
37. $6 - 2\frac{1}{3}$
38. $4 - 3\frac{1}{2}$
39. $3 - 1\frac{5}{8}$
40. $5 - 2\frac{6}{7}$
41. $10 - 8\frac{3}{4}$
42. $9 - 5\frac{1}{6}$
43. $8 - 6\frac{7}{10}$
44. $7 - 3\frac{1}{8}$
45. $8\frac{4}{5} - 6\frac{1}{5}$
46. $4\frac{6}{7} - 3\frac{2}{7}$
47. $5\frac{3}{10} - 2\frac{9}{10}$
48. $5\frac{1}{4} - 2\frac{3}{4}$
49. $9\frac{3}{5} - 2\frac{1}{2}$
50. $6\frac{1}{2} - 1\frac{3}{4}$
51. $6\frac{1}{6} - 4\frac{1}{3}$
52. $4\frac{1}{2} - 1\frac{1}{3}$
53. $8\frac{3}{4} - 2\frac{1}{3}$
54. $7\frac{1}{10} - 5\frac{3}{5}$
55. $6\frac{2}{3} - 2\frac{5}{6}$
56. $8\frac{1}{4} - 2\frac{5}{6}$
57. $5\frac{3}{8} - 1\frac{7}{12}$
58. $4\frac{1}{4} - 1\frac{7}{10}$
59. $8\frac{3}{16} - 4\frac{5}{8}$
60. $9\frac{4}{5} - 7\frac{3}{4}$
61. $15\frac{1}{4} - 7\frac{3}{5}$
62. $8\frac{1}{10} - 2\frac{5}{6}$
63. $16\frac{5}{6} - 8\frac{1}{9}$
64. $11\frac{3}{8} - 9\frac{2}{3}$
65. $16\frac{1}{4} - 12\frac{3}{8}$
66. $18\frac{5}{6} - 13\frac{7}{12}$
67. $18\frac{3}{4} - 10\frac{5}{12}$
68. $11\frac{2}{3} - 5\frac{3}{4}$
69. $15\frac{3}{4} - 8\frac{4}{9}$
70. $13\frac{7}{12} - 9\frac{5}{8}$
71. $16\frac{1}{20} - 15\frac{4}{5}$
72. $18\frac{1}{10} - 6\frac{3}{5}$

skills file

Ratio and proportion, pages 30-31

Find the cross products. Tell whether the ratios are equal.

1. $\frac{2}{3}$ $\frac{6}{9}$
2. $\frac{5}{9}$ $\frac{11}{18}$
3. $\frac{5}{13}$ $\frac{4}{12}$
4. $\frac{2}{15}$ $\frac{6}{45}$
5. $\frac{4}{5}$ $\frac{12}{16}$
6. $\frac{10}{12}$ $\frac{4}{6}$
7. $\frac{15}{24}$ $\frac{5}{8}$
8. $\frac{7}{12}$ $\frac{28}{48}$
9. $\frac{8}{5}$ $\frac{28}{15}$
10. $\frac{20}{45}$ $\frac{4}{9}$
11. $\frac{11}{12}$ $\frac{35}{36}$
12. $\frac{8}{11}$ $\frac{40}{43}$
13. $\frac{6}{14}$ $\frac{15}{35}$
14. $\frac{24}{15}$ $\frac{16}{10}$
15. $\frac{39}{73}$ $\frac{13}{21}$
16. $\frac{12}{15}$ $\frac{26}{30}$
17. $\frac{14}{38}$ $\frac{21}{57}$
18. $\frac{.2}{5}$ $\frac{.3}{7}$
19. $\frac{6}{1.8}$ $\frac{.3}{9}$
20. $\frac{8}{12}$ $\frac{2.4}{3.2}$
21. $\frac{1.8}{2.7}$ $\frac{42}{63}$
22. $\frac{9}{2.1}$ $\frac{21.3}{5}$
23. $\frac{2}{.3}$ $\frac{42}{6.3}$
24. $\frac{4.8}{5.6}$ $\frac{18}{21}$
25. $\frac{12}{28}$ $\frac{1.6}{4.2}$
26. $\frac{2.5}{7}$ $\frac{4}{11.2}$
27. $\frac{.8}{3}$ $\frac{2.7}{10}$
28. $\frac{44}{1.1}$ $\frac{12}{.3}$
29. $\frac{7.5}{6}$ $\frac{4}{3.2}$
30. $\frac{1.35}{3.6}$ $\frac{1.5}{4}$
31. $\frac{7.9}{4}$ $\frac{16.1}{8.6}$
32. $\frac{17}{1.5}$ $\frac{8.3}{.6}$
33. $\frac{1.8}{16.5}$ $\frac{.6}{5.5}$
34. $\frac{.8}{3.5}$ $\frac{2.4}{10.5}$
35. $\frac{2.8}{4.5}$ $\frac{2.1}{3.5}$

Solve and check.

36. $\frac{c}{15} = \frac{2}{5}$
37. $\frac{2}{3} = \frac{n}{18}$
38. $\frac{14}{s} = \frac{7}{9}$
39. $\frac{65}{10} = \frac{13}{m}$
40. $\frac{9}{10} = \frac{r}{30}$
41. $\frac{50}{a} = \frac{10}{3}$
42. $\frac{34}{72} = \frac{17}{n}$
43. $\frac{d}{45} = \frac{7}{9}$
44. $\frac{22}{t} = \frac{66}{27}$
45. $\frac{6}{1} = \frac{78}{h}$
46. $\frac{f}{16} = \frac{45}{48}$
47. $\frac{19}{57} = \frac{k}{21}$
48. $\frac{30}{4} = \frac{36}{x}$
49. $\frac{w}{4} = \frac{9}{24}$
50. $\frac{18}{15} = \frac{v}{18}$
51. $\frac{8}{y} = \frac{5}{9}$
52. $\frac{s}{18} = \frac{8}{15}$
53. $\frac{.5}{.9} = \frac{b}{2.7}$
54. $\frac{2.4}{r} = \frac{.8}{1.7}$
55. $\frac{.04}{.14} = \frac{18}{t}$
56. $\frac{.12}{.45} = \frac{f}{.3}$
57. $\frac{.04}{g} = \frac{.32}{.56}$
58. $\frac{.2}{.7} = \frac{.6}{b}$
59. $\frac{x}{16} = \frac{2.4}{3.2}$
60. $\frac{5.6}{c} = \frac{1.4}{7.3}$
61. $\frac{.5}{8.9} = \frac{36}{n}$
62. $\frac{a}{1.26} = \frac{4}{.72}$
63. $\frac{.08}{.6} = \frac{t}{3.3}$
64. $\frac{.2}{.15} = \frac{7}{w}$
65. $\frac{h}{8} = \frac{23.7}{3}$
66. $\frac{7.52}{4} = \frac{m}{6}$
67. $\frac{.8}{y} = \frac{4.8}{9}$
68. $\frac{d}{5.6} = \frac{1.4}{2.8}$
69. $\frac{.18}{.29} = \frac{2.88}{x}$
70. $\frac{9.6}{4.7} = \frac{t}{2.35}$

skills file

Writing percents, decimals, and fractions, pages 34-35

Write as a decimal.

1. 27%
2. 45%
3. 74%
4. 53%
5. 20%
6. 90%
7. 7%
8. 4%
9. 16.9%
10. 81.8%
11. 51.3%
12. 20.7%
13. 7.2%
14. 3.9%
15. 8.23%
16. 1.04%
17. $7\frac{1}{2}\%$
18. $4\frac{3}{4}\%$
19. $23\frac{1}{4}\%$
20. $6\frac{1}{8}\%$
21. 900%
22. 130%
23. 256%
24. 108%

Write as a fraction in lowest terms.

49. 80%
50. 10%
51. 75%
52. 30%
53. 90%
54. 25%
55. 62%
56. 49%
57. 31%
58. 58%
59. 43%
60. 99%
61. 23%
62. 88%
63. 11%
64. 64%
65. 78%
66. 91%
67. 66%
68. 73%
69. 110%
70. 103%
71. 140%
72. 250%

Write as a percent.

25. .37
26. .48
27. .65
28. .19
29. .02
30. .07
31. .8
32. .3
33. .096
34. .353
35. .727
36. .941
37. .503
38. .802
39. .6492
40. .2734
41. .8077
42. .1209
43. .0188
44. .0566
45. 1.08
46. 6.39
47. 7.149
48. 3.027

Write as a percent.

73. $\frac{10}{20}$
74. $\frac{1}{2}$
75. $\frac{3}{4}$
76. $\frac{3}{5}$
77. $\frac{1}{25}$
78. $\frac{1}{4}$
79. $\frac{2}{5}$
80. $\frac{3}{20}$
81. $\frac{37}{50}$
82. $\frac{21}{25}$
83. $\frac{13}{20}$
84. $\frac{12}{50}$
85. $\frac{16}{25}$
86. $\frac{7}{20}$
87. $\frac{1}{5}$
88. $\frac{4}{25}$
89. $\frac{49}{50}$
90. $\frac{1}{8}$
91. $\frac{5}{8}$
92. $\frac{1}{32}$
93. $\frac{3}{16}$
94. $\frac{15}{16}$
95. $\frac{29}{32}$
96. $\frac{23}{4}$
97. $\frac{15}{2}$
98. $\frac{17}{5}$
99. $\frac{51}{25}$

skills file

Percent problems, pages 36-38

1. 60% of 30 is ▒.
2. 25% of 60 is ▒.
3. 90% of 50 is ▒.
4. 6% of 77 is ▒.
5. 89% of 351 is ▒.
6. $7\frac{1}{4}\%$ of 800 is ▒.
7. $9\frac{1}{2}\%$ of 420 is ▒.
8. 43% of 1341 is ▒.
9. Find 82% of 12.
10. Find 8% of 91.
11. Find 65% of 200.
12. Find 20% of 790.
13. Find 14% of 660.
14. Find 73% of 555.
15. Find 3% of 309.
16. Find 56% of 56.
17. What number is 7% of 81?
18. What number is 23% of 57?
19. What number is 68% of 2700?
20. What number is 52% of 900?
21. What number is 7.2% of 500?
22. What number is 9.6% of 780?
23. What number is 3.5% of 655?
24. 5% of ▒ is 2.
25. 80% of ▒ is 26.
26. 40% of ▒ is 81.
27. 14% of ▒ is 21.
28. 13% of ▒ is 21.84.
29. 30% of ▒ is 99.
30. 40% of ▒ is 21.
31. 24% of ▒ is 11.04.
32. 17% of ▒ is 40.8.
33. 80% of ▒ is 39.
34. $8\frac{1}{2}\%$ of ▒ is 51.
35. $5\frac{1}{4}\%$ of ▒ is 42.
36. 60% of what number is 18?
37. 8% of what number is 10?
38. 17% of what number is 85?
39. $37\frac{1}{2}\%$ of what number is 63?
40. $67\frac{1}{2}\%$ of what number is 3375?
41. 6.3 is 20% of what number?
42. 8.4 is 70% of what number?
43. 95 is $6\frac{1}{4}\%$ of what number?
44. 27 is $12\frac{1}{2}\%$ of what number?
45. ▒% of 50 is 24.
46. ▒% of 25 is 17.
47. ▒% of 51 is 1.53.
48. ▒% of 50 is 4.
49. ▒% of 80 is 12.
50. ▒% of 66 is 36.3
51. ▒% of 115 is 23.
52. ▒% of 520 is 364.
53. ▒% of 25 is 13.
54. ▒% of 30 is 2.4.
55. ▒% of 35 is .7.
56. ▒% of 200 is 64.
57. What percent of 90 is 18?
58. What percent of 40 is 6?
59. What percent of 48 is 18?
60. What percent of 56 is 35?
61. What percent of 50 is 47?
62. 42 is what percent of 48?
63. 70 is what percent of 80?
64. 18.4 is what percent of 23?
65. 12 is what percent of 32?

tables

Metric System

Length

10 millimeters (mm) = 1 centimeter (cm)
10 centimeters, 100 millimeters = 1 decimeter (dm)
10 decimeters, 100 centimeters = 1 meter (m)
1000 meters = 1 kilometer (km)

Area

100 square millimeters (mm^2) = 1 square centimeter (cm^2)
10,000 square centimeters = 1 square meter (m^2)
100 square meters = 1 are (a)
10,000 square meters = 1 hectare (ha)

Volume

1000 cubic millimeters (mm^3) = 1 cubic centimeter (cm^3)
1000 cubic centimeters = 1 cubic decimeter (dm^3)
1,000,000 cubic centimeters = 1 cubic meter (m^3)

Mass

1000 milligrams (mg) = 1 gram (g)
1000 grams = 1 kilogram (kg)
1000 kilograms = 1 metric ton (t)

Capacity

1000 milliliters (mL) = 1 liter (L)
1000 liters = 1 kiloliter (kL)

United States Customary System

Length

12 inches (in.) = 1 foot (ft.)
3 feet, 36 inches = 1 yard (yd.)
1760 yards, 5280 feet = 1 mile (mi.)
6076 feet = 1 nautical mile

Area

144 square inches (sq. in.) = 1 square foot (sq. ft.)
9 square feet = 1 square yard (sq. yd.)
4840 square yards = 1 acre (A.)

Volume

1728 cubic inches (cu. in.) = 1 cubic foot (cu. ft.)
27 cubic feet = 1 cubic yard (cu. yd.)

Weight

16 ounces (oz.) = 1 pound (lb.)
2000 pounds = 1 ton (T.)

Capacity

8 fluid ounces (fl. oz.) = 1 cup (c.)
2 cups = 1 pint (pt.)
2 pints = 1 quart (qt.)
4 quarts = 1 gallon (gal.)

Symbols

$\approx$	approximately equal to
$\overline{AB}$	segment AB
$\angle G$	angle G
45°	45 degrees
∟	right angle
$\sqrt{25}$	square root of 25

Geometric Formulas

Perimeter
rectangle $P = 2l + 2w$

Circumference
circle $C = \pi d$ or $C = 2\pi r$

Area
rectangle $A = lw$
square $A = s^2$
parallelogram $A = bh$
triangle $A = \frac{1}{2}bh$
trapezoid $A = \frac{1}{2}h(a + b)$
circle $A = \pi r^2$

Surface area
rectangular prism $A = 2lw + 2lh + 2wh$
cube $A = 6s^2$
cylinder $A = 2\pi rh + 2\pi r^2$

Volume
rectangular prism $V = lwh$
cube $V = s^3$
cylinder $V = \pi r^2 h$
rectangular pyramid $V = \frac{1}{3}lwh$
cone $V = \frac{1}{3}\pi r^2 h$
sphere $V = \frac{4}{3}\pi r^3$

SINGLE PERSONS – Weekly Pay Period

And the wages are–		Exemptions claimed										
At least	But less than	0	1	2	3	4	5	6	7	8	9	10 or more
		The amount of income tax to be withheld shall be—										
$0	$25	$0	$0	$0	$0	$0	$0	$0	$0	$0	$0	$0
25	26	.10	0	0	0	0	0	0	0	0	0	0
26	27	.20	0	0	0	0	0	0	0	0	0	0
27	28	.40	0	0	0	0	0	0	0	0	0	0
28	29	.60	0	0	0	0	0	0	0	0	0	0
29	30	.70	0	0	0	0	0	0	0	0	0	0
30	31	.90	0	0	0	0	0	0	0	0	0	0
31	32	1.00	0	0	0	0	0	0	0	0	0	0
32	33	1.20	0	0	0	0	0	0	0	0	0	0
33	34	1.40	0	0	0	0	0	0	0	0	0	0
34	35	1.50	0	0	0	0	0	0	0	0	0	0
35	36	1.70	0	0	0	0	0	0	0	0	0	0
36	37	1.80	0	0	0	0	0	0	0	0	0	0
37	38	2.00	0	0	0	0	0	0	0	0	0	0
38	39	2.20	0	0	0	0	0	0	0	0	0	0
39	40	2.30	0	0	0	0	0	0	0	0	0	0
40	41	2.50	.20	0	0	0	0	0	0	0	0	0
41	42	2.60	.30	0	0	0	0	0	0	0	0	0
42	43	2.80	.50	0	0	0	0	0	0	0	0	0
43	44	3.00	.70	0	0	0	0	0	0	0	0	0
44	45	3.10	.80	0	0	0	0	0	0	0	0	0
45	46	3.30	1.00	0	0	0	0	0	0	0	0	0
46	47	3.40	1.10	0	0	0	0	0	0	0	0	0
47	48	3.60	1.30	0	0	0	0	0	0	0	0	0
48	49	3.80	1.50	0	0	0	0	0	0	0	0	0
49	50	3.90	1.60	0	0	0	0	0	0	0	0	0
50	51	4.10	1.80	0	0	0	0	0	0	0	0	0
51	52	4.20	1.90	0	0	0	0	0	0	0	0	0
52	53	4.40	2.10	0	0	0	0	0	0	0	0	0
53	54	4.60	2.30	0	0	0	0	0	0	0	0	0
At least	But less than	0	1	2	3	4	5	6	7	8	9	10 or more
54	55	4.70	2.40	.10	0	0	0	0	0	0	0	0
55	56	4.90	2.60	.30	0	0	0	0	0	0	0	0
56	57	5.00	2.70	.40	0	0	0	0	0	0	0	0
57	58	5.20	2.90	.60	0	0	0	0	0	0	0	0
58	59	5.40	3.10	.70	0	0	0	0	0	0	0	0
59	60	5.50	3.20	.90	0	0	0	0	0	0	0	0
60	62	5.80	3.50	1.10	0	0	0	0	0	0	0	0
62	64	6.10	3.80	1.50	0	0	0	0	0	0	0	0
64	66	6.40	4.10	1.80	0	0	0	0	0	0	0	0
66	68	6.70	4.40	2.10	0	0	0	0	0	0	0	0
68	70	7.10	4.70	2.40	.10	0	0	0	0	0	0	0
70	72	7.50	5.10	2.70	.40	0	0	0	0	0	0	0
72	74	7.90	5.40	3.10	.80	0	0	0	0	0	0	0
74	76	8.30	5.70	3.40	1.10	0	0	0	0	0	0	0
76	78	8.70	6.00	3.70	1.40	0	0	0	0	0	0	0
78	80	9.10	6.30	4.00	1.70	0	0	0	0	0	0	0
80	82	9.50	6.70	4.30	2.00	0	0	0	0	0	0	0
82	84	9.90	7.00	4.70	2.40	0	0	0	0	0	0	0
84	86	10.30	7.40	5.00	2.70	.40	0	0	0	0	0	0
86	88	10.70	7.80	5.30	3.00	.70	0	0	0	0	0	0
88	90	11.10	8.20	5.60	3.30	1.00	0	0	0	0	0	0
90	92	11.50	8.60	5.90	3.60	1.30	0	0	0	0	0	0
92	94	11.90	9.00	6.30	4.00	1.60	0	0	0	0	0	0
94	96	12.30	9.40	6.60	4.30	2.00	0	0	0	0	0	0
96	98	12.70	9.80	6.90	4.60	2.30	0	0	0	0	0	0
98	100	13.10	10.20	7.30	4.90	2.60	.30	0	0	0	0	0
100	105	13.80	10.90	8.00	5.50	3.20	.90	0	0	0	0	0
105	110	14.80	11.90	9.00	6.30	4.00	1.70	0	0	0	0	0
110	115	15.80	12.90	10.00	7.20	4.80	2.50	.20	0	0	0	0
115	120	16.90	13.90	11.00	8.20	5.60	3.30	1.00	0	0	0	0

SINGLE PERSONS - Weekly Pay Period

And the wages are-		Exemptions claimed										
At least	But less than	0	1	2	3	4	5	6	7	8	9	10 or more
		The amount of income tax to be withheld shall be—										
$120	$125	$18.00	$14.90	$12.00	$9.20	$6.40	$4.10	$1.80	$0	$0	$0	$0
125	130	19.20	15.90	13.00	10.20	7.30	4.90	2.60	.20	0	0	0
130	135	20.30	17.00	14.00	11.20	8.30	5.70	3.40	1.00	0	0	0
135	140	21.50	18.20	15.00	12.20	9.30	6.50	4.20	1.80	0	0	0
140	145	22.60	19.30	16.00	13.20	10.30	7.40	5.00	2.60	.30	0	0
145	150	23.80	20.50	17.10	14.20	11.30	8.40	5.80	3.40	1.10	0	0
150	160	25.50	22.20	18.90	15.70	12.80	9.90	7.00	4.60	2.30	0	0
160	170	27.80	24.50	21.20	17.80	14.80	11.90	9.00	6.20	3.90	1.60	0
170	180	30.10	26.80	23.50	20.10	16.80	13.90	11.00	8.10	5.50	3.20	.90
180	190	32.40	29.10	25.80	22.40	19.10	15.90	13.00	10.10	7.20	4.80	2.50
190	200	34.50	31.40	28.10	24.70	21.40	18.10	15.00	12.10	9.20	6.40	4.10
200	210	36.60	33.50	30.40	27.00	23.70	20.40	17.10	14.10	11.20	8.30	5.70
210	220	38.70	35.60	32.60	29.30	26.00	22.70	19.40	16.10	13.20	10.30	7.50
220	230	40.80	37.70	34.70	31.60	28.30	25.00	21.70	18.40	15.20	12.30	9.50
230	240	42.90	39.80	36.80	33.80	30.60	27.30	24.00	20.70	17.40	14.30	11.50
240	250	45.20	41.90	38.90	35.90	32.80	29.60	26.30	23.00	19.70	16.30	13.50
250	260	47.80	44.00	41.00	38.00	34.90	31.90	28.60	25.30	22.00	18.60	15.50
260	270	50.40	46.60	43.10	40.10	37.00	34.00	30.90	27.60	24.30	20.90	17.60
270	280	53.00	49 20	45.50	42.20	39.10	36.10	33.10	29.90	26.60	23.20	19.90
280	290	55.80	51.80	48.10	44.30	41.20	38.20	35.20	32.10	28.90	25.50	22.20
290	300	58.80	54.50	50.70	46.90	43.30	40.30	37.30	34.20	31.20	27.80	24.50
300	310	61.60	57.50	53.30	49.50	45.80	42.40	39.40	36.30	33.30	30.10	26.80
310	320	64.80	60.50	56.20	52.10	48.40	44.60	41.50	38.40	35.40	32.40	29.10
320	330	67.80	63.50	59.20	54.80	51.00	47.20	43.60	40.50	37.50	34.50	31.40
330	340	70.80	66.50	62.20	57.80	53.60	49.80	46.10	42.60	39.60	36.60	33.60
340	350	73.80	69.50	65.20	60.80	56.50	52.40	48.70	44.90	41.70	38.70	35.70
350	360	77.40	72.50	68.20	63.80	59.50	55.20	51.30	47.50	43.80	40.80	37.80
360	370	81.00	75.80	71.20	66.80	62.50	58.20	53.90	50.10	46.40	42.90	39.90
370	380	84.60	79.40	74.20	69.80	65.50	61.20	56.90	52.70	49.00	45.20	42.00
380	390	88.20	83.00	77.80	72.80	68.50	64.20	59.90	55.50	51.60	47.80	44.10
At least	But less than	0	1	2	3	4	5	6	7	8	9	10 or more
390	400	91.80	86.60	81.40	76.20	71.50	67.20	62.90	58.50	54.20	50.40	46.70
400	410	95.40	90.20	85.00	79.80	74.60	70.20	65.90	61.50	57.20	53.00	49.30
410	420	99.00	93.80	88.60	83.40	78.20	73.20	68.90	64.50	60.20	55.90	51.90
420	430	102.60	97.40	92.20	87.00	81.80	76.60	71.90	67.50	63.20	58.90	54.60
430	440	106.20	101.00	95.80	90.60	85.40	80.20	75.00	70.50	66.20	61.90	57.60
440	450	109.80	104.60	99.40	94.20	89.00	83.80	78.60	73.50	69.20	64.90	60.60
450	460	113.40	108.20	103.00	97.80	92.60	87.40	82.20	77.00	72.20	67.90	63.60
460	470	117.00	111.80	106.60	101.40	96.20	91.00	85.80	80.60	75.40	70.90	66.60
470	480	120.60	115.40	110.20	105.00	99.80	94.60	89.40	84.20	79.00	73.90	69.60
480	490	124.20	119.00	113.80	108.60	103.40	98.20	93.00	87.80	82.60	77.40	72.60
490	500	127.80	122.60	117.40	112.20	107.00	101.80	96.60	91.40	86.20	81.00	75.80
500	510	131.40	126.20	121.00	115.80	110.60	105.40	100.20	95.00	89.80	84.60	79.40
510	520	135.00	129.80	124.60	119.40	114.20	109.00	103.80	98.60	93.40	88.20	83.00
520	530	138.60	133.40	128.20	123.00	117.80	112.60	107.40	102.20	97.00	91.80	86.60
530	540	142.20	137.00	131.80	126.60	121.40	116.20	111.00	105.80	100.60	95.40	90.20
540	550	145.80	140.60	135.40	130.20	125.00	119.80	114.60	109.40	104.20	99.00	93.80
550	560	149.40	144.20	139.00	133.80	128.60	123.40	118.20	113.00	107.80	102.60	97.40
560	570	153.00	147.80	142.60	137.40	132.20	127.00	121.80	116.60	111.40	106.20	101.00
570	580	156.60	151.40	146.20	141.00	135.80	130.60	125.40	120.20	115.00	109.80	104.60
580	590	160.20	155.00	149.80	144.60	139.40	134.20	129.00	123.80	118.60	113.40	108.20
590	600	163.80	158.60	153.40	148.20	143.00	137.80	132.60	127.40	122.20	117.00	111.80
600	610	167.40	162.20	157.00	151.80	146.60	141.40	136.20	131.00	125.80	120.60	115.40
610	620	171.00	165.80	160.60	155.40	150.20	145.00	139.80	134.60	129.40	124.20	119.00
620	630	174.60	169.40	164.20	159.00	153.80	148.60	143.40	138.20	133.00	127.80	122.60
630	640	178.20	173.00	167.80	162.60	157.40	152.20	147.00	141.80	136.60	131.40	126.20
		36 percent of the excess over $640 plus—										
$640 and over		180.00	174.80	169.60	164.40	159.20	154.00	148.80	143.60	138.40	133.20	128.00

MARRIED PERSONS - Weekly Pay Period

And the wages are-		Exemptions claimed										
At least	But less than	0	1	2	3	4	5	6	7	8	9	10 or more
		The amount of income tax to be withheld shall be—										
$0	$48	$0	$0	$0	$0	$0	$0	$0	$0	$0	$0	$0
48	49	.10	0	0	0	0	0	0	0	0	0	0
49	50	.20	0	0	0	0	0	0	0	0	0	0
50	51	.40	0	0	0	0	0	0	0	0	0	0
51	52	.60	0	0	0	0	0	0	0	0	0	0
52	53	.80	0	0	0	0	0	0	0	0	0	0
53	54	.90	0	0	0	0	0	0	0	0	0	0
54	55	1.10	0	0	0	0	0	0	0	0	0	0
55	56	1.30	0	0	0	0	0	0	0	0	0	0
56	57	1.40	0	0	0	0	0	0	0	0	0	0
57	58	1.60	0	0	0	0	0	0	0	0	0	0
58	59	1.80	0	0	0	0	0	0	0	0	0	0
59	60	1.90	0	0	0	0	0	0	0	0	0	0
60	62	2.20	0	0	0	0	0	0	0	0	0	0
62	64	2.50	.10	0	0	0	0	0	0	0	0	0
64	66	2.90	.40	0	0	0	0	0	0	0	0	0
66	68	3.20	.80	0	0	0	0	0	0	0	0	0
68	70	3.60	1.10	0	0	0	0	0	0	0	0	0
70	72	3.90	1.40	0	0	0	0	0	0	0	0	0
72	74	4.20	1.80	0	0	0	0	0	0	0	0	0
74	76	4.60	2.10	0	0	0	0	0	0	0	0	0
76	78	4.90	2.50	0	0	0	0	0	0	0	0	0
78	80	5.30	2.80	.40	0	0	0	0	0	0	0	0
80	82	5.60	3.10	.70	0	0	0	0	0	0	0	0
82	84	5.90	3.50	1.00	0	0	0	0	0	0	0	0
84	86	6.30	3.80	1.40	0	0	0	0	0	0	0	0
86	88	6.60	4.20	1.70	0	0	0	0	0	0	0	0
88	90	7.00	4.50	2.10	0	0	0	0	0	0	0	0
90	92	7.30	4.80	2.40	0	0	0	0	0	0	0	0
92	94	7.60	5.20	2.70	.30	0	0	0	0	0	0	0
At least	But less than	0	1	2	3	4	5	6	7	8	9	10 or more
94	96	8.00	5.50	3.10	.60	0	0	0	0	0	0	0
96	98	8.30	5.90	3.40	1.00	0	0	0	0	0	0	0
98	100	8.70	6.20	3.80	1.30	0	0	0	0	0	0	0
100	105	9.40	6.80	4.30	1.90	0	0	0	0	0	0	0
105	110	10.40	7.70	5.20	2.70	.30	0	0	0	0	0	0
110	115	11.40	8.60	6.00	3.60	1.10	0	0	0	0	0	0
115	120	12.40	9.60	6.90	4.40	2.00	0	0	0	0	0	0
120	125	13.40	10.60	7.70	5.30	2.80	.40	0	0	0	0	0
125	130	14.40	11.60	8.70	6.10	3.70	1.20	0	0	0	0	0
130	135	15.40	12.60	9.70	7.00	4.50	2.10	0	0	0	0	0
135	140	16.40	13.60	10.70	7.80	5.40	2.90	.50	0	0	0	0
140	145	17.40	14.60	11.70	8.80	6.20	3.80	1.30	0	0	0	0
145	150	18.40	15.60	12.70	9.80	7.10	4.60	2.20	0	0	0	0
150	160	19.90	17.10	14.20	11.30	8.40	5.90	3.50	1.00	0	0	0
160	170	21.90	19.10	16.20	13.30	10.40	7.60	5.20	2.70	.30	0	0
170	180	23.90	21.10	18.20	15.30	12.40	9.50	6.90	4.40	2.00	0	0
180	190	25.60	23.10	20.20	17.30	14.40	11.50	8.60	6.10	3.70	1.20	0
190	200	27.30	24.80	22.20	19.30	16.40	13.50	10.60	7.80	5.40	2.90	.50
200	210	29.00	26.50	24.10	21.30	18.40	15.50	12.60	9.80	7.10	4.60	2.20
210	220	30.70	28.20	25.80	23.30	20.40	17.50	14.60	11.80	8.90	6.30	3.90
220	230	32.40	29.90	27.50	25.00	22.40	19.50	16.60	13.80	10.90	8.00	5.60
230	240	34.10	31.60	29.20	26.70	24.30	21.50	18.60	15.80	12.90	10.00	7.30
240	250	35.80	33.30	30.90	28.40	26.00	23.50	20.60	17.80	14.90	12.00	9.10
250	260	37.50	35.00	32.60	30.10	27.70	25.20	22.60	19.80	16.90	14.00	11.10
260	270	39.20	36.70	34.30	31.80	29.40	26.90	24.50	21.80	18.90	16.00	13.10
270	280	41.70	38.40	36.00	33.50	31.10	28.60	26.20	23.70	20.90	18.00	15.10
280	290	44.20	40.60	37.70	35.20	32.80	30.30	27.90	25.40	22.90	20.00	17.10
290	300	46.70	43.10	39.50	36.90	34.50	32.00	29.60	27.10	24.70	22.00	19.10
300	310	49.20	45.60	42.00	38.60	36.20	33.70	31.30	28.80	26.40	23.90	21.10
310	320	51.70	48.10	44.50	40.90	37.90	35.40	33.00	30.50	28.10	25.60	23.10

MARRIED PERSONS - Weekly Pay Period

And the wages are-		Exemptions claimed										
At least	But less than	0	1	2	3	4	5	6	7	8	9	10 or more
		The amount of income tax to be withheld shall be—										
$320	$330	$54.20	$50.60	$47.00	$43.40	$39.80	$37.10	$34.70	$32.20	$29.80	$27.30	$24.90
330	340	56.70	53.10	49.50	45.90	42.30	38.80	36.40	33.90	31.50	29.00	26.60
340	350	59.20	55.60	52.00	48.40	44.80	41.20	38.10	35.60	33.20	30.70	28.30
350	360	62.00	58.10	54.50	50.90	47.30	43.70	40.10	37.30	34.90	32.40	30.00
360	370	64.80	60.80	57.00	53.40	49.80	46.20	42.60	39.00	36.60	34.10	31.70
370	380	67.60	63.60	59.50	55.90	52.30	48.70	45.10	41.50	38.30	35.80	33.40
380	390	70.40	66.40	62.30	58.40	54.80	51.20	47.60	44.00	40.40	37.50	35.10
390	400	73.20	69.20	65.10	61.10	57.30	53.70	50.10	46.50	42.90	39.30	36.80
400	410	76.00	72.00	67.90	63.90	59.80	56.20	52.60	49.00	45.40	41.80	38.50
410	420	78.80	74.80	70.70	66.70	62.60	58.70	55.10	51.50	47.90	44.30	40.70
420	430	81.60	77.60	73.50	69.50	65.40	61.40	57.60	54.00	50.40	46.80	43.20
430	440	84.50	80.40	76.30	72.30	68.20	64.20	60.20	56.50	52.90	49.30	45.70
440	450	87.70	83.20	79.10	75.10	71.00	67.00	63.00	59.00	55.40	51.80	48.20
450	460	90.90	86.30	81.90	77.90	73.80	69.80	65.80	61.70	57.90	54.30	50.70
460	470	94.10	89.50	84.90	80.70	76.60	72.60	68.60	64.50	60.50	56.80	53.20
470	480	97.30	92.70	88.10	83.50	79.40	75.40	71.40	67.30	63.30	59.30	55.70
480	490	100.50	95.90	91.30	86.60	82.20	78.20	74.20	70.10	66.10	62.10	58.20
490	500	103.70	99.10	94.50	89.80	85.20	81.00	77.00	72.90	68.90	64.90	60.80
500	510	107.10	102.30	97.70	93.00	88.40	83.80	79.80	75.70	71.70	67.70	63.60
510	520	110.70	105.50	100.90	96.20	91.60	87.00	82.60	78.50	74.50	70.50	66.40
520	530	114.30	109.10	104.10	99.40	94.80	90.20	85.60	81.30	77.30	73.30	69.20
530	540	117.90	112.70	107.50	102.60	98.00	93.40	88.80	84.20	80.10	76.10	72.00
540	550	121.50	116.30	111.10	105.90	101.20	96.60	92.00	87.40	82.90	78.90	74.80
550	560	125.10	119.90	114.70	109.50	104.40	99.80	95.20	90.60	86.00	81.70	77.60
560	570	128.70	123.50	118.30	113.10	107.90	103.00	98.40	93.80	89.20	84.60	80.40
570	580	132.30	127.10	121.90	116.70	111.50	106.30	101.60	97.00	92.40	87.80	83.20
580	590	135.90	130.70	125.50	120.30	115.10	109.90	104.80	100.20	95.60	91.00	86.30
590	600	139.50	134.30	129.10	123.90	118.70	113.50	108.30	103.40	98.80	94.20	89.50
600	610	143.10	137.90	132.70	127.50	122.30	117.10	111.90	106.70	102.00	97.40	92.70
610	620	146.70	141.50	136.30	131.10	125.90	120.70	115.50	110.30	105.20	100.60	95.90
At least	But less than	0	1	2	3	4	5	6	7	8	9	10 or more
620	630	150.30	145.10	139.90	134.70	129.50	124.30	119.10	113.90	108.80	103.80	99.10
630	640	153.90	148.70	143.50	138.30	133.10	127.90	122.70	117.50	112.40	107.20	102.30
640	650	157.50	152.30	147.10	141.90	136.70	131.50	126.30	121.10	116.00	110.80	105.60
650	660	161.10	155.90	150.70	145.50	140.30	135.10	129.90	124.70	119.60	114.40	109.20
660	670	164.70	159.50	154.30	149.10	143.90	138.70	133.50	128.30	123.20	118.00	112.80
670	680	168.30	163.10	157.90	152.70	147.50	142.30	137.10	131.90	126.80	121.60	116.40
680	690	171.90	166.70	161.50	156.30	151.10	145.90	140.70	135.50	130.40	125.20	120.00
690	700	175.50	170.30	165.10	159.90	154.70	149.50	144.30	139.10	134.00	128.80	123.60
700	710	179.10	173.90	168.70	163.50	158.30	153.10	147.90	142.70	137.60	132.40	127.20
710	720	182.70	177.50	172.30	167.10	161.90	156.70	151.50	146.30	141.20	136.00	130.80
720	730	186.30	181.10	175.90	170.70	165.50	160.30	155.10	149.90	144.80	139.60	134.40
730	740	189.90	184.70	179.50	174.30	169.10	163.90	158.70	153.50	148.40	143.20	138.00
740	750	193.50	188.30	183.10	177.90	172.70	167.50	162.30	157.10	152.00	146.80	141.60
750	760	197.10	191.90	186.70	181.50	176.30	171.10	165.90	160.70	155.60	150.40	145.20
760	770	200.70	195.50	190.30	185.10	179.90	174.70	169.50	164.30	159.20	154.00	148.80
770	780	204.30	199.10	193.90	188.70	183.50	178.30	173.10	167.90	162.80	157.60	152.40
780	790	207.90	202.70	197.50	192.30	187.10	181.90	176.70	171.50	166.40	161.20	156.00
790	800	211.50	206.30	201.10	195.90	190.70	185.50	180.30	175.10	170.00	164.80	159.60
800	810	215.10	209.90	204.70	199.50	194.30	189.10	183.90	178.70	173.60	168.40	163.20
810	820	218.70	213.50	208.30	203.10	197.90	192.70	187.50	182.30	177.20	172.00	166.80
820	830	222.30	217.10	211.90	206.70	201.50	196.30	191.10	185.90	180.80	175.60	170.40
830	840	225.90	220.70	215.50	210.30	205.10	199.90	194.70	189.50	184.40	179.20	174.00
840	850	229.50	224.30	219.10	213.90	208.70	203.50	198.30	193.10	188.00	182.80	177.60
850	860	233.10	227.90	222.70	217.50	212.30	207.10	201.90	196.70	191.60	186.40	181.20
860	870	236.70	231.50	226.30	221.10	215.90	210.70	205.50	200.30	195.20	190.00	184.80
		36 percent of the excess over $870 plus—										
$870 and over		238.50	233.30	228.10	222.90	217.70	212.50	207.30	202.10	197.00	191.80	186.60

Annual rate	Monthly payment per $1 borrowed					
	6 mo.	12 mo.	18 mo.	24 mo.	30 mo.	36 mo.
7%	.17008	.08653	.05869	.04477	.03643	.03088
8%	.17058	.08699	.05914	.04523	.03689	.03134
8.5%	.17082	.08722	.05937	.04546	.03712	.03157
9%	.17107	.08745	.05960	.04568	.03735	.03180
9.5%	.17131	.08768	.05983	.04591	.03758	.03203
10%	.17156	.08792	.06006	.04614	.03781	.03227
11%	.17205	.08838	.06052	.04661	.03828	.03274
12%	.17255	.08885	.06098	.04707	.03875	.03321
14%	.17354	.08979	.06192	.04801	.03970	.03418
16%	.17453	.09073	.06286	.04896	.04066	.03516
18%	.17553	.09168	.06381	.04992	.04164	.03615
20%	.17652	.09263	.06476	.05090	.04263	.03716
22%	.17752	.09359	.06573	.05188	.04363	.03819

1976 Tax Table

Based on Taxable Income For Persons with Taxable Incomes of $20,000 or less

If line 15 (taxable income) is— Over	But not over	And you are— Single	Married filing separately	Head of a household	Married filing jointly *
		Your tax is—			
0	4	0	0	0	0
4	25	2	2	2	2
25	50	5	5	5	5
50	75	9	9	9	9
75	100	12	12	12	12
100	125	16	16	16	16
125	150	19	19	19	19
150	175	23	23	23	23
175	200	26	26	26	26
200	225	30	30	30	30
225	250	33	33	33	33
250	275	37	37	37	37
275	300	40	40	40	40
300	325	44	44	44	44
325	350	47	47	47	47
350	375	51	51	51	51
375	400	54	54	54	54
400	425	58	58	58	58
425	450	61	61	61	61
450	475	65	65	65	65
475	500	68	68	68	68
500	525	72	72	72	72
525	550	76	76	75	75
550	575	79	79	79	79
575	600	83	83	82	82
600	625	87	87	86	86
625	650	91	91	89	89
650	675	94	94	93	93
675	700	98	98	96	96
700	725	102	102	100	100
725	750	106	106	103	103
750	775	109	109	107	107
775	800	113	113	110	110
800	825	117	117	114	114
825	850	121	121	117	117
850	875	124	124	121	121
875	900	128	128	124	124
900	925	132	132	128	128
925	950	136	136	131	131
950	975	139	139	135	135
975	1,000	143	143	138	138
1,000	1,025	147	147	142	142
1,025	1,050	151	151	146	146
1,050	1,075	155	155	150	149
1,075	1,100	159	159	154	153
1,100	1,125	163	163	158	157
1,125	1,150	167	167	162	161
1,150	1,175	171	171	166	164
1,175	1,200	175	175	170	168
1,200	1,225	179	179	174	172
1,225	1,250	183	183	178	176
1,250	1,275	187	187	182	179

If line 15 (taxable income) is— Over	But not over	And you are— Single	Married filing separately	Head of a household	Married filing jointly *
		Your tax is—			
1,275	1,300	191	191	186	183
1,300	1,325	195	195	190	187
1,325	1,350	199	199	194	191
1,350	1,375	203	203	198	194
1,375	1,400	207	207	202	198
1,400	1,425	211	211	206	202
1,425	1,450	215	215	210	206
1,450	1,475	219	219	214	209
1,475	1,500	223	223	218	213
1,500	1,525	227	227	222	217
1,525	1,550	231	231	226	221
1,550	1,575	236	236	230	224
1,575	1,600	240	240	234	228
1,600	1,625	244	244	238	232
1,625	1,650	248	248	242	236
1,650	1,675	253	253	246	239
1,675	1,700	257	257	250	243
1,700	1,725	261	261	254	247
1,725	1,750	265	265	258	251
1,750	1,775	270	270	262	254
1,775	1,800	274	274	266	258
1,800	1,825	278	278	270	262
1,825	1,850	282	282	274	266
1,850	1,875	287	287	278	269
1,875	1,900	291	291	282	273
1,900	1,925	295	295	286	277
1,925	1,950	299	299	290	281
1,950	1,975	304	304	294	284
1,975	2,000	308	308	298	288
2,000	2,025	312	312	302	292
2,025	2,050	317	317	307	296
2,050	2,075	322	322	311	300
2,075	2,100	327	327	316	304
2,100	2,125	331	331	320	308
2,125	2,150	336	336	325	312
2,150	2,175	341	341	329	316
2,175	2,200	346	346	334	320
2,200	2,225	350	350	338	324
2,225	2,250	355	355	343	328
2,250	2,275	360	360	347	332
2,275	2,300	365	365	352	336
2,300	2,325	369	369	356	340
2,325	2,350	374	374	361	344
2,350	2,375	379	379	365	348
2,375	2,400	384	384	370	352
2,400	2,425	388	388	374	356
2,425	2,450	393	393	379	360
2,450	2,475	398	398	383	364
2,475	2,500	403	403	388	368
2,500	2,525	407	407	392	372
2,525	2,550	412	412	397	376
2,550	2,575	417	417	401	380

If line 15 (taxable income) is— Over	But not over	And you are— Single	Married filing separately	Head of a household	Married filing jointly *
		Your tax is—			
2,575	2,600	422	422	406	384
2,600	2,625	426	426	410	388
2,625	2,650	431	431	415	392
2,650	2,675	436	436	419	396
2,675	2,700	441	441	424	400
2,700	2,725	445	445	428	404
2,725	2,750	450	450	433	408
2,750	2,775	455	455	437	412
2,775	2,800	460	460	442	416
2,800	2,825	464	464	446	420
2,825	2,850	469	469	451	424
2,850	2,875	474	474	455	428
2,875	2,900	479	479	460	432
2,900	2,925	483	483	464	436
2,925	2,950	488	488	469	440
2,950	2,975	493	493	473	444
2,975	3,000	498	498	478	448
3,000	3,050	505	505	485	454
3,050	3,100	514	514	494	463
3,100	3,150	524	524	503	471
3,150	3,200	533	533	512	480
3,200	3,250	543	543	521	488
3,250	3,300	552	552	530	497
3,300	3,350	562	562	539	505
3,350	3,400	571	571	548	514
3,400	3,450	581	581	557	522
3,450	3,500	590	590	566	531
3,500	3,550	600	600	575	539
3,550	3,600	609	609	584	548
3,600	3,650	619	619	593	556
3,650	3,700	628	628	602	565
3,700	3,750	638	638	611	573
3,750	3,800	647	647	620	582
3,800	3,850	657	657	629	590
3,850	3,900	666	666	638	599
3,900	3,950	676	676	647	607
3,950	4,000	685	685	656	616
4,000	4,050	695	696	665	625
4,050	4,100	706	707	674	634
4,100	4,150	716	718	684	644
4,150	4,200	727	729	693	653
4,200	4,250	737	740	703	663
4,250	4,300	748	751	712	672
4,300	4,350	758	762	722	682
4,350	4,400	769	773	731	691
4,400	4,450	779	784	741	701
4,450	4,500	790	795	750	710
4,500	4,550	800	806	760	720
4,550	4,600	811	817	769	729
4,600	4,650	821	828	779	739
4,650	4,700	832	839	788	748
4,700	4,750	842	850	798	758

*This column is to be used by a qualifying widow(er).

Continued on next page

If line 15 (taxable income) is—		And you are—			
Over	But not over	Single	Married filing separately	Head of a household	Married filing jointly *
		Your tax is—			
4,750	4,800	853	861	807	767
4,800	4,850	863	872	817	777
4,850	4,900	874	883	826	786
4,900	4,950	884	894	836	796
4,950	5,000	895	905	845	805
5,000	5,050	905	916	855	815
5,050	5,100	916	927	864	824
5,100	5,150	926	938	874	834
5,150	5,200	937	949	883	843
5,200	5,250	947	960	893	853
5,250	5,300	958	971	902	862
5,300	5,350	968	982	912	872
5,350	5,400	979	993	921	881
5,400	5,450	989	1,004	931	891
5,450	5,500	1,000	1,015	940	900
5,500	5,550	1,010	1,026	950	910
5,550	5,600	1,021	1,037	959	919
5,600	5,650	1,031	1,048	969	929
5,650	5,700	1,042	1,059	978	938
5,700	5,750	1,052	1,070	988	948
5,750	5,800	1,063	1,081	997	957
5,800	5,850	1,073	1,092	1,007	967
5,850	5,900	1,084	1,103	1,016	976
5,900	5,950	1,094	1,114	1,026	986
5,950	6,000	1,105	1,125	1,035	995
6,000	6,050	1,116	1,136	1,046	1,005
6,050	6,100	1,128	1,149	1,057	1,014
6,100	6,150	1,140	1,161	1,068	1,024
6,150	6,200	1,152	1,174	1,079	1,033
6,200	6,250	1,164	1,186	1,090	1,043
6,250	6,300	1,176	1,199	1,101	1,052
6,300	6,350	1,188	1,211	1,112	1,062
6,350	6,400	1,200	1,224	1,123	1,071
6,400	6,450	1,212	1,236	1,134	1,081
6,450	6,500	1,224	1,249	1,145	1,090
6,500	6,550	1,236	1,261	1,156	1,100
6,550	6,600	1,248	1,274	1,167	1,109
6,600	6,650	1,260	1,286	1,178	1,119
6,650	6,700	1,272	1,299	1,189	1,128
6,700	6,750	1,284	1,311	1,200	1,138
6,750	6,800	1,296	1,324	1,211	1,147
6,800	6,850	1,308	1,336	1,222	1,157
6,850	6,900	1,320	1,349	1,233	1,166
6,900	6,950	1,332	1,361	1,244	1,176
6,950	7,000	1,344	1,374	1,255	1,185
7,000	7,050	1,356	1,386	1,266	1,195
7,050	7,100	1,368	1,399	1,277	1,204
7,100	7,150	1,380	1,411	1,288	1,214
7,150	7,200	1,392	1,424	1,299	1,223
7,200	7,250	1,404	1,436	1,310	1,233
7,250	7,300	1,416	1,449	1,321	1,242
7,300	7,350	1,428	1,461	1,332	1,252
7,350	7,400	1,440	1,474	1,343	1,261
7,400	7,450	1,452	1,486	1,354	1,271
7,450	7,500	1,464	1,499	1,365	1,280
7,500	7,550	1,476	1,511	1,376	1,290
7,550	7,600	1,488	1,524	1,387	1,299
7,600	7,650	1,500	1,536	1,398	1,309
7,650	7,700	1,512	1,549	1,409	1,318
7,700	7,750	1,524	1,561	1,420	1,328

If line 15 (taxable income) is—		And you are—			
Over	But not over	Single	Married filing separately	Head of a household	Married filing jointly *
		Your tax is—			
7,750	7,800	1,536	1,574	1,431	1,337
7,800	7,850	1,548	1,586	1,442	1,347
7,850	7,900	1,560	1,599	1,453	1,356
7,900	7,950	1,572	1,611	1,464	1,366
7,950	8,000	1,584	1,624	1,475	1,375
8,000	8,050	1,596	1,637	1,486	1,386
8,050	8,100	1,609	1,651	1,497	1,397
8,100	8,150	1,621	1,665	1,509	1,408
8,150	8,200	1,634	1,679	1,520	1,419
8,200	8,250	1,646	1,693	1,532	1,430
8,250	8,300	1,659	1,707	1,543	1,441
8,300	8,350	1,671	1,721	1,555	1,452
8,350	8,400	1,684	1,735	1,566	1,463
8,400	8,450	1,696	1,749	1,578	1,474
8,450	8,500	1,709	1,763	1,589	1,485
8,500	8,550	1,721	1,777	1,601	1,496
8,550	8,600	1,734	1,791	1,612	1,507
8,600	8,650	1,746	1,805	1,624	1,518
8,650	8,700	1,759	1,819	1,635	1,529
8,700	8,750	1,771	1,833	1,647	1,540
8,750	8,800	1,784	1,847	1,658	1,551
8,800	8,850	1,796	1,861	1,670	1,562
8,850	8,900	1,809	1,875	1,681	1,573
8,900	8,950	1,821	1,889	1,693	1,584
8,950	9,000	1,834	1,903	1,704	1,595
9,000	9,050	1,846	1,917	1,716	1,606
9,050	9,100	1,859	1,931	1,727	1,617
9,100	9,150	1,871	1,945	1,739	1,628
9,150	9,200	1,884	1,959	1,750	1,639
9,200	9,250	1,896	1,973	1,762	1,650
9,250	9,300	1,909	1,987	1,773	1,661
9,300	9,350	1,921	2,001	1,785	1,672
9,350	9,400	1,934	2,015	1,796	1,683
9,400	9,450	1,946	2,029	1,808	1,694
9,450	9,500	1,959	2,043	1,819	1,705
9,500	9,550	1,971	2,057	1,831	1,716
9,550	9,600	1,984	2,071	1,842	1,727
9,600	9,650	1,996	2,085	1,854	1,738
9,650	9,700	2,009	2,099	1,865	1,749
9,700	9,750	2,021	2,113	1,877	1,760
9,750	9,800	2,034	2,127	1,888	1,771
9,800	9,850	2,046	2,141	1,900	1,782
9,850	9,900	2,059	2,155	1,911	1,793
9,900	9,950	2,071	2,169	1,923	1,804
9,950	10,000	2,084	2,183	1,934	1,815
10,000	10,050	2,097	2,198	1,946	1,826
10,050	10,100	2,110	2,214	1,959	1,837
10,100	10,150	2,124	2,230	1,971	1,848
10,150	10,200	2,137	2,246	1,984	1,859
10,200	10,250	2,151	2,262	1,996	1,870
10,250	10,300	2,164	2,278	2,009	1,881
10,300	10,350	2,178	2,294	2,021	1,892
10,350	10,400	2,191	2,310	2,034	1,903
10,400	10,450	2,205	2,326	2,046	1,914
10,450	10,500	2,218	2,342	2,059	1,925
10,500	10,550	2,232	2,358	2,071	1,936
10,550	10,600	2,245	2,374	2,084	1,947
10,600	10,650	2,259	2,390	2,096	1,958
10,650	10,700	2,272	2,406	2,109	1,969
10,700	10,750	2,286	2,422	2,121	1,980

If line 15 (taxable income) is—		And you are—			
Over	But not over	Single	Married filing separately	Head of a household	Married filing jointly *
		Your tax is—			
10,750	10,800	2,299	2,438	2,134	1,991
10,800	10,850	2,313	2,454	2,146	2,002
10,850	10,900	2,326	2,470	2,159	2,013
10,900	10,950	2,340	2,486	2,171	2,024
10,950	11,000	2,353	2,502	2,184	2,035
11,000	11,050	2,367	2,518	2,196	2,046
11,050	11,100	2,380	2,534	2,209	2,057
11,100	11,150	2,394	2,550	2,221	2,068
11,150	11,200	2,407	2,566	2,234	2,079
11,200	11,250	2,421	2,582	2,246	2,090
11,250	11,300	2,434	2,598	2,259	2,101
11,300	11,350	2,448	2,614	2,271	2,112
11,350	11,400	2,461	2,630	2,284	2,123
11,400	11,450	2,475	2,646	2,296	2,134
11,450	11,500	2,488	2,662	2,309	2,145
11,500	11,550	2,502	2,678	2,321	2,156
11,550	11,600	2,515	2,694	2,334	2,167
11,600	11,650	2,529	2,710	2,346	2,178
11,650	11,700	2,542	2,726	2,359	2,189
11,700	11,750	2,556	2,742	2,371	2,200
11,750	11,800	2,569	2,758	2,384	2,211
11,800	11,850	2,583	2,774	2,396	2,222
11,850	11,900	2,596	2,790	2,409	2,233
11,900	11,950	2,610	2,806	2,421	2,244
11,950	12,000	2,623	2,822	2,434	2,255
12,000	12,050	2,637	2,839	2,447	2,266
12,050	12,100	2,652	2,857	2,460	2,279
12,100	12,150	2,666	2,875	2,474	2,291
12,150	12,200	2,681	2,893	2,487	2,304
12,200	12,250	2,695	2,911	2,501	2,316
12,250	12,300	2,710	2,929	2,514	2,329
12,300	12,350	2,724	2,947	2,528	2,341
12,350	12,400	2,739	2,965	2,541	2,354
12,400	12,450	2,753	2,983	2,555	2,366
12,450	12,500	2,768	3,001	2,568	2,379
12,500	12,550	2,782	3,019	2,582	2,391
12,550	12,600	2,797	3,037	2,595	2,404
12,600	12,650	2,811	3,055	2,609	2,416
12,650	12,700	2,826	3,073	2,622	2,429
12,700	12,750	2,840	3,091	2,636	2,441
12,750	12,800	2,855	3,109	2,649	2,454
12,800	12,850	2,869	3,127	2,663	2,466
12,850	12,900	2,884	3,145	2,676	2,479
12,900	12,950	2,898	3,163	2,690	2,491
12,950	13,000	2,913	3,181	2,703	2,504
13,000	13,050	2,927	3,199	2,717	2,516
13,050	13,100	2,942	3,217	2,730	2,529
13,100	13,150	2,956	3,235	2,744	2,541
13,150	13,200	2,971	3,253	2,757	2,554
13,200	13,250	2,985	3,271	2,771	2,566
13,250	13,300	3,000	3,289	2,784	2,579
13,300	13,350	3,014	3,307	2,798	2,591
13,350	13,400	3,029	3,325	2,811	2,604
13,400	13,450	3,043	3,343	2,825	2,616
13,450	13,500	3,058	3,361	2,838	2,629
13,500	13,550	3,072	3,379	2,852	2,641
13,550	13,600	3,087	3,397	2,865	2,654
13,600	13,650	3,101	3,415	2,879	2,666
13,650	13,700	3,116	3,433	2,892	2,679
13,700	13,750	3,130	3,451	2,906	2,691

*This column is to be used by a qualifying widow(er).

Continued on next page

If line 15 (taxable income) is—		And you are—				If line 15 (taxable income) is—		And you are—				If line 15 (taxable income) is—		And you are—			
Over	But not over	Single	Married filing separately	Head of a household	Married filing jointly *	Over	But not over	Single	Married filing separately	Head of a household	Married filing jointly *	Over	But not over	Single	Married filing separately	Head of a household	Married filing jointly *
		Your tax is—						Your tax is—						Your tax is—			
13,750	13,800	3,145	3,469	2,919	2,704	15,950	16,000	3,822	4,320	3,533	3,254	18,150	18,200	4,573	5,249	4,216	3,869
13,800	13,850	3,159	3,487	2,933	2,716	16,000	16,050	3,839	4,341	3,548	3,267	18,200	18,250	4,591	5,271	4,232	3,883
13,850	13,900	3,174	3,505	2,946	2,729	16,050	16,100	3,856	4,362	3,563	3,281	18,250	18,300	4,609	5,294	4,248	3,897
13,900	13,950	3,188	3,523	2,960	2,741	16,100	16,150	3,873	4,383	3,579	3,295	18,300	18,350	4,627	5,316	4,264	3,911
13,950	14,000	3,203	3,541	2,973	2,754	16,150	16,200	3,890	4,404	3,594	3,309	18,350	18,400	4,645	5,339	4,280	3,925
14,000	14,050	3,218	3,560	2,987	2,766	16,200	16,250	3,907	4,425	3,610	3,323	18,400	18,450	4,663	5,361	4,296	3,939
14,050	14,100	3,233	3,579	3,001	2,779	16,250	16,300	3,924	4,446	3,625	3,337	18,450	18,500	4,681	5,384	4,312	3,953
14,100	14,150	3,249	3,599	3,015	2,791	16,300	16,350	3,941	4,467	3,641	3,351	18,500	18,550	4,699	5,406	4,328	3,967
14,150	14,200	3,264	3,618	3,029	2,804	16,350	16,400	3,958	4,488	3,656	3,365	18,550	18,600	4,717	5,429	4,344	3,981
14,200	14,250	3,280	3,638	3,043	2,816	16,400	16,450	3,975	4,509	3,672	3,379	18,600	18,650	4,735	5,451	4,360	3,995
14,250	14,300	3,295	3,657	3,057	2,829	16,450	16,500	3,992	4,530	3,687	3,393	18,650	18,700	4,753	5,474	4,376	4,009
14,300	14,350	3,311	3,677	3,071	2,841	16,500	16,550	4,009	4,551	3,703	3,407	18,700	18,750	4,771	5,496	4,392	4,023
14,350	14,400	3,326	3,696	3,085	2,854	16,550	16,600	4,026	4,572	3,718	3,421	18,750	18,800	4,789	5,519	4,408	4,037
14,400	14,450	3,342	3,716	3,099	2,866	16,600	16,650	4,043	4,593	3,734	3,435	18,800	18,850	4,807	5,541	4,424	4,051
14,450	14,500	3,357	3,735	3,113	2,879	16,650	16,700	4,060	4,614	3,749	3,449	18,850	18,900	4,825	5,564	4,440	4,065
14,500	14,550	3,373	3,755	3,127	2,891	16,700	16,750	4,077	4,635	3,765	3,463	18,900	18,950	4,843	5,586	4,456	4,079
14,550	14,600	3,388	3,774	3,141	2,904	16,750	16,800	4,094	4,656	3,780	3,477	18,950	19,000	4,861	5,609	4,472	4,093
14,600	14,650	3,404	3,794	3,155	2,916	16,800	16,850	4,111	4,677	3,796	3,491	19,000	19,050	4,879	5,631	4,488	4,107
14,650	14,700	3,419	3,813	3,169	2,929	16,850	16,900	4,128	4,698	3,811	3,505	19,050	19,100	4,897	5,654	4,504	4,121
14,700	14,750	3,435	3,833	3,183	2,941	16,900	16,950	4,145	4,719	3,827	3,519	19,100	19,150	4,915	5,676	4,520	4,135
14,750	14,800	3,450	3,852	3,197	2,954	16,950	17,000	4,162	4,740	3,842	3,533	19,150	19,200	4,933	5,699	4,536	4,149
14,800	14,850	3,466	3,872	3,211	2,966	17,000	17,050	4,179	4,761	3,858	3,547	19,200	19,250	4,951	5,721	4,552	4,163
14,850	14,900	3,481	3,891	3,225	2,979	17,050	17,100	4,196	4,782	3,873	3,561	19,250	19,300	4,969	5,744	4,568	4,177
14,900	14,950	3,497	3,911	3,239	2,991	17,100	17,150	4,213	4,803	3,889	3,575	19,300	19,350	4,987	5,766	4,584	4,191
14,950	15,000	3,512	3,930	3,253	3,004	17,150	17,200	4,230	4,824	3,904	3,589	19,350	19,400	5,005	5,789	4,600	4,205
15,000	15,050	3,528	3,950	3,267	3,016	17,200	17,250	4,247	4,845	3,920	3,603	19,400	19,450	5,023	5,811	4,616	4,219
15,050	15,100	3,543	3,969	3,281	3,029	17,250	17,300	4,264	4,866	3,935	3,617	19,450	19,500	5,041	5,834	4,632	4,233
15,100	15,150	3,559	3,989	3,295	3,041	17,300	17,350	4,281	4,887	3,951	3,631	19,500	19,550	5,059	5,856	4,648	4,247
15,150	15,200	3,574	4,008	3,309	3,054	17,350	17,400	4,298	4,908	3,966	3,645	19,550	19,600	5,077	5,879	4,664	4,261
15,200	15,250	3,590	4,028	3,323	3,066	17,400	17,450	4,315	4,929	3,982	3,659	19,600	19,650	5,095	5,901	4,680	4,275
15,250	15,300	3,605	4,047	3,337	3,079	17,450	17,500	4,332	4,950	3,997	3,673	19,650	19,700	5,113	5,924	4,696	4,289
15,300	15,350	3,621	4,067	3,351	3,091	17,500	17,550	4,349	4,971	4,013	3,687	19,700	19,750	5,131	5,946	4,712	4,303
15,350	15,400	3,636	4,086	3,365	3,104	17,550	17,600	4,366	4,992	4,028	3,701	19,750	19,800	5,149	5,969	4,728	4,317
15,400	15,450	3,652	4,106	3,379	3,116	17,600	17,650	4,383	5,013	4,044	3,715	19,800	19,850	5,167	5,991	4,744	4,331
15,450	15,500	3,667	4,125	3,393	3,129	17,650	17,700	4,400	5,034	4,059	3,729	19,850	19,900	5,185	6,014	4,760	4,345
15,500	15,550	3,683	4,145	3,407	3,141	17,700	17,750	4,417	5,055	4,075	3,743	19,900	19,950	5,203	6,036	4,776	4,359
15,550	15,600	3,698	4,164	3,421	3,154	17,750	17,800	4,434	5,076	4,090	3,757	19,950	20,000	5,221	6,059	4,792	4,373
15,600	15,650	3,714	4,184	3,435	3,166	17,800	17,850	4,451	5,097	4,106	3,771						
15,650	15,700	3,729	4,203	3,449	3,179	17,850	17,900	4,468	5,118	4,121	3,785						
15,700	15,750	3,745	4,223	3,463	3,191	17,900	17,950	4,485	5,139	4,137	3,799						
15,750	15,800	3,760	4,242	3,477	3,204	17,950	18,000	4,502	5,160	4,152	3,813						
15,800	15,850	3,776	4,262	3,491	3,216	18,000	18,050	4,519	5,181	4,168	3,827						
15,850	15,900	3,791	4,281	3,505	3,229	18,050	18,100	4,537	5,204	4,184	3,841						
15,900	15,950	3,807	4,301	3,519	3,241	18,100	18,150	4,555	5,226	4,200	3,855						

*This column is to be used by a qualifying widow(er).

metric system

Length

The base unit of length is the meter. The width of a door is about one meter.

Millimeter, centimeter, and kilometer are other commonly used units of length.

The thickness of the wire in a paper clip is about one millimeter.

The diameter of an ordinary piece of chalk is almost one centimeter.

A distance of five city blocks is about one kilometer. It takes about ten minutes to walk one kilometer.

Time

The base unit of time is the second. Other units of time in the metric system are familiar units such as minutes and hours.

Mass

The base unit of mass is the kilogram.* The mass of this butter is about one kilogram.

Gram is another commonly used unit of mass. The mass of an aspirin is about one gram.

Temperature

The base unit of temperature is the kelvin. However, the Celsius scale is commonly used in countries employing the metric system.

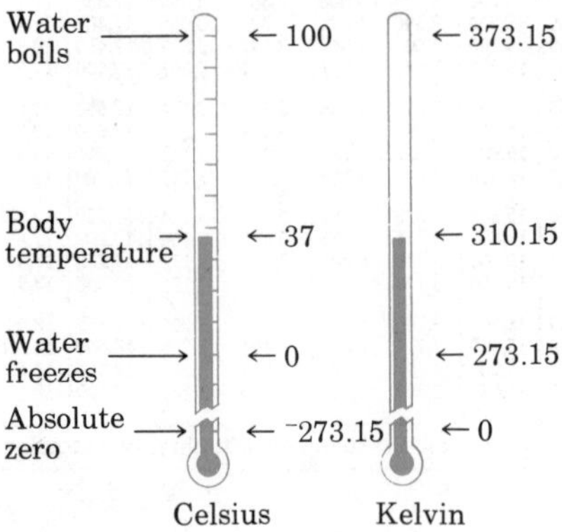

*The mass of an object is the same on the moon as it is on the earth. The gravitational force on an object is less on the moon than it is on the earth.

In common usage, units of mass are often referred to as units of weight. The term *weight* is also used to mean the gravitional force on an object.

Area

Square meter and square centimeter are commonly used units of area. The area of this thumbnail is about one square centimeter.

1 square centimeter

Volume

Cubic meter and cubic centimeter are commonly used units of volume. The amount of water in this eyedropper is one cubic centimeter, or one milliliter. The mass of the water is one gram.

1 cubic centimeter
1 milliliter
1 gram

Cubic decimeter is another unit of volume. This carton holds almost one cubic decimeter, or one liter. If it were filled with water, the mass of the water would be about one kilogram.

1 cubic decimeter
1 liter
1 kilogram

Prefixes and symbols

This table shows the most commonly used prefixes in the metric system.

Prefix	Symbol	Meaning
mega-	M	million
kilo-	k	thousand
hecto-	h	hundred
deka-	da	ten
deci-	d	tenth
centi-	c	hundredth
milli-	m	thousandth
micro-	μ	millionth

Here are symbols for some of the metric units of measure. Periods are not used after these symbols, and an *-s* is not added for the plural form.

Unit of measure	Symbol
meter*	m
kilometer	km
centimeter	cm
millimeter	mm
liter*	L
milliliter	mL
kilogram	kg
gram	g
milligram	mg
square meter	m^2
square centimeter	cm^2
square millimeter	mm^2
cubic meter	m^3
cubic decimeter	dm^3
cubic centimeter	cm^3
cubic millimeter	mm^3

*The root words *meter* and *liter* may be spelled "metre" and "litre." The "-er" spelling appears in this book and is in common usage in the United States.

careers chart

This four-page chart gives information about jobs in eight career clusters: Trades, Technical, Science, Health, Arts, Social Service, Business Contact, and Business Detail.* These clusters cover most of the occupations and educational programs which people enter.

The following code is used under the heading "Qualifications."

C 4 years or more of college required
S Special training required (technical or vocational school, junior college, or apprenticeship)
— No college or special training required

Trades	Qualifications	Estimated employment in 1970	Average annual openings to 1980
Air-conditioning, refrigeration, or heating mechanic	S	115,000	7900
Aircraft mechanic	S	140,000	6000
Appliance service person	—	220,000	11,000
Assembler	—	865,000	44,000
Automobile mechanic	—	610,000	23,300
Bricklayer	S	175,000	8500
Carpenter	S	830,000	46,000
Electrician (construction)	S	190,000	12,000
Industrial machinery repair person	S	180,000	9000
Inspector	S	665,000	29,700
Instrument repair person	S	95,000	5900
Machine tool operator	—	425,000	9600
Machinist	S	530,000	16,600
Maintenance electrician	S	250,000	11,000
Meatcutter	S	190,000	5000
Millwright	S	80,000	3100
Painter or paperhanger	—	390,000	22,000
Plumber or pipefitter	S	350,000	20,000
Power truck operator	—	200,000	5100
Supervisor	S	1,488,000	56,500
Television or radio service technician	S	132,000	4500
Tool and die maker	S	165,000	4700
Truck and bus mechanic	—	115,000	5200
Welder or oxygen and arc cutter	—	535,000	22,000

*Cluster titles are from the American College Testing Career Planning Profile, 1971. Information about jobs is from the "Occupational Outlook Handbook in Brief," *Occupational Outlook Quarterly,* vol. 16, no. 1, Spring, 1972 and the *Occupational Outlook Handbook, 1974–75 Edition.*

Technical	Qualifications	Estimated employment in 1970	Average annual openings to 1980
Aerospace engineer	C	65,000	1500
Air traffic controller	C	20,000	800
Chemical engineer	C	50,000	1700
Civil engineer	C	185,000	10,000
Drafter	S	310,000	16,300
Electrical engineer	C	235,000	12,200
Engineering and science technician	S	650,000	33,000
Forester	C	22,000	1000
Industrial engineer	C	125,000	8000
Mechanical engineer	C	220,000	10,100
Pilot or copilot	S	49,000	4800
Technical writer	C	20,000	1000

Science			
Chemist	C	137,000	9400
Economist	C	33,000	2300
Geologist	C	23,000	500
Home economist	C	105,000	6700
Life scientist	C	180,000	9900
Mathematician	C	75,000	4600
Physicist	C	48,000	3500

Health			
Dental assistant	—	91,000	9200
Dentist	C	103,000	5400
Dietitian	C	30,000	2300
Medical assistant	—	175,000	20,000
Medical laboratory worker	C	110,000	13,500
Pharmacist	C	129,000	5100
Physician	C	305,000	22,000
Radiologic technologist	S	80,000	7700
Registered nurse	S,C	700,000	69,000
Surgical technician	—	25,000	2600
Veterinarian	C	25,000	1500

Arts	Qualifications	Estimated employment in 1970	Average annual openings to 1980
Commercial artist	S	60,000	2500
Dancer	S	23,000	1500
Musician or music teacher	S,C	210,000	11,100
Photographer	—	65,000	2000
Radio or television announcer	—	17,000	1000
Singer or singing teacher	S,C	75,000	4300

Social Service

Automobile parts stock clerk	—	68,000	2600
Automobile sales agent	—	120,000	4300
Barber	S	180,000	7700
Bartender	—	160,000	8700
Building custodian	—	1,110,000	70,000
College or university teacher	C	336,000	22,000
Cook or chef	—	740,000	49,000
Cosmetologist	S	484,000	43,000
Firefighter	—	180,000	11,800
Gasoline service station attendant	—	410,000	13,300
Guard	—	200,000	15,700
Hospital attendant	—	830,000	111,000
Kindergarten or elementary school teacher	C	1,260,000	52,000
Lawyer	C	280,000	14,000
Librarian	C	125,000	11,500
Licensed practical nurse	S	370,000	58,000
Model	—	58,000	1900
Personnel worker	C	160,000	9100
Police officer (municipal)	—	332,000	17,000
Private household worker	—	1,558,000	16,000
Real estate sales agent or broker	S	226,000	14,800
School counselor	C	54,000	5200
Secondary school teacher	C	1,015,000	38,000
Social worker	C	170,000	18,000
State police officer	—	41,000	2900
Taxi driver	—	100,000	1800
Telephone operator	—	420,000	28,000
Waiter or waitress	—	1,040,000	67,000

Business Contact	Qualifications	Estimated employment in 1970	Average annual openings to 1980
Advertising worker	C	141,000	5400
Bank clerk	—	510,000	29,600
Bank officer	C	174,000	11,000
Bank teller	—	153,000	14,700
Conductor (railroad)	—	37,500	1200
Local truckdriver	—	1,200,000	35,000
Manufacturers sales representative	—	510,000	25,000
Marketing research worker	C	23,000	2600
Motel manager or assistant	C	195,000	14,400
Public relations worker	C	75,000	4400
Purchasing agent	C	167,000	5400
Retail sales worker	—	2,500,000	131,000
Securities salesworker	S	200,000	11,800
Shipping and receiving clerk	—	379,000	12,000
Stock clerk	—	500,000	23,000
Supervisor of newspaper carriers	—	240,000	2600
Traffic agent or clerk (civil aviation)	—	45,000	4800
Truck driver, over-the-road	—	665,000	21,000
Wholesale trade salesworker	—	539,000	27,700

Business Detail			
Accountant	C	491,000	31,200
Bookkeeping worker	—	1,340,000	74,000
Cashier	—	847,000	64,000
Electronic computer operator	—	200,000	34,200
File clerk	—	169,000	15,300
Front office clerk (hotel)	—	61,000	4500
Industrial traffic manager	C	18,000	700
Office machine operator	—	365,000	20,800
Programmer	S,C	200,000	34,700
Receptionist	—	298,000	23,500
Systems analyst	S,C	100,000	22,700
Stenographer or secretary	—	2,833,000	247,000
Typist	—	671,000	61,000

glossary

Brief descriptions of certain important terms are listed in this Glossary. These descriptions need not be considered formal, complete definitions.

amortization table
Table showing repayment of a loan and the breakdown of each payment into interest and principal.

annual
For one year, or 12 months.

annual yield
Percent of interest earned for 1 year; the rule is

$$\frac{\text{amount earned in 1 year}}{\text{amount invested}}.$$

The answer is expressed as a percent.

area
Measure of an amount of surface, given in square units.

assessed valuation
Value of property, usually a percentage of actual market value, upon which the property tax is based.

average annual depreciation
Average yearly loss in value of an article or piece of property; for a car, divide the total amount of depreciation by the number of years the car has been owned.

average daily balance
Average of the daily unpaid amounts in an account; used to determine the finance charge.

bank statement
Record from a bank showing deposits, canceled checks, and other information concerning an account.

bearings
Position and direction of something, such as the boundaries of a piece of property.

beneficiary
Person named in an insurance policy to receive benefits if the insured person dies.

bodily-injury insurance
Type of liability insurance that protects a car owner financially if someone is injured by the car.

bond
Type of investment in which a person loans money to a company or a government agency that will repay the amount of the loan with interest.

broker
Person who buys and sells for other people; stocks, bonds, and real estate are often handled by brokers.

budget
Organized spending plan.

calorie
Unit of heat used to express the fuel value of food.

canceled checks
Checks, written on an account, that have been paid by the bank, marked "paid," and returned to the depositor with the bank statement.

capacity
Greatest number of units a container can hold.

cash on delivery
Amount paid at the time of delivery of a purchase.

cash value
Amount of money that can be collected from a life insurance policy by the insured if the policy is canceled.

CD
Certificate of deposit.

certificate of deposit
Savings account of a specified size (often a multiple of $1000) that earns interest at a rate higher than that of a regular savings account.

charge account
Allows a customer to buy goods or services and pay at a later date or on an installment plan.

check
Written order to a bank directing the bank to pay out money from a depositor's account.

checking account
Bank account into which money is deposited; the money is withdrawn by using forms called checks.

check register
Depositor's record that a check has been written; similar to the check stub.

check stub
Depositor's record that a check has been written; similar to the check register but stays in the checkbook.

classified ads
Short advertisements placed in a special section of newspapers or magazines; the ads concern such things as jobs available, jobs wanted, and property for rent or for sale. Also called want ads.

closing costs
Various fees and taxes that must be paid to complete the purchase of real estate.

collision insurance
Type of insurance that pays for repairs on the owner's car in case of an accident.

commission
Straight commission: a percentage of total sales that is paid to a salesperson as wages.
Graduated commission: a wage in which the rate of commission varies, depending on the total sales.

common stock
Share of a business bought as an investment.

compound interest
Interest computed on the principal and on the interest previously earned.

comprehensive auto insurance
Type of insurance that pays for damage caused to a car by fire, theft, vandalism, or acts of nature.

consumer
Any person who buys or rents goods and services offered to the public.

cross-products
The cross-products for the ratios below are 3×8 and 4×6; two ratios are equal if their cross-products are equal.
$\frac{3}{4} = \frac{6}{8}$ because $3 \times 8 = 4 \times 6$.

data
Information such as scores, values, and measurements.

deductible amount
Amount subtracted from an insured loss and not replaced by the insurance; \$50 and \$100 are common deductible amounts.

deductions
Money withheld from a person's pay for taxes, insurance, social security, and so on; also, amounts a person may subtract from gross income when computing income tax.

deferred-payment price
Sum of the down payment and the total paid in monthly installments.

denominator
In the fraction $\frac{5}{6}$, the denominator is 6.

deposit
Money given to a bank to open or to add to a checking or a savings account; also, an amount paid when a person places an order to buy an item.

depreciation
Decrease in value of a piece of property because of age and wear; for automobiles, the greatest depreciation usually occurs in the first two years.

discount
Amount deducted from list price to obtain sale price; a percent of the list price.

dividend
In $820 \div 20 = 41$, the dividend is 820.

dividends (stock)
Part of a company's profits that is paid periodically to stockholders.

divisor
In $820 \div 20 = 41$, the divisor is 20.

down payment
Amount paid at the time of an installment purchase to reduce the amount of loan needed.

endorse
Write one's name and perhaps instructions on the reverse side of a check made out to one; this must be done before the check is cashed, deposited, or directed to someone else.

equation
Mathematical sentence that uses the equal sign; examples are $5 + 6 = 11$ and $4n = 28$.

exemptions
Persons claimed by a taxpayer as legally dependent on the taxpayer for support; the number of exemptions entitles the taxpayer to a certain income-tax deduction.

factor
Number used in multiplication; in $18 \times 4 = 72$, the numbers 18 and 4 are factors.

Federal Insurance Contributions Act (FICA)
Commonly called social security; provides retirement income, medical payments, and survivors' benefits to those who qualify.

FICA deduction
Amount withheld from a person's pay for social security.

finance charge
Amount charged for buying an item on credit or on an installment plan.

financing
Purchasing goods or services through installment buying.

fixed monthly expenses
Costs that require the same amount to be paid every month, such as rent.

fuel consumption
Distance traveled divided by amount of gasoline consumed; usually stated in km/L or mi./gal.

graph
Picture used to show data; the picture could be a bar, line, or circle graph or a pictograph. A graph might also be points on a grid matched with given ordered pairs of numbers.

gross pay
Income before any deductions are made.

hourly rate
Dollar amount paid for each hour worked or fraction thereof.

insurance
Provides protection against financial loss; common types of insurance are health, life (term, straight, limited payment, endowment), automobile, homeowner's, and personal-property.

insured
Person covered by an insurance policy.

interest
Amount paid for the use of money; usually a percent of the amount invested, loaned, or borrowed.

investment
Expenditure of money for something that is expected to produce a profit.

itemized deductions
Expenses a taxpayer may list on which no tax is paid; used instead of standard deduction.

landlord
Person who owns land or buildings that are rented to others.

lease
Right to use real estate or other property for a given length of time with a payment of rent.

level-payment loan
Loan that is repaid in equal monthly installments.

liability insurance
Automobile insurance that includes bodily-injury insurance and property-damage insurance.

list price
Original price or regular price before discounts, fees, or commissions are subtracted.

loan
Amount of money that is borrowed for a certain period of time and upon which interest is usually paid.

mean
Average; the sum of a set of numbers divided by the number of addends.

median
Middle number in a set of numbers arranged in order.

minimum payment
Least amount that can be paid on a monthly bill for credit-card expenses.

mode
Number occurring most often in a set of numbers.

mortgage loan
Money borrowed to buy a home.

mutual fund
Investment company that sells shares and combines the investors' money in order to buy a large variety of stocks and bonds.

net deposit
Amount deposited in an account less cash received.

net pay
Amount left after all deductions have been subtracted from gross pay; sometimes called take-home pay.

numerator
In the fraction $\frac{5}{6}$, the numerator is 5.

ordinary method
Method used by banks to express time on promissory notes; each year has 12 months of 30 days each (a 360-day year).

overtime
Time worked beyond the regular hours; an increase in the hourly rate is often given for this time.

percent
Fraction with denominator of 100; *percent* means "hundredths" or "out of 100."
$\frac{4}{100} = .04 = 4\%$

perimeter
Measure of the distance around a closed figure.

policy (insurance)
Written agreement between the person being insured and the insurer.

premium
Cost of an insurance policy; premiums can be paid monthly, semiannually, or annually.

principal
Amount of money upon which interest is computed.

product
Answer in a multiplication problem; in $8 \times 12 = 96$, the product is 96.

promissory note
Written statement that is signed by a borrower and tells to whom, how much, and when payment will be made.

property-damage insurance
Type of liability insurance that protects the car owner financially if the car damages the property of others.

property tax
Tax based upon the value of property owned.

proportion
Statement that two ratios are equal; an example is
$\frac{3}{8} = \frac{9}{24}$.

protractor
Instrument used to draw or measure angles.

quarterly
Every 3 months, or 4 times a year.

quotient
Answer in a division problem; in $48 \div 6 = 8$, the quotient is 8.

reconciling a bank statement
Procedure used by the depositor to see that the checkbook balance and the bank statement agree; this verifies the balance left in the account.

remainder
When 15 is divided by 6, the remainder is 3.

$$6\overline{)15}\ \text{ = 2 R3}$$

salary
Fixed amount paid to an employee at regular intervals for regular hours of work; usually paid every week, every 2 weeks, or every month.

sales tax
Tax imposed by state or local government on the retail price of certain goods and services.

savings account
Account at a bank or other savings institution into which money is deposited to earn interest.

scale drawing
Drawing in which all distances are measured and are in a constant ratio to the actual distances.

semiannual
Every 6 months, or twice a year.

service charge
Amount charged by a bank for handling an account; the service charge is printed on the bank statement.

short-form tax return
Form 1040A; a simplified federal tax return for persons who use the standard deduction instead of itemized deductions.

simple-interest formula
Basic method of computing interest; the interest (I) equals the principal (p) times the rate (r) times the time (t) expressed in years.
$I = p \times r \times t$

social security
See Federal Insurance Contributions Act.

standard deduction
Allowance for certain personal expenses on which no income tax is required; used instead of itemized deductions.

statistics
Collection of data, usually numbers, relating to any topic.

sticker price
Quoted price of a car including the base price and the cost of optional equipment.

surveyor
Person who accurately determines boundaries, measures distances, and makes scale drawings of land.

taxable income
Income on which tax is payable; total income minus all allowances equals taxable income.

tax credit
Amount that can be subtracted from the income tax that is based on taxable income.

tenant
Person paying rent for the use of land or buildings.

time and a half
Overtime rate of pay—1.5 times the regular hourly rate.

tip
Small amount of money in excess of regular charges paid by a customer for a service, such as a tip paid to a waiter or a waitress for serving a meal.

town house
One of several houses, often of two stories, built in a row or a cluster and attached to one another.

trade-in allowance
Amount of money allowed for a used article as part of the purchase price of a new item.

unit price
Price per unit of measure of an item.

utilities
Public-service items, such as gas, electricity, water, or telephone service, that are usually paid for by the individual consumer.

variable monthly expenses
Costs that change from month to month; most of a person's expenses are variable to some extent.

volume
Measure of an amount of space, given in cubic units.

wage and tax statement
Form W-2; a form, issued by an employer to an employee, that states the income earned and taxes withheld for the employee during the calendar year.

want ads
See classified ads.

selected answers

page 5

set A **1.** 2000; 1500; 1540 **3.** 5000; 4900; 4870 **5.** 1000; 900; 930 **7.** 6000; 6000; 6010 **9.** 7000; 7000; 7000

set B **11.** 13; 12.7; 12.68 **13.** 14; 13.9; 13.88 **15.** 48; 48.0; 47.97 **17.** 321; 320.7; 320.71 **19.** 100; 100.1; 100.08

set C **21.** \$6; \$6.04 **23.** \$27; \$26.85 **25.** \$124; \$124.37 **27.** \$70; \$70.05 **29.** \$50; \$50.50 **31.** 16

page 7

set A **1.** 110; 109 **3.** 100; 104 **5.** 160; 154 **7.** 210; 203 **9.** 150; 160 **11.** 1170; 1165

set B **13.** 6; 5.98 **15.** 28; 27.98 **17.** 6; 6.59 **19.** 11; 10.81 **21.** 17; 17.86 **23.** 2; 1.73

set C **25.** 10; 15 **27.** 30; 25 **29.** 26; 26.1 **31.** 9; 8.8 **33.** 31; 31.61 **35.** 41; 41.34 **37.** 67; 66.79 **39.** 31; 30.614 **41.** 12; 12.4 **43.** 15; 15.1 **45.** 45; 44.8

set D **47.** \$6

page 9

set A **1.** 4500 **3.** 16,000 **5.** 72,000 **7.** 480,000 **9.** 5,400,000 **11.** 40,000 **13.** 1800 **15.** 81,000 **17.** 2400 **19.** 320,000 **21.** 66,000 **23.** 8400 **25.** 1,530,000 **27.** 465,000

set B **29.** 1500; 1378 **31.** 1200; 1026 **33.** 1200; 950 **35.** 3000; 3298 **37.** 16,000; 13,800 **39.** 5000; 6071 **41.** 18,000; 17,632 **43.** 32,000; 34,486 **45.** 100,000; 108,072 **47.** 60,000; 69,996 **49.** 350,000; 353,792 **51.** 50,000; 54,135 **53.** 720,000; 775,782 **55.** 1,600,000; 1,384,346 **57.** 2,000,000; 2,127,224 **59.** 12,000 bushels **61.** 1240 chairs

page 11

set A **1.** .08 **3.** .064 **5.** .032 **7.** 0 **9.** .18 **11.** .035 **13.** .02 **15.** .01 **17.** .0024 **19.** .00001

set B **21.** 42 **23.** 270 **25.** 150 **27.** 30 **29.** 4000 **31.** 490 **33.** 24 **35.** 3.6 **37.** 7.7 **39.** 2.5

set C **41.** 24; 23.994 **43.** .1; .13412 **45.** 120; 90.65 **47.** .45; .42394 **49.** 24; 25.7712 **51.** .012; .0138243 **53.** .24; .250046 **55.** .018; .0157982 **57.** .0024; .0025636 **59.** .1; .0936144

set D **61.** \$8000 **63.** \$20.85

page 13

set A **1.** 356 **3.** 126 R3 **5.** 680 R5 **7.** 216 **9.** 49 R53 **11.** 208 R34 **13.** 6004 **15.** 5007 R7

set B **17.** 1.971 **19.** .043 **21.** .564 **23.** 4.435 **25.** .534 **27.** 300 **29.** 9.157 **31.** 1.386

set C **33.** 5 cans

page 15

set A **1.** $\frac{5}{6}$ **3.** $\frac{2}{5}$ **5.** $\frac{8}{9}$ **7.** $\frac{3}{5}$ **9.** $\frac{5}{8}$ **11.** $\frac{1}{2}$

set B **13.** $\frac{1}{4}$ **15.** $\frac{3}{4}$ **17.** $\frac{1}{5}$ **19.** $\frac{7}{9}$ **21.** $\frac{3}{4}$

set C **23.** $4\frac{2}{3}$ **25.** $1\frac{1}{3}$ **27.** $3\frac{3}{11}$ **29.** $1\frac{7}{16}$

set D **31.** $\frac{7}{4}$ **33.** $\frac{26}{3}$ **35.** $\frac{4}{1}$ **37.** $\frac{37}{10}$ **39.** $\frac{81}{16}$

set E **41.** $\frac{3}{4}''$

page 17

set A **1.** $\frac{5}{12}$ **3.** $\frac{1}{2}$ **5.** $\frac{4}{5}$ **7.** 5; $2\frac{2}{3}$ **9.** 4; $4\frac{1}{2}$ **11.** 2; $3\frac{1}{16}$ **13.** 18; $17\frac{1}{2}$ **15.** 1; $\frac{5}{24}$

set B **17.** $\frac{3}{4}$ **19.** $1\frac{1}{14}$ **21.** 8 **23.** 2; $2\frac{1}{7}$ **25.** 1; $\frac{20}{27}$ **27.** 3; $2\frac{1}{4}$ **29.** 3; $2\frac{1}{2}$

set C **31.** 10 pounds

page 19

set A **1.** $\frac{11}{24}$ **3.** $\frac{13}{14}$ **5.** $1\frac{3}{16}$ **7.** $\frac{29}{36}$ **9.** $1\frac{23}{24}$ **11.** 7; $7\frac{1}{6}$ **13.** 13; $13\frac{1}{24}$ **15.** 3; $2\frac{17}{20}$ **17.** 10; $10\frac{7}{12}$ **19.** 11; $10\frac{15}{16}$ **21.** 8; $7\frac{19}{20}$

set B **23.** $\frac{1}{8}$ **25.** $\frac{1}{4}$ **27.** $\frac{1}{24}$ **29.** $\frac{1}{24}$ **31.** $3\frac{2}{5}$ **33.** 3; $3\frac{1}{4}$ **35.** 12; $11\frac{5}{8}$ **37.** 5; $5\frac{2}{9}$ **39.** 14; $13\frac{13}{16}$ **41.** 8; $7\frac{17}{20}$ **43.** 5; $5\frac{11}{24}$

set C **45.** $4\frac{1}{2}$ quarts; $1\frac{1}{2}$ quarts

page 20 **1.** .833 **3.** .846 **5.** .625 **7.** .389 **9.** .288 **11.** 1.071 **13.** 2.622 **15.** 7.6 **17.** 10.875 **19.** 27.688 **21.** 40.056 **23.** 3.556 **25.** 20.297 **27.** 12.04 **29.** 8.172

page 21 **1.** 7000; 7500; 7480 **2.** 24; 23.7; 23.72 **3.** 141 **4.** 8.28 **5.** 34 **6.** 41.46 **7.** 21,000 **8.** 24,192 **9.** 3.5 **10.** 35.041 **11.** 411 R6 **12.** 582 **13.** 6.23 **14.** 350.42 **15.** $\frac{5}{12}$ **16.** $\frac{2}{3}$ **17.** $\frac{1}{3}$ **18.** $\frac{3}{5}$ **19.** $9\frac{1}{3}$ **20.** $5\frac{5}{6}$ **21.** $\frac{5}{3}$ **22.** $\frac{23}{5}$ **23.** $\frac{5}{21}$ **24.** $3\frac{1}{9}$ **25.** $3\frac{3}{4}$ **26.** $2\frac{4}{5}$ **27.** $\frac{19}{20}$ **28.** $6\frac{5}{24}$ **29.** $\frac{47}{72}$ **30.** $3\frac{5}{9}$

page 25
set A **1.** $a = 3.9$ **3.** $c = 6.3$ **5.** $f = 1.53$
set B **7.** $g = 23$ **9.** $k = .79$ **11.** $n = 24$
set C **13.** $m = 12$ **15.** $t = .93$ **17.** $s = 5.6$ **19.** $w = 51.19$ **21.** $y = 53$ **23.** $p = 91$ **25.** $b = 2.76$ **27.** $z = 9.05$ **29.** $g = 33.4$ **31.** $x + \$.27 = \$6.35$; $x = \$6.08$

page 27
set A **1.** $a = 47$ **3.** $c = 17$ **5.** $z = .9$
set B **7.** $f = .6$ **9.** $r = 15.2$
set C **11.** $a = 3$ **13.** $t = 9$ **15.** $x = 12$
set D **17.** $x = 50$ **19.** $y = 0$ **21.** $z = 90$ **23.** $s = 4$ **25.** $x = 0$ **27.** $f = .096$ **29.** $k = 0$ **31.** $\$.35x = \$61.25$; $x = 175$

page 29
set A **1.** $a = 1$ **3.** $n = 9$ **5.** $b = 3.5$
set B **7.** $a = 36$ **9.** $c = 52$
set C **11.** $z = 8$ **13.** $y = 8$ **15.** $x = 10.89$ **17.** $b = 10$ **19.** $m = .2$ **21.** $x = 2$ **23.** $x = .18$ **25.** $g = .14$ **27.** $w = 19$ **29.** $\$2.75x + \$24.75 = \$55$; $x = 11$

page 31
set A **1.** 84; 84; equal **3.** 210; 222; not equal **5.** 192; 192; equal **7.** 528; 528; equal **9.** 2.4; 2.4; equal **11.** 21.6; 21.6; equal **13.** .1; .1; equal **15.** 453.6; 420; not equal
set B **17.** $a = 15$ **19.** $d = 9$ **21.** $x = 3.75$ **23.** $h = 4.2$ **25.** $x = 40$ **27.** $s = 20$ **29.** $t = .006$ **31.** $y = .5$
set C **33.** 5 teaspoons

page 32 **1.** $n = 336$ **3.** $n = 189$ **5.** $n = 273$ **7.** $n = 459$ **9.** $n = 126$ **11.** $n = 23.7$ **13.** $n = 3.71$ **15.** $n = 2.22$ **17.** $n = 39.6$ **19.** $n = 11.676$ **21.** $n = 3.8376$ **23.** $n = 20.4$ **25.** 6 days **27.** 18 packs

page 35

set A **1.** .23 **3.** .02 **5.** .135 **7.** .0875 **9.** .035 **11.** .3225 **13.** 1.35 **15.** 1.07

set B **17.** 71% **19.** 10% **21.** 31.4% **23.** 46.8% **25.** 23.25% **27.** 3.75% **29.** 374%

set C **31.** $\frac{1}{10}$ **33.** $\frac{1}{4}$ **35.** $\frac{2}{5}$ **37.** $\frac{3}{5}$ **39.** $\frac{21}{100}$ **41.** $\frac{9}{50}$ **43.** $\frac{93}{100}$ **45.** $\frac{107}{100}$

set D **47.** 50% **49.** 80% **51.** 68% **53.** 5% **55.** 62.5% **57.** 37.5% **59.** 220%

set E **61.** 13.25%

pages 37–38

set A **1.** 2.25 **3.** 2.331 **5.** $7.50 **7.** 4.48 **9.** 4.2

set B **11.** 3.5% **13.** 75% **15.** 8% **17.** 6%

set C **19.** 200 **21.** 120 **23.** 11 **25.** 30 **27.** 6.25

set D **29.** 64 grams **31.** 45 grams **33.** 2921 people **35.** 26% **37.** Store B

page 39 **1.** $d = 4.5$ **2.** $m = 8.5$ **3.** $f = 7.99$ **4.** $g = 7.95$ **5.** $x = 53$ **6.** $t = 7$ **7.** $b = 2.16$ **8.** $a = 4$ **9.** $c = 5$ **10.** $y = 8$ **11.** $w = 15$ **12.** $x = 6$ **13.** 250; 260; not equal **14.** 28.8; 28.8; equal **15.** $c = 24$ **16.** $t = 88$ **17.** .57 **18.** .0575 **19.** 6% **20.** 46.5% **21.** $\frac{41}{100}$ **22.** $\frac{19}{50}$ **23.** 76% **24.** 56.25% **25.** 31.62 **26.** 24 **27.** 15% **28.** 87.5% **29.** 45 **30.** 150

page 43

set A **1.** 3.87 km **3.** 300 cm **5.** 14 mm **7.** 2130 km

set B **9.** 4590 km **11.** 60 m **13.** 4 mm

set C **15.** Answers will vary. **17.** Answers will vary. **19.** 3 cm

page 45

set A **1.** 392 mm^2 **3.** 9.4 km^2 **5.** 322.5 m^2

set B **7.** 73.6 m^3 **9.** 185.8 m^3

set C **11.** 7350 m^2 **13.** 17,760 mm^3 **15.** 8.1 m^2

page 47

set A **1.** 250 mL **3.** 40 L **5.** 350 mg

set B **7.** 3.5 kg **9.** 2 kg **11.** 4 L

set C **13.** 4–8 L **15.** 450–675 g

page 49

set A **1.** 500 **3.** 93 **5.** 1275 **7.** 500 **9.** 2100

set B **11.** 0.935 **13.** 0.429 **15.** 6.7 **17.** 0.084 **19.** 1.375

set C **21.** 23,000 **23.** 180 **25.** 0.06 **27.** 0.25 **29.** 1.296 **31.** No

page 51

set A **1.** 19°C **3.** 21°C **5.** 39.8°C

set B **7.** 225°C **9.** 125°C **11.** 225°C

set C **13.** ⁻28°C **15.** ⁻32°C and ⁻33°C **17.** Water skiing

page 53

set A **1.** 8 hours 35 minutes **3.** 8 hours 20 minutes

set B **5.** 3:30 P.M.

set C **7.** 3 hours 10 minutes **9.** 6 hours 35 minutes

set D **11.** 3 hours 20 minutes **13.** 8 hours 5 minutes

15. 1:50 P.M. **17.** Yes

page 55

set A **1.**

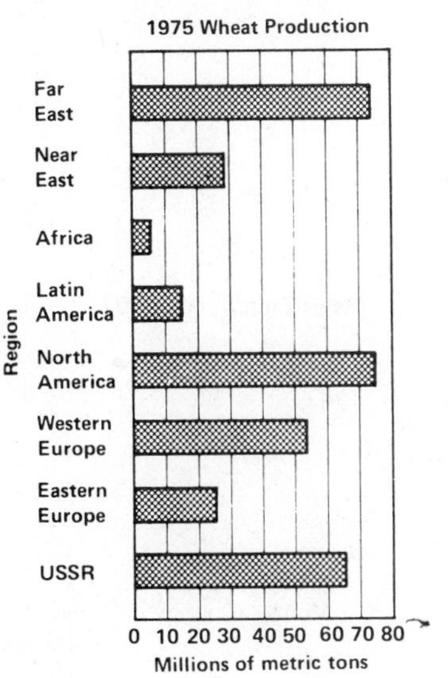

3.

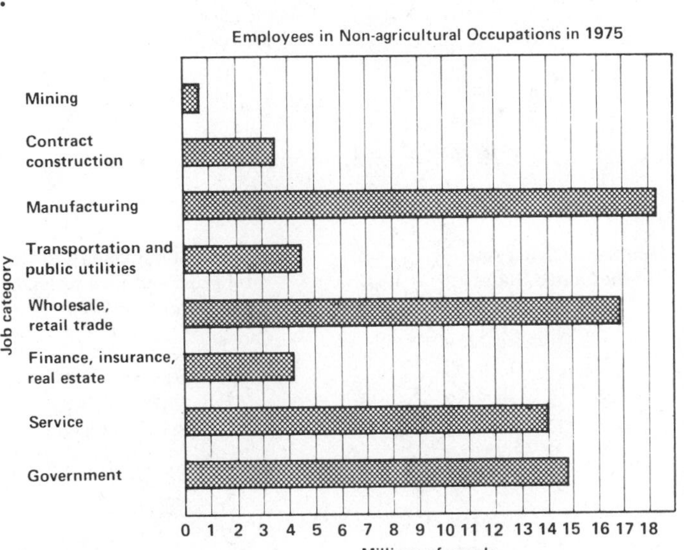

page 55 continued

set B 5. 7. 9.

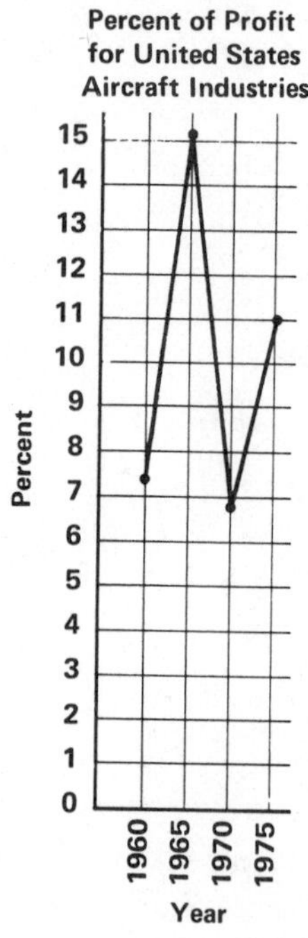

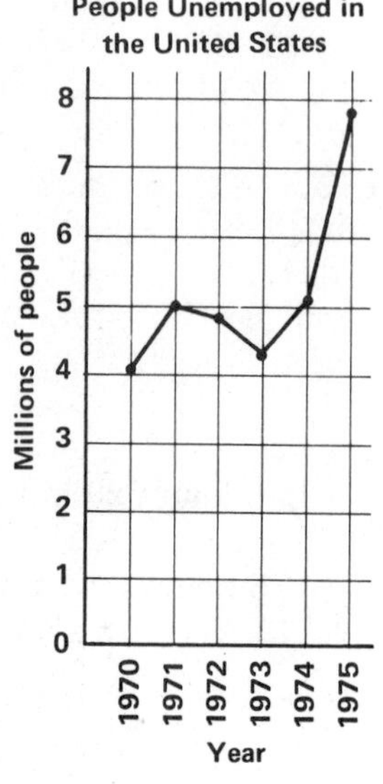

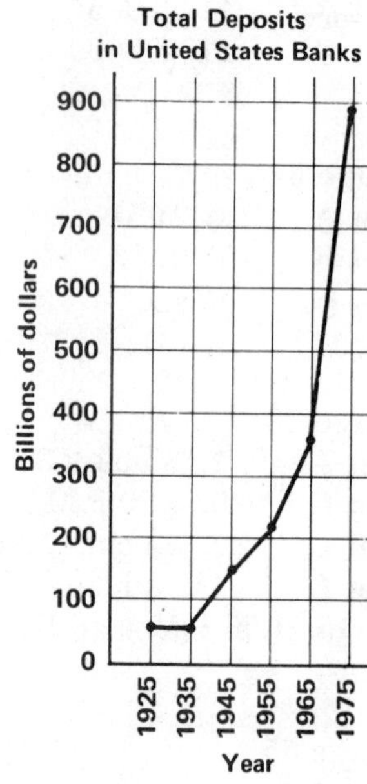

page 57

set A 1. 1,079,906 3. 4,559,603 5. 317 7. 24

set B 9. 11. set C 13.

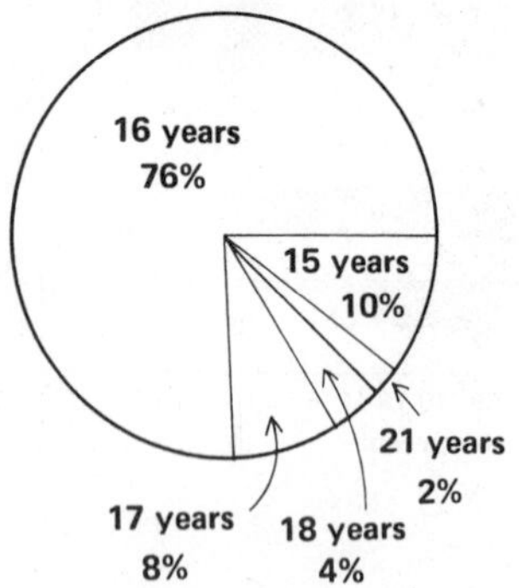

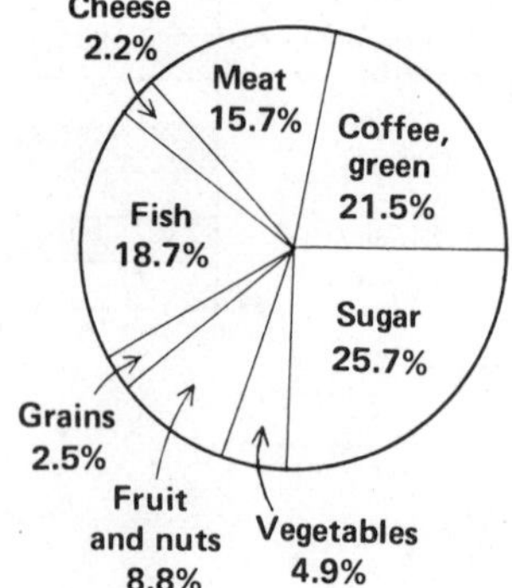

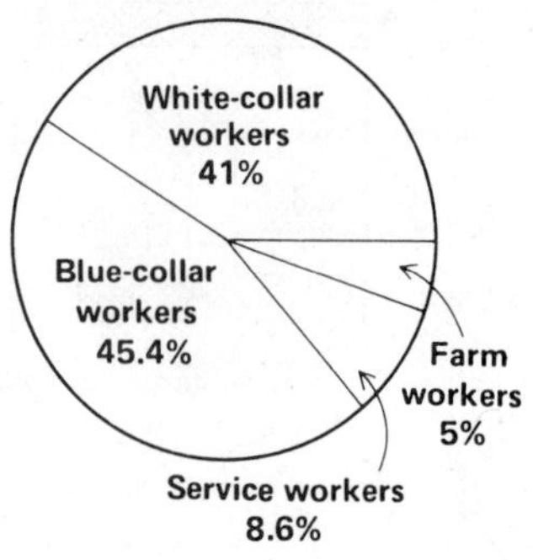

page 57 continued

set C **15.** White-collar workers: 21,004,300; blue-collar workers: 23,258,420; service workers: 4,405,780; farm workers: 2,561,500

page 59

set A **1.** 7 **3.** 21 **5.** 10.01 **7.** No mode **9.** 2.5

set B **11.** 6 **13.** 37.2 **15.** 10.13 **17.** 8 **19.** 2.29

set C **21.** 7 **23.** 21 **25.** 10.1

set D **27.** 8 **29.** 2.3

set E **31.** Mean, 73.71; median, 80; mode, 93

page 60 **1.** 600.5 **3.** 4567 **5.** 50,883.6 **7.** 68,802.06 **9.** 241.31 **11.** 1757 **13.** 56,501 **15.** 1,084,673

page 61 **1.** 3 cm **2.** 24 m **3.** 33.6 m^2 **4.** 576.576 cm^3 **5.** 13 L **6.** 5 kg **7.** 200 mL **8.** 600 g **9.** .34 **10.** 7630 **11.** $^{-}10$°C **12.** 3 hours 45 minutes

13.

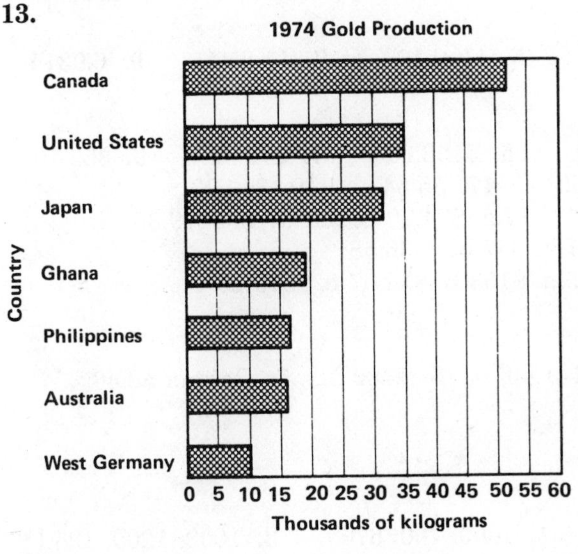

14.

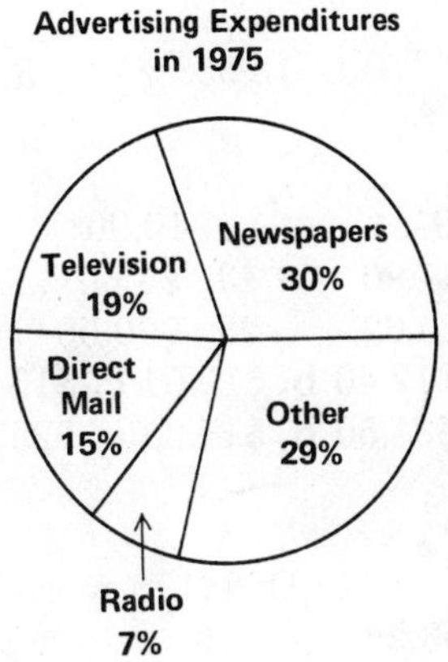

15. 20 **16.** 22

page 69 **1.a.** $251.20 **b.** $9.42 **c.** $0 **d.** $251.20 **3.a.** $171.20 **b.** $6.42 **c.** $32.10 **d.** $203.30 **5.a.** $167.20 **b.** $6.27 **c.** $50.16 **d.** $217.36 **7.a.** $222.40 **b.** $8.34 **c.** $20.02 **d.** $242.42 **9.a.** $192 **b.** $7.20 **c.** $25.20 **d.** $217.20 **11.a.** $183.20 **b.** $6.87 **c.** $35.72 **d.** $218.92

page 71 **1.** $360 **3.** $239.20 **5.** $268.20 **7.** $241.48 **9.** $341.25

page 73 **1.** $1.12 **3.** $.98 **5.** $1.18 **7.** $.69 **9.** $.20 **11.a.** $10.40 **b.** $4.16 **13.a.** $4.50 **b.** $1.80 **15.a.** $9 **b.** $3.60 **17.a.** $4.50 **b.** $1.80

page 75 **1.** $189 **3.** $281.50 **5.** $245.57 **7.** $298.92 **9.** $109 **11.** $634

page 76 **1.** $920 **3.** $975 **5.** $1114.75

page 77 **1.** 13.958% **3.** 14.283% **5.** 11.451% **7.** 11.85% **9.** 6.931%

pages 79–81 **1.** $10.90 **3.** $23.50 **5.** $106.20 **7.** $72.30 **9.** $55.10 **11.** $41.90 **13.** $3.60 **15.** $96.60 **17.** $5.54 **19.** $13.27 **21.** $10.62 **23.** $90.50 **25.** $0 **27.a.** $74.20 **b.** $21.97 **c.** $279.35 **29.a.** $12.40 **b.** $10.51 **c.** $154.50 **31.a.** $67 **b.** $366.58 **33.a.** $34.50 **b.** $17.25 **c.** $233.40 **35.a.** $153 **b.** $33.07 **c.** $379.20

page 83 **1.** D; $4175 more **3.** $3141.40 **5.** $480 **7.** Gain of $8.40 **9.** $153.28

page 84
Rounding whole numbers and decimals **1.** 1000; 700; 670 **3.** 1000; 1200; 1250 **5.** 5000; 5000; 5040 **7.** 65,000; 65,200; 65,190 **9.** 1000; 900; 880 **11.** 3; 3.3; 3.28 **13.** 75; 74.5; 74.52 **15.** 153; 152.8; 152.80 **17.** 391; 391.5; 391.48 **19.** 85; 84.7; 84.67

page 84 continued
Subtracting whole numbers and decimals **1.** 31 **3.** 66 **5.** 9 **7.** 12.5
9. 12.71 **11.** 15.81 **13.** 3.482 **15.** 17.345 **17.** .353 **19.** .6
21. 5.103 **23.** 71.4 **25.** 4.39
Multiplying whole numbers **1.** 1500 **3.** 42,000 **5.** 540,000 **7.** 180,000
9. 3,400,000 **11.** 344,000 **13.** 144,000 **15.** 442 **17.** 7857
19. 31,635 **21.** 97,226 **23.** 344,284 **25.** 6,397,424

page 85 **1.** $194.40 **2.** $288 **3.** $155.82 **4.** $234 **5.** $190
6. $477.50 **7.** $32.80 **8.** $16.93 **9.** $237.38 **10.** A; $11 more

page 89 **1.a.** $70.31 **b.** $70.31 **3.a.** $419.19 **b.** $344.19 **5.** $182.07

7.
Pay to the order of
Valley National Bank
for deposit only.
James B. Jones

9.
Pay to the order of
State Bank of Georgetown
for deposit only.
Cynthia Ann Wallace

pages 90–91 **1.** Twenty-seven and $\frac{81}{100}$ **3.** Sixty and $\frac{00}{100}$ **5.** Fifteen and $\frac{00}{100}$
7. Three hundred ninety-five and $\frac{13}{100}$ **9.** One thousand two and $\frac{30}{100}$
11.a. $146.86 **b.** $97.91 **13.** $438.80

page 93 **1.** Balance: $182.22 **3.** Balance: $136.28 **5.** Balance: $314.42
7. Balance: $307.97 **9.** Balance: $231.38 **11.** $245.52

page 96 **1.** $74.29 **3.** $39.61 **5.** $174.72

page 97 **1.** Balance after check no. 118: $35.91

page 99 **1.** $.33 **3.** $34.13 **5.** $28.28 **7.** $27.25 **9.** $84.11
11. $90.63 **13.** $1015.63 **15.** $135.30

pages 100–101 **1.** $31.08 **3.** $101.46 **5.** $207.95 **7.** $20.38 **9.** $148.59 **11.** $114.62 **13.** $30.45

page 103 **1.** $21.55 **3.** $1629.15 **5.** $136.04 **7.** $787.69 **9.** $971.80 **11.** $872.10

page 104
Multiplying decimals **1.** .35 **3.** .016 **5.** .0018 **7.** .00008 **9.** 140 **11.** 32 **13.** 2.1 **15.** .00002 **17.** 4.4 **19.** 34.944 **21.** .243 **23.** 153.51063 **25.** 1.574944
Ratio and proportion **1.** 120; 120; equal **3.** 140; 144; not equal **5.** .064; .033; not equal **7.** $n = 36$ **9.** $x = 15$ **11.** $d = 21$ **13.** $y = 81$
Writing percents, decimals, and fractions **1.** .17 **3.** .01 **5.** .96 **7.** .99 **9.** .0775 **11.** .125 **13.** .0675 **15.** .328 **17.** .0575 **19.** .375 **21.** 8.56 **23.** 1.6 **25.** $\frac{1}{2}$ **27.** $\frac{7}{20}$ **29.** $\frac{3}{5}$ **31.** $\frac{6}{25}$ **33.** $\frac{1}{5}$ **35.** $\frac{9}{100}$ **37.** $\frac{33}{100}$ **39.** $\frac{9}{20}$ **41.** $\frac{19}{20}$ **43.** $1\frac{1}{10}$ **45.** $3\frac{1}{2}$

page 105 **1.a.** $81.18 **b.** $56.18 **2.a.** $206.62 **b.** $131.42 **3.** Balance: $248.56 **4.** Balance: $384.74 **5.** $109.11 **6.** No **7.** $45 **8.** $216.32 **9.** $61.37 **10.** $164.24

page 109 **1.** $17 **3.** $9.13 **5.** $.50 **7.** $69 **9.** $43.75 **11.** $48 interest; $1848 total due **13.** $540 interest; $2940 total due

page 111 **1.a.** $47.16 **b.** $.71 **c.** $47.87 **3.a.** $106.38 **b.** $1.60 **c.** $107.98 **5.a.** $22.33 **b.** $.33 **c.** $47.32 **7.a.** $73.77 **b.** $1.11 **c.** $104.52 **9.a.** $0 **b.** $0 **c.** $20.94 **11.a.** $0 **b.** $0 **c.** $35.60

page 114 **1.** Finance charge, $1.35; new balance, $131.35 **3.** Finance charge, $2.36; new balance, $348.44 **5.** Finance charge, $0; new balance, $8.67 **7.** Finance charge, $1.21; new balance, $64.35 **9.** Finance charge, $1.31; new balance, $128.64

page 115 **1.a.** $459.75 **3.a.** $409.75 **b.** 4 **c.** $1639 **5.a.** $422.06 **b.** 8 **c.** $3376.48 **7.a.** $441.05 **b.** 4 **c.** $1764.20 **9.a.** $456.84 **b.** 2 **c.** $913.68 **11.** $431.26 **13.** $463.31

page 117 **1.a.** $42.16 **b.** $54.70 **c.** $10 **3.a.** $107.36 **b.** $194.47 **c.** $20 **5.a.** $190.93 **b.** $193.79 **c.** $20 **7.a.** $9.68 **b.** $9.83 **c.** $9.83 **9.a.** $326.27 **b.** $465.93 **c.** $93.19

pages 118-119 **1.** $85.41 **3.** $119.92 **5.** $13.09 **7.** $46.51 **9.** $159.53 **11.a.** $1.88 **b.** $252.81 **c.** $201.49 **13.a.** $151.68 **b.** $1.14 **c.** $152.82 **d.** $101.50 **15.a.** $50.94 **b.** $.38 **c.** $51.32 **d.** $0

page 121 **1.a.** $250.92 **b.** $25.17 **3.a.** $469.95 **b.** $574.08 **c.** $104.13 **5.a.** $134.20 **b.** $171.60 **c.** $37.40 **7.a.** $322.74 **b.** $431.64 **c.** $108.90 **9.a.** $257.21 **b.** $344.16 **c.** $86.95 **11.a.** $45.37 **b.** $544.44 **c.** $44.44 **13.a.** $17.58 **b.** $632.88 **c.** $132.88 **15.a.** $24.96 **b.** $599.04 **c.** $99.04 **17.a.** $29.38 **b.** $705.12 **c.** $105.12

page 123 **1.** $66.63 **3.** Plan A **5.** $23.75 **7.** $79.40 **9.** 12% for 36 months **11.** $31.46 **13.** $9.20 **15.** Savings and loan

page 124

Dividing whole numbers **1.** 2604 **3.** 183 **5.** 1653 R2 **7.** 44 R57 **9.** 104 R43 **11.** 41 R10 **13.** 458 **15.** 209 R25 **17.** 45 R26 **19.** 679 **21.** 5785 R50 **23.** 8276 R10 **25.** 87 R96

Dividing decimals **1.** 1.838 **3.** .656 **5.** .091 **7.** .019 **9.** .108 **11.** 6.392 **13.** 4.567 **15.** 280 **17.** 5.649 **19.** .784 **21.** .054 **23.** 1.389 **25.** 7.228

Multiplying fractions and mixed numbers **1.** $\frac{2}{15}$ **3.** $\frac{1}{5}$ **5.** $\frac{1}{2}$ **7.** $6\frac{2}{3}$ **9.** $1\frac{4}{5}$ **11.** 5 **13.** $3\frac{1}{8}$ **15.** 6 **17.** $15\frac{3}{4}$ **19.** $\frac{5}{14}$

page 125 **1.** $25.50 **2.** $1825.50 **3.** $1.61 **4.** $70.60 **5.** $110.83 **6.** $20 **7.** $36.59 **8.** $337.64 **9.** $404.40 **10.** $66.76

page 133 **1.a.** $36.25 **b.** $831.75 **3.a.** $60 **b.** $2087.50 **5.a.** $130.20 **b.** $2014.20 **7.a.** $3739.95 **9.a.** $69.13 **b.** $2936.78 **11.a.** $36.80 **b.** $13.80 **c.** $990.10 **13.** $1839.75 **15.** $30.15

page 135 **1.** $5672 **3.** $5901 **5.** $5835; no **7.** AM-FM radio, $142; steel-belted, blackwall tires, N.E.C.; rear-seat speaker (single), $21
9. AM-FM stereo radio with front and rear dual speakers, $233; steel-belted, wide-oval, billboard-lettered tires, $69

page 137 **1.** $5625 **3.** $6916.50 **5.** $4419 **7.** $5283 **9.** $3771
11. $358.80 **13.** $178.25

page 139 **1.a.** $2625 **b.** $2730 **c.** $2740; Suburban Ltd. **3.a.** $3170
b. $3275 **c.** $3115; Heritage Ltd. **5.a.** $5630 **b.** $5525 **c.** $5650; Prospect Sales **7.a.** Lowest **b.** Middle **9.a.** Middle **b.** Highest
11.a. Highest **b.** Highest

page 141 **1.a.** $4894.64 **b.** $354.64 **3.a.** $6621.30 **b.** $281.30
5.a. $5878.04 **b.** $143.04 **7.a.** $8436 **b.** $1221 **9.a.** $5894.96
b. $269.96

page 143 **1.a.** $887.50 **b.** $120 **c.** $1007.50 **3.a.** $1206.25 **b.** $240
c. $1446.25 **5.a.** $1468.75 **b.** $300 **c.** $1768.75 **7.a.** $1133.75
b. $195 **c.** $1328.75 **9.a.** $1266.25 **b.** $255 **c.** $1521.25
11.a. $831.25 **b.** $110 **c.** $941.25 **13.** $956.25 **15.** $1125.25

page 144 **1.a.** $367.81 **b.** $6988.47 **3.a.** $867.65 **b.** $4916.71
5.a. $184.64 **b.** $3508.09 **7.a.** $927.44 **b.** $3709.77 **9.a.** $187.27
b. $3558.12

page 146
Subtracting whole numbers and decimals **1.** 34 **3.** 24 **5.** 67
7. 21.1 **9.** 18.2 **11.** 20.97 **13.** 3.781 **15.** 21.272 **17.** .363
19. .9 **21.** 5.789 **23.** 26.6 **25.** 1.96
Writing percents, decimals, and fractions **1.** .29 **3.** .09 **5.** .82
7. .73 **9.** .1842 **11.** .675 **13.** .0825 **15.** .184 **17.** .0825
19. .205 **21.** 4.05 **23.** 2.5 **25.** 56% **27.** 3% **29.** 50%
31. 49% **33.** 5.3% **35.** 33.9% **37.** 90.6% **39.** 1.25% **41.** 32.25%
43. 90.54% **45.** 506% **47.** 112.1%
Percent problems **1.** 4.9 **3.** 39 **5.** 207 **7.** 237.5 **9.** 796
11. 1200 **13.** 3 **15.** 21 **17.** 15 **19.** 12 **21.** 96

page 147 **1.** \$73.75 **2.** \$1634.50 **3.** \$5551 **4.** \$3861 **5.** \$3675 **6.** \$6337.76 **7.** \$612.76 **8.** \$903 **9.** \$195 **10.** \$1098

page 151 **1.** 729.5 km **3.** 4.4 km/L **5.** 4.1¢/km **7.a.** 349.5 **b.** 6.1 **c.** 3.3¢ **9.a.** 242.0 **b.** 4.0 **c.** 5.1¢ **11.a.** 342.5 **b.** 4.5 **c.** 4.4¢

pages 153-155 **1.a.** \$3500 **b.** \$2750 **c.** \$2100 **d.** \$1650 **e.** \$1250 **f.** \$3750
3.a. \$4060 **b.** \$3190 **c.** \$2436 **d.** \$1914 **e.** \$1450 **f.** \$4350
5.a. \$4340 **b.** \$3410 **c.** \$2604 **d.** \$2046 **e.** \$1550 **f.** \$4650
7.a. \$4970 **b.** \$3905 **c.** \$2982 **d.** \$2343 **e.** \$1775 **f.** \$5325
9.a. \$5950 **b.** \$4675 **c.** \$3570 **d.** \$2805 **e.** \$2125 **f.** \$6375
11. Total, \$2320; average, \$773 **13.** Total, \$2182; average, \$1091
15. Total, \$3785; average, \$946 **17.** Total, \$4576; average, \$763
19. Total, \$7140; average, \$1020 **21.** \$3123 **23.** \$1094 **25.** \$3120
27. \$3125 **29.** \$4186 **31.** \$2340

pages 158-159 **1.** \$31 **3.** \$7.50 **5.** \$12.40 **7.** \$7.46 **9.** \$83.04 **11.** \$65 **13.** \$180.79 **15.** \$348.30

page 161 **1.** \$25,000 **3.** \$10,000 **5.** \$126.35 **7.** \$148.20 **9.** \$176 **11.** \$202.70 **13.** \$155 **15.** \$310.20 **17.** \$355.36

page 163 **1.a.** \$185 **b.** \$60 **c.** \$245 **3.a.** \$115 **b.** \$10 **c.** \$125 **5.a.** \$60 **b.** \$9 **c.** \$69 **7.a.** \$140 **b.** \$25 **c.** \$165 **9.a.** \$350 **b.** \$115 **c.** \$465

pages 165-166 **1.** \$765 **3.** \$687.39 **5.** 16,000 km **7.** Depreciation **9.** \$663 **11.** \$706.53 **13.** 15,000 km **15.** No loan payment **17.** 8000 km **19.** \$3180.63 **21.** 31.8¢/km **23.** \$73.93 **25.** \$153.34

page 167 **1.** 8.63 km/L **3.** 7.62 km/L **5.** 6.03 km/L **7.** 7.44 km/L **9.** 6.31 km/L **11.a.** 7.31 **b.** 6.85 **c.** .46 **d.** 6.72% **13.a.** 8.50 **b.** 6.94 **c.** 1.56 **d.** 22.48% **15.a.** 10.45 **b.** 8.70 **c.** 1.75 **d.** 20.11%

page 169 **1.** \$55.60 **3.** \$24 **5.** \$22 **7.** \$54 **9.** 2.7¢/km **11.** \$2340 **13.** \$4140 **15.** \$2544 **17.** \$4440 **19.** \$3096 **21.** \$5340

page 170

Adding whole numbers and decimals **1.** 52 **3.** 157 **5.** 189 **7.** 232 **9.** 320 **11.** 1732 **13.** 1566 **15.** 12.85 **17.** 59.51 **19.** 18.87 **21.** 21.6 **23.** 1.68 **25.** 7.904

Multiplying decimals **1.** .18 **3.** .036 **5.** .003 **7.** .00024 **9.** 320 **11.** 3.6 **13.** 5.6 **15.** .00003 **17.** 8.4 **19.** 34.452 **21.** .3588 **23.** 35.2772 **25.** 6.268648

Renaming fractions and mixed numbers **1.** $2\frac{1}{4}$ **3.** $1\frac{1}{2}$ **5.** $2\frac{1}{6}$ **7.** $4\frac{2}{3}$ **9.** $4\frac{1}{3}$ **11.** $1\frac{5}{16}$ **13.** $2\frac{3}{8}$ **15.** $1\frac{4}{5}$ **17.** $7\frac{4}{9}$ **19.** $\frac{11}{8}$ **21.** $\frac{17}{6}$ **23.** $\frac{26}{5}$ **25.** $\frac{19}{2}$ **27.** $\frac{32}{9}$ **29.** $\frac{5}{1}$ **31.** $\frac{55}{12}$ **33.** $\frac{62}{7}$ **35.** $\frac{85}{12}$

page 171 **1.** 5.5 km/L **2.** 3.5¢/km **3.** $2352 **4.** $3248 **5.** $35.25; $8.10 **6.** $308.20 **7.** $143 **8.** $4132.48 **9.** 27.5¢/km **10.** $45.10

pages 174–175 **1.** 309 km; 4 h **3.** 205 km; 2.5 h **5.** 493 km; 6 h **7.** 703 km; 9 h **9.** 60 km **11.** 195 km **13.** 210 km **15.a.** 108 km **b.** 90 km **17.a.** 38 km **b.** 30 km **19.** 120 km; 1.5 h

page 177 **1.** 4737 km **3.** 1534 km **5.** 4300 km **7.** 2245 km **9.** 4693 km **11.** 5208 km **13.** 4576 km

page 179 **1.a.** $16.60 **b.** $4 **c.** $0 **d.** $0 **e.** $20.60 **3.a.** $153.40 **b.** $100 **c.** $288 **d.** $15 **e.** $556.40 **5.** $67.75

page 181 **1.** $82 **3.** $203 **5.** $1024 **7.** $250 **9.** $356

page 182 **1.** $116 **3.** $106 **5.** $232.44 **7.** $190.50 **9.** Same number of days and kilometers

page 183 **1.a.** 828 km **b.** $107.64 **c.** $119 **d.** $226.64 **3.a.** 544 km **b.** $76.16 **c.** $72 **d.** $148.16 **5.a.** 379 km **b.** $56.85 **c.** $63 **d.** $119.85 **7.** $125 **9.** $179 **11.** $197.20 **13.** $345 **15.** Special rate; $91

page 185 **1.** $80.45 **3.** $100 **5.** $210.90 **7.** $269 **9.** $78 **11.** $150.45 **13.** $196

page 186

Dividing decimals **1.** 5.925 **3.** .562 **5.** .062 **7.** .068 **9.** .129 **11.** 2.031 **13.** 5.657 **15.** 170 **17.** .522 **19.** 1.182 **21.** .006 **23.** 2.011 **25.** 7.936

Adding fractions and mixed numbers **1.** $1\frac{1}{12}$ **3.** $1\frac{1}{3}$ **5.** $1\frac{1}{14}$ **7.** $1\frac{11}{36}$ **9.** $4\frac{1}{15}$ **11.** $8\frac{1}{3}$ **13.** $7\frac{5}{6}$ **15.** $6\frac{14}{15}$ **17.** $8\frac{3}{16}$ **19.** 19

Subtracting fractions and mixed numbers **1.** $\frac{1}{2}$ **3.** $\frac{3}{8}$ **5.** $\frac{17}{24}$ **7.** $\frac{1}{14}$ **9.** $2\frac{3}{8}$ **11.** $2\frac{1}{2}$ **13.** $4\frac{1}{3}$ **15.** $9\frac{9}{16}$ **17.** $6\frac{7}{15}$ **19.** $6\frac{1}{3}$

page 187 **1.** 118 km **2.** 1.5 h **3.** 2202 km **4.** 203 L; $40.60 **5.** $105.60 **6.** $219 **7.** $438 **8.** $155.49 **9.** $475.50 **10.** $478

pages 196–197 **1.** $252 **3.** $300 **5.** $224 **7.** $208 **9.** $183.25 **11.** $217.79 **13.** $188 **15.** $220 **17.** $157 **19.** $322

page 199 **1.** $232 **3.** $245 **5.** $195 **7.** Colony Point, $195; The Villas, $225; Summit, $232; Georgetown, $237; Cranbrook Square, $245; Meadow Green, $255; 750 Nichols Road, $260 **9.** $122.50

page 201 **1.** 58915 **3.** 60279 **5.** 62750 **7.** 64431 **9.** Feb.–March, 677; April–May, 643; June–July, 1828; Aug.–Sept., 1134; Oct.–Nov., 547 **11.** Use of air conditioning in summer months

page 202 **1.** $172.81 **3.** $74.92 **5.** $49.36 **7.** $14.87 **9.** $1.60 **11.** $40.67 **13.** $56.89 **15.** $14.83 **17.** $3.52 **19.** $.66 **21.** $.02

page 205 **1.a.** 37 m^2 **b.** 13.5 m^2 **c.** 50.5 m^2 **d.** 6 L **3.a.** 15.6 m^2 **b.** 2.4 m^2 **c.** 18 m^2 **d.** 2 L **5.a.** 45.9 m^2 **b.** 12.3 m^2 **c.** 5 L **d.** 2 L **7.** $114.69

page 207 **1.** 45.75 m^2 **3.** 3 **5.** $76.57 **7.** 21 **9.** 18 rolls **11.** 3 rolls

pages 208–209 For ex. 1–5, answers are given in this order: length, width, total.
1. 8; 5; 40 **3.** $10\frac{1}{2}$; 11; $115\frac{1}{2}$ **5.** $14\frac{1}{2}$; $9\frac{1}{2}$; $137\frac{3}{4}$ **7.** $183.60
9. $173\frac{1}{2}$ tiles **11.** $160.20 **13.** $320.40

page 211 **1.** 17 cm **3.** 7.7 cm × 4.3 cm **5.** 7.5 cm × 2.9 cm
7. 6.4 cm × 3 cm **9.** 7.8 cm × 5.4 cm **11.** 2.6 cm × 1.8 cm
13. 6.7 cm × 1.9 cm **15.** Outline should be 14.4 cm × 13.8 cm.

page 213 **1.** $90 **3.** $57.20 **5.** $68 **7.** $131.25 **9.** $339.70
11. $129.50 **13.** $279.50 **15.** $38.25

page 214
Dividing whole numbers **1.** 511 **3.** 324 R4 **5.** 4742 **7.** 126 R28
9. 108 R21 **11.** 121 R47 **13.** 44 **15.** 207 **17.** 80 R32
19. 1203 R3 **21.** 7814 R16 **23.** 4285 R86 **25.** 204
Multiplying fractions and mixed numbers **1.** $\frac{5}{24}$ **3.** $\frac{2}{7}$ **5.** $\frac{1}{12}$ **7.** $3\frac{1}{2}$
9. $1\frac{1}{5}$ **11.** $1\frac{1}{4}$ **13.** 27 **15.** 9 **17.** $24\frac{2}{5}$ **19.** $10\frac{1}{2}$
Ratio and proportion **1.** 24; 28; not equal **3.** 1200; 1280; not equal
5. 117.6; 144; not equal **7.** $a = 30$ **9.** $c = 3$ **11.** $n = 5.3$
13. $n = 400$

page 215 **1.** $270 **2.** $223 **3.** 24936 **4.** 55.5 m^2 **5.** 6 L
6. 12 rolls **7.** $262\frac{1}{2}$ tiles **8.** 22.5 cm **9.** $292 **10.** $192

page 219 **1.** $37,500; yes **3.** $23,400; no **5.** $29,900; yes
7. $35,360; yes **9.** $18,200; no **11.** No **13.** Yes

page 221 **1.a.** $8000 **b.** $32,000 **c.** $240.64 **3.a.** $7200 **b.** $28,800
c. $241.92 **5.a.** $13,000 **b.** $39,000 **c.** $327.99 **7.a.** $14,900
b. $59,600 **c.** $565.60 **9.** $4000 **11.** $11.44 **13.** $42,300 **15.** $36.15

page 223 **1.a.** 300 **b.** $72,540 **c.** $42,540 **3.a.** 300 **b.** $74,070
c. $44,070 **5.a.** $216.98 **b.** 360 **c.** $78,112.80 **d.** $52,312.80
7.a. $433.62 **b.** 360 **c.** $156,103.20 **d.** $110,603.20 **9.** $21,348
11. $68,088 **13.** 2.8

page 224 **1.** \$262.36 **3.** \$34,961.36 **5.** \$19.54 **7.** \$262.06 **9.** \$34,922.13

page 225 **1.a.** \$262.36 **b.** \$19.39 **c.** \$34,961.36 **3.a.** \$34,941.82 **b.** \$262.06 **c.** \$19.69 **d.** \$34,922.13 **5.a.** \$34,902.30 **b.** \$261.77 **c.** \$19.98 **d.** \$34,882.32 **7.a.** \$100.67 **b.** \$181.08 **c.** \$13,241.77 **9.a.** \$13,059.33 **b.** \$97.94 **c.** \$183.81 **d.** \$12,875.52 **11.a.** \$27,971.58 **b.** \$192.30 **c.** \$28.62 **d.** \$27,942.96 **13.a.** \$27,914.15 **b.** \$191.91 **c.** \$29.01 **d.** \$27,885.14

page 227 **1.** \$8.10 **3.** \$1.32 **5.** \$151.07 **7.** \$1.76 **9.** \$17.60 **11.** \$5.72 **13.** \$27.83 **15.** \$176.67 **17.** \$5.50 **19.** \$6.75 **21.** \$12.59 **23.** \$14.72

page 229 **1.a.** \$18,500 **b.** \$508.75 **3.a.** \$24,250 **b.** \$715.38 **5.a.** \$25,680 **b.** \$1063.15 **7.a.** \$13,725 **b.** \$715.07 **9.a.** \$14,550 **b.** \$1102.31 **11.** \$55.39

page 231 **1.** \$337.50 **3.** \$90 **5.** \$225 **7.** \$231 **9.** \$146.25 **11.** \$19.25 **13.** \$448 **15.** \$700 **17.** \$2480.50

pages 233-235 **1.** \$50,900 **3.** \$56,700 **5.** \$52,200 **7.** \$500 **9.** \$6385.50 **11.** \$11,110 **13.a.** \$16,182 **b.** \$20,648 **c.** \$4466 **15.** \$2600 **17.** San Francisco-Oakland; Los Angeles-Long Beach; Washington, D.C.-Maryland, Virginia; Dallas; Boston; New York-Northeastern New Jersey; Denver; Minneapolis-St. Paul; Houston; Atlanta; Chicago-Northwestern Indiana; Miami; Baltimore; Seattle-Everett; Cleveland; Philadelphia; Detroit; St. Louis

page 236

Multiplying whole numbers **1.** 3200 **3.** 3000 **5.** 280,000 **7.** 450,000 **9.** 8,400,000 **11.** 175,000 **13.** 3,440,000 **15.** 816 **17.** 2037 **19.** 17,696 **21.** 216,544 **23.** 368,760 **25.** 1,285,309

Renaming fractions and mixed numbers **1.** $\frac{1}{2}$ **3.** $\frac{3}{4}$ **5.** $\frac{2}{3}$ **7.** $\frac{3}{8}$ **9.** $\frac{1}{3}$ **11.** $\frac{1}{9}$ **13.** $\frac{1}{8}$ **15.** $\frac{7}{8}$ **17.** $\frac{1}{5}$ **19.** $4\frac{1}{2}$ **21.** $3\frac{1}{2}$ **23.** $1\frac{1}{2}$ **25.** $6\frac{1}{2}$ **27.** $2\frac{1}{2}$ **29.** $3\frac{7}{8}$ **31.** $4\frac{4}{11}$ **33.** $1\frac{1}{3}$ **35.** $6\frac{1}{2}$

page 236 continued

Dividing fractions and mixed numbers **1.** $1\frac{1}{2}$ **3.** $1\frac{1}{8}$ **5.** $\frac{24}{35}$ **7.** $7\frac{1}{2}$
9. 16 **11.** $6\frac{1}{4}$ **13.** $1\frac{7}{9}$ **15.** $1\frac{8}{15}$ **17.** $\frac{25}{34}$ **19.** $\frac{3}{4}$

page 237 **1.** \$38,740; yes **2.** \$38,800 **3.** \$332.52 **4.** \$61,894
5. \$180 **6.** \$26,971.56 **7.** \$129.05 **8.** \$744.19 **9.** \$239
10. \$55,400

page 241

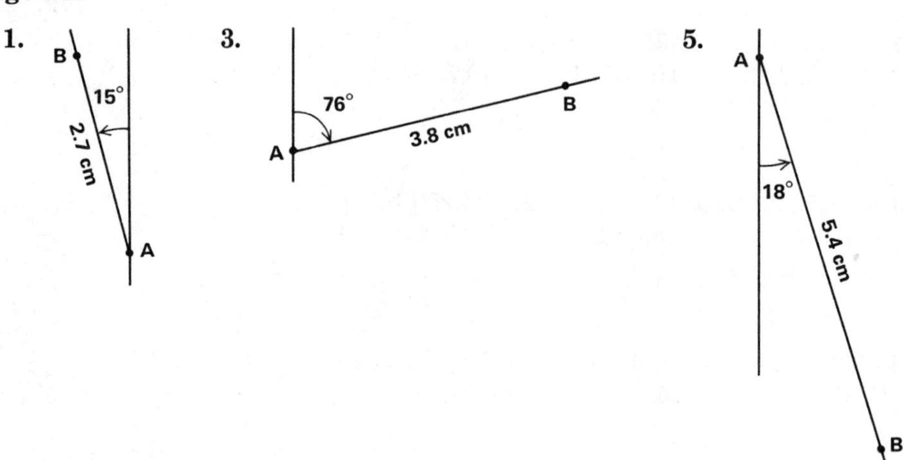

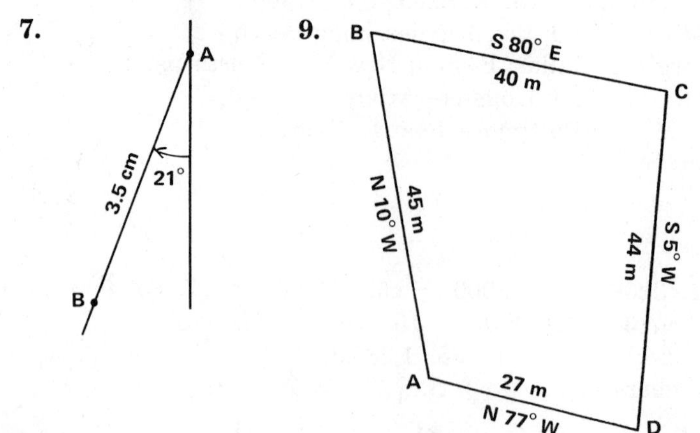

page 241 continued

11.

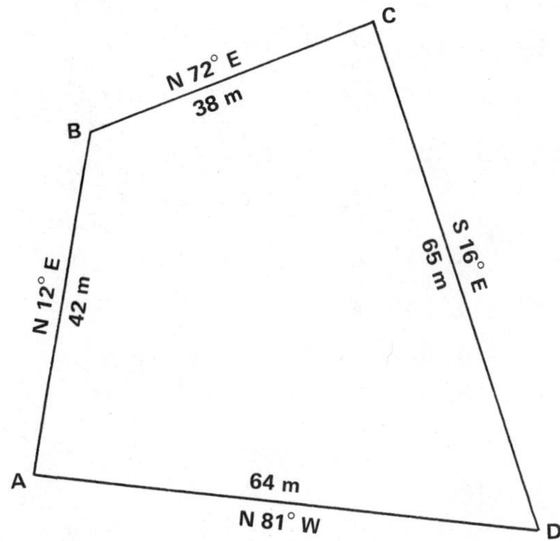

pages 243–244 **1.** 725 sq. ft. **3.** $797\frac{1}{2}$ sq. ft. **5.** $49,197.50 **7.** $3690 **9.** 564 sq. ft. **11.** 624 sq. ft. **13.** $50,460 **15.** $3792.50

page 245 **1.a.** $55,125 **b.** $5625 **c.** $60,750 **3.a.** $54,375 **b.** $3612.50 **c.** $57,987.50 **5.a.** $56,420 **b.** $5535 **c.** $61,955 **7.a.** $71,225 **b.** $5850 **c.** $77,075 **9.a.** $48,647.50 **b.** $5557.50 **c.** $54,205 **11.a.** $54,825 **b.** $4972.50 **c.** $59,797.50

page 247 **1.** $16\frac{1}{2}$ sq. ft. **3.** $319\frac{1}{2}$ sq. ft. **5.** 1011 sq. ft. **7.** $404.40 **9.** 611 sq. ft. **11.** $39\frac{3}{16}$ sq. ft. **13.** $15\frac{3}{4}$ sq. ft. **15.** $10\frac{1}{8}$ sq. ft. **17.** 1531 sq. ft. **19.** $612.40

page 251 **1.a.** 15; 975 **b.** 25; 1000 **c.** None **d.** None; allowance: 1000 **3.** $3\frac{1}{4}$; allowance: 975 **5.a.** None **b.** $235\frac{3}{4}$; allowance: 707 **7.** 500; allowance: 1500 **9.** 10,041

page 252
Multiplying fractions and mixed numbers **1.** $\frac{7}{16}$ **3.** $\frac{2}{5}$ **5.** $\frac{3}{8}$ **7.** 8 **9.** $\frac{5}{8}$ **11.** $2\frac{2}{5}$ **13.** $38\frac{1}{3}$ **15.** $18\frac{6}{7}$ **17.** $22\frac{1}{4}$ **19.** $1\frac{1}{2}$

page 252 continued

Adding fractions and mixed numbers **1.** $\frac{3}{4}$ **3.** $1\frac{5}{12}$ **5.** $\frac{17}{18}$ **7.** $1\frac{1}{5}$ **9.** $2\frac{7}{12}$ **11.** $3\frac{1}{2}$ **13.** $9\frac{5}{24}$ **15.** $13\frac{13}{15}$ **17.** $10\frac{2}{15}$ **19.** 7

Subtracting fractions and mixed numbers **1.** $\frac{1}{2}$ **3.** $\frac{1}{10}$ **5.** $\frac{1}{6}$ **7.** $\frac{3}{16}$ **9.** $8\frac{2}{3}$ **11.** $2\frac{2}{3}$ **13.** $2\frac{1}{8}$ **15.** $3\frac{11}{18}$ **17.** $2\frac{17}{18}$ **19.** $1\frac{5}{6}$

page 253 **1.**

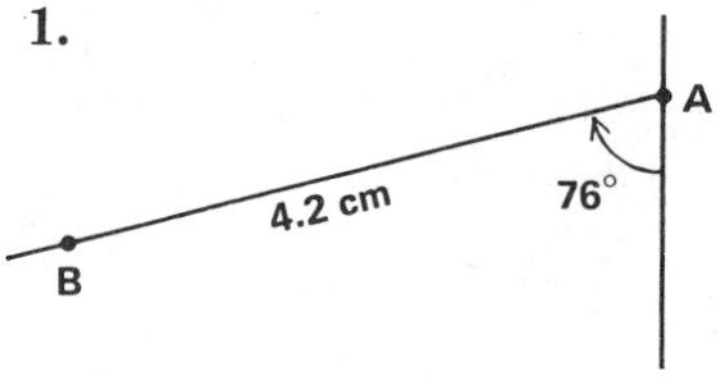

A
4.2 cm
76°
B

2. 429 sq. ft. **3.** $897\frac{3}{4}$ sq. ft. **4.** $46,445 **5.** $822\frac{1}{4}$ sq. ft. **6.** $9\frac{1}{2}$ sq. ft. **7.** 841 sq. ft. **8.** $756.90 **9.** 788 **10.** 495

page 262 **1.** $22 **3.** $8759 **5.** $10,107

page 263 **1.** $0 **3.** $5629 **5.** $14,454 **7.** $7455 **9.** $10,202 **11.** $321 **13.** $4968 **15.** $17,394

pages 265–267 **1.** $0 **3.** $82 **5.** $1054 **7.** $4065 **9.** $2268 **11.** Refund: $245 **13.** Balance due: $11 **15.** Balance due: $124 **17.** Refund: $2 **19.** Refund: $128 **21.** Refund: $230 **23.** Refund: $419 **25.** Balance due: $343 **27.** Refund: $233 **29.** Balance due: $153

pages 269–270 **1.** Standard, $1700; Itemized, $273 **3.** Standard, $1700; Itemized, $347 **5.** Standard, $2352; Itemized, $1094 **7.** Standard, $2800; Itemized, $4856 **9.** Standard, $2120; Itemized, $2244

page 273 **1.** $87 billion **3.** $16 billion **5.** $10 billion **7.** $23 billion **9.** $15 billion **11.** 27% **13.** 10%

page 275 **1.** $17.90 **3.** $1344.55 **5.** $225 **7.** $63.50 **9.** $372.37 **11.** $793.36 **13.** $58.46 **15.** $199.80

page 276

Rounding whole numbers and decimals **1.** 1000; 800; 830 **3.** 1000; 600; 560 **5.** 10,000; 9600; 9600 **7.** 1000; 1100; 1070 **9.** 1000; 600; 600 **11.** 7; 7.4; 7.37 **13.** 37; 36.9; 36.91 **15.** 783; 783.1; 783.14 **17.** 547; 546.8; 546.80 **19.** 60; 59.6; 59.61

Subtracting whole numbers and decimals **1.** 52 **3.** 48 **5.** 5 **7.** 48.6 **9.** 66.2 **11.** 69.42 **13.** 7.638 **15.** 11.089 **17.** 3.315 **19.** .8 **21.** 2.612 **23.** 2.5 **25.** 25.58

Writing percents, decimals, and fractions **1.** $\frac{3}{25}$ **3.** $\frac{11}{20}$ **5.** $\frac{47}{100}$ **7.** $\frac{31}{50}$ **9.** $\frac{4}{25}$ **11.** $\frac{7}{10}$ **13.** $\frac{27}{100}$ **15.** $\frac{13}{20}$ **17.** $2\frac{1}{4}$ **19.** $1\frac{3}{100}$ **21.** 50% **23.** 10% **25.** 60% **27.** 70% **29.** 38% **31.** 55% **33.** 75% **35.** 87.5% **37.** 425% **39.** 760%

page 277 **1.** $1814 **2.** $8771 **3.** $3521 **4.** Refund: $239 **5.** $2800 **6.** $4051 **7.** Total of itemized deductions **8.** $13 billion **9.** $398 **10.** $146.20

page 281 **1.a.** $392 **b.** $148 **3.a.** $3510 **b.** $590 **5.a.** $1360 **b.** $390 **7.a.** $1707 **b.** $569 **9.a.** $846.40 **b.** $133.60 **11.** $209 **13.** $282.70

page 283 **1.** $25.90 **3.** $279.20 **5.** $151.50 **7.** $72.60 **9.** $1715 **11.** $312.50 **13.** $25,000; $565 **15.** $12,000

pages 285–287 **1.** $275.80 **3.** $383.40 **5.** $165.75 **7.** $135.03 **9.** $289.68 **11.** $69.96 **13.** $100.40 **15.** $1263.60 **17.** $2424 **19.** $1032 **21.** $44,572.50 **23.** $1160 **25.** $4830

page 289 **1.** $29.97 **3.** $38.82 **5.** $236.03 **7.** $13.26 **9.** $1268.10 **11.** $1268.40

page 290 **1.a.** $15.09 **b.** $181.08 **c.** $8.59 **3.a.** $11.15 **b.** $133.80 **c.** $6.34 **5.a.** $13.02 **b.** $156.24 **c.** $7.47 **7.a.** $10.90 **b.** $130.80 **c.** $6.25 **9.a.** $40.93 **b.** $163.72 **c.** $6.30 **11.a.** $38.66 **b.** $154.64 **c.** $5.93 **13.a.** $51.34 **b.** $205.36 **c.** $7.91 **15.a.** $98.64 **b.** $197.28 **c.** $3.86 **17.a.** $158.97 **b.** $317.94 **c.** $6.23 **19.a.** $167.84 **b.** $335.68 **c.** $6.59

pages 292–293 **1.** \$68,000; \$16,388 **3.** \$81,000; \$18,468 **5.** \$37,000; \$9694 **7.** \$40,000; \$12,920 **9.** \$68,000; \$19,448 **11.** \$32.81 **13.** \$21,978.04 **15.** \$15,655

pages 295–297 **1.** \$3505.20 **3.** \$3790.80 **5.** \$4753.20 **7.** \$3486 **9.** \$4712.40 **11.** \$7610.53 **13.** \$5200.80 **15.** \$130,020 **17.** \$3668.40 **19.** After 15 years, the total benefits from retiring at 63 are \$55,026, and the total benefits from retiring at 65 are \$55,036.80.

page 298
Adding whole numbers and decimals **1.** 55 **3.** 170 **5.** 108 **7.** 120 **9.** 231 **11.** 1737 **13.** 2232 **15.** 21.94 **17.** 115.66 **19.** 16.05 **21.** 17.81 **23.** 1.49 **25.** 11.269
Multiplying whole numbers **1.** 1400 **3.** 20,000 **5.** 210,000 **7.** 420,000 **9.** 12,000,000 **11.** 68,000 **13.** 340,000 **15.** 1872 **17.** 2936 **19.** 29,488 **21.** 329,280 **23.** 147,288 **25.** 643,405
Percent problems **1.** 9.4 **3.** 20 **5.** 1.78 **7.** 90 **9.** 8.2 **11.** 7.2 **13.** 350 **15.** 410 **17.** 95 **19.** 85 **21.** 3.5

page 299 **1.** \$421.31 **2.** \$408.75 **3.** \$465.30 **4.** \$8850 **5.** \$33.66 **6.** \$19.20 **7.** \$51,000 **8.** \$18,481.60 **9.** \$5192.40 **10.** \$19,428

page 303 **1.a.** \$37.50 **3.a.** \$75 **b.** \$225 **5.a.** \$37.50 **b.** \$225 **7.a.** \$75 **b.** \$225 **9.a.** \$7500 **b.** \$15,000 **11.** \$21.71 **13.** \$75.60 **15.** \$84.56 **17.** \$60.18 **19.** \$892.40 **21.** \$122.32

pages 305–306 **1.a.** 1.07250 **b.** \$1072.50 **c.** \$72.50 **3.a.** 1.08057 **b.** \$10,805.70 **c.** \$805.70 **5.a.** 1.03130 **b.** \$4125.20 **c.** \$125.20 **7.a.** 1.01866 **b.** \$2037.32 **c.** \$37.32 **9.** \$39.60 **11.a.** 7.25% **13.a.** 6.45% **15.a.** \$115.04 **b.** 5.75% **17.a.** \$114.24 **b.** 5.71% **19.** \$1000 CD paying \$61.83 each year

page 307 **1.a.** \$2919.08 **3.a.** \$3154.27 **b.** \$3408.41 **5.a.** \$3683.03 **b.** \$3979.77 **7.a.** \$4300.42 **b.** \$4646.90 **9.a.** \$5021.30 **b.** \$5425.87 **11.a.** \$5863.03 **b.** \$6335.41 **13.a.** \$6845.85 **b.** \$7397.42 **15.a.** \$7993.43 **b.** \$8637.46 **17.a.** \$9333.38 **b.** \$10,085.37 **19.** 9; 15

pages 309–311 **1.** $193.88 **3.** $533.75 **5.** $2057.75 **7.** $11,915 **9.** $6278.50 **11.** $145 **13.** $2130.25 **15.** $3136.75 **17.** $12,539 **19.** $559 **21.** −$23.75 **23.** $177 **25.** $158 **27.** $119.75 **29.** $1212.25 **31.a.** $120 **b.** 5.71% **33.a.** $159 **b.** 3.98% **35.a.** $361.20 **b.** 5.16%

page 313 **1.a.** $110 **b.** 10% **3.a.** $100 **b.** 9.95% **5.a.** $39 **b.** 4.48% **7.a.** $116 **b.** 10.27% **9.a.** $45 **b.** 6.25%

page 315 **1.a.** $19.91 **b.** $99.55 **3.a.** $14.26 **b.** $213.90 **5.a.** $4.50 **b.** $337.50 **7.a.** $8.34 **b.** $100.08 **9.a.** $24.97 **b.** $399.52 **11.** $381.50 **13.** $.93 **15.** 111.1111 shares

page 316
Rounding whole numbers and decimals **1.** 1000; 700; 720 **3.** 3000; 3500; 3490 **5.** 9000; 9400; 9360 **7.** 56,000; 56,200; 56,200 **9.** 1000; 1000; 1000 **11.** 6; 5.6; 5.63 **13.** 47; 47.5; 47.46 **15.** 376; 376.3; 376.29 **17.** 765; 765.0; 764.97 **19.** 68; 68.0; 68.02
Dividing decimals **1.** 3.033 **3.** .899 **5.** .091 **7.** .016 **9.** .222 **11.** 2.769 **13.** 3.638 **15.** 80 **17.** 4.683 **19.** .391 **21.** .183 **23.** 2.204 **25.** 24.421
Ratio and proportion **1.** 9; 10; not equal **3.** 36; 14; not equal **5.** 183.6; 180; not equal **7.** $a = 24$ **9.** $n = 63$ **11.** $x = 24$ **13.** $y = 16$

page 317 **1.** $56.25 **2.** $80.19 **3.** $67.12 **4.** 6.21% **5.** $3790.25 **6.** $3132.25 **7.** $132.25 profit **8.** 4.69% **9.** 8.09% **10.** $297

page 325 **1.** 530 cal. **3.** 480 cal. **5.** 730 cal. **7.** 1765 cal.

page 327 **1.** 1248 cal. **3.** 142 cal. **5.** 1180 cal. **7.** 454 cal. **9.** 408 cal. **11.** 503 cal. **13.** 3030 cal.

pages 329–330 **1.** $1.85 **3.** $2.13 **5.** $1.34 **7.** $1.24 **9.** Large **11.** Large **13.** Store brand, $1.89 **15.** Prepackaged, $3.83 **17.** Medium, $1.44 **19.** 300-gram can, $1.86 **21.** Name brand, $.64 **23.** 300-gram box, $.94 **25.** 2.5-kilogram bag, $2.94 **27.** $22.81

page 331 **1.** .17¢/g; .16¢/g **3.** .12¢/g; .09¢/g **5.** .08¢/mL; .07¢/mL **7.** .09¢/mL; .10¢/mL **9.** 49.5¢/L; 18.64¢/L

page 333 **1.a.** $234 **b.** 91 kg **c.** $2.57 **3.a.** $207.50 **b.** 95 kg **c.** $2.18 **5.a.** $288.75 **b.** 123.75 kg **c.** $2.33

page 335 **1.a.** 15.4 kg **b.** $61.45 **3.a.** 12.5 kg **b.** $22.38 **5.a.** 8.5 kg **b.** $29.67 **7.a.** 7.1 kg **b.** $38.98 **9.a.** 2.9 kg **b.** $8.09 **11.a.** 0.4 kg **b.** $.44 **13.** $259 **15.** $308.50

page 337 **1.** $6.05 **3.** $8.95 **5.** $4.20 **7.** $10.95

page 338
Multiplying decimals **1.** .3 **3.** .009 **5.** .0035 **7.** .00004 **9.** 120 **11.** 18 **13.** 1.2 **15.** .00004 **17.** 6.6 **19.** 11.076 **21.** .4935 **23.** 110.79138 **25.** 13.732136
Dividing fractions and mixed numbers **1.** $\frac{4}{5}$ **3.** $\frac{2}{3}$ **5.** $2\frac{3}{16}$ **7.** 8 **9.** 16 **11.** $2\frac{1}{2}$ **13.** $2\frac{15}{16}$ **15.** $\frac{6}{7}$ **17.** $1\frac{11}{16}$ **19.** $2\frac{9}{10}$
Percent problems **1.** 1.25 **3.** 15 **5.** 17.5 **7.** 3.3 **9.** 7.2 **11.** 28 **13.** 37 **15.** 120 **17.** 95 **19.** 50 **21.** 25

page 339 **1.** 355 cal. **2.** 605 cal. **3.** $.60 **4.** Large **5.** $280 **6.** 115.2 kg **7.** $2.43 **8.** 10.8 kg **9.** $49.57 **10.** $9.45

pages 343-344 **1.** $38.69 **3.** 2 lb. 5 oz. **5.** $41.49 **7.** $2.25 **9.** $1.14 **11.** $24.66 **13.** 3 lb. 8 oz. **15.** $27.75

page 345 **1.a.** $63 **b.** 20 lb. 10 oz. **3.a.** $28.80 **b.** 10 lb. 8 oz. **5.a.** $65.24 **b.** 26 lb. 11 oz. **7.a.** $32.40 **b.** 10 lb. 8 oz. **9.a.** $608.71 **b.** 141 lb. 4 oz. **11.** $9.87

page 347 **1.** $11\frac{1}{4}$ yd. **3.** 5 yd. **5.** $53\frac{5}{8}$ yd. **7.** $85.80 **9.** $3.80 **11.** 43 packages **13.** $5.40 **15.** $357.38 **17.** $610.78

page 349 **1.a.** January, July, December **b.** \$2.70 **c.** \$15.30 **3.a.** March **b.** \$64.99 **c.** \$194.96 **5.a.** February, September **b.** \$113.99 **c.** \$455.96 **7.a.** May, July **b.** \$2.63 **c.** \$14.87 **9.a.** July **b.** \$9.21 **c.** \$17.09

page 351 **1.** \$37.93 **3.** \$30.31 **5.** \$25.40

page 353 **1.a.** \$.30 **b.** \$3.00 **3.a.** \$5.50 **5.a.** \$392 **7.a.** \$34.20 **9.a.** \$3.20 **b.** \$5.12 **c.** \$7.84 **11.a.** \$.20 **b.** \$.70 **13.** \$684.89

page 355 **1.** \$14 **3.** \$6 **5.** \$24 **7.** \$13.50 **9.** \$4.50 **11.** 8 years **13.** 19 hours

page 356
Dividing whole numbers **1.** 2188 **3.** 888 R1 **5.** 194 **7.** 42 R19 **9.** 699 **11.** 114 R15 **13.** 69 R20 **15.** 28 R54 **17.** 74 R13 **19.** 3192 R26 **21.** 11,908 R5 **23.** 12,277 R65 **25.** 225 R48
Adding fractions and mixed numbers **1.** $\frac{14}{15}$ **3.** $\frac{17}{24}$ **5.** $\frac{5}{6}$ **7.** $1\frac{1}{4}$ **9.** $1\frac{1}{18}$ **11.** $7\frac{4}{5}$ **13.** $8\frac{1}{6}$ **15.** $20\frac{5}{6}$ **17.** $6\frac{17}{24}$ **19.** $18\frac{7}{20}$
Subtracting fractions and mixed numbers **1.** $\frac{1}{3}$ **3.** $\frac{17}{24}$ **5.** $\frac{1}{24}$ **7.** $\frac{2}{21}$ **9.** $14\frac{1}{7}$ **11.** $3\frac{1}{2}$ **13.** $9\frac{2}{5}$ **15.** $\frac{5}{24}$ **17.** $7\frac{5}{12}$ **19.** $16\frac{5}{6}$

page 357 **1.** \$57.90 **2.** \$2.90 **3.** 5 lb. 4 oz. **4.** \$1.45 **5.** \$62.25 **6.** $11\frac{1}{4}$ yd. **7.** \$293.25 **8.** \$21.64 **9.** \$12 **10.** \$8.75

pages 361–363 **1.** \$35 **3.** \$13 **5.** \$109 **7.** \$29 **9.** \$16 **11.** \$150 **13.** \$19 **15.** \$32 **17.** \$329 **19.** \$22 **21.** \$70 **23.** \$27 **25.** \$12

pages 364–365 **1.** \$35 **3.** \$10 **5.** \$105 **7.** \$30 **9.** \$15 **11.** \$150 **13.** \$18 **15.** \$25 **17.** \$325 **19.** \$20 **21.** \$70 **23.** \$30 **25.** \$20

pages 367–369 **1.** \$105 **3.** \$17 **5.** No **7.** \$2215 **9.** \$503 **11.** \$185 **13.** No **15.** \$457 **17.** \$1666

page 371 **1.** $40 **3.** $178 **5.** $40 **7.** $50 **9.** $1438 **11.** $540 **13.** $550 **15.** $40 **17.** $20 **19.** $8 **21.** $15 **23.** $170 **25.** $0 **27.** $200 **29.** $50 **31.** $0 **33.** $790 **35.** $176 **37.** Yes

page 373 **1.** $296 **3.** $6 **5.** $509 **7.** $50 **9.** $1519 **11.** No

page 375 **1.a.** $3850 **b.** $5040 **3.a.** $1430 **b.** $1925 **c.** $1920 **5.a.** $1100 **b.** $2275 **c.** $4320

page 376

Adding whole numbers and decimals **1.** 72 **3.** 161 **5.** 199 **7.** 202 **9.** 233 **11.** 1649 **13.** 778 **15.** 18.07 **17.** 98.61 **19.** 17.85 **21.** 20.07 **23.** 1.56 **25.** 10.499

Renaming fractions and mixed numbers **1.** $\frac{3}{4}$ **3.** $\frac{3}{4}$ **5.** $\frac{5}{9}$ **7.** $\frac{5}{6}$ **9.** $\frac{7}{12}$ **11.** $\frac{1}{2}$ **13.** $\frac{1}{3}$ **15.** $\frac{5}{6}$ **17.** $\frac{3}{8}$ **19.** $\frac{1}{4}$ **21.** $\frac{1}{2}$ **23.** $\frac{3}{4}$ **25.** $\frac{1}{2}$ **27.** $\frac{7}{8}$ **29.** $\frac{1}{4}$ **31.** $\frac{5}{8}$ **33.** $\frac{4}{5}$ **35.** $\frac{3}{4}$

Dividing fractions and mixed numbers **1.** $\frac{3}{4}$ **3.** $\frac{3}{5}$ **5.** $\frac{3}{20}$ **7.** 8 **9.** $9\frac{1}{3}$ **11.** 7 **13.** $\frac{3}{25}$ **15.** $\frac{3}{5}$ **17.** $\frac{6}{7}$ **19.** $\frac{16}{49}$

page 377 **1.** $12 **2.** $22 **3.** $42 **4.** $72 **5.** $27 **6.** $43 **7.** $147 **8.** No **9.** $29 **10.** $3901

page 386 **1.** 1000; 600 **3.** 1000; 500 **5.** 1000; 700 **7.** 1000; 1400 **9.** 6000; 5900 **11.** 4000; 3700 **13.** 2000; 2400 **15.** 8000; 7600 **17.** 3000; 2800 **19.** 7000; 7100 **21.** 5000; 5400 **23.** 2000; 2000 **25.** 9000; 8700 **27.** 97,000; 96,900 **29.** 43,000; 43,000 **31.** 85,000; 84,900 **33.** 67,000; 67,400 **35.** 31,000; 30,900 **37.** 26,000; 26,400 **39.** 75,000; 74,900 **41.** 68,000; 68,100 **43.** 81,000; 80,900 **45.** 52,000; 52,400 **47.** 47,000; 47,200 **49.** 1000; 600 **51.** 1000; 900 **53.** 1000; 1300 **55.** 5000; 5100 **57.** 92,000; 91,700 **59.** 35,000; 35,500 **61.** 3; 3.49 **63.** 8; 8.09 **65.** 2; 1.79 **67.** 6; 5.82 **69.** 9; 9.42 **71.** 2; 2.06 **73.** 7; 6.74 **75.** 3; 2.80 **77.** 1; 1.25 **79.** 5; 4.93 **81.** 62; 62.29 **83.** 94; 94.01 **85.** 68; 68.26 **87.** 38; 37.89 **89.** 55; 55.01 **91.** 26; 26.38 **93.** 91; 90.54 **95.** 72; 72.48 **97.** 65; 65.07 **99.** 20; 20.37 **101.** 912; 912.05 **103.** 746; 745.92 **105.** 568; 567.61 **107.** 193; 193.25 **109.** 808; 808.35 **111.** 447; 446.50 **113.** 881; 880.92 **115.** 671; 671.41 **117.** 466; 466.06 **119.** 248; 248.34

page 387 **1.** 79 **3.** 83 **5.** 140 **7.** 86 **9.** 90 **11.** 72
13. 146 **15.** 177 **17.** 95 **19.** 84 **21.** 285 **23.** 591 **25.** 1181
27. 639 **29.** 913 **31.** 2098 **33.** 11.96 **35.** 14.17 **37.** 13.83
39. .8 **41.** 8.0 **43.** 11.41 **45.** 20.98 **47.** 19.09 **49.** 14.54
51. 22.51 **53.** 7.72 **55.** 12.888 **57.** 16.322 **59.** 15.62
61. 10.275 **63.** 15.536

page 388 **1.** 34 **3.** 48 **5.** 6 **7.** 43 **9.** 25 **11.** 29 **13.** 8
15. 244 **17.** 347 **19.** 394 **21.** 227 **23.** 5075 **25.** 4591
27. 1873 **29.** 44.3 **31.** 26.5 **33.** .6 **35.** 60.19 **37.** 47.55
39. .57 **41.** 23.62 **43.** 10.52 **45.** 14.321 **47.** 81.646 **49.** 15.035
51. 21.315 **53.** 14.069 **55.** 69.488 **57.** 33.314 **59.** 24.806
61. 16.325 **63.** 22.49 **65.** 18.51 **67.** 9.216 **69.** 12.078
71. 1.886 **73.** 8.237 **75.** 75.734 **77.** 31.71 **79.** 57.721
81. 20.7 **83.** 41.16

page 389 **1.** 1600 **3.** 2800 **5.** 1000 **7.** 2100 **9.** 18,000
11. 7000 **13.** 40,000 **15.** 720,000 **17.** 60,000 **19.** 240,000
21. 90,000 **23.** 240,000 **25.** 450,000 **27.** 40,000 **29.** 900,000
31. 700,000 **33.** 6,300,000 **35.** 1,600,000 **37.** 100,000 **39.** 880,000
41. 14,800,000 **43.** 96 **45.** 86 **47.** 264 **49.** 3078 **51.** 4832
53. 4285 **55.** 676 **57.** 2680 **59.** 2072 **61.** 14,658 **63.** 43,602
65. 28,676 **67.** 55,182 **69.** 724,240 **71.** 242,305 **73.** 342,186
75. 78,642 **77.** 461,674 **79.** 2,881,216 **81.** 4,912,128 **83.** 1,631,168

page 390 **1.** .21 **3.** .08 **5.** .1 **7.** .036 **9.** .035 **11.** .081
13. .0048 **15.** .0006 **17.** .004 **19.** .0018 **21.** .0024 **23.** .003
25. .00028 **27.** .00025 **29.** .00032 **31.** .000012 **33.** .000072
35. 240 **37.** 14 **39.** 5.4 **41.** 7.7 **43.** 29.6 **45.** 18.72
47. 1.74 **49.** 9 **51.** 13.32 **53.** 12.217 **55.** 17.272 **57.** 18.574
59. 3.7022 **61.** 17.0502 **63.** 12.4218 **65.** 2.3219 **67.** 1.5232
69. .4878 **71.** 36.57006 **73.** .92254 **75.** 22.63174 **77.** .044888
79. .39501 **81.** 3.43674 **83.** .0047448

page 391 **1.** 255 **3.** 117 R2 **5.** 77 R3 **7.** 1453 R5 **9.** 1463 R2
11. 6390 R4 **13.** 25,685 **15.** 5014 R1 **17.** 122,374 R2 **19.** 117,747 R5
21. 42,918 R3 **23.** 142 R26 **25.** 139 R24 **27.** 45 R60 **29.** 277 R8
31. 63 **33.** 90 R52 **35.** 96 R8 **37.** 308 R26 **39.** 117 R42
41. 58 R74 **43.** 1231 R2 **45.** 515 R39 **47.** 753 R17 **49.** 555 R20
51. 962 R22 **53.** 378 R13 **55.** 3379 R1 **57.** 738 R6 **59.** 350 R2
61. 459 R45 **63.** 616 R35 **65.** 31,653 **67.** 60,548 R7 **69.** 5289 R15

page 391 continued **71.** 20,009 R3 **73.** 4975 R7 **75.** 3589 R81
77. 5846 R59 **79.** 105 R161 **81.** 278 **83.** 197 R98 **85.** 86 R404
87. 46 R633 **89.** 98 R92 **91.** 35 R249 **93.** 755 R180 **95.** 1048 R432
97. 682 **99.** 2940 R149 **101.** 899 R9 **103.** 507 R801 **105.** 326 R891

page 392 **1.** 5.257 **3.** 3.189 **5.** 7.533 **7.** 11.263 **9.** 7.983
11. 3.123 **13.** .806 **15.** .788 **17.** 2.007 **19.** .167 **21.** .334
23. .079 **25.** .113 **27.** .067 **29.** .024 **31.** .276 **33.** .043
35. .176 **37.** 1.508 **39.** .867 **41.** 23.966 **43.** 11.871 **45.** 7.627
47. 8.149 **49.** 1.288 **51.** .698 **53.** .381 **55.** .058 **57.** 2.396
59. .511 **61.** 173.333 **63.** 126.667 **65.** 68.571 **67.** 74.444
69. 3.052 **71.** .983 **73.** .504 **75.** 2.087 **77.** 1.063 **79.** .645
81. .129 **83.** .107 **85.** .308 **87.** .013 **89.** .572 **91.** .114
93. 3.065 **95.** 17.634 **97.** .978 **99.** 116.838

page 393 **1.** $\frac{1}{2}$ **3.** $\frac{1}{3}$ **5.** $\frac{1}{4}$ **7.** $\frac{1}{6}$ **9.** $\frac{2}{3}$ **11.** $\frac{2}{3}$ **13.** $\frac{1}{3}$
15. $\frac{7}{10}$ **17.** $\frac{7}{9}$ **19.** $\frac{1}{2}$ **21.** $\frac{1}{5}$ **23.** $\frac{1}{4}$ **25.** $\frac{5}{6}$ **27.** $\frac{1}{2}$ **29.** $\frac{4}{7}$
31. $\frac{1}{3}$ **33.** $\frac{3}{5}$ **35.** $\frac{2}{3}$ **37.** $\frac{4}{5}$ **39.** $\frac{5}{8}$ **41.** $\frac{1}{5}$ **43.** $\frac{1}{3}$ **45.** $\frac{2}{3}$
47. $\frac{7}{8}$ **49.** $3\frac{1}{3}$ **51.** $2\frac{1}{4}$ **53.** $3\frac{1}{6}$ **55.** $5\frac{2}{5}$ **57.** $5\frac{3}{7}$ **59.** $1\frac{11}{18}$
61. $3\frac{2}{7}$ **63.** $1\frac{7}{12}$ **65.** $14\frac{1}{3}$ **67.** $12\frac{3}{7}$ **69.** $21\frac{4}{5}$ **71.** $4\frac{1}{5}$ **73.** $24\frac{1}{2}$
75. $11\frac{1}{5}$ **77.** $\frac{13}{4}$ **79.** $\frac{11}{4}$ **81.** $\frac{28}{3}$ **83.** $\frac{26}{5}$ **85.** $\frac{45}{7}$ **87.** $\frac{26}{3}$
89. $\frac{55}{7}$ **91.** $\frac{67}{12}$ **93.** $\frac{62}{9}$ **95.** $\frac{67}{16}$ **97.** $\frac{153}{5}$ **99.** $\frac{47}{3}$ **101.** $\frac{113}{8}$
103. $\frac{65}{3}$ **105.** $\frac{343}{4}$

page 394 **1.** $\frac{1}{16}$ **3.** $\frac{3}{20}$ **5.** $\frac{1}{9}$ **7.** $\frac{1}{7}$ **9.** $\frac{3}{10}$ **11.** $\frac{7}{12}$ **13.** $\frac{5}{12}$
15. $\frac{7}{12}$ **17.** $\frac{1}{2}$ **19.** $\frac{1}{2}$ **21.** $\frac{1}{6}$ **23.** $\frac{4}{7}$ **25.** $\frac{5}{8}$ **27.** $7\frac{1}{2}$
29. $\frac{7}{8}$ **31.** 5 **33.** 14 **35.** $31\frac{1}{2}$ **37.** 9 **39.** 30 **41.** $33\frac{3}{5}$
43. $\frac{3}{4}$ **45.** $\frac{3}{5}$ **47.** 3 **49.** $1\frac{1}{2}$ **51.** $1\frac{1}{8}$ **53.** 4 **55.** $1\frac{31}{35}$ **57.** $\frac{7}{9}$
59. $8\frac{1}{3}$ **61.** $1\frac{6}{7}$ **63.** 6 **65.** $8\frac{1}{6}$ **67.** 30 **69.** 3 **71.** $8\frac{3}{4}$
73. 23 **75.** $4\frac{4}{9}$ **77.** $18\frac{1}{3}$ **79.** $4\frac{1}{2}$ **81.** $13\frac{1}{2}$ **83.** $11\frac{1}{4}$ **85.** 18
87. 104 **89.** $30\frac{2}{3}$ **91.** $\frac{3}{5}$ **93.** $1\frac{2}{3}$ **95.** $2\frac{4}{5}$ **97.** $4\frac{2}{5}$ **99.** $\frac{2}{3}$
101. $24\frac{2}{3}$ **103.** $23\frac{1}{3}$ **105.** $32\frac{1}{2}$

page 395 **1.** $\frac{3}{4}$ **3.** 3 **5.** $\frac{1}{2}$ **7.** $\frac{4}{5}$ **9.** $1\frac{1}{2}$ **11.** $\frac{2}{3}$ **13.** $\frac{3}{8}$
15. $\frac{6}{7}$ **17.** $\frac{21}{50}$ **19.** $\frac{9}{14}$ **21.** $\frac{9}{10}$ **23.** $\frac{2}{3}$ **25.** $\frac{5}{6}$ **27.** $5\frac{1}{4}$
29. $\frac{8}{15}$ **31.** $\frac{63}{80}$ **33.** $\frac{1}{5}$ **35.** $\frac{1}{6}$ **37.** $\frac{5}{12}$ **39.** $\frac{3}{10}$ **41.** $\frac{2}{27}$
43. 12 **45.** 8 **47.** 5 **49.** $2\frac{1}{2}$ **51.** 16 **53.** $10\frac{1}{2}$ **55.** $\frac{2}{5}$
57. $\frac{2}{13}$ **59.** 15 **61.** 10 **63.** $7\frac{1}{9}$ **65.** $\frac{8}{9}$ **67.** $\frac{2}{5}$ **69.** $\frac{5}{8}$
71. $5\frac{1}{3}$ **73.** $7\frac{1}{2}$ **75.** 35 **77.** 5 **79.** $1\frac{7}{8}$ **81.** $1\frac{3}{5}$ **83.** 4
85. $1\frac{3}{5}$ **87.** 6 **89.** $\frac{2}{3}$ **91.** $1\frac{3}{5}$ **93.** $1\frac{1}{2}$ **95.** $1\frac{7}{12}$ **97.** 2
99. $\frac{3}{7}$ **101.** $3\frac{8}{9}$ **103.** $1\frac{17}{25}$ **105.** $11\frac{1}{40}$

page 396 **1.** $1\frac{1}{8}$ **3.** $\frac{7}{10}$ **5.** $1\frac{1}{4}$ **7.** $\frac{13}{15}$ **9.** $\frac{5}{12}$ **11.** $\frac{13}{24}$ **13.** $1\frac{1}{6}$
15. $\frac{13}{15}$ **17.** $1\frac{5}{16}$ **19.** $1\frac{13}{24}$ **21.** $1\frac{1}{3}$ **23.** $1\frac{4}{9}$ **25.** $2\frac{3}{8}$ **27.** $8\frac{7}{8}$
29. $7\frac{7}{15}$ **31.** $6\frac{5}{12}$ **33.** $5\frac{1}{10}$ **35.** $13\frac{1}{2}$ **37.** 8 **39.** $6\frac{1}{6}$ **41.** $13\frac{7}{18}$
43. $11\frac{13}{16}$ **45.** $13\frac{2}{3}$ **47.** $8\frac{17}{21}$ **49.** $9\frac{1}{20}$ **51.** $13\frac{3}{10}$ **53.** $16\frac{1}{6}$
55. $14\frac{11}{30}$ **57.** $9\frac{5}{6}$ **59.** $18\frac{1}{2}$ **61.** $5\frac{1}{8}$ **63.** $5\frac{9}{10}$ **65.** $10\frac{7}{12}$ **67.** $14\frac{7}{8}$

page 397 **1.** $\frac{1}{4}$ **3.** $\frac{1}{10}$ **5.** $\frac{11}{20}$ **7.** $\frac{5}{12}$ **9.** $\frac{1}{8}$ **11.** $\frac{1}{4}$ **13.** $\frac{4}{9}$
15. $\frac{19}{30}$ **17.** $\frac{1}{15}$ **19.** $\frac{17}{24}$ **21.** $\frac{5}{14}$ **23.** $\frac{3}{16}$ **25.** $\frac{8}{35}$ **27.** $\frac{3}{16}$
29. $4\frac{7}{10}$ **31.** $\frac{1}{5}$ **33.** $2\frac{5}{6}$ **35.** $8\frac{1}{3}$ **37.** $3\frac{2}{3}$ **39.** $1\frac{3}{8}$ **41.** $1\frac{1}{4}$
43. $1\frac{3}{10}$ **45.** $2\frac{3}{5}$ **47.** $2\frac{2}{5}$ **49.** $7\frac{1}{10}$ **51.** $1\frac{5}{6}$ **53.** $6\frac{5}{12}$ **55.** $3\frac{5}{6}$
57. $3\frac{19}{24}$ **59.** $3\frac{9}{16}$ **61.** $7\frac{13}{20}$ **63.** $8\frac{13}{18}$ **65.** $3\frac{7}{8}$ **67.** $8\frac{1}{3}$ **69.** $7\frac{11}{36}$
71. $\frac{1}{4}$

page 398 **1.** 18; 18; equal **3.** 60; 52; not equal **5.** 64; 60; not equal
7. 120; 120; equal **9.** 120; 140; not equal **11.** 396; 420; not equal
13. 210; 210; equal **15.** 819; 949; not equal **17.** 798; 798; equal
19. 54; .54; not equal **21.** 113.4; 113.4; equal **23.** 12.6; 12.6; equal
25. 50.4; 44.8; not equal **27.** 8; 8.1; not equal **29.** 24; 24; equal
31. 67.94; 64.4; not equal **33.** 9.9; 9.9; equal **35.** 9.8; 9.45; not equal
37. $n = 12$ **39.** $m = 2$ **41.** $a = 15$ **43.** $d = 35$ **45.** $h = 13$
47. $k = 7$ **49.** $w = 1.5$ **51.** $y = 14.4$ **53.** $b = 1.5$ **55.** $t = 63$
57. $g = .07$ **59.** $x = 12$ **61.** $n = 640.8$ **63.** $t = .44$ **65.** $h = 63.2$
67. $y = 1.5$ **69.** $x = 4.64$

page 399 **1.** .27 **3.** .74 **5.** .2 **7.** .07 **9.** .169 **11.** .513
13. .072 **15.** .0823 **17.** .075 **19.** .2325 **21.** 9 **23.** 2.56
25. 37% **27.** 65% **29.** 2% **31.** 80% **33.** 9.6% **35.** 72.7%
37. 50.3% **39.** 64.92% **41.** 80.77% **43.** 1.88% **45.** 108% **47.** 714.9%
49. $\frac{4}{5}$ **51.** $\frac{3}{4}$ **53.** $\frac{9}{10}$ **55.** $\frac{31}{50}$ **57.** $\frac{31}{100}$ **59.** $\frac{43}{100}$ **61.** $\frac{23}{100}$
63. $\frac{11}{100}$ **65.** $\frac{39}{50}$ **67.** $\frac{33}{50}$ **69.** $1\frac{1}{10}$ **71.** $1\frac{2}{5}$ **73.** 50% **75.** 75%
77. 4% **79.** 40% **81.** 74% **83.** 65% **85.** 64% **87.** 20% **89.** 98%
91. 62.5% **93.** 18.75% **95.** 90.625% **97.** 750% **99.** 204%

page 400 **1.** 18 **3.** 45 **5.** 312.39 **7.** 39.9 **9.** 9.84 **11.** 130
13. 92.4 **15.** 9.27 **17.** 5.67 **19.** 1836 **21.** 36 **23.** 22.925
25. 32.5 **27.** 150 **29.** 330 **31.** 46 **33.** 48.75 **35.** 800
37. 125 **39.** 168 **41.** 31.5 **43.** 1520 **45.** 48% **47.** 3%
49. 15% **51.** 20% **53.** 52% **55.** 2% **57.** 20% **59.** 37.5%
61. 94% **63.** 87.5% **65.** 37.5%

index